Canadian Small Business Kit

Business Kit

for
dummies®
A Wiley Brand

Canadian Small Business Kit

4th Edition

by Andrew Dagys, Margaret Kerr, and JoAnn Kurtz

for dummies®
A Wiley Brand

Canadian Small Business Kit For Dummies®, 4th Edition

Published by: **John Wiley & Sons, Inc.,** 111 River Street, Hoboken, NJ 07030-5774, www.wiley.com

Copyright © 2019 by John Wiley & Sons, Inc., Hoboken, New Jersey

Published simultaneously in Canada

For general information on our other products and services, please contact our Customer Care Department within the U.S. at 877-762-2974, outside the U.S. at 317-572-3993, or fax 317-572-4002. For technical support, please visit https://hub.wiley.com/community/support/dummies.

Wiley publishes in a variety of print and electronic formats and by print-on-demand. Some material included with standard print versions of this book may not be included in e-books or in print-on-demand. If this book refers to media such as a CD or DVD that is not included in the version you purchased, you may download this material at http://booksupport.wiley.com. For more information about Wiley products, visit www.wiley.com.

Library of Congress Control Number: 2019939298

ISBN 978-1-119-57589-4 (pbk); ISBN 978-1-119-57584-9 (ebk); ISBN 978-1-119-57587-0 (ebk)

Manufactured in the United States of America

C10009967_050119

Contents at a Glance

Table of Contents

Introduction

Starting a business is an exciting — and often frightening — adventure. Who knows where you may end up? To keep from getting lost on your journey exploring business opportunities, you need help setting up your business — choosing the right vehicle, charting the right course, and heading out with the right equipment. This book gives you a head start on your voyage.

About This Book

According to Industry Canada's recent *Key Small Business Statistics,* the Canadian economy totalled 1.17 million businesses. Of these, 1.14 million (97.9 percent) were small businesses — namely, enterprises with fewer than 100 employees. But for just about every one of the 100,000 new businesses created each year, there are others that no longer operate due to bankruptcy, insolvency, retirement, or other reasons. In fact, these statistics also show that about 85 percent of small businesses survive for three years, and 70 percent survive for five years. That's a pretty high failure rate.

In addition to external circumstances beyond anyone's control, exits from small businesses are commonly driven by the fact that many small business owners are poorly prepared to go into business. They don't know the things they need to know that will allow their businesses to succeed. This book isn't long enough to tell you everything you need to know about going into business for yourself, but it gives you a really good head start and addresses many of the root cause "knowledge gaps" often attributed to business failures.

Within this book, you may note that some web addresses break across two lines of text. If you're reading this book in print and want to visit one of these web pages, simply key in the web address exactly as it's noted in the text, pretending as though the line break doesn't exist. If you're reading this as an e-book, you've got it easy — just click the web address to be taken directly to the web page.

Foolish Assumptions

We wrote this book for people who want to go into business for themselves. You have aspirations of being an entrepreneur, but that's all we know about you. We don't assume that you know where your business will be located, or even what it will be. We don't assume that you have any background knowledge about law or risk management or insurance or accounting or marketing or anything else for that matter. We do assume that you have a computer with Internet access, although we don't assume that you're a techno-nerd. We assume that you are intelligent and self-motivated. And we assume that you're aware that this book is just the start of a long journey that will entail a lot of work but will hopefully confer great rewards, too.

Icons Used in This Book

Scattered along the left-hand side of this book are little icons. Here's a guide to what they mean:

REMEMBER

This icon draws your attention to important information you've probably already forgotten if we've told you about it before, or to information that we want you to remember in the future.

TECHNICAL STUFF

This icon suggests that we're going to say something that will make your eyes glaze over. But we use it sparingly — instead we try to make sure to cover technical points in understandable language, so you hardly know you've hit a technical bump at all.

TIP

This icon tells you to sit up and pay attention. We're telling you something that's worth acting on or keeping in mind.

WARNING

This icon says that you're heading for trouble and should reconsider your flight path!

Beyond the Book

In addition to the material in the print or e-book you're reading right now, this product also comes with some access-anywhere goodies on the web.

Check out the free Cheat Sheet for help on determining whether you have a small business personality, a list of five great websites for setting up a Canadian small business, and five reasons why small businesses fail. To get the Cheat Sheet, just go to www.dummies.com and type **Canadian Small Business Kit For Dummies Cheat Sheet** in the Search box.

This book includes companion downloadable content. You can find just about every form, table, questionnaire, and contract that we mention in this book on the Downloads tab at www.dummies.com/go/csbkfd4e.

Where to Go from Here

You don't have to read this book in order. Each chapter is self-contained, so you can pick up some information here and some information there about a topic that's of particular interest to you. For example, if you're interested in buying a franchise, have a look at Chapter 5. If you're keen to incorporate, take a peek at Chapter 6. Worried about where you're going to get the money for everything you need to run your business? Check out Chapters 9 and 10. If you're forward-thinking, and you're already envisioning how your business will expand, go to Chapter 18.

But if you're really thinking of starting a business and you haven't been in business before, we recommend that you begin at the beginning and read until you reach the end.

1
Small Business Essentials

IN THIS CHAPTER

» Knowing the upsides and downsides of small business ownership

» Identifying a good idea and business opportunity

» Assessing your true entrepreneurial spirit

» Looking at timing and resources

» Deciding if you should keep your day job

Chapter **1**

Do You Have the Right Stuff?

S o you're thinking of starting your own business! Every year, lots of Canadians of all ages and backgrounds get the entrepreneurial urge and take the leap to start businesses. Some of those businesses become very successful, and some of them fail.

Business success or failure isn't the result of fate, or random chance. A business does well for good reasons — like providing a great product or service, having a solid marketing plan, and having an owner with good management skills.

Likewise, when a business goes under, you can often identify the reasons — lack of money to get properly started, poor timing or location for entering the market, or a wipeout on the customer service front. Whatever the reason for a business failure, it usually boils down to this: The business owner didn't look carefully before leaping into a new business frontier.

This chapter and the others in this section of the book help you think about going into business before you hit the ignition button and blast off. Think of this first section as "countdown."

Weighing the Pros and the Cons of Small Business Ownership

People start up their own businesses for different reasons. One of the best reasons is that they've found a business opportunity and idea that are just too attractive to pass up. A good reason is that they want to work for themselves rather than for someone else. A discouraging — but still valid — reason is that their other job options are poor (the number of small business start-ups always rises when the economy sinks or stinks).

Whatever your reason is for wanting to become an entrepreneur, you should know that life as an entrepreneur is a bit of a mixed bag. Don't say we didn't warn you! Running your own business has some great advantages, but it also has its share of disadvantages.

The pros

Here are some of the good things about going into business for yourself:

>> **You're free!** You'll have the freedom to

- Make your own decisions — you're in charge now. Only investors (see Chapter 9), customers and clients (see Chapter 13), government regulators (see Chapter 6), and so on will tell you what to do.

- Choose your own work hours — in theory, anyway. You may not be able to get away with sleeping in until noon or concentrating your productive hours around 3 a.m. But you're more likely to be able to pick up the kids from school at 3 p.m., or exercise from 10 a.m. to 11 a.m., or grocery shop during normal office hours.

- Create your own work environment (see Chapters 7 and 8) — surround yourself with dirty coffee cups and empty candy wrappers if you feel like it.

>> **You can be creative!** You can build your business from scratch following your own ideas rather than following someone else's master plan. (See Chapter 3.)

>> **You'll face new challenges!** Every day. And twice as many on days that end in a *y*. You'll never be able to say that work is always the same old boring routine.

>> **Your job will be secure . . . as long as you have a business!** Your business may fail — but no one can fire you. You can ask yourself to resign, though. (See Chapter 20 for information about the depressing prospect of running out of money.)

>> **You'll have increased financial opportunities!** If your business is successful, you have the potential to make more than you could as an employee.

>> **You'll have tax advantages!** This is especially true if your business is not incorporated (a sole proprietorship or a partnership), but it's also true in a different way if your business is incorporated (see Chapter 6).

The cons

Do you think we used enough exclamation marks in the exuberant section just before this one? Bet they got you all enthused and excited about entrepreneurship. But calm down for a minute — being an entrepreneur has plenty of disadvantages, too. For some people, they outweigh the advantages. For example:

>> **You may not make a lot of money.** You may make enough money to live on, but it may not come in regularly like an employment paycheque, so you'll have cash flow predictability and budgeting problems. Or you may not make enough money to live on. You may not even make any money at all. You may go bankrupt and lose not only your business, but most of your personal possessions as well. See Chapter 20 for comfort (or failing comfort, at least for information).

>> **You lose easy and inexpensive access to employment benefits if you don't hang on to employment elsewhere.** These may be benefits that you have come to count on — extended health and dental benefits, disability insurance, life insurance, a pension plan, and so on.

>> **You'll have to work really hard.** That is, if you want to succeed — and you won't just be working at the business your business is about. You'll also have to do stuff you may not be trained to do, such as accounting, sales, and collection work. (But see Chapters 13 and 17 for some help.)

>> **You may not have a lot of free time.** You may see less of your friends, family, and pets (even if you're working at home) and have less time for your favourite activities. Getting a business up and running takes more than hard work; it also takes your time and commitment. Don't scoff that you won't let that happen to you, at least not until you've put in hours filling out government paperwork (GST/HST for example — see Chapter 16) on a beautiful sunny day that would be perfect for, well, almost anything else. By the way, you don't get paid for your sacrificed time, either.

>> **You may have to put a lot of your own money into starting up the business.** And even if you can borrow the money, unless the lender is The Bank of Mom and Dad, you'll have to give personal guarantees that the money will be repaid (with interest) within a certain time. The pressure is

building! (For more on borrowing, see Chapter 9.) By the way, not to add to the pressure or anything, but you should know that you might lose your own money or not be able to repay borrowed money because of factors beyond your control. You could get sick (and now you probably don't have disability insurance), be flattened by a competitor, squashed by a nose-diving economy, or whacked by a partner who pulls out on you. (See Chapter 20 for advice on how to deal with some of these problems).

>> **You are the bottom line.** No excuses — success is up to you, and failure is your fault. You'll have to keep on top of changes in your field, the impact of new technology, economic fluctuations. . . .

>> **Your personal life can stick its nose into your business life in a major way.** If you and your spouse split up, your spouse may be able to claim a share of your business under equalization provisions in the family law of some provinces. You might have to sell your home, your business, or your business assets (business property) to pay off your spouse. (Chapter 21 looks at selling your business.)

Choosing Your Business

After you're aware of the upside and the downside to running your own business, start considering how people choose a business to go into.

Five main kinds of businesses exist:

>> **Service:** Doing things for others, including the professions (doctors, engineers, lawyers, dentists, architects, accountants, pilots); skilled trades (plumbers, electricians, carpet installers, bookkeepers, renovators, truckers, carpenters, landscapers); and a huge range of other things for which you might need a lot of training and skill, or at least some talent and willingness. We're talking about teachers, data scientists, financial planners, real estate agents, painters, insurance brokers, management consultants, taxi and Uber drivers, travel agents, dry cleaners, caterers, event planners, hairdressers, equipment repairers, commercial printers, photographers, gardeners, snow removers . . . this list could go on.

>> **Retail:** Selling things to the general public, such as jewellery, groceries, clothing, appliances, books, furniture, antiques and collectibles, toys, hardware, cards and knick-knacks, garden accessories, plants, cars . . . this list could also go on.

>> **Wholesale:** Buying large quantities of goods from manufacturers at a discount and selling in smaller quantities to others — usually retailers — for a higher price. For example, you could buy nails in bulk from a manufacturer and resell them to hardware stores. Wholesalers sometimes also sell to the general public, usually without the frills of a retail establishment (for example, bulk food, carpets, and clothing).

>> **Manufacturing:** Making things from scratch — from designing and sewing baby clothes for sale through a local children's clothing store to making furniture in a workshop to manufacturing steel ingots in a mammoth industrial plant.

>> **Extraction:** Harvesting natural resources, including agriculture, fishing, logging, and mining.

If you're a glutton for detail, the five general types of businesses we outline here are actually broken down by the North American Industry Classification System (NAICS) into 928 specific Canadian industries. You can access this list to help you brainstorm small business ideas at www.statcan.gc.ca/eng/concepts/industry.

WARNING

Note that e-commerce is not a new and separate kind of business. E-commerce is simply a tool and channel to help transact business in a more efficient, effective, and economical way.

REMEMBER

Small businesses are most likely to concentrate in service and retail. Service, in particular, is usually the cheapest business to start up, because it requires less financial, human, and physical capital, so it attracts a lot of entrepreneurs.

Now, most people don't look at a short list of the 5, or even a ginormous list of 928, kinds of businesses or industries and wonder, "Service or extraction? Retail or manufacturing? Electronics or sporting goods? What best expresses my personality?" Instead, they have an idea that happens to fit into one of the five categories. At least, having an idea helps. And most people do, but others don't.

Those who have a clue

Most people who are thinking seriously about going into business for themselves have an idea about what they want to do before they start thinking seriously. Many people get their idea from a job they've held and decide to develop a new product or service similar to a former employer's, or become a consultant in the field.

WARNING

If you're going into the same field as your previous employer, be careful not to breach any confidentiality agreement or noncompetition agreement you may have entered into. And do not infringe your previous employer's copyright or trademark (see Chapter 3).

TIP

The idea may come from your skills:

>> If you have professional training or training in a skilled trade, you can set up your own business instead of joining a firm.

>> If you have a hobby, you may be able to expand it into a business.

>> If you invent something, you may be able to create a business around it.

>> If you have always wanted to start a particular kind of business, maybe now is the time.

Or you may have become aware of an excellent business opportunity. It may or may not be related to your training or a hobby or your "dream" business. Or in your travels, you may have seen a good idea that hasn't hit your hometown yet. Tim Hortons, for instance, was once confined to Hamilton, believe it or not.

Those who are clueless

Some people are serious about going into business but haven't decided on the business yet. If you're one of these people and you're looking for ideas . . . you probably need to look further than this chapter, or even this book. So here are some suggestions about where to look for an appealing business start-up idea.

To get a business idea in the first place, you can

>> Look around the field in which you have work experience to see if any opportunities are waiting to be explored. Maybe you've noticed that customers would be delighted if they could get a specific product or service that no one's offering right now.

>> Look around a field in which you have play experience to scope out opportunities — a few thousand people's hobby could become one person's successful business. Parlay your love of mountain climbing into an outfitting or guiding business, for example.

>> Take out your pet peeves and look them over. You may not be the only person who wishes someone would make/import/distribute a better pair of dog boots.

>> Read newspapers and magazines, trade publications, newsletters, and online publications and blogs to find out what's going on in the business world.

>> Visit trade shows, inventors' shows, conventions, or conferences to find out what's going on in a particular field.

>> Go on field trips (in your own city or town or in the wide world) to see what businesses exist and how they're doing.

>> Look for government or other lists of licensing opportunities.

>> Ask friends and acquaintances for ideas.

After you have an idea, you need to evaluate it by considering the following factors.

What to look for in a business start-up

To begin with, try to aim toward something you'll enjoy doing. Starting a business is hard enough without choosing a business that you're pretty sure you'll loathe, even if you think it could make a lot of money.

Next, look for something people want . . . as opposed to something they don't want, or that they'll have to be carefully educated to want. It should also be something they'll want tomorrow and next week as well as today — in other words, don't base your business on a product or service that's going out of use or out of style. Ideally, your product or service is something that people want often, rather than occasionally or only once.

Especially in Canada, consider offering a product or service that isn't completely seasonal like skate sharpening or outdoor ice cream stands. Choose something with a good distribution and advertising system in place: For example, a product you manufacture should be one that established retailers will be happy to carry; a product you sell should be one that already benefits from a national marketing campaign by the manufacturer; a service you offer should be positioned within a network that will bring you lots of referrals.

TIP

Look for a business with a high profit margin. You'd like your direct cost of performing the work or supplying the product to be a small percentage of what you charge the client or customer. (The service industry lends itself to robust profit margins; manufacturing and corner grocery stores do not.)

What to avoid in a business start-up

While you're searching for a business with lots of advantages, you also have to avoid a business with too many disadvantages.

You'll probably be happier if you stay away from a business that will be immediately overwhelmed by the existing competition. If the field is competitive (as are most fields worth going into), look for a niche where you have a competitive advantage (say, because you have a lot of natural talent or you've acquired great skills and experience; or because you have exclusive manufacturing or distribution rights). Don't go head-to-head with the established players and imagine you'll knock them down! They already enjoy first-mover advantage.

You also don't want a business that will be overwhelmed by regulation — by the federal, provincial, or municipal government — or by the governing body of a professional or skilled trade. You'll find regulation in any type of business, but it's worse in some than in others. For example, food and drug manufacturing are heavily regulated by the federal government, as are telecommunications and commercial aviation. Medical, dental, and many other professional services industries are likewise heavily regulated by provincial and federal bodies. Canada's growing cannabis industry has also joined the ranks of the strongly regulated, and rightly so. (We discuss this dynamic sector in Chapter 19.) Alternately, if you open a restaurant or bar, municipal food inspectors and provincial liquor inspectors will visit you regularly. Look into the extent of regulation when you research the area of business in which you are interested. We tell you about getting information geared to your specific business in Chapter 2.

You might prefer to avoid a business that will require expensive insurance from the start (this describes most of the professions, and the manufacture of products that are potentially harmful). (See Chapter 12 for more about insurance.)

Unless you've got guaranteed access to a big wad of cash, you'll certainly also want to avoid a business with high start-up costs. You may think you can build a better steel mill, but you can't do it on a $25,000 loan. Consider how much money you have to invest in starting up a business, or how much you can raise by borrowing. If you have almost nothing to invest and realistically don't expect anyone else will want to invest a lot in you and your business, choose a business that requires almost no initial investment (that's usually service).

You'll probably also want to steer clear of a business with immediate high labour needs. Paying employees isn't just a matter of cash flow (although that's pretty important). As an employer, you'll also have to deal with a lot of regulations and paperwork — such as income tax, Employment Insurance, Canada or Quebec Pension Plan, provincial workers' compensation, and occupational health and safety rules — and you may already have enough on your plate. (See Chapter 15 for more about the responsibilities of being an employer.)

Think about these trendy areas for business start-ups:

- **Become an alter-ego for people who have money but no time.** Be a concierge or personal assistant (do chores for people, like picking up dry cleaning or getting tickets to a show); personal shopper; closet organizer; handyman-for-hire; drop-in cook (shop for ingredients, go to the client's home and spend a few hours cooking meals for the entire week); or personal dating service operator or matchmaker.

- **Sell the promise of health, youth, and beauty to an aging population.** Be a personal trainer; spa service provider (massage, manicure, pedicure, makeup, facials); a plastic surgery consultant or coordinator; a tattoo artist or tattoo removal specialist or body piercer. Or be a manufacturer of exercise equipment, comfortable furniture, sun-protection clothing, or sports clothing.

- **Be an outsource for other people's businesses.** Provide telephone and email surveys, market surveys, data processing, technical support, secretarial support, bookkeeping, website design, or help in using social media sites.

- **Go the eco-entrepreneur route.** Manufacture, distribute, or sell ecologically sound cleaning products, recycling systems, or energy sources that are environmentally friendly or recyclable.

- **Provide specialty travel arrangements.** Organize seniors' tours, educational tours, eco-tours, or singles' tours.

- **Look after other people's kids, parents, or pets.** Provide a chauffeur service for kids (to get them to school, practices and games, after-school lessons, or appointments); offer dog walking, house-sitting, babysitting (rent-a-parent), or health-care coordination for the elderly; provide tutoring, keyboarding/typing, music lessons, computer lessons, or test preparation help; or provide sports coaching, a summer camp program, party planning and preparation, or a party place.

Determining If You Have the Small Business Personality

Whatever your reason for wanting to go into business for yourself, and whatever the business you decide to go into, stop and check whether you have the right personality for the adventure before you start. This is true whether you really want to go into business for yourself or whether you think you have no choice but to do so. And it will give you an excuse to put off figuring out your finances.

REMEMBER

Realizing that you don't have the right stuff to run your own business is better done before you sink a lot of time and effort, and maybe even money, into a business. You can always pursue other options.

And if you find you're not going to be the perfect entrepreneur, but you're determined to go ahead anyway, then a self-assessment will tell you where your weaknesses lie and show you where you need to improve or get outside help.

An entrepreneur needs most of the following qualities — whether you were born with them, or developed them, or are about to get working on them now:

>> **Self-confidence:** You have to believe in yourself and your abilities . . . no matter what other people might think. You have to believe that your success depends on the good work you know you can do and not on matters beyond your control. However, your self-confidence should be realistic and not induced by whatever weird thing they put in the coffee at your current workplace.

>> **Goal-orientation:** You have to know what you want, whether it's to revolutionize a particular industry or to be home when your children return from school. However, if your main goals are money, power, and prestige, you probably need to reorient yourself toward something a little more attainable in the small business sector.

>> **Drive to be your own boss:** The burning desire and the ability to be your own boss — if you need or even want direction about what to do next, you won't make it in your own business. You have to be able to make your own plans and carry them out.

>> **Independence:** The ability to work independently rather than as part of a team. You've probably had propaganda pounded into your head since you were a kid that teamwork is really important, and maybe even better than working on your own. It isn't if you're an entrepreneur.

>> **Survival skills:** The ability to survive without a social group is handy. When you start up your own business, you'll probably be working by yourself for some time. If you need people around you to chat with, or else you start to go crazy . . . then you may go crazy.

>> **People skills:** Even though you have to be able to get along without being surrounded by people all the time, you still have to get along with people. You'll be dealing directly with customers and clients (see Chapter 13), investors (see Chapter 9), suppliers (see Chapter 14), associates (see Chapter 6), and employees (see Chapter 15), and you need their willing cooperation.

>> **Determination and persistence:** You have to want to succeed, and you have to plan to succeed and keep working at succeeding. It's that "fire in the belly" stuff you hear about from people who look like they haven't slept in the past eight months.

>> **Self-discipline:** You can't let yourself be distracted from your work by nice weather, phone calls from family and friends, earthquakes, or wrestling matches on TV.

>> **Reliability:** You'll build most of your important business relationships by always meaning what you say and doing what you promise.

>> **Versatility:** You have to be prepared to do many different things in short periods of time, probably constantly switching from task to task.

>> **Creativity:** You have to want to do something new or something old in a new way. If copying what someone else is already doing is the best you can manage, you may not go far.

>> **Resourcefulness:** Creativity's country cousin, resourcefulness, means being prepared to try different ways of doing things if the first way doesn't work.

>> **Organizational talents:** You'll be plunged into chaos if you can't organize your goals, your time, or your accounts, to name just a few things.

>> **Risk-management instincts:** You have to be able to spot risks, weigh them, and come up with a plan to steer around them or soften their impact in case of a collision. (See Chapter 12 for some help in managing risk.)

>> **Nerves of steel in a crisis:** Nerves of granite, titanium, oak, and so on are acceptable. Nerves of rubber, talc, or pasta al dente are not. Crises won't necessarily be frequent, but they will occur. Don't count on gin or prescription drugs to stiffen your spine during a crisis. And you can't collapse until the crisis is over.

>> **Pick-yourself-up-itiveness — a combination of optimism and grit:** You're going to have failures, some of them caused by your own mistakes; and you have to see failures as valuable experiences rather than as signs that you and your business are doomed.

>> **Opportunism:** You need to not only recognize opportunities when they come along, but you also need to seek them out — and even create them yourself.

>> **Success-management instincts:** You can't let yourself be bowled over or lulled by success. You have to be able to see each success as a platform on which you can build your next success. (See Chapter 19.)

>> **Objectivity:** For a business owner, it's always reality-check time. You have to have the courage to stare down reality's throat and acknowledge your own mistakes. You also have to corner reality by getting feedback about your

business and how you run it from customers and clients, suppliers, professional advisors, competitors, employees, and even your mother-in-law. Then you have to have the strength to make necessary changes.

That's a long list! And you'll also need a Zen-like calm about not having a regular paycheque. Not only will you not get a bank deposit once a month, but you won't get paid for sick days, personal days off, or days when you show up at the office but are too zonked to work.

In addition, it helps if your parents (or close relatives or close friends) are or were in business for themselves. You may have absorbed some business know-how from them, plus you may have easy access to advice.

And to finish you off, good health and physical stamina can do an entrepreneur no harm.

The small business personality aptitude test

You may have taken a personality aptitude test before. Perhaps you took one when you sought employment in a large company to see if you would fit in, or before you got married to see if you were truly compatible with your future life partner. Taking a small business personality aptitude test is similar. It's not unlike taking a test to see if you would get along being "married" to your own small business! It's all about fit and alignment to your needs, wants, and objectives.

TIP

A great free resource is the online entrepreneurial assessment provided by the Business Development Bank of Canada. Go to www.bdc.ca, hover your mouse over Articles and Tools, and click Entrepreneur's Toolkit. From there, click the Entrepreneurial Potential Self-Assessment link. This robust questionnaire includes 50 statements that will take you about 15 minutes to thoughtfully complete. The questions are not binary — there is no right or wrong answer. All the tool requires is your honest response. When you finish the questionnaire, your answers are summarized in a way that helps you to self-assess your entrepreneurial traits, motivations, aptitudes, and attitudes.

Considering Other Factors Before Starting Your Business

Even if you're a potential paragon of entrepreneurship, think about the following before leaping into business for yourself:

>> Would your personal life allow you to take the entrepreneurial plunge right now?

>> Do you have the practical resources to go into the particular business you have your heart set on?

>> Is this a good time (for economic and market reasons) for anyone to go into this particular business?

Your personal life

What's going on in your personal life right now? Starting a small business makes more sense at some times than at others. Think about the following questions:

>> Do you need a steady income right now — maybe because you have small children and your spouse has given up paid employment to stay home with them, or because you have debts to repay?

>> Do you need a steady and conventional lifestyle right now because all hell is breaking loose in the rest of your life?

>> Do you need to be physically present in your home more (maybe because you want to spend time with your young children after school or you have to look after an elderly parent), so a home-based business makes more sense than working outside your home?

>> Do you have some money to throw around right now, perhaps from an inheritance or a buyout package from your employer?

>> Would you have trouble raising the necessary cash to start a business — say, because you've just gone bankrupt?

TIP

If you have a spouse, or someone who depends on your income or companionship, ask him or her to list the pros and cons of your going into business for yourself right now — from his or her own point of view. You might as well get it all out in the open.

Your practical resources

Do you really have what it takes to start this business? Ask yourself now, before you invest time, money, and effort and maybe pass up other work or opportunities for which you're better suited.

For starters, if you go into any business, you'll have to

>> Find customers; identify customer needs; develop new product and service ideas; decide on prices; and develop promotional strategies. (This is *marketing* — see Chapters 4 and 11.)

>> Persuade customers to buy. (This is *sales* — see Chapter 13.)

>> Do good work so customers will (a) be more likely to pay you and (b) come back to you. (This is *commitment to excellence* — see Chapter 13 again.)

>> Enter into contracts to buy and provide goods and services — you need to know what has to go into the contract, even if you don't draft it yourself. (This is *business law* — see Chapters 13 and 14.)

>> Have a working knowledge of the law so you don't break it and it doesn't break you (for example, you need to know about different kinds of taxes and levies; see Chapter 16), non-discrimination in providing goods and services (Chapter 13) or in hiring (see Chapter 15), breach of the *Competition Act* in your advertising (see Chapter 11), and arrest of shoplifters (see Chapter 12).

>> Understand the financial side of your business and keep proper accounts (payable and receivable) (see Chapter 17), collect and pay taxes (see Chapter 16), borrow money, manage cash flow, handle credit, and create and stick to a budget (see Chapter 9). (This is *accounting* and *money management*.)

>> Keep track of the product or service you provide or sell (if it's a service, you provide your time) and purchase supplies and materials on time. (This is *inventory management*.)

>> Buy and use a computer and software. (This is *computer literacy*.)

>> Get money owed to you by deadbeat customers and clients. (This is *collections* — see Chapter 13.)

>> Eventually hire, supervise, train, motivate, and evaluate employees. (This is *human resources management* — see Chapter 15.)

If you don't have these skills, you'll have to fill in the blanks. We give you some ideas about that in Chapter 2. (Don't get into a funk! You may be surprised at how many of the skills you've already acquired through courses at school, jobs you've held, participation in clubs or organizations, and even just from running your own life.)

You'll also need a set of skills to run the particular kind of business you have in mind. Ask yourself these questions:

>> **Do I need particular skills, talents, years of experience, expertise, or connections to succeed in this business?** Or, in some cases, do I need all this just to get my foot in the door of this business?

>> **Is this business heavily regulated?** Do I need particular education, training, or other official qualifications before I start? Do I need government approval that may not be automatic?

>> **Is this business expensive?** Do I need a lot of money to get set up? (For example, will it cost a lot to develop the product or service, to manufacture the product, or to find customers or develop a distribution system?)

HEY, KIDS, TRY THIS AT HOME!

After you have a good idea of what you need to get into and run the business of your choice, do this exercise to put off doing really useful work for a while. First, write a job description for starting this business. What education, background, and skills are required to do the job now and as it grows? What experience would be useful? What personal characteristics should the owner have? Be objective. Forget that you're the only person to whom you're going to offer the job.

Then apply for the job by writing your own résumé:

- Detail your formal education.

- List the jobs you've held and tasks you performed in those jobs. (You can include jobs that aren't normally considered paid employment, such as running a household.)

- List the skills you've acquired through formal education and training, jobs, and personal interests and activities (hobbies, sports, membership in organizations, and so on) and through life experience.

- Finish up with your character by listing your strengths and weaknesses.

Compare your résumé with the job description. Are you up to the job? Would you hire yourself? If you think the job applicant is on kind of shaky ground, maybe you're heading into the wrong business.

But don't despair. If you don't qualify for the job yet, ask yourself what reasonable steps you could take to improve your qualifications. Maybe you can get some training or experience, even as you start to set up the business.

If you don't know the answers to these questions, you need to do your homework. Speak to people who are already in this business, read trade papers or publications about the business, or contact government offices and professional or trade associations. We help you out with some of this in Chapter 2.

The broader economy, the industry, and the specific market

Your personal life and practical resources may be in just the right shape for you to start your own business, but the business world will chew up and spit out a navel-gazer. You also need to look at the economy generally, and at the market for your proposed product or service in particular. If the economy's tanking, the time probably isn't right to launch a luxury business . . . but the time may be exactly right to start a business that will appeal to penny-pinchers. If the market for your product is jammed with competitors or if demand has started to dry up, you're headed for trouble if you stay on course. But if the market is just about to expand in a big way, you may have hit on a sure-fire success.

Easing into It: Knowing If and When to Give Up Your Day Job

Should you start a business and keep your day job (if you've got one)?

Conventional wisdom says that you shouldn't give up your day job until absolutely necessary (that's the point when you have to devote the time to your business or give it up) or until you don't need a day job (that's the point when you're making a living from your business). Conventional wisdom also urges entrepreneurs not to go it alone until they've saved up about six months' salary. That's a good joke! It would take most of us years to save six months' salary, unless we were offered a fantastic buyout package.

Even if you're dying to tell your current employer "I quit!" think about the following questions:

>> **Do you have to have the money from employment?** Even if your business turns out to be a success, you may not have much, or even any, income when you first start your business.

>> **Do you want to keep your employment contacts?** The business you're starting might be something your employer or fellow employees could assist or patronize.

>> **Do you have the time to hold down a job and start a business (and still have time to eat and sleep)?**

>> **Would starting your own business and keeping your day job be problematic because of**

- Your employer's requirement (in your employment contract) that you not carry on any kind of a competing business while you're an employee?

- Your employer's requirement (in your employment contract) that you put your full effort toward your employment work?

- Suspicious superiors and co-workers who would assume you were goofing off by focusing on your own business instead of doing what you were paid to do?

>> **Do you want to be able to fall back on your day job if your business venture doesn't work out?** Remember, if you quit to start a business, you might not get hired back.

IN THIS CHAPTER

» **Searching for information**

» **Getting information about business in general**

» **Investigating your own field**

» **Building your skill set with education**

» **Finding experts to help you**

» **Looking for potential customers and suppliers**

Chapter **2**

Seeking Out Helpful Business Information

How do you find the information you need to start your business? In this chapter, we tell you how to collect data about the following areas:

» Starting and carrying on a business

» Acquiring general business skills

» Acquiring skills for your chosen business field

» Choosing potential customers and suppliers

We also help you line up a team of experts: a lawyer, an accountant, and an insurance agent. You need their help to get your business off the ground.

Getting Started

The amount of information about business can appear to be infinite. How do you zero in on the information that's useful to you?

TIP

The first step is to get general information about starting and carrying on a business. Our advice is to find a fairly comprehensive and self-contained start-to-finish source, such as a book — hey, this book is a great choice! — or a business resource centre, or a website. You've already got the book, so below are our suggestions for resource centres and websites. We start with the superstars, such as the Government of Canada's business resource portal. But we also tell you about provincial and private-sector resources.

The Government of Canada: Core resources for entrepreneurs

The Government of Canada maintains an online portal, referred to as Canada Business (www.canadabusiness.ca), that provides access to both government and general business information, relevant to both start-up entrepreneurs and established, small to medium-size businesses in any field. In this section, we show you what you can expect to find there.

Taking a look at the services offered

The Canada Business website provides information on government services, programs, and regulations pertaining to business. It has an extensive and up-to-date reference collection of general business information from government and non-government sources — topics include starting a business, writing a business plan, finding financing, marketing, exporting, and being an employer. Service centres located across Canada have information officers to help you navigate your way through everything they offer.

In addition, you can get products, services, publications, and referrals to experts. Here are some examples of the products and services the service centres provide:

>> **Info guides:** These free guides on different topics provide brief overviews of services and programs.

>> **How-to guides:** These guides provide information about the potential licence, permit, and registration requirements for specific types of businesses.

>> **Fact sheets:** These fact sheets contain information about starting and running a business and are available online.

>> **BizPaL online business permits and licences service:** This online service provides information about business permits and licence requirements from all levels of government.

>> **Specialized Research Service:** This limited business research service is free and provides access to information on topics such as business associations, Canadian demographics, company data, consumer spending, and sample business plans.

Some of the service centres also offer low-cost seminars and workshops on a variety of business topics.

Getting access to the resources you need

You can obtain resources in three ways:

>> **Website:** The government's website (www.canadabusiness.ca) contains information about business-related programs and services of federal and provincial agencies. The site allows you to input your province, industry and/or demographic group and receive information tailored to the location and nature of your business, and provides links to the individual websites maintained by some provinces. The main site contains information on such topics as

- Starting a business
- Looking at growth and innovation in your business
- Getting financial assistance through grants, loans, and financing
- Managing federal and provincial taxes
- Complying with business regulations
- Obtaining licences and permits
- Exporting and importing
- Hiring and managing staff
- Creating a business plan
- Managing and operating a business
- Conducting market research and getting access to statistics
- Doing marketing and sales
- Managing intellectual property
- Exiting your business

Some of the provincial sites also provide information about and let you register for business workshops and seminars, as well as links to other useful websites.

>> **Email:** Send questions by email from the main website under Contact Us.

>> **In person:** At the offices of your provincial/territorial service centre, you can use the resource materials on your own or with the help of a business information officer. These provincial service centres also have arrangements with existing business service organizations in communities across Canada to provide relevant information. Contact your Canada Business network service centre for the location nearest you. You can find information for your region at http://canadabusiness.ca/about/contact.

Provincial/territorial government websites

Each provincial and territorial government maintains a website. Some of the provincial sites contain good general business information that you can use to get started.

For example, the Nova Scotia site contains an "Access to Business" page with links to publications on planning, starting, and operating a business in Nova Scotia. The Manitoba site contains a "Business" page with links to information about starting, financing, and operating a business. The Ontario government site is particularly helpful; its "Business" page contains links to many useful sources, including an online book entitled "Your Guide to Small Business."

Here are the websites:

>> **Alberta:** www.gov.ab.ca

>> **British Columbia:** www.gov.bc.ca

>> **Manitoba:** www.gov.mb.ca

>> **New Brunswick:** www.gov.nb.ca

>> **Newfoundland and Labrador:** www.gov.nl.ca

>> **Northwest Territories:** www.gov.nt.ca

>> **Nova Scotia:** www.gov.ns.ca

>> **Nunavut:** www.gov.nu.ca

>> **Ontario:** www.gov.on.ca

>> **Prince Edward Island:** www.gov.pe.ca

>> **Quebec:** www.quebec.ca

>> **Saskatchewan:** www.gov.sk.ca

>> **Yukon:** www.gov.yk.ca

Bank and trust company websites

The major banks' and trust companies' websites have information about the products and services they provide to small businesses. Some have information about general business topics, as well. For example, the Bank of Montreal site (www.bmo.com) contains links to a number of small business resources such as podcasts, planning guides, articles, tips, Internet resources, and business FAQs.

A particularly good example is the Royal Bank of Canada (RBC) website (www.rbc.com). It contains information about many general business topics such as starting a business, expanding a business, and business succession. It also has several web pages promoting entrepreneurship for women. The RBC website has its own "Resource Centre" for businesses to guide you through the steps of developing a business plan. It even provides sample business plans for several different types of businesses. Other bank websites include TD Canada Trust (www.td.com), CIBC (www.cibc.com), HSBC (www.hsbc.com), and Bank of Nova Scotia, or Scotiabank as it is better known (www.scotiabank.com).

Small business or entrepreneurship centres

A number of small business or entrepreneurship centres provide support and training to start-up and small businesses, for example:

>> **Centennial College Centre of Entrepreneurship:** This Toronto-based centre provides entrepreneurial training, business plan development, analysis of proposed acquisitions, as-needed business advice and consulting, and international business training. It also offers a New Business Start-up Program, designed to provide entrepreneurs with the basic principles and practices of business, along with the skills to market, operate, and control a business. Visit www.centennialcollege.ca/pdf/new-website/coe/be-your-own-boss.pdf to find out more.

>> **Centre for Entrepreneurship Education & Development Incorporated (CEED):** This Nova Scotia not-for-profit society is devoted to helping people discover and use entrepreneurship as a vehicle to become self-reliant. Its services include technical assistance, entrepreneurship consulting, and entrepreneurship courses. CEED's website (www.ceed.ca) has more information.

>> **Ontario Small Business Enterprise Centres:** These Ontario government centres are located throughout the province and provide entrepreneurs with support to start and grow their businesses. They offer a wide variety of support resources, including consultations with qualified business consultants, workshops and seminars, and mentoring and networking opportunities. Visit www.ontario.ca/page/small-business-enterprise-centre-and-community-based-provider-locations for more information.

>> **The Stu Clark Centre for Entrepreneurship:** The University of Manitoba's Asper School of Business (www.umanitoba.ca/asper) operates this centre. It aims to encourage the development of new businesses and entrepreneurial thinking among Canadians. The centre supports a variety of programs aimed at youth, as well as undergraduate students and adults. Its Manitoba Venture Challenge (MVC) is a province-wide competition open to new and established businesses in Manitoba whose owners are seeking outside investment or need advice to start or grow their businesses. The specific web page is www.umanitoba.ca/faculties/management/academic_depts_centres/centres_institutes/entrepreneurship/index.html.

Business incubators

A *business incubator* is a business-mentoring facility that nurtures small- and medium-sized businesses during the start-up period. Business incubators provide management assistance, education, technical and business support services, and financial advice. They may also provide flexible rental space and flexible leases.

Over 1,300 business incubators exist in North America, with about 170 located throughout Canada. Most Canadian business incubators are non-profit and sponsored by government, economic development organizations, and academic institutions. Some examples of business incubators are

>> **CDEM Business Incubator:** Run by the Economic Development Council for Manitoba Bilingual Municipalities and located in St. Boniface, Manitoba. Visit www.cdem.com/en for more information.

>> **The Genesis Centre:** Located at the Memorial University of Newfoundland in St. John's. Their website is www.genesiscentre.ca.

>> **Northern Alberta Business Incubator:** Created by and located in the city of St. Albert, Alberta. Its website is www.nabi.ca.

>> **Toronto Business Development Centre (TBDC):** Started by the City of Toronto, TBDC's Business Incubation Program supports the growth of new businesses by providing useful resources, including business advisory support, dedicated office space, and participation in a robust community of successful entrepreneurs from around the world. Its website is www.tbdc.com.

The business incubator process usually has three stages:

>> **Pre-incubation:** Applicants are screened for ability and compatibility with the business incubator's goals and may be referred for business skills training.

> » **Incubation:** The business becomes a tenant of the business incubator and has access to the incubator's services for about three years.
>
> » **Graduation:** The business moves into the community.

TECHNICAL STUFF

Incubators are also known as *accelerators.* The slight nuance lies in the stage of start-ups they accept. Incubators are a resource for the "childhood" of a start-up, whereas accelerators can guide small business entrepreneurs from "adolescence" to "adulthood."

Getting Information Geared to Your Specific Business

After you find out about starting and carrying on a business in general, you can find out more about your field of business in particular. For example, you might want to know these facts:

» What skills you need for this business

» What government regulations apply to this business

» How much it will cost to run this kind of business

» What the demand is for the goods or services you'll be supplying

» Who the likely customers are for the goods and services you'll be providing

» What the competition is like for this type of business

» What supplies and equipment you require for this type of business

You need a good gateway into the sector you're interested in. Here are our recommendations.

Innovation, Science, and Economic Development Canada

The Innovation, Science, and Economic Development Canada website (www. ic.gc.ca) is particularly useful at the preliminary stage of starting a business because, in addition to general business information, it also contains information on a wide variety of businesses, organized by sector. Each type of business has its own page, with additional pages on a number of subtopics. The subtopics vary for each business category but cover areas such as the following:

>> **Company directories:** Links to lists of Canadian companies carrying on business in the field

>> **Contacts:** Links to major trade associations in the field

>> **Electronic business:** Links to a variety of information about e-business and e-commerce

>> **Events:** Links to major trade shows in a particular business field

>> **Grants:** Links to information about ways to fund your business with government assistance

>> **Industry news:** Links to Canada and U.S. trade periodicals

>> **Regulations and standards:** Links to relevant government regulations and standards organizations

>> **Statistics, analysis, and industry profiles:** Links to North American Industry Classification definitions and to selected Canadian statistics on topics such as the Canadian market, imports, and exports

>> **Trade and exporting:** Links to relevant international trade agreements and export information

Trade and professional associations

Trade and professional associations are another great source of information about particular fields of business. Thousands of associations exist in North America, many of them based in the United States. Whatever your field of business, a related association probably exists. A good association will give you access to industry-specific information. Most associations maintain a website, setting out the services the association provides and membership information. Simon Fraser University has a web page with a repository of trade and professional associations that can be found at www.lib.sfu.ca/help/research-assistance/subject/business/associations. More general resources can be accessed at www.cpmdq.com/htm/org.canada2.htm and www.canadiancareers.com/sector.html.

TIP

The Internet is the best way to track down the trade or professional associations in your field. Use a search engine such as Google (www.google.com) or Bing (www.bing.com) by typing in the name of the specific field you're interested in plus the word **association** — for example, **giftware association**. You can also get information about associations on the Industry Canada website by following the Contact link for your business field.

AVOID GETTING LOST IN CYBERSPACE

TIP

The Internet is the best way to get the information you need. You can find what you're looking for on the Internet reasonably easily — once! What seems to be remarkably hard is finding the same information a second time.

We can't tell you how many times we've found a wonderful site on the web — just to have it vanish into a black hole when we decide to return for a bit more information. We can never remember the website address or re-create the search that got us there. Don't let that happen to you. Here are some tips:

- Note the website address of any site that seems useful. Bookmark the site, but be warned that websites often move — sometimes without leaving a forwarding address.

- Mark your trail. If you found a site through a web search, make a note of the keywords you used. Also, make a note of the search engine! The same keywords on a different search engine may not turn up the site you're looking for. Not all sites turn up in all search engines. And the same site may be locatable with different keywords in different search engines.

- Print anything useful. If you find information, print it or save it to a file. Then you won't have to go looking for it again.

Trade and professional journals

Many trade and professional associations publish journals or newsletters with current information about the field. They also contain ads for equipment and supplies that the business uses, and some list business opportunities (businesses for sale, partners wanted, premises for lease, equipment for sale, and so on). You may be able to get information about trade and professional journals on the Innovation, Science, and Economic Development Canada website by following the Industry News link offered for some industry sectors.

Workshops and seminars

Many trade and professional associations hold seminars and workshops on topics of specific interest to members. Some offer courses leading to a designation or certification in the field.

Trade shows

Most trade associations hold an industry-wide trade show at least once a year. Trade shows are good places to make contacts in the industry and learn about the latest trends in the field.

Obtaining Essential Business Skills

After you research your chosen business field, you may realize that you need some training before you can start your business. You may need skills specific to your chosen business field (such as how to frame a picture if you're going into the framing business, or how to mediate if you're going into family counselling), or you may want to pick up some general business skills and knowledge such as simple bookkeeping, basic computer skills, or how to prepare a business plan.

When people think of education, they usually think of universities, community colleges, career colleges, vocational schools, and boards of education. But in fact, many different places offer business education and skills training. You may be able to pick up the skills you need from a trade association, a partnering Canada Business network service centre, or the little place in your local mall that teaches keyboarding. In fact, you may want to avoid many of the educational institutions, because they often offer certificate or diploma programs more suited to people looking for a job, rather than individual courses focused on the specific skills an entrepreneur needs.

Where you go to get your training will depend on the kind of skill you're trying to acquire.

Skills for your particular business

You may be able to pick up the special skills required for your particular business in a day, a weekend, or a week. Or you may need a certificate or diploma in the field that will take months or years to get.

You may be able to find out not only what skills you need, but also where to get them, from Innovation, Science, and Economic Development Canada or from the relevant trade or professional association. Or you can use a search engine such as Google, Bing, or Yahoo! by typing in the name of the specific field you're interested in and the word **education** or **training**.

If you're not required to have a degree, diploma, or certificate offered by a university or community college, you may want to consider programs offered by privately run career colleges or vocational schools. These programs tend to be shorter than university and community college programs, but be warned — these courses are usually more expensive, sometimes much more expensive!

The trade or professional association in your field may offer short workshops or seminars on individual topics of interest to you as well as complete training programs designed specifically for your field.

General business skills

To acquire in-depth business skills, you can enroll in degree, diploma, or certificate programs offered by colleges and universities. These programs run over the course of a year, or from two to three years. You probably won't be able to take one course of interest to you without taking another course as a prerequisite or without signing on for the entire program.

TIP

If you want to acquire some business skills as quickly as possible, look for *continuing education* courses offered by your local university or community college. For example, the University of Toronto (http://learn.utoronto.ca) and most other Canadian post-secondary institutions offer courses (usually with classes held once a week for about three months) in a wide variety of business-related areas, including Accounting Fundamentals, Business Law and Insurance, Business Management, Business Strategy, Social Media Starter, Taxation for Canadian Business, and Understanding and Resolving Conflict. The University of Calgary (http://conted.ucalgary.ca) has seminars on numerous topics, including Time Management, Accounting for Non-Financial Managers, Building Great Customer Relationships, Writing Skills for Business, and Creative Negotiating.

Your local board of education may offer courses in business skills as part of its continuing education programs, and you should have no problem enrolling in individual courses rather than in programs. Classes will probably be scheduled once a week over several months.

You may also be able to find weekend workshops or evening seminars offered by your trade or professional association, or through your provincial Canada Business network service centre.

Finding Professional and Other Help

Planning a business start-up takes a lot of work. But you don't have to do it all alone. You can and should get professional help with many of the tasks involved. In this section, we help you determine whom you need on your team, and how to find the best candidates.

Determining whom you need to help you

At the very least, you'll need a lawyer, a Chartered Professional Accountant (CPA), and a licensed insurance agent or broker. We also offer suggestions for other professionals you might find useful.

Lawyer

Almost everything that happens in the business world has legal implications. A lawyer can help you navigate through every stage of your business odyssey.

When you're setting up your business, a lawyer can

>> Help you decide whether or not to incorporate (see Chapter 6)

>> Help you form a corporation or partnership (see Chapter 6)

>> Review start-up documents such as loan agreements (see Chapter 9), leases (see Chapter 8), and franchise agreements (see Chapter 5)

>> Draft standard forms for contracts to use in your business (see Chapters 12, 13, and 14)

When you're in business, a lawyer can be of further assistance by

>> Helping you negotiate contracts (see Chapters 9, 12, 13, 14, and 18)

>> Giving you advice about hiring and firing employees (see Chapter 15)

>> Helping you collect your unpaid accounts (see Chapter 13)

>> Acting for you in a lawsuit if you sue or are sued (see Chapter 20)

Even if you decide to get out of the business, you'll still need a lawyer to help you sell it, or give it to your children, or wind it up (see Chapter 21).

Accountant

REMEMBER

In Canada, anyone can call himself or herself an accountant. What you want is a professional accountant — a chartered professional accountant, or CPA. Professional accountants are licensed and regulated by CPA Canada (www.cpacanada.ca).

You'll probably need an accountant to help you

>> Buy an existing business (see Chapter 5)

>> Set up a bookkeeping system (see Chapter 17)

>> Prepare budgets and cash-flow statements (see Chapters 10 and 16)

>> Prepare financial statements (see Chapter 17)

>> Prepare your income tax returns (see Chapter 16)

>> Deal with the Canada Revenue Agency (CRA) from time to time (see Chapter 16)

Insurance agent or broker

You'll need insurance for your business, including

>> Property insurance to cover loss or damage to your business property

>> Business interruption insurance to cover your loss of earnings if your business premises are damaged

>> General liability insurance to cover claims made if you cause injury to a customer, supplier, or innocent bystander

>> Key person insurance to tide over your business in case you, a partner, or an important employee dies or becomes disabled

>> Cyber insurance in case your personal data or intellectual property is hacked by some kid in his mother's basement

We tell you more about insurance in Chapter 12.

An *insurance agent* (a person who deals with and sells the policies of only one insurance company) or *insurance broker* (a person who deals with and sells the policies of several insurance companies) can give you advice about what kind of insurance you need and how much. Both agents and brokers are regulated and licensed by provincial governments.

Other assistance

Depending on the nature of your business, you may also want help from any of the following professionals (in no particular order):

>> **Advertising firm and/or media relations firm:** To help you get the word out about your business

>> **Business coach:** To help you do various things such as acquire presentation skills, get pointers on power dressing, pick up business etiquette, and even improve your table manners (for those four-fork lunches with potential investors and customers)

>> **Business valuation expert:** To help you decide on the value of a business you are thinking of buying

>> **Computer systems consultant:** To help you choose and set up your computer equipment and choose and install your software

>> **Graphic designer:** To help you design a business logo, your business cards, and letterhead

>> **Human resources specialist (also known as a head-hunter):** To help you hire staff

- ≫ **Interior designer:** To help you set up your business premises attractively

- ≫ **Management consultant:** To help you polish your management skills

- ≫ **Marketing consultant:** To help you identify the market for your product or service and determine how best to reach that market

- ≫ **Website designer:** To help you create a great website for your business

Identifying the right people

Whatever kind of help you're looking for, you want to find someone who has experience in small business matters, someone with whom you'll feel comfortable, and someone who will charge you a reasonable fee.

TIP

Take these steps before you hire a professional:

1. **Get recommendations.**

   Ask your friends, relatives, or business associates for names of good people.

2. **Investigate.**

   Call each recommended person's office to find out more about his or her area of expertise, experience with business start-ups, fees, and location (if the person doesn't make client calls but expects you to come to him or her).

3. **Interview.**

   Meet the top two or three candidates in person. You want not only more information than you collected in Step 2, but also to see how you react to each individual personally.

Finding peer support

Even though you're going it alone in the business universe, you may want to seek out the companionship of fellow travellers with whom you can share your experiences and from whom you can get advice. Whatever demographic group you fall into, you'll likely find a business organization for you. These organizations provide opportunities to network and get advice geared to your demographic.

Here's a sampling:

- ≫ **Canadian Association of Women Executives & Entrepreneurs:** An organization that provides networking, support, mentoring, and professional development to businesswomen at all stages of their careers (www.cawee.net)

- **》 Canadian Council for Aboriginal Business:** A national, non-profit organization that promotes the full participation of Aboriginal individuals in the Canadian economy (www.ccab.com)

- **》 Canadian Gay & Lesbian Chamber of Commerce:** An organization designed to improve opportunities for gay, lesbian, bisexual, transgender, transsexual, two-spirited, and intersex owned/operated/friendly businesses (www.cglcc.ca)

- **》 Futurpreneur Canada:** A national, non-profit organization that provides financing, mentoring, and support tools to aspiring business owners ages 18 to 39. A mentoring program exists to match young entrepreneurs with a business expert from a network of almost 3,000 volunteer mentors (www.futurpreneur.ca/en)

Getting the Scoop on Customers and Suppliers

A lot of information is available about your potential customers and suppliers — much of it produced by the customers and suppliers themselves. You just need to know how to tap into it.

Customers

This early stage is a good time to do some research to help you figure out who your customers will be and what you'll have to do to persuade them to buy what you sell. (We tell you more about marketing your goods and services in Chapter 4.)

Who will your customers be?

Earlier in this chapter, we tell you about the Innovation, Science, and Economic Development Canada website, and that it has a separate page for each of many business sectors. You can do a search specific to a particular industry for major buying groups, wholesalers, and retailers. The pages for many sectors provide information on selling to government.

What can you find out about your potential customers?

If your prospective customers are businesses or government, you'll probably be able to learn a great deal without having to get up from your computer.

If you hope to sell your goods or services to the government of Canada, go to Buyandsell.gc.ca (http://buyandsell.gc.ca). This site was created to improve supplier and buyer awareness of federal business opportunities and of the Government of Canada procurement system. The site contains information, for suppliers who want to do business with the federal government, about how the government does its buying. Important updates about new international trade rules such as the Comprehensive Economic and Trade Agreement (CETA) can also be found there.

TIP

If you hope to sell your goods or services to a provincial government, find out if the province has a centralized purchasing department that handles purchases of goods and services on behalf of various government departments. Examples are the Purchasing Services Branch of the British Columbia government or the Purchasing Branch of the Saskatchewan government. Search the provincial website for a page on procurement or purchasing.

TIP

In addition, bidding services provide information on tenders being sought by the federal and provincial governments, as well as the municipal, academic, school, and hospital sectors. Examples are BIDS (www.bids.ca), MERX (www.merx.com), and Biddingo (www.biddingo.com).

If you hope to sell your goods or services to another business, find out as much as you can about the business. If it has a website, visit it. Large purchasers such as retail chains may provide information to prospective suppliers. For example, Walmart provides a Supplier Proposal Packet and Supplier Standards on its website. Even if the business you're targeting is not quite that helpful, you can still pick up information about the business's operations and needs that will help you fine-tune your sales pitch to the business.

Suppliers

As you research your particular type of business, you'll get a sense of the equipment and supplies you need to get set up. (See Chapter 7 for general advice on equipping your business.) You can then search the Internet for suppliers of that kind of equipment and supplies. The websites of major and many minor suppliers have online catalogues that include specifications, pricing, and shipping information. Some major suppliers offer consultants to help you choose the right equipment for your business.

IN THIS CHAPTER

» **Thinking about business ideas**

» **Learning that ideas can have (possessive) owners**

» **Understanding how to protect your ideas**

» **Using your own business idea without fear that someone else will steal it**

» **Using someone else's idea in your business without getting whacked with a lawsuit**

Chapter **3**

What's the Big Idea? Intellectual Property and You

anada's resource and manufacturing sectors are experiencing some growth and labour stagnation, and workers are even being laid off, but the knowledge sector is growing across all regions in Canada. This growth is especially pronounced in Ontario, Quebec, British Columbia, and central Canada. Leaders in knowledge sectors and areas like information technology, public and private research and development, engineering, and education are eager to hire the skilled Canadians and engage the innovative small businesses that operate in these spheres. This area of Canada's economy has a long way to go in terms of reaching its potential, but this reality creates tremendous small business opportunities.

More likely than not, the more you think about your business-to-be, the more evident it will be to you that at least some aspect of it will involve knowledge, or as it's often referred to, intellectual property (IP). This may be IP that you own, or it may be the IP of others that you use in your business. This chapter explains why it's important not to ignore the IP side of your business.

As your idea takes shape in your mind, you'll no doubt have notions about a product or service you want to manufacture or sell, a name or slogan to identify the business, information to include in an instruction manual, a favourite quotation you'll use on your website, or a cartoon you'll incorporate into presentations or your newsletter. You may even consider background music you'll play on the phone when you put clients on hold, and customer lists you can get your hands on. Some of these notions may just be whims, but others may be fundamental to the business.

Before moving ahead on these ideas at the speed of light, pause for just a minute! These ideas may already be owned by someone else. If they are, you can't use them without the owner's permission. And if they're your own original ideas, you'll want to make sure that nobody else can pirate them. This chapter shows you what you can and should consider.

What a Fine Idea

An idea's just an idea; it's not a gold mine or an expensive piece of equipment, right? Right, it's an idea. . . . Wrong! It's not "just" an idea. Many ideas are commercially valuable, and the owner of a valuable idea may go to great lengths to prevent anyone else from using it. And you may need to go to great lengths to keep someone else from stealing an idea out from under your nose — and making off with an important asset of your business.

Investigating the value of an idea

Need some convincing that an idea can have immense value? What do you think the word-ideas and music-ideas combined into the song "Yesterday" are worth? What about the chemical formula-idea for the drug Viagra? What about the name-idea for Coca-Cola, or the logo-idea for Nike? If you tried to buy any of these ideas, they'd cost you millions of dollars.

Of course, lots of ideas have no commercial value. The chemical formula for a drug that doesn't work (or worse, causes harm to a person who takes it) doesn't have much value; neither does the crawling worm logo for Fred and Mike's Pizzeria and Fish Bait Stand. The value of an idea is linked to its ability to sell products. An idea that sells a lot of products is very valuable; an idea that sells few products is not.

Determining who owns an idea

The general rule is that only the *owner* of an idea (or someone with whom the owner has a legal agreement) can legally use the idea. So before you decide to use an idea in your business, you need to know who the owner is. Only the owner can give permission to use the idea. If the owner isn't you (or nobody), you can get into hot water if you use the idea without permission.

Even if you personally came up with an original idea, you're not necessarily the owner. The owner of an idea could be the creator, the person who had the idea first; or it could be someone who hired the creator to have ideas; or it could be someone who bought ownership of the idea from its original owner. Check out the Government of Canada's Intellectual Property Database at `www.canada.ca/en/services/business/ip/databases.html` to search out trademarks, patents, copyrights, and other protected intellectual property.

Creator versus owner

If the creator was working independently when the idea sprang from his or her brain, the creator usually owns the idea.

If the creator was hired for the purpose of creating an idea, the person who hired the creator typically owns the idea (even if no written agreement exists to this effect).

If the creator created the idea in the course of his or her employment, the idea normally belongs to the employer (unless the employer and the employee-creator have a prior agreement that the creator rather than the employer owns the idea). If this idea involves possible high stakes (for instance, it's worth a lot or ownership of valuable IP is unclear), our advice throughout this chapter is to spend the extra money to hire a professional, accredited, and experienced lawyer who specializes in IP.

EXCUSE ME, MAY I PLEASE USE YOUR IDEA?

Permission to use an idea is given in the form of a *licence agreement* negotiated between the owner and the user. Licence agreements are usually long and incomprehensible legal documents. One of the long and incomprehensible clauses in the document says that in exchange for the right to use the idea, the user will pay the owner an upfront fee plus a royalty. A *royalty* is a percentage of the money made from the use of the idea. If the creator or other owner has sold or otherwise transferred the idea by *legal agreement* (assignment) to someone else — such as a business that wants the idea — then the other party to the agreement owns the idea. Engage a lawyer to help you craft a proper licence agreement, which normally includes matters such as responsibilities, revenue sharing, duration, and many other important details.

Ownerless ideas

Some ideas are orphans — they no longer have an owner. An idea without an owner is said to be in the *public domain*, which means that anyone can use it freely. An idea moves into the public domain once its legal protection expires (ideas are protected only for a limited number of years; more about that further on in this chapter) or, for certain kinds of ideas, if the idea has been made public before it got the right legal protection.

Beethoven's symphonies and Shakespeare's plays, for example, are in the public domain. Anyone can publish them or perform them because legal protection ended years ago. Similarly, the drug penicillin is in the public domain (and can be manufactured as a generic drug) because legal protection for the drug formula has ended. Sometimes the creator of an idea accidentally or deliberately puts the idea into the public domain by making the idea public without first arranging for protection. This could happen, for example, if the creator of a drug published the chemical formula in a journal of chemistry without first applying for patent protection (we talk about patents later in this chapter). Linux is another example of open source IP or protocol that lives in the public domain on purpose — to create even better software products and technologies.

Protecting ideas from unauthorized use

An owner can protect an idea in two ways. One is to keep the idea secret — if nobody else knows about the idea, then nobody else can use it. The other way is to sue the pants off anybody who uses the idea without permission. So when we talk about *protection,* it turns out that we mainly mean "the exclusive right to sue anybody else who uses the idea." (The lawsuit is for infringement.) This exclusive right to sue comes with official ownership of an idea.

Official ownership of ideas is given through different methods. They include copyright, industrial design registration, patent, and trademark. Following is a brief primer on intellectual property law. Again, to really be sure where you stand on your idea, or the use of someone else's idea, seek qualified legal advice.

Manufacturing or Selling a Product in Your Business

If you want to set up a business to manufacture or sell a product, you can't just fire up the assembly line and start churning out the product or go out and take orders. You have to make sure you have the right to make or sell the product in the country in the first place.

Manufacturing or selling a product from a design

If you've found or created a design for a product you want to manufacture, you could run into two different problems if you just go ahead and start manufacturing:

>> Someone else already may have registered that same design as an industrial design and can prevent you from manufacturing and distributing your product.

>> If you've come up with an original design, another manufacturer who sees your product on the market might think it looks pretty good and might start making and selling something very similar (maybe at a lower price). To prevent that, you need to register your design as an industrial design.

An *industrial design* is an original artistic shape, or pattern, or ornamentation that is to be applied to a mass-produced useful article. (The design itself is not supposed to be useful, only ornamental.) Industrial design registration protects the right to *mass-produce* — produce more than 50 copies of — a designed article. If a design has not been registered, anyone can imitate it and sell it, and the owner of the design has no legal means of stopping them. But if a design has been registered, the owner can sue those who make or sell a product with the design, and force them to stop making or selling it.

Industrial design protection isn't automatic; it's short-lived and it isn't renewable indefinitely. Protection has to be bought country by country. In Canada, registration protects the design for a maximum period of ten years. Specifically, Canadian industrial design registrations are valid for an initial five-year term and can be renewed for one further five-year term (for a total possible term of ten years). In the United States, a design patent protects the design for 14 years. This is another area where engaging a lawyer with intellectual property experience and credentials is crucial.

For more information about industrial design, see the Canadian Intellectual Property Office (CIPO) website at www.cipo.ic.gc.ca. You can also access more information at www.canadian-patent.com/designs. If you're interested in manufacturing or distributing a product in the United States, see the United States Patent and Trademark Office (USPTO) website at www.uspto.gov. Some other countries have similar websites, such as the United Kingdom Intellectual Property Office site at www.ipo.gov.uk.

A product from your own design

If you decide to register your design before you get into the manufacturing process, first check whether your design is new and original, or whether something very similar already has industrial design protection. You can do this through the Internet, free of charge, by using the Canadian Industrial Designs Database on the CIPO website (www.cipo.ic.gc.ca/iddatabase). You can conduct searches using the classification code, classification text, client reference number, court order number, name of current owner, date of registration, description, interested parties, and title of the design. The process of registering your design takes from six months to a year, or even longer. You have to apply to register your design no more than one year after your design has been made public. If you need help with an industrial design application, consult with an intellectual property lawyer.

After your design is registered, you can mark it with a D followed by your name as owner. If you have registered your design, you can sue anyone who produces your design to force them to stop. If you've registered and marked your design, you can sue to stop another user, and you can also get financial compensation for the harm they've caused you.

A product from someone else's design

If the design you want to use has been protected in a country, you need the owner's permission to manufacture or sell the product in that country. You may be able to tell if a product is protected: for example, if the product is marked. Because industrial design protection doesn't last very long, the protection may have expired. The only way of being sure about the status of protection is to do a search in that country's industrial design office.

Manufacturing a product that you've invented

Suppose your business isn't going to manufacture or sell a product with just a new look. Suppose it's going to manufacture a product that's new, period — something that you've dreamed up that hasn't been made before. In this case, you're manufacturing an invention.

In Canada, *inventions* include any kind of product (and that extends to a machine for making a product, or a chemical formula, or even a non-human life form such as a genetically modified mouse) and also an improvement on a product. In the United States, in addition to products and improvements, inventions can include a business method or a surgical method. For examples of inventions, just look around you — computer hardware and software, appliances, machines and machine parts, the shampoo you use, prescription and over-the-counter drugs, DNA sequences — you're surrounded by inventions wherever you go.

If you don't arrange to protect your invention before you start telling the neighbours about it, you're letting your invention slip into the public domain. When it's in the public domain, anybody who can figure out the invention can make it and sell it — without your permission and certainly without paying you anything.

You can protect an invention in two different ways: by secrecy or by patent.

Should you keep your invention secret?

You don't have to get patent protection for an invention if you think you can keep others from using (and making money from) your invention by keeping it a secret (Coca-Cola, for example, has never patented its recipe for Coke Classic). This kind of secret is known as a *trade secret.*

However, a secret that's totally and completely secret isn't going to be all that useful to a business. The secret has to be used in some way in order to generate revenue. It may be possible for the owner of the secret to use it without revealing it to anyone else, but in most cases the secret eventually has to be shared if it's going to be used. For example, the owner of a secret recipe for a soft drink will eventually have to tell some people what the recipe is — an investor, a chemist who will scale the recipe up for mass production, or a manufacturer who will produce the drink according to specifications.

The trick to manufacturing a product using a trade secret is to keep the secret reasonably safe. Here are some tips for keeping things under wraps:

>> If you're going to tell your secret to anyone (including employees and outsiders), first get an agreement with them in writing that this is confidential information that belongs to you and that they cannot reveal it to others or use it themselves without your written permission.

>> You'll find a sample confidential disclosure agreement in the free downloads available online; just look for Form 3-1. (Refer to the Introduction of this book for instructions on how to access this material.) This sample agreement may or may not work for you. **Remember:** Consult with your own lawyer before telling your valuable secrets to anyone.) Stamp any document relating to your secret with the word "CONFIDENTIAL." And don't tell the secret to anyone who doesn't actually need to know the secret to carry out his or her job.

>> Keep your secret physically safe — lock confidential documents in a drawer or a safe when you're not using them. Password protect your computer. Keep your office doors locked when you're not in the office, and don't allow anyone to poke around, even when you're there.

If your secret gets out anyway, you can try locking the barn door after the horse is stolen. If you had a confidentiality agreement with the person who made off with your secret, you can take that person to court and ask the judge to prevent the person from using or revealing the information any further, and/or you can ask for money damages to compensate you for losses you've suffered.

But even if you keep your secret safe from the people you work with, when your product is in the marketplace, competitors will be able to look at it and try to duplicate it. If they succeed, then they can just go ahead and use the idea — you can't stop them or get any money from them.

Should you patent your invention?

If you *patent* an invention, you give up your exclusive knowledge of how the invention works in exchange for an exclusive right to make money from the invention for a period of years.

Maybe the first question to ask in this section should be "*Can* you patent your invention?" You can't if the invention hasn't been "reduced to practice" yet. (Essentially, this means that the invention hasn't been described through written text and pictures in such a way that a skilled person reading the description can re-create the invention. The description of the invention forms the main part of a patent application.) You also can't patent an invention if someone has already patented it — you can't patent the exact same thing that's already patented — even if you invented it without knowing anything about the patent or the other inventor's work. You can, however, patent an improvement on the patented invention.

Even if no one has already patented your invention, a patent will be granted only for an invention that meets the test of "novelty, utility, and ingenuity." The invention has to be something new — something that hasn't been seen before (in many countries this means something that has never been made public before, although in Canada and the United States it can have been publicly disclosed by the inventor no more than one year before the patent application is filed), something useful, and something that wasn't obvious to a skilled person in the field.

Now that we've dealt with "can you" a bit, let's go back to "should you." Patent protection is not automatic in Canada or anywhere else. In fact, it involves a long and expensive process with no guarantees that a patent will be granted. The entire process, from filing a patent application to receiving a patent, takes at least two years and can quite easily take five or six years, or more. If a patent is granted, patent protection can extend back to the date the application was *published* (made public by the patent office as part of the application process). If you see a product marked *patent pending*, it means that an application has been filed, but the patent had not yet been granted when the product was marked. If a patent is not granted, the invention never had any protection at any time. And once your patent application is published by the patent office, everyone in the world will be able to see how your invention works.

An invention has patent protection only in the country where a patent has been granted. A patent application has to be made in every country where the owner of the invention wants protection. In Canada, most invention owners file an application in Canada or the United States first, and then file in a few additional countries (often including countries in the European Union or East Asia). After the deadline for filing a patent in a country has passed, the invention is in the public domain in that country, even though it's protected elsewhere against use without the owner's permission.

REMEMBER

The cost of getting patent protection is high. Getting a patent in the United States alone might cost up to $20,000 (Canadian) in patent lawyers' fees and filing fees. Getting a patent in additional countries might cost $10,000 to $15,000 per country — or more. So in total, getting a patent in the United States and a handful of other countries can cost about $100,000. Even well-heeled corporations balk at doing widespread patenting. Patenting is worthwhile only in a country with a big market where you have a good chance of making lots of money from the invention. (Think at least twice, and preferably three or four times, about spending money to patent something that will be obsolete in a couple of years, as is often the case with computer software or fad products.) If you personally don't have the money to patent your invention, you may be able to interest an investor in paying the bill if your invention is potentially worth a lot. In return, the investor will almost certainly want part ownership of the patent and a guaranteed share of any revenues that flow from the patent.

After you go to all the trouble of getting a patent, patent protection doesn't last very long — only 20 years from the date the patent application was first filed! But once you've got a patent, you can sue anyone who manufactures or sells your patented product in the country. Except that . . . sometimes you can be forced to let someone else use your patent. In some countries, you may be required to license the invention to a local manufacturer.

TIP

For more information about patents, you can visit the following websites: the Canadian Intellectual Property Office (CIPO) at www.cipo.ic.gc.ca; the United States Patent and Trademark Office (USPTO) at www.uspto.gov; and the European Patent Office (EPO) at www.epo.org. A very important web page to refer to relates to amendments to the Canadian Patent Act (www.ic.gc.ca/eic/site/cipointernet-internetopic.nsf/eng/wr03892.html) to ensure that you stay current; or just Google "changes to Canadian patent law."

Manufacturing or selling a product that someone else has invented

Not everybody has a great new idea for a product, and that may include you. But not having your own idea doesn't necessarily mean you can't manufacture or sell the product of your choice. Many inventors and patent owners are keen to find someone who will manufacture or distribute their product.

Using someone else's patent

If you want to use an invention that is under patent in the country where you're going to manufacture and sell it, you have to get the permission of the patent owner if you don't want to risk being sued. If a product is subject to patent protection, it may have the words "patent" or "patent pending" on it somewhere. Or you can do a patent search if you don't have the product itself at hand.

After you've located the patent owner, you can start negotiating for use of the invention. If the owner is willing to let you use it, the owner will want you to pay an initial fee and/or a royalty on sales of the product in return.

TIP

If the invention is patented (or patent pending) in one or more countries, but a patent application was not filed in the country where you want to make or market the invention, you don't need the owner's permission. You can just go ahead and do your thing. The published patent application should contain all the information that you'll need to make the invention. So you can search for the patent in the patent office of the country where the patent was registered. (Canadian, U.S., and European Union patents are available through online databases. See the website addresses in the "Should you patent your invention?" section earlier.) The Canadian Patents Database (available via the CIPO website at www.cipo.ic.gc.ca or directly at www.canada.ca/en/services/business/ip/databases) provides access to over 75 years of patent descriptions and images, and allows you to search, retrieve, and study more than 2,000,000 patent documents.

You can also just go ahead if the patent protection has expired. Again, you'll want to search for the patent in the country's patent office to make sure that the patent really has expired and to get the specifications of the invention. And you might be wise to approach the patent owner for a discussion anyway; the owner may have some valuable information about making or marketing the product, and might provide it in exchange for a payment of some kind.

Using someone else's unpatented invention

If an invention is in the public domain, anyone can use it. It's in the public domain, for example, if it's been published in a journal or been presented at a conference or trade show before the owner applied for patent protection (although in Canada and the United States an inventor has a year after publishing or presenting an invention to file for patent protection); or if patent protection has expired.

But what if the invention isn't patented but it's not exactly in the public domain either? In other words, what if it's somebody else's trade secret?

Theoretically, you could use someone else's trade secret under the following conditions:

» You're not an employee of the owner of the trade secret. Unless you're an industrial spy, the place you'll most likely acquire trade secrets is from your own employer — and employees have a legal and moral duty (typically under an employment contract, as well as a corporate code of conduct) not to use their employer's trade secrets even if they haven't signed a confidentiality agreement. (We tell you about confidentiality agreements under the heading "Should you keep your invention secret?" earlier in this chapter.)

» You're not an ex-employee of the owner of the trade secret who picked up the trade secret during your employment. If you removed or copied documents containing information about the secret, you could probably be charged with theft. If you held a senior management position with the employer, you likely had a legal duty of faithfulness to the employer and you could be sued for breach of fiduciary duty if you use the secret for your own gain.

» You were never an employee of the owner of the trade secret and you didn't sign a confidentiality agreement with the owner saying that you wouldn't use or reveal the secret; or, if you did sign such an agreement, it has expired (typically confidentiality agreements last for a limited period of time, say five or ten years).

Using a Name or Word in Your Business

The manufacture and sale of products are a couple of places where you can get into trouble when you're starting up a business, but they're not the only ones. Something as apparently minor as a name or word you want to use in your business can cause you major headaches.

A name or word could get mixed up in your business in a number of ways. You might want a name for the business, or you might want to use a catchy word or phrase to identify your product or service, or you might want a domain name for your business's website. But woe betide you if you jump in without thinking and use a name that somebody else already owns.

Naming your business

An incorporated business has a corporate name. That's the business's legal name and it's taken at the time of incorporation. It can be a name made up of words, or it can be a "number name." (For more on incorporating a business, see Chapter 6.)

A business that isn't incorporated can be carried on under the name of its owner(s) — the sole proprietor or the partners. (For more on starting an unincorporated business, see Chapter 6.)

An incorporated or unincorporated business can also be carried on under a trade name, which is kind of like an alias.

When it comes to naming a business, you can have problems not just with someone who's already using the name, but also with the government authorities who register names . . . and who've made up a slew of rules about acceptable names.

Choosing a corporate name

The authorities that incorporate businesses (the federal and the provincial governments) have rules about choosing a word name. Check them out in the Business Corporations Act of your province if you're incorporating provincially, or the *Canada Business Corporations Act* if you're incorporating federally. One of the numerous rules is that the name has to include the word *Incorporated*, or *Inc.*, or *Corporation*, or *Corp.*, or *Limited*, or *Ltd.* But even if the name you choose meets all the rules, the incorporation authorities won't allow another business to take a name that is "confusingly similar" to the name of an existing corporation. For, example the name "Smearnoff Vodka" would be considered confusingly similar to "Smirnoff Vodka."

TIP

Before you try to register a corporate word name, you have to search a registry of names to make sure the name you want isn't already taken or isn't confusingly similar to another name. In Canada, this involves paying to have a Government of Canada NUANS search done. For federal incorporations only, you can order your own NUANS report from the NUANS "Do it yourself" Real-Time System (RTS) or you can get help from a registered NUANS member. For provincial incorporations, you have no choice but to use a registered NUANS member to conduct the search for you. See www.nuans.com for more about performing a NUANS search and to find a registered NUANS member.

There are a lot of businesses, but only so many great business names. Most of the great names you've thought of are probably already in use. Many business owners get tired of searching for a name that will be allowed by the authorities and just incorporate with a *number name*. Every corporation is assigned a number at the time of incorporation. (The incorporator doesn't get to choose it like a lucky lottery number; it's just the next available number in sequence, as if you took a ticket at the meat counter or the passport office.) This number, when combined with the name of the incorporating jurisdiction and the word *Limited*, is the corporation's number name — such as "123456 Ontario Limited" or "654321 Canada Ltd."

Choosing a trade name

An incorporated or unincorporated business can carry on business under a trade name. A trade name can be any word or phrase the business owner likes (although an unincorporated business can't use a word like *Inc.,* or *Ltd.,* or *Corporation* in its trade name, because only corporations can use those words). However, someone else may own the trade name already and be able to prevent others from using confusingly similar names. In some cases, a trade name has actually been trademarked by another business and the trademark owner can sue to prevent others from using the name (we tell you more about trademarks a little later on).

Selecting a name, slogan, or logo that identifies your business or product

Maybe you want to generate some excitement around your business by giving your product a neat-o name or attaching a cool logo to it.

A *trademark* is a distinctive word, phrase, symbol, or design (or a combination of some or all of these) that is marked on a business's goods or displayed with its services. The trademark identifies the business's goods and services in the mind of the consumer (and that's why confusingly similar trademarks are a problem). A trademark usually appears on packaging or in advertisements, accompanied by ® (for registered trademark) or MD (*marque déposée* = registered trademark), or by TM (trademark), or SM (service mark), or MC (*marque de commerce*). For example, "Bell Mobility" is a trademark of Bell Canada, "Windows" is a trademark of Microsoft Corp., "The Document Company" is a trademark of Xerox Corporation, and a tiny little polo player is a trademark of Ralph Lauren.

For more information about trademarks, see the Canadian Intellectual Property Office website at www.cipo.ic.gc.ca and the United States Patent and Trademark Office website at www.uspto.gov/trademarks/index.jsp.

Choosing a trademark

Telling you what you *can't* choose as a trademark is easier than telling you what you *can* choose. Visit the Canadian Intellectual Property Office (CIPO) website for more information. Generally, you cannot trademark

>> **A person's name (not even your own)** — although an exception occurs if you can show that the name has become linked in the public mind with certain products or services (think McDonald's and Ralph Lauren).

>> **Words that are simply descriptive** — so you couldn't trademark words such as "hot" soup or "soothing" lotion.

>> **A geographical name** — so you couldn't trademark a name, for example, "Atlantic" cod.

>> **A business's name** — unless the name is used to identify the business's products or services (for example, "Xerox" is a trademark of the Xerox Corporation, and "Microsoft" is a trademark of Microsoft Corp.) You definitely can't trademark words or symbols that are confusingly similar to someone else's existing trademark. Other rules also apply to choosing a trademark, so visit the CIPO website for more information.

TIP

Before you choose a trademark, search the Canadian Trade-marks Database on the CIPO website to see whether a trademark that's the same or similar is already registered. (It's similar if it has a slightly different spelling, sounds the same when pronounced, or has the same words in different order.) If you're planning on doing business in the United States, search the U.S. trademark database on the United States Patent and Trademark website, too. You might want to get a lawyer familiar with trademarks, or a trademark agent, to do the search for you. If you're thinking of doing business in other countries, you probably won't be able to do the search by Internet; you'll have to get the help of a trademark agent.

WARNING

If you search trademark databases and find nothing, you could still run into an unregistered trademark. A trademark owner doesn't have to register the trademark to have the right to prevent another business from using it in the geographical area where the owner does business. Finding out about unregistered trademarks is harder, but you could try the following:

>> Search the Internet for domain names that are the same as or very similar to the word or phrase you want to use, and check to see where the business associated with the domain name is located.

>> Search business name registers — NUANS for Canada or ThomasNet (www. thomasnet.com) for the United States — for similar names and the location of the business.

>> Search in your local phone book if you're feeling very low-tech (or the phone book for any area where you want to do business — available at some public libraries. Or, if you're feeling higher-tech, search online at www.yellowpages.ca for business names. If the companies are in the phone book, you can assume they do business in the neighbourhood.

Protecting your trademark

To become the owner of a trademark, a business simply has to be the first to use it. Then it's protected as the business's trademark in the geographical areas where it's in use.

You can register a trademark for more complete protection. If an owner registers a trademark in a country, then it's protected throughout that country for a specified period of time (15 years in Canada, for example; 10 years in the United States). Once registered, a trademark can be renewed as many times as you want. In Canada, your registration can, therefore, be renewed every 15 years; and in the United States, every 10 years. A registered trademark is stronger than an unregistered trademark.

If your trademark is registered in a country, you can sue a competitor anywhere in that country to make the competitor stop using your trademark. A court will give a registered trademark much more protection than it will give to an unregistered trademark. If your trademark is not registered, you can sue only a competitor who's using your trademark in the particular geographical area(s) where you do business.

To register a trademark, you have to file an application for registration with the country's trademarks office. In Canada, the registration fee is several hundred dollars. (If you use a trademark agent, you'll have to pay his or her fees as well.) You have to file a new trademark application in each country where you want protection.

You'll find an example of the CIPO Application for Registration of a Proposed Trademark in the free downloads available online; just look for Form 3-2. Form 3-3 is an example of the CIPO Application for Registration of a Trademark in Use in Canada. (Refer to the Introduction of this book for instructions on how to access this material.)

Using someone else's trademark

The fact that someone already owns the trademark you want doesn't necessarily mean you can't use it.

If you're going to use the trademark in relation to a completely different product, you will probably be able to use it. So, if you find someone is already using the term or logo you'd like to use, consider these questions:

>> Is the trademark well known and owned by a business that has lots of money to sue you?

>> Will your goods or services compete with the goods or services being sold, or even simply registered, under the trademark in use? (For example, are both of the businesses selling sports equipment, or is one selling sports equipment and the other musical instruments?)

>> Will your use of the trademark confuse customers, even though your goods or services are not competing directly with those of the trademark owner? (Will people think an ad for your product is an ad for the trademark owner's product, or vice versa?)

If the answer to any of these questions is yes, you should probably look for another trademark — unless you currently receive so little mail that you'd look forward to getting a chilly letter from the trademark owner's lawyers.

You can also use someone else's trademark if they are not using it in the geographical area in which you plan to use it, as long as they haven't registered it with the federal government. (If the trademark is registered, the owner doesn't have to use it to get protection.)

Or you can arrange with the trademark owner for permission to use the trademark. For example, if you're a franchisee, you can use the franchisor's trademark. The trademark is one of the most important things the franchisee gets under the franchise agreement. (For more about franchises, see Chapter 5.) Even without a franchise agreement, you can arrange to manufacture or sell a product under licence from the owner of the trademark and to display the trademark on the product. (Maple Leaf Sports and Entertainment, for example, licenses lots of businesses to sell things with the Toronto Maple Leafs, Toronto Raptors, Toronto FC, and Argonauts trademarks.)

Registering an Internet domain name

If you're starting up a website to go with your business, you need a name for it. You can register pretty well any domain name you like, as long as it's not the same as an existing domain name. But once you've registered a domain name, you could run into trouble if it's the same as or confusingly similar (either deliberately or accidentally similar) to another business's trademark. You could be forced by the owner of the trademark to stop using your domain name. For example, if your name is Sam McDonald and your business partner's name is Wayne Burger, you may both be in for a very rough ride if you chose the domain name of www.mcdonald-burger.com. No one would confuse your website with that of McDonald's the fast-food chain — but McDonald's may still prefer that you use a different name, and it would cost you a lot of money to argue with them.

CHOOSING A DOMAIN NAME

TIP

Before you choose a distinctive domain name, check whether your name is going to be the same as or confusingly similar to another business's trademark or name or trade name. The Internet Corporation for Assigned Names and Numbers (ICANN) can get shirty with anyone who registers a domain name in bad faith (this is called "cybersquatting" and "cyberpiracy"). ICANN has the power to cancel a domain name registration if a complainant can prove that the domain name was registered for the purpose of trying to sell the name to the complainant or a competitor of the complainant, or to keep the complainant from using a trademark as a domain name, or to disrupt a competitor's business, or to confuse Internet users and attract them to the registrant's site, rather than the complainant's, for commercial gain. See www.icann.org for more information. You can also check out Resolutions Canada (www.resolutioncanada.ca), a Toronto-based company that specializes in resolving disputes over domain names in the dot-ca domain.

USING SOMEONE ELSE'S DOMAIN NAME

If you want to use a domain name that someone else is already using, see if you can buy it from the owner. Check for contact information on their website. If the website doesn't provide contact information, you may be able to find it using the WHOIS Lookup (www.whois.net) and typing in the domain name. You can also find websites where people offer to sell their domain names (try www.great domains.com or register.com).

For more information about domain names, see Chapter 11.

Using Written Materials in Your Business

Unless you and your customers and suppliers have all entered the post- postmodern commercial age and are conducting business entirely by cellphone and Skype videoconferencing, your business will probably use some written materials.

Understanding copyright

Written materials are protected by *copyright*. Copyright is the exclusive right to copy or reproduce, publish, translate, adapt, or perform a work. Copyrightable works include books, articles, manuals, plays, screenplays, scripts, music, and computer software programs. They don't have to be printed (typeset) or published to be copyrighted. They can be written by hand, or they can be virtual text on the Internet.

Facts or ideas cannot be copyrighted. That means that the actual information contained in a written or otherwise recorded document is not protected. It's really the way that the information is *expressed* that is protected. Copyright also does not protect a name, character, or slogan you might want to associate with your business (these are protectable by trademark — we talk about trademarks earlier in this chapter).

Copyright is automatic. Once text is written, copyright exists. And it exists not only in Canada but also in nearly every country in the world. Almost all countries have signed one of the several international copyright treaties littering the landscape. (If you wish, however, you can register a copyright with the federal government.)

Form 3-4 is the CIPO Application for Registration of a Copyright. (Refer to the Introduction of this book for instructions on how to access this book's free downloadable content.)

Copyright also lasts a long time — at least 50 years from the date of creation or performance, and often more than twice that long. (Exactly how long depends on what the copyrighted material is and the circumstances of its creation.) After you register your copyright, you may choose to get a certificate issued by the Canadian Intellectual Property Office that can be used in court as physical evidence that you own the copyright.

You may be wondering why copyright is so easy to get, and free, and lasts so long, when a patent is hell to get, costs the earth, and lasts for the blink of an eye. Invention owners all wonder exactly the same thing — and nobody seems to have a good answer.

TIP

For more information about copyright, see the website of the Canadian Intellectual Property Office (www.cipo.ic.gc.ca). You can also go to the website of the United States Copyright Office (www.copyright.gov) or the website of the World Intellectual Property Organization (www.wipo.int).

Using someone else's written material

If you want to reproduce software — for example, if you want to make and distribute copies of someone else's computer program as part of your business activities — you have to get the copyright owner's permission. Software is very easy and cheap to reproduce, so it's no wonder that the world is full of pirated software. Don't confuse "easy and cheap" with "legal."

TIP

If you want to reprint text from a book, or manual, or screenplay, or newspaper article, or website rant in a document you distribute or on your own website, again you have to get permission from the copyright owner. To find the copyright owner, start by searching Library and Archives Canada (www.bac-lac.gc.ca) or the Library of Congress (www.loc.gov) to find an author's publisher(s); or do an Internet search under the author's name to find the author's or publisher's website. You can also contact organizations of creators or publishers (you can find links to them at www.accesscopyright.ca).

YOU MAY NOT NEED PERMISSION

You don't always need permission to use a copyrighted work. "Fair dealing" allows you to use another's work for purposes such as criticism, review, or news reporting. (That's why a newspaper doesn't have to get permission to quote a passage from a book that it's reviewing.) So you may be able to quote in your newsletter or on your website a short passage that someone else has written, as long as you identify the source of the quotation and credit the author. But fair dealing is quite a limited exception, so don't try to push it too far.

Even if you have permission to use copyrighted material, you can't use the material in a way that interferes with the original creator's "moral rights" in the work. So you have to mention the creator's name in connection with the material, and you can't mess around with the material without the creator's permission. For example, if you have the right to use someone's love poem, you can't change the words and turn it into a jingle for transmission repairs.

If all you want to do is photocopy materials to distribute to potential or actual clients or customers or others, contact Access Copyright, the Canadian Copyright Licensing Agency, for permission. It's a not-for-profit collective that administers Canadian creators' and publishers' reproduction rights, and it also represents foreign creators and publishers through agreements with similar organizations in other countries, including the United States, Great Britain, Australia, and France. Again, Access Copyright's website can be found at www.accesscopyright.ca.

Using someone else's confidential materials

You may have come into contact with materials at your (perhaps former) place of employment that could be quite useful in your new business. We're not talking about government publications or the phone book. We're talking about materials that are valuable to the business and that the business wants to keep confidential. Can you use an employer's or former employer's materials in your own business — without getting permission?

WARNING

When you leave an employer, or you stay but start up your own business on the side, you can't take away copies of confidential documents such as customer lists, market reports, and financial projections. That's theft, and the company could sue you or possibly even have you charged criminally.

After employment ends, unless you've signed a written agreement with your employer that you won't compete with the employer or won't use the employer's confidential information for your own gain, an employer would probably have difficulty preventing you from using information (as opposed to documents or other property) you picked up as an employee. For example, a former sales manager who knows the names of customers can approach them to pitch her own business. But beware if you held a fairly high management position with your former employer! If you use your employer's confidential information — such as information about a great business opportunity — to start up your own business, you could be sued for "breach of fiduciary duty."

Using your own written materials

Before you use copyrighted work that you think is your own, check it out. If you created the work as an employee, it probably belongs to your employer, and you can't use it without the employer's permission. The same is true if you were hired to create the work (for example, if you were commissioned to provide a report or manual). If the work is definitely your own, then you can go ahead and use it as you like.

Using Pictures and Drawings in Your Business

Pictures and drawings are subject to copyright just like written works. Copyright also covers film or video, paintings, sculpture, maps, photographs, and designs. So if you want to use someone else's picture or drawing for business purposes, you'll have to get the copyright owner's permission.

If you're just looking for something to liven up your business stationery or a newsletter or presentation, you can easily find pictures and cartoons that you can license with a minimum amount of effort and trouble. On the Internet, you'll find sites that offer licences to use cartoons (such as *New Yorker* cartoons, at www.cartoonbank.com) and photographs (for example, at Getty Images at www.gettyimages.ca).

CLIP ART

Many Internet websites offer access to "clip art." (To find some, just type **clip art** into a search engine.) For most commercial purposes, you don't have to ask special permission to use clip art, and you can download and use an image instantly. You should check the terms of use set out on the website, however, to find out what you can and can't do with the clip art.

You can also find drawings and pictures that you can use without special permission and without paying a licence fee. See the "Clip art" sidebar.

Using Music in Your Business

If you're not actually in the music business, you might think that you're not going to use music in your business and you might skip this section. But suppose you want to make public use of musical works that you choose — maybe you want to play a tape of classical music in your restaurant during dining hours, or have pop music or Christmas music in your retail store, or have a karaoke night at your bar, or play rap on your phone line when customers are on hold, or run a jazz theme when someone enters your website, or blast a rock 'n' roll song out at the beginning of a presentation, or have background music in your radio or TV ad, or hire a group to play hits from the '80s in front of your store during a street festival?

Music is also subject to copyright, and that applies not only to the composer. So what if Mozart has been dead for hundreds of years and his music is in the public domain? The orchestra that recorded his works ten years ago isn't dead, and the orchestra expects to be paid royalties for the use of the performance.

TIP

If you want to use music publicly for a business purpose, contact SOCAN (The Society of Composers, Authors and Music Publishers of Canada). SOCAN can give you the right to use or present performances of copyright-protected music in a public setting. SOCAN can get you rights not only to Canadian music, but also, through its agreements with similar foreign organizations, to music from all over the world. See the SOCAN website at www.socan.ca.

Chapter **4**

Choosing a Product or Service

Your business will be in big trouble if you offer a product or service that not a soul wants, or that your chosen customer group is not interested in. In this chapter, we help you avoid those problems and give you hints on how to develop a product or service tailored for your target customers or clients.

Developing Your Product or Service with a Market in Mind

To start a business, you need a product or service to sell. And it needs to be something that customers or clients want to buy.

Developing a product or service requires quite a chunk of your time and energy. You'll need to take on some tasks that may seem kind of challenging, such as researching potential customers and existing competition.

Eureka!

To start at the beginning, where do ideas for products or services come from in the first place? Very innocent entrepreneurs believe that the stork brings ideas, or that ideas are found in the garden under the fallen leaves of maple trees. But entrepreneurs who've been introduced to the facts of life know that ideas really come from the following sources:

>> **Potential customers:** If you're not actually in business yet, you don't have customers, but you're probably already in contact with people who would be glad to be your customers if only you'd provide a product or service they need. Keep your ears open in your current job — maybe your employer or your employer's competitors or your employer's customers or suppliers are making wistful comments about not being able to find Product X, or Person Y to perform Service Z.

>> **Trade shows, trade journals — even the daily newspaper or a TV program:** A great idea may already be out there. It just needs you to develop it.

>> **Your fertile imagination:** You may have had a real *eureka!* moment, when you thought up a solution to a problem or you created an invention that people have been desperately hoping for — or that they don't even know they need yet.

Asking yourself some sobering questions

After the *eureka!* moment has passed and your heart rate has returned to normal, you need to rationally evaluate the idea. Love at first sight can cost you a lot in business (just like in real life), so you have to make sure that this is the idea for you to get hitched up with. In this section we look at deciding whether

>> This is the right idea for you and your business personality.

>> A market exists for the product or service you envision.

>> You can compete successfully.

>> The idea is financially viable.

TIP

If your idea is new and innovative, you may be able to get assistance with the evaluation, for example from The Canadian Innovation Centre (CIC) (www. innovationcentre.ca) in Waterloo, Ontario, an organization that grew out of the invention commercialization activities of the University of Waterloo. Their website has information for inventors as well as links to other useful organizations such as the U.S. National Inventor Fraud Center (www.inventor-fraud.com), which offers advice on how to steer away from invention marketing companies that are set up only to scam inventors.

WARNING

Don't get mixed up with a company that combines high-pressure sales tactics with a low success rate.

Is this idea right for you?

Or is this a good idea at all, when you get right down to it? For example, is it legal? (And if it's legal now, will it become illegal once it takes off? Remember radar detectors for the travelling public?) Is it hands-off? The reverse is also true. In Chapter 19, we discuss the whole area of cannabusiness, a business sphere that was generally illegal just a while ago, but is now legal. The idea may already be patented (refer to Chapter 3) and the patent owner doesn't want to license to you. Are you legal? Some products and services can be provided only by a licensed individual or business. Is the product or service safe — or will you cause harm to someone and end up getting sued? And if everything's legal, hands-on, and safe, do you have the reputation or expertise needed to develop the idea into a business and reel in customers or clients?

Does anyone want the product or service?

Your idea may seem wonderful to you, but you're going to need a slightly larger market than yourself to prosper. So you have to do some *customer research* — identify a target market for the product or service and estimate the size of the market. Here's a brief guide to doing customer research.

First, think generally about who your customers or clients might be (keep in mind that you could be wrong about this, though). For example, are they

» **Other businesses?** A whole bunch of them or just one or two? Are the businesses service providers or retailers or manufacturers?

» **Individuals?** Do the individuals live in a particular neighbourhood or geographic area, or do they live all over the country or around the world? Are they men only? Women only? The young? Older people? The well-to-do, or just anyone with a buck to spend?

After you've identified a starting point, you can proceed with your customer/client research to find out if anybody would want your product or service. Different research methods exist, so try a combination of them. From the least expensive to most expensive, here they are:

>> **Review of publicly available information:** This includes websites (including blogs), TV programs, newspapers, trade journals, newsletters, and market analysis materials from the business reference section of a public or university library.

>> **Direct observation of potential customers or clients:** You can use your own personal knowledge of a business you're in or have followed, you can visit stores and trade shows, or you can attend presentations and conferences.

>> **Interviews with experts in the field or with potential customers or clients:** This isn't as hard to do as you think. If you start with people you know and ask for names of other people who wouldn't mind talking to you, if you just ask for an opinion or advice and don't try to sell anything, and if you keep the interview polite and brief, you will very likely meet people who will agree to give you 20 minutes or half an hour of their time. It's really amazing how many people are open and amenable to sharing their thoughts and insights, especially if you compliment them by referring to them as experts or thought leaders in their field. Try to meet face-to-face if you can — the interviewee will remember you better if it later turns out that she needs the product or service you want to provide.

>> **Focus groups:** See if you can lure groups of potential customers or clients together to talk about the product or service. The lure should be something significant, like a free meal or a chance to win a prize. Unless you can find friends and acquaintances who'll participate in a focus group, you may be better off hiring a market analysis firm to run focus groups than trying to corner strangers on your own.

>> **Surveys and questionnaires:** These are short written, telephone or online questionnaires distributed or conducted on a large scale. You'll have to come up with the right questions to ask, and pay for printing and distribution of written materials, find your nerve to make calls or hire trained interviewers to phone people at dinnertime, and then you'll have to analyze the results . . . if anyone answers the questions (a lot of paper surveys will be considered garbage and thrown out, and a lot of people won't answer telephone interviewers). (See Chapter 11 for more about online surveys.)

Doing door-to-door surveys in a neighbourhood, or approaching people on the street in a business or shopping area, will probably earn you a lot of suspicion and brush-offs. As with focus groups, you may prefer to have a professional market analysis firm handle a survey. (Surveys and questionnaires are easier to handle yourself if you've already got an established customer base.)

At the conclusion of your market research, ideally you should have an idea about whether the product or service is attractive to some target group or groups, and you should also be able to estimate roughly the size of your market. Your market is the number of customers you'll win times the number of sales per customer.

Who's the competition?

And what are they up to? This information is known as "competitive intelligence." Your competitors may already have claimed all of the customers or clients you identified by doing your market research. Or they may not. You can find out by assessing your potential market share.

To start with the question we just asked (Who's the competition?), your competition is made up of the following:

>> **Direct competitors** — who offer exactly the same product or service

>> **Indirect competitors** — who offer an alternative product that more or less meets the same need as your product

>> **Who-was-that-masked-man? competitors** — who offer something completely different that potential customers will spend their money on instead of on your product or a similar product, much to your regret and amazement

>> **Inertia** — the tendency of customers and clients to do nothing at all when brought face-to-face with your wonderful product or service

As an example, if you want to offer a service tutoring children in math or reading, your direct competition is other private tutoring services, your indirect competition is the public and private schools in the area (they may be doing a fine job of teaching, in which case your services won't be required); your who-was-that-masked-man? competition is social media and video games; and inertia is parents letting their kids sink or swim through school on their own.

TIP

Look carefully at your direct and indirect competitors and see if you can find out whether

>> They've cornered the market and are doing such a good job at such a good price that you haven't much hope of taking market share away from them. Or whether you should be able to relieve them of market share because you can offer better value — for example, a lower price, a higher-quality product or service, a more convenient location, greater expertise, friendlier service, and so on. Sometimes the first competitor into the market may just have collected and educated your potential clients for you!

>> Their business is profitable — are they growing or shrinking?

>> They're big enough and mean enough to run you out of town if you show your face on the street (have you noticed how small airlines regularly get eaten?).

How much money can you put behind this idea?

You likely can't get your idea off the ground for free. So the last sober second thought involves figuring out

>> **Approximately how much it will cost to launch your business:** This involves adding up your start-up costs plus bridge financing for your operating expenses until your business is generating income. We cover start-up costs for equipment in Chapter 9, for premises in Chapter 10, and for purchase of an existing business in Chapter 5. We look at operating costs in Chapter 7.

>> **Approximately how much money is available to you for a business start-up:** The cash you have on hand or can raise through family contributions may be enough to get your particular business up and running; or you may need a bank loan for a larger amount; or you may need a significant investment from an angel investor or venture capital firm. (See Chapter 9 for sources of start-up money.)

How much you'll be able to raise (especially from outsiders) is linked to the likely return on investment for your idea. So just because it will take $1 million to build a plant to produce your product doesn't mean you should scrap the idea. It could be full steam ahead if an investor believes that your business could generate profits of $2 million annually after a couple of years or that the business might be worth $50 million in five years.

Tinker with your idea

After you've had all these second thoughts, you have to decide whether to forget your idea altogether or rework it in light of what you've discovered about your target market and your competition. If you decide to keep going with your idea, you may be thinking about how you can do the following:

>> Redesign or add value to the product or service so that it appeals more to your target market

>> Provide the product or service more efficiently than the competition or at a price that potential customers or clients will find more attractive

>> Redesign or reposition your product or service so that it doesn't meet a powerful competitor head-on

>> Redesign or present the product or service so that it appeals to a potential investor

After you've tinkered, you may need to re-evaluate.

Finding the Best Route to Your Target Market

Okay, so you think you've got a product or service that can go the distance. Now you have to figure out how to get it from you to the person who will actually use it — so you have to decide on one or more distribution channels. You have two basic choices:

>> **Distribute directly:** The product or service goes from your business to your buyer (most services and products take this route).

>> **Distribute indirectly:** The product or service goes from your business to another business to the buyer. Although your target market is the buyer, your customer is the "middleman" business.

From your business directly to your customer

If you choose direct distribution, you can deal with customers or clients in two ways:

>> **Face-to-face:** In your retail store or your office.

>> **Facelessly:** Through an order system that uses a website, email, mail, phone, or even fax. If you choose this option, remember that you'll need a place to keep your inventory, such as a room in a warehouse, and you'll need a delivery system, such as mail or courier. (Certain kinds of services provided this way — such as essays or advice for the lovelorn — may be deliverable electronically.)

From your business to another business to your target customer

If your customer is a middleman, you'll probably need fewer customers to make a go of your business. However, a middleman may be more demanding about low prices, so your profit margin may be lower.

Middlemen include

>> **Retailers**

>> **Wholesalers or distributors** — who in turn sell to retailers, and sometimes to the general public

>> **Re-packagers** — who also sell to retailers after — you guessed it — repackaging the products they buy from you

You may be able to or may want to sell directly to the middleman yourself, or you may want to employ a manufacturer's agent or representative to do the selling for you (on commission). First you'll have to choose an agent who sells to the kind of middleman you want in the regions you want. Then you'll have to persuade the agent to carry your line and talk it up to customers.

Pricing Your Product or Service

You can make a profit in different ways — for example, by combining a small profit on each item or service provided with high sales volume, or by combining a low sales volume with a big profit on each transaction. (Best, of course, is high profit on each unit and high sales volume, but not many businesses are that lucky.) But if you underprice, you'll lose money on every sale even if you sell a gazillion units; if you overprice, no one will buy at all. How do you figure this whole thing out? In this section, we talk about how to settle on the right price to charge.

Deciding on the minimum price you can charge

Minimum price is not all that difficult to figure out. As a rule, you don't want to charge less for your product or service than it costs to produce. (An exception to the rule is offering the product or service as a loss leader, to lure customers in — but you can't keep that up for long, and certainly not on an important part of your line.) The formula that tells you, as the owner of a start-up business, your cost to produce (your *break-even cost*) is

> Total direct and indirect costs over a given period (say, one to three months) ÷ Total number of products or services that it would be reasonable for you to provide over the given period = Your break-even cost for that period

Your break-even cost for the period is the amount you need to charge for each unit of your product or service to pay your direct and indirect costs. (See the sidebar, "A sample break-even chart.")

Direct costs, also known as variable costs, include

>> Materials required to manufacture the product, and cost of shipping the materials to your site

>> Lease payments for factory space or storage space

>> Energy (or other utility) costs of production (for example, electricity, water)

>> Wages paid to subcontractors or employees to produce the product or service

>> Cost of delivering the product or service to your customer

Indirect costs, also known as fixed costs or overhead, include administrative expenses such as the following:

>> Wages for office staff

>> Electricity, telephone, and other office utilities

>> Office supplies

>> Advertising expenses

>> Rent on your office space

If your business involves supplying a service rather than manufacturing a product, you'll probably have higher indirect costs than direct costs.

Deciding on the maximum price you can charge

Now over to the other end of the price scale. Here, the ceiling for your price is the value of your product or service to the customer or client. Value is what the customer perceives that he or she is getting in exchange for the cost of the product, and includes things such as quality and reliability of the product or service, image or prestige associated with the product or service, uniqueness of the product or service, backup from your business such as support and guarantees, convenience of dealing with your business (such things as good location or inexpensive delivery or the helpfulness of your staff), and incentives such as rebates (money back following a purchase), discounts (money off the purchase price), and other freebies.

If customers believe that your price (their cost) is greater than the value of your product or service (the benefit to them), customers won't buy from you. Ouch!

Form 4-1 is a sample break-even chart (like the one we show in the sidebar, "A sample break-even chart") that you can use to calculate the sales volume at which you'll break even. Head to this book's Introduction for instructions on how to access the free downloadable content.

A SAMPLE BREAK-EVEN CHART

At what sales price will your business break even?

Direct or variable cost per month of producing total number of units you think it would be reasonable to produce and sell in a month (let's say 1,000, at $10 per unit)	$10,000
PLUS	
Indirect or fixed cost per month of producing the units	$5,000
EQUALS	
Total cost per month of producing the units	$15,000
DIVIDED BY	
Number of units of product or service produced and sold per month	1,000
EQUALS	
Break-even cost, or the minimum *price* you need to charge per unit	$15

You can fiddle with the figures in the different boxes, increasing or decreasing the numbers to see how your break-even cost is affected by changes. This is referred to as a *sensitivity analysis,* and it's a great tool for making scenario-based decisions. For example, if your direct cost is $12,000 instead of $10,000, your minimum price becomes $17. Or if the number of units produced and sold is 800 instead of 1,000, your minimum price becomes $18.75 instead of $15. A Microsoft Excel flowchart is a great tool to use for these types of arithmetic gymnastics.

Setting your price

Setting a price comes down to supply and demand. If a product is essential or useful and it's hard to find, the price can be higher and the product will still sell (until people run out of money). If a product is not a must-have or is readily available, the price has to be lower if you want to sell. Higher or lower than what? The competition's price.

So see what your competition is charging. Once you know that, then you can implement one of the following three strategies:

» **Charge more than the competition.** This will work only if your product is seen as more valuable than the competition's. You can increase the value of the same product or service offered by the competition by (for example) creating a higher-end image for your business or by trading on your reputation as an expert.

» **Charge the same as the competition.** But you still need to increase the value of your product over the competition's to drive actual sales. You could do this, for example, by offering a more convenient location to your target customers.

» **Charge less than the competition.** Just be careful not to undercut your own cost of production, and keep in mind that you'll acquire a "reputation." Whether it's true or not, customers and clients will tend to associate lower prices with lower value. Only in rare cases will people think they've made a marvellous discovery of a business that carries exactly the same product as the competition, but at a lower price. It's also a good idea to keep prices fluid. Flexibility never hurts.

2

Getting Started

IN THIS PART . . .

Find out about buying an existing business or starting one from scratch.

Dig into the legal ownership side of setting up a business.

Shop for the basic equipment your business needs to get started.

Decide where your business will be located.

Get the money you need to finance your enterprise.

Discover the importance of having a business plan.

Make a marketing splash.

IN THIS CHAPTER

» **Thinking about buying a business instead of building your own business**

» **Finding a business to buy**

» **Knowing what to look for when you're buying a business**

» **Placing a value on an existing business**

» **Putting together the deal to buy a business**

» **Contemplating a franchise**

Chapter **5**

Custom-Made Business — or Off-the-Shelf?

uilding your own business is a lot of work. In addition to coming up with a business concept, you have to find a good location, prepare your business premises (see Chapter 8), buy equipment (see Chapter 7), and find and attract clients or customers (see Chapter 11). And when you custom-build your business, you have no one to give you on-the-job training or to pass on wisdom gained from experience about what works and what doesn't.

But custom-building a business is not the only way to go into business. You can buy an existing business instead. In this chapter, we weigh the advantages and disadvantages of each approach.

Why Buy an Existing Business?

You might want to buy an existing business for a number of reasons:

» You already know of a business that you want to own. Perhaps you're an employee and the owner wants to sell, or the owner is a relative or friend who is retiring and looking for a successor, or you've been a customer or a client of the business and you know the owner would look favourably on an offer to buy.

» You'll be able to eliminate a lot of the difficult, early work involved in building a business, and hit the ground running. If you buy an established business, you may not have to find a location or buy equipment or hunt for customers or hire employees or develop a new marketing plan.

» You may be able to tap into a source of advice about how to run a business because the original owner may be willing to stay on with you for a while.

» You may be able avoid some of the risks of starting a new business:

  • When you buy a successful business, you know that the product or service you will be offering already has a market.

  • When you buy an existing business, your immediate money situation may be better — borrowing money may be easier, because banks know that the risks of failure are lower for an established business than for a start-up. And you may need less money than you would for a new business if the business has an established income stream.

» You may be able to get rights you couldn't otherwise get — buying a business may be the only way to get the right to distribute a specific product in a particular area, or the licence to manufacture a particular item.

But before you go rushing off to buy a business, know that buying a business has its disadvantages, as well:

» You won't be able to buy a successful business cheap. (A business that's in trouble will be less expensive to buy, but you have to be realistic about your chances of turning the business around.) And on top of the price for the business itself, you'll have to pay professional fees — for an accountant, lawyer, and a business valuation expert at least, and maybe for others, as well.

» A successful business may not continue to be successful for you. The success may have been based on the personality and/or skill of the current owner. When he leaves, he may take the success with him. Or the business, although it pays the current owner well, may not generate enough income to give you a reasonable return on your investment (if you pay cash) or to be profitable after you make your loan payments (if you borrow money to buy the business).

>> You'll inherit any problems the business has. Even successful businesses have problems, such as difficult employees, inefficient business practices, unreliable suppliers, or troublesome clients or customers. The previous owner may have learned to live with these problems, but they may drive you crazy — and your efforts at reform may cause resentment among employees, suppliers, or clients.

Shopping for a Business

If you don't already have your eye on a particular business, where do you look for one that's for sale?

>> **Read the ads:** Look in the classified section of your newspaper under Business Opportunities or Businesses for Sale. Check ads in industry journals, newsletters, and magazines.

>> **Search the Internet:** Find websites that list Canadian businesses for sale. You can search for Canadian sites on Google, Bing, Kijiji, or Yahoo! Canada by using the search terms "buy business Canada" or "small business for sale Alberta."

>> **Place an ad:** Consider advertising online or in print in your local newspaper, or in industry publications under Businesses Wanted.

>> **Visit trade shows and conventions:** The program may contain ads for businesses for sale, or exhibitors may know of some. Tell people you meet that you're looking for a business to buy. Word may reach someone who's looking to sell.

>> **Tell business professionals that you're interested in buying:** Speak to any lawyers, accountants, financial advisors, consultants, or bank managers you know. One of them may work with a business owner who's looking for a buyer.

>> **Ask a business owner if he or she wants to sell:** If you know of a business that interests you, consider asking the owner if she's interested in selling. Just because a business isn't for sale doesn't mean that the owner won't consider an offer. You can at least plant this seed of possibility.

>> **Use a business broker:** Business brokers help business owners sell their businesses and they can tell you about the businesses their clients are selling. If you work with a broker, keep in mind that he's interested in making a sale so he can earn a commission, and that his job is to make his clients' businesses look as attractive as possible to a prospective buyer. You can find a business broker on Google, Bing, or Yahoo! by using the search terms "business brokers Canada."

Looking Carefully at Potential Existing Businesses

Before the owner agrees to answer your questions, show you around the business premises, and let you see documents, he or she may ask you to sign a *confidential disclosure agreement*. By signing the agreement you agree not to tell anyone else what you find out about the business, and usually you also agree not to use the information for any purpose but assessing the business for a possible purchase. The information and the business are protected if you decide you don't want to buy, because the owner can sue you if you don't honour the agreement.

Take a very careful, even cynical, look at any business before deciding to buy. In the upcoming sections, we set out some questions to guide your examination of a business that's up for sale.

Why is the owner selling the business?

This may be the most important and fundamental question to ask. Many reasons exist for selling a business, but from the buyer's point of view, some are better than others.

These reasons shouldn't set off alarm bells for you:

>> The owner is retiring because he or she no longer needs to work, or because of age or ill-health (. . . as long as the business didn't cause the ill-health).

>> The owner wants to pursue a different career or business opportunity (unless a problem with this business triggered that desire).

>> The owner is having marital problems.

These reasons may signal trouble:

>> The business is not profitable.

>> The owner cannot raise enough money to finance the business.

>> Competition for the business is heating up.

>> Markets for the business's product or service are drying up.

>> The work hours are too long and/or the work is unpleasant.

TIP

The owner may be very forthcoming about her reasons for selling, or she may be reluctant to talk. Even if she does talk, don't just believe what she tells you. Seek internally consistent information from others in the same industry — business owners, employees, suppliers, and customers.

What is the reputation of the business?

TIP

A major reason for buying an established business is to get the benefit of its reputation. You hope that it has a base of loyal customers and suppliers who will continue to deal with you. Speak to the business's customers and suppliers to find out what they think of the business. Contact the Better Business Bureau (www.bbb. org), industry associations, and any federal or provincial licensing bodies to see if any complaints have been made against the business. Search on Google, Bing, or Yahoo! for reviews of the business.

What is the reason for the success of the business?

You want to make sure that the business has been successful because of a lasting reason. So here are some areas to check out:

>> Does the business have a great product or service — or was it built on a passing fad?

>> If the business was built on a small number of enthusiastic clients or customers, are they likely to stay on with you?

>> If the business was built on exports, what's the economic and political outlook for the countries where the exports go?

>> If the business has done well because it had little competition, is competition likely to increase in the future?

How's the neighbourhood?

Perhaps your main reason for buying the business is that it has a wonderful location that draws customers like a magnet, or it's perfectly placed for receiving supply deliveries and shipping out products. If so, be sure to check the terms of the lease for the location:

>> Is the rent reasonable?

>> How much time is left on the lease — and does the lease contain any rights to renew?

>> If the business is located in a mall, does the lease protect you from competition by other tenants?

>> Does the lease affect the hours you can or have to work? Some retail mall leases require storeowners to operate whenever the mall is open, and that may include evening and weekend hours you do not want to work. Access to office, industrial, or warehouse space may be restricted to certain hours, and even if you can get in, the power, light, heat, air-conditioning, and elevators may not be operational.

If the location of the business is not the main reason you want the business, then make sure that the location is not a reason you'll come to regret your purchase:

>> If this business has been at its location for only a short while, what happened to the business that was there before? Does this location have a history of failed businesses? You want to be sure that the past success of the business wasn't tied to its previous location.

>> Does the municipality or landlord have any plans for the property that will affect traffic, parking, or access to the property? A major renovation of the building or major road construction or anything else that limits customer or supplier access could be bad news for you.

What do the financial statements tell you?

When you're looking over a business, you should ask to see its audited and otherwise vetted financial statements for the preceding three to five years.

The financial statements of a business contain information that will be very useful to you in deciding whether the business is worth buying at all, and, if it is, in deciding on the price you should pay. But you have to be able to understand the financial statements. We talk about financial statements in Chapter 17, and if you don't know very much — or anything — about financial statements, flip to Chapter 17 now and read about them before continuing.

TIP

Have a professional accountant (Chartered Professional Accountant) or business valuation expert (Chartered Business Valuator) review the financial statements before you make a final decision to buy — even if you think you've got the business's financials all figured out yourself.

In the following sections, we tell you what to look for in two types of statements: the income statement and the balance sheet. For a more detailed look at these statements, check out the latest edition of *Bookkeeping For Canadians For Dummies* by Lita Epstein and Cécile Laurin (Wiley).

The income statement

The *income statement*, also called a profit and loss statement, sets out a business's revenues and expenses over a stated period of time (a month, quarter, or year). The *revenues* (also called sales) is the money paid by customers or clients for products or services. The *expenses* are the costs of doing business. A business's *profit* (also called income) equals revenues minus expenses.

Look at the revenues of the business, and ask

>> **How profitable is the business?** Don't look at just the total dollar amount of the profit. Look at the *profit margin* (profit divided by revenues times 100 gives you the percentage that is the profit margin). If it's low for this kind of business (see the section "Sources of information for valuing a business" for help with questions like this), that may indicate that the business is not run efficiently. Also factor out non-cash items like depreciation expense or a one-time gain on a sale of a fixed asset to get a better picture of actual profitability. By doing so, the resulting adjusted net income figure will more closely mirror actual net "cash" flows. Hopefully, it's an inflow!

>> **Have revenues increased over the past while?** If they have, that's certainly good news, but try to get a sense of why. You want to see an increase in the amount of business, not simply an increase in the price the business has charged for its goods or services.

>> **Will the profits give you a reasonable return on your investment?** Compare the profits to the price you'd be willing to pay for the business. If you invested the price in something else, would the profit you see in these financial statements be a reasonable return on your investment?

Look at the expenses, and ask

>> **Have expenses as a percentage of revenues gone up, remained steady, or gone down over the past while?** If expenses have gone up, does a particular category of expenses seem to be getting out of control?

>> **Could you cut some expenses? Would you want to increase any expenses?** Some expenses may be discretionary (typically entertainment, travel, car expenses, and club memberships), and if you can cut expenses, you'll be able to increase profits. But if you increase expenses, the profits will go down.

>> **How much has the owner been paying himself or herself?** How does that salary compare to what you intend to take? The business may show a profit only because the owner has been taking little or no salary. But if the owner has been taking a higher salary than you need, you'll be able to increase the profits of the business by taking a lower salary.

The balance sheet

The *balance sheet* is a financial snapshot at a point in time that lists and shows a value for everything a business owns (its *assets*) and everything it owes (its *liabilities*), usually the last day of the company's *fiscal* year. (This is called its year-end. A fiscal year has 365 days in it, but it doesn't have to match up with the calendar year. March 31 and June 30 are common fiscal year-ends.)

Assets fall into two categories, current assets and fixed assets. *Current assets* are cash, and assets that are intended to be and can be turned into cash easily and quickly. *Fixed assets* are assets the business intends to hold onto for a long time.

With the balance sheet in one hand and the income statement in the other, have a look at the business's assets to find out more about the financial shape the business is in:

>> One current asset is *accounts receivable* — amounts billed out to customers or clients but not yet paid. Is the accounts receivable, over time, becoming a larger percentage of the business's revenue? High accounts receivable are a sign of problems. Perhaps the customers or clients have no money. (You don't want to buy a business that has deadbeat customers.) Or maybe the customers aren't paying because they're not happy with the business's product or service. (You don't want to buy a business that has a poor reputation.)

>> Another current asset in a retail or manufacturing business is *inventory* (unsold goods). (The balance sheet will not list the inventory in detail, but will show how much the unsold inventory cost to buy.) Have inventory levels been going up or down over the past years? You should be concerned if the inventory levels are going up more than revenues. Too much inventory may be a sign that business isn't good because nobody's buying the product. Even if the business is not in trouble, with high levels of inventory, some of the inventory may be out-of-date and, therefore, not worth as much as more

recent inventory. Actually go and look over the inventory to see if it actually exists and to evaluate its condition.

>> Fixed assets include equipment. The value shown on the balance sheet for fixed assets is called book value. *Book value* reflects the purchase price of the assets less *depreciation* (reduction in the value of the assets year by year to take into account their age), but doesn't necessarily reflect the true value of the assets. Look at the book value of equipment and then look at the equipment itself. Does it appear to be worth its book value? You don't want to overpay for assets. Does the business have too much equipment? You don't want to pay for equipment you don't need (and excess equipment may be a sign that business is declining). Does the business lack equipment or have obsolete equipment? You may have to buy new equipment when you take over the business, adding to expenses. And anyway, you don't want to pay for something you can't use.

Liabilities, or debts owed, are categorized as current liabilities and long-term liabilities. *Current liabilities* are debts that will be paid within a year such as *accounts payable* (money the business owes to suppliers), current wages, current taxes, and the portion of any long-term debt that's currently payable. *Long-term liabilities* are debts that will not be paid off within a year.

Look at the balance sheet again and ask

>> **Who actually owns the business — the owner or the creditors?** To find this out, divide the total amount of debt (current and long-term) by the net worth of the business. You calculate the net worth, also called the *owner's equity* in the business, by subtracting the total liabilities of the business from the total assets of the business. When you divide the debt by the net worth, you get the *debt-to-equity* or *debt-to-net-worth* ratio. A ratio of 1:1 (that is, the owner owns as much of the business as the creditors do) or less is what you'd like to see.

>> **How easy will it be to borrow money?** Lenders look at the debt-to-equity ratio to decide whether or not to cough up the cash when a business asks to borrow. If the ratio is too high (2:1 or higher), you may find it hard to persuade a lender to part with its money.

>> **How quickly could the business get cash without borrowing, if it needed to?** Divide the business's current assets by its current liabilities to get the business's current ratio. The *current ratio* measures the business's *liquidity* — its ability to quickly raise cash by disposing of assets that are fairly easy to sell. The higher the current ratio, the more liquid the business, and the more easily it can come up with a fistful of dollars. A ratio of 4:1 or 5:1 is very healthy; a ratio of less than 2:1 should cause you some concern.

What is the "corporate culture"?

The employees of every business develop attitudes that govern the way they deal with management, customers, suppliers, and each other. In some businesses, management, staff, suppliers, and customers may treat each other like family. (We mean like family who like each other.) In others, they may treat each other very formally and follow a rigid structure. In a few, they may be engaged in guerrilla, or even open, warfare. Do you like what you see of the corporate culture? If you don't, do you think you will be able to change the culture — and still keep the business's staff, customers, and suppliers?

Deciding on a Price for a Business

If you've checked out the business and are pleased with it, don't just say, "I'll take it!" You must first decide what the business is worth and what price you're willing to pay. Buying a good business for the wrong price can be as big a mistake as buying a bad business. In this section, we tell you about different approaches to valuing businesses and where to find information on the value of a business.

TIP

Don't make a final decision to buy a business without getting professional help — from a Chartered Professional Accountant (CPA) and/or a Chartered Business Valuator (CBV) and/or a lawyer — perhaps from all three.

>> An accountant and/or a business valuation expert can help you decide what the business is worth.

>> A CPA and/or a lawyer can help you decide how to structure the deal.

>> A lawyer can draft the contract to buy and complete the transaction to make sure that you get what you're supposed to.

If you're wondering how you'll actually come up with the money to buy the business, go to Chapter 7.

What's a business worth?

When you buy a business as a going concern, you're buying more than the physical assets of the business. You're also buying the business's *goodwill* — the likelihood that the business will be successful in the future. So in arriving at a price for a business, you have to find a price that includes both.

Valuing assets

You can value physical (or "tangible") assets in different ways, including the following:

>> **Fair market value** — the price you would have to pay on the open market for equipment or inventory of the same age and condition. This is usually the best way to determine what the assets are "worth," but the owner may expect you to pay more than the fair market value of the assets in order to get the business as a going concern.

>> **Replacement value** — the price you would have to pay for new inventory and equipment to replace what the business currently has. Generally, you would not pay replacement value when purchasing used assets. However, if the assets of the business are difficult to replace, that drives their value up.

>> **Book value** — the value at which the assets are shown in the business's balance sheet. It may be higher or lower than the fair market value of the assets.

Another is *liquidation value* — the price for which the equipment and inventory could be sold if the business were liquidated (turned into cash), for example in a bankruptcy. However, liquidation value is not normally used when the business is a going concern, because it's lower than fair market value.

Note that if you will be taking over the debts of the company (and that's the usual scenario if you buy a going concern), to arrive at a value for the assets you have to deduct the amount of debts from the value of the assets.

Valuing goodwill

If you're buying a business as a going concern, you're not just shopping for some equipment and inventory. You also want the business's goodwill, which is an "intangible" (untouchable) asset of the business. Goodwill is valuable because it affects the business's continuing success. Theoretically, goodwill is often defined as the likelihood that customers will keep coming back if you ceased advertising and promotion. From an accounting perspective, goodwill is the amount of money you pay to buy the business minus the fair market value of the tangible assets, the intangible assets that can be identified and valued, and the liabilities obtained in the purchase.

All of the following affect a business's goodwill:

>> The customer base it has established

>> The business's age and reputation, including its name and any trademarks or intellectual property that it possesses

>> The location

>> The exclusive rights the business might hold

>> The talent of its employees

>> The reliability of its suppliers

>> The amount of competition the business faces

How do you place a value on the business, including goodwill? Most valuation methods involve examining the past earnings of the business as the best indicator of what future earnings are likely to be.

One valuation method that's often used is the *multiple of earnings* method. With this method, the business's earnings (its revenues less its expenses) over the past three to five years are averaged, and then that average is multiplied by a given number to arrive at a value for the business as a whole, not just for goodwill. The given number (known as a "multiple") varies from industry to industry. The best way to figure out the multiple for the business you're thinking of buying is to get information about recent sales of comparable businesses. (We give you some suggestions for finding that information in the "Sources of information for valuing a business" section.) Divide the price for which a business sold by its average annual earnings. That will give you a multiple to use for this particular type of business. Other business valuation methods include discounted cash flow and capitalized cash flow, both outside the scope of this book but well within the scope of the work of a CBV or even a CPA.

TIP

After you come up with a proposed purchase price, check how reasonable it is by calculating the return you would likely get on your investment if you bought the business for that price. Take the average annual earnings of the company over the past three to five years and divide them by the proposed purchase price. That will give you the rate of return you may reasonably expect from your investment. (For example, if you're thinking about paying $250,000 for a business that has had average earnings of $15,000, the rate of return is 6 percent.) How does the rate of return compare to what you might earn on the same sum put into a different investment? Is the rate of return worth it when you take into account the work and risk involved in this particular business?

Sources of information for valuing a business

TIP

The best way to figure out what a business is worth is to find out how much comparable businesses have sold for. Unfortunately, getting sales information about businesses is harder than getting it about homes. Here are some possible sources of information about sale prices, and also about valuing businesses generally.

Trade publications

Trade publications for the industry you're interested in will probably have articles about how to value businesses within that industry, and may have information about actual sales.

Businesses that you've looked at

Keep track of any businesses you've looked at but decided not to buy. If a business is sold, try to find out the price by talking to the previous owner. This is a bit of a long shot, because most businesspeople don't like to gab about their financial affairs.

Accountants, lawyers, and consultants

Speak to accountants, lawyers, and consultants who work with business buyers and sellers. They may have information on comparable sales if they have been involved in sales of businesses similar to the one you're thinking of buying.

Business brokers

If you've been looking at businesses with a business broker he or she should have information about sales of similar businesses — at least those sold through the broker's office. Keep in mind that the broker is working on commission for the seller and the commission is based on the price you agree to pay for the business — so the broker has an interest in getting you to pay the highest possible price.

Chartered Business Valuators

TIP

Using a CBV is probably your best bet. If you've reached the point where you're ready to make an offer, you should seriously consider hiring a CBV who will, for a fee, estimate the value of the business you're interested in. The amount of the fee varies with the size and complexity of the business, but may well be several thousand dollars. Your lawyer, accountant, or business consultant may be able to refer you to an appraiser or valuator. Or you can contact the Canadian Institute of Chartered Business Valuators (https://cbvinstitute.com) for a list of members in your province.

Putting the Deal Together

REMEMBER

After you find a business you want to buy and you've figured out how much it's worth, you negotiate a deal with the owner. If you haven't already called in your lawyer and your accountant, do so now.

In this section, we give you some background on how a business purchase is structured, so you'll understand why you need professional help.

Buy assets or buy shares?

The business you're interested in buying is one of the following:

>> A sole proprietorship

>> A partnership

>> A corporation

(We tell you more about these different forms of business in Chapter 6.)

If the business is run as a sole proprietorship or as a partnership, you have to buy the business by buying the assets of the business. However, if you're buying a corporation, you have a choice between buying the assets of the business and buying the shares of the corporation.

A share purchase

Buying all the shares of a corporation makes the buyer the owner of the corporation. The corporation continues to exist just as before, and continues to own all its assets and owe all its debts. If the corporation was a party to any contracts, they will continue in effect. (This works in theory. Some of the contracts may allow the other party to withdraw from the contract if the corporation changes ownership.)

An asset purchase

Buying all the assets of a corporation does not make the buyer the owner of the corporation. The buyer will have no relationship with the corporation itself. The corporation continues to exist. It has no assets, but it's still responsible for its debts (except for those that the buyer agrees to take over — for example, a mortgage on real property or lease on a piece of equipment). The buyer does not get the benefit of any of the corporation's contracts unless the corporation assigns (transfers) them to the buyer. (The consent of the other party to the contract is usually required for an assignment.)

Deciding between a share purchase and an asset purchase

If you can choose either a share purchase or an asset purchase, how do you decide? Common wisdom is that buyers prefer asset purchases while sellers prefer share purchases. (The preference has to do with Canadian tax consequences, which we explain later in this chapter.) So chances are that you'll want to purchase assets and the seller will want to sell shares.

Some of the usual advantages of an asset purchase if you're the buyer are

>> You can pick and choose the assets you want to buy — well, in theory. The seller may refuse to sell you the assets you want to buy unless you also agree to take some or all of the other assets he or she wants to sell.

>> You don't automatically take on the debts and liabilities of the business. However, you may want to take on some debts (for example, a favourable mortgage as a way to help finance the purchase of a particular asset). You may also want to take on some liabilities (for example, warranty responsibilities, so that you don't aggravate your newly acquired customers by telling them to buzz off if they previously bought faulty products from the business).

>> You can negotiate the value assigned to each asset to try to get the maximum tax advantage (see the next section, "Allocation of the purchase price in an asset purchase").

Some disadvantages of an asset purchase if you're the buyer are

>> You'll usually have to contend with a lot of legal paperwork in an asset purchase, because each individual asset has to be identified and transferred separately, and because the purchase must comply with provincial legislation to protect creditors of the business.

>> You'll have to pay GST and provincial retail sales tax, or HST, on the equipment you buy, and land transfer tax on any real property you buy.

>> You'll have to go through the process of hiring any employees you want to keep. (Unfortunately, the opposite is not true — because of provincial legislation, you may find yourself stuck with some employees you don't want to keep and you'll have to pay them off to let them go.)

>> You may not be able to buy certain assets without the consent of a third party. For example, the landlord's consent may be required before you can take over the lease for the business premises.

And despite the common wisdom, a share purchase has advantages if you're the buyer. For example:

>> You may face less paperwork than in an asset purchase . . . although that probably won't translate into lower professional fees because a thorough investigation of the corporation and its ownership of the assets must still occur.

>> You likely won't have to pay GST, HST, provincial sales tax, or land transfer tax.

>> You won't have to hire anyone, because the employment relationship between employees and the corporation doesn't change — although employees you'd like to keep may choose to leave because of the change in ownership (and, naturally, employees you'd like to part ways with may choose to stay).

>> You won't have to get third-party consent to the sale, because the assets do not change ownership (although some leases may contain a condition that the lease ends if the corporation changes ownership).

>> You may find that buying the entire corporation is the only way to acquire a licence or contract that by its terms cannot be transferred by the corporation to anyone else.

>> You may be able to get a tax reduction if the business has lost money in past years — if the corporation now has a loss carry forward, it can be applied against the corporation's future profits to reduce income taxes. Of course, you have to turn the business around and generate some profits first!

Allocation of the purchase price in an asset purchase

If you proceed by way of an asset purchase, negotiating a price with the seller has two parts. First you have to decide what you think the business is worth as a whole and come to an agreement with the seller on an overall price. Then, you must allocate the amount of the purchase price among the various assets included in the sale (in other words, you must assign a price to each asset).

You may be thoroughly sick of us telling you about all the complicated and expensive steps involved in buying a business, so you probably feel like tossing this book into a garbage can, pouring lighter fluid all over it, and lighting a match. But that would waste the book *and* the lighter fluid — and furthermore, what we have to tell you can reduce your Canadian taxes! Interested now? If so, see the sidebar "Reducing your taxes in an asset purchase."

The dear departed — can you control the former owner?

Whether you decide on a share purchase or an asset purchase, you need to cover off certain matters with the soon-to-be-ex-owner to increase your chance of success after you take over the business.

REDUCING YOUR TAXES IN AN ASSET PURCHASE

One way to reduce the tax you pay on your business income is to increase your deductions. (See Chapter 16 for more on taxes.) So when you buy the assets of a business, you want to structure the deal so that in future years your deductions from income will be as high as possible.

Many of the assets of a business are *capital property* (property with long-term value that is bought to keep). You can deduct the cost of capital property from business income, but you can't deduct the full cost of it in the year of purchase. Instead, you're allowed annual deductions for capital cost allowance (which is a different name for, but pretty much the same thing as, *depreciation* or *amortization,* or decrease in value as the asset ages). Each year the Canada Revenue Agency (CRA) allows you to claim a deduction for *capital cost allowance* on capital property. Different rates of depreciation apply to different classes of assets. For example, the rate that applies to land is 0 percent (because land doesn't depreciate in value), to buildings 4 percent or more in some cases, to equipment 20 percent, and to computer hardware and systems software 45 percent to 55 percent depending on a few nuances in tax regulations. And inventory can be fully deducted as an expense in the year of purchase.

In an asset purchase, the price you allocate to each asset determines the asset's *adjusted cost base*, which is the figure used to calculate the capital cost allowance for that asset. As a buyer, you want to allocate a higher price to inventory and to assets that have a higher rate of capital cost allowance, and a lower price to assets that have a lower rate of capital cost allowance. That way, you deduct more dollars at a faster pace.

The seller, however, will want to allocate a lower price to assets that have a higher rate of capital cost allowance and a higher price to assets that have a lower rate of capital cost allowance. Sellers are very stubborn about this, but they're not just trying to annoy buyers. They've got a reason.

The general rule in an asset sale is that the seller has to pay only *capital gains tax* on the assets sold — which means that 50 percent of the increase in value of the asset since the seller acquired it is added to the seller's income and taxed. But if the sale price allocated to an asset is higher than the depreciated value of the asset (the purchase price less the capital cost allowance claimed over the years), 100 percent of the extra amount of capital cost allowance that the seller has claimed is added to the seller's taxable income as *recaptured capital cost allowance*. Think of this as the seller paying back the CRA excessive CCA she claimed in the past. In addition, 100 percent of any amount allocated to inventory is added to the seller's taxable income. So allocating the purchase price among assets is not going to be easy.

Non-competition agreement

TIP

When you buy a business as a going concern, you want to keep the business's customers — so the last thing you want is for the seller to set up a competing business next door. To make sure that doesn't happen, you must have *a non-competition agreement* with the seller. Without one, nothing can stop the vendor from competing with you and taking your customers away.

If you've got a non-competition agreement and the ex-owner starts competing with you, you'll have to sue to stop him or her. But a non-competition agreement will stand up in court only if it's reasonable — you'll be able to prevent the seller from setting up a similar business only for a reasonable period of time and only within a reasonable distance of your business location. What's reasonable will depend on the nature of the business (although you should always think in terms of months rather than decades and in kilometres rather than provinces). For example, preventing the seller of a convenience store or hair salon from competing only in the immediate neighbourhood is probably reasonable. Or, preventing the seller of an advertising agency with a national clientele from competing anywhere in Canada for one year may also be reasonable.

An agreement that gives the seller a stake in the business

TIP

Another way of discouraging the seller from competing with you is to structure the deal so that the seller has a stake in the continued success of the business. The seller will have a stake in your success if you can persuade him or her to take back a mortgage or promissory note for part of the purchase price, or if part of the purchase price is made payable at a future time and is tied to the business's income.

Consulting agreement

You might like the former owner of the business to stay on as a consultant for a limited time after the sale. The former owner will be able to give you advice about running the business (if you think you need some help), and his or her presence may encourage customers to keep on dealing with the business while they get to know you.

A consulting contract can also be used to turn some of the purchase price into consulting fees and spread it out over the period of the contract. This has two advantages, one for you and one for the former owner. You don't have to come up with the full purchase price at the time of the sale, and the owner gets to spread taxes on the profit from the sale over two or more taxation years.

Considering a Franchise

A *franchise* isn't exactly an off-the-shelf business. It's more like a pre-packaged business — you add water and stir. The *franchisor* (the company that created and developed the original business) owns the business name and trademarks and practices and procedures; the *franchisee* (the "buyer" of the franchise that is essentially granted the rights to the franchise) gets a licence to use them. The franchisee pays an up-front franchise fee and then also makes continuing payments (royalties) based on the franchise's earnings. The franchisee sets up his or her own business, but sets it up as if it were part of a chain with one name and with standardized products, design, service, and operations.

Checking out the advantages of a franchise

Being granted the rights to an established franchise provides the benefits of belonging to a large organization, while still being your own boss, including

>> A business concept that has been thought out, and a product or service that has been researched and developed

>> A recognized business name, centralized advertising, and sophisticated marketing

>> Assistance, training, and support in management and production

>> Economies of scale in buying supplies and services, because purchasing is centralized

>> Assistance in choosing a business location (reputable franchises check out the strength of the local market before selling a new franchise in an area)

Investigating the disadvantages of a franchise

Buying a franchise can sometimes lead to trouble for the franchisee because

>> Franchises like Harvey's are standardized operations, and standardization can be stifling to a business owner who has his or her own ideas.

>> Successful franchises like McDonald's are very expensive — and new franchises are a gamble because costs may be higher than expected and/or profits lower than expected.

>> Franchise agreements are always drafted by the franchisor and they favour the franchisor over the franchisee.

>> The franchisor may promise training and support, but they may not be as good or thorough as promised.

>> Franchisees may be charged more than the going market rate for supplies if they have to be purchased through the franchisor or specified suppliers.

>> Franchisees are often required to pay substantial amounts for advertising and they may not see that they're getting anything in return.

>> Sometimes the franchisor leases premises for a franchise location and subleases them to the franchisee. Then the franchisor can use its rights as a landlord to lock the franchisee out of the premises without notice if the franchisee doesn't make all the payments required under the franchise agreement.

>> If the franchisor opens too many coffee shops in one area, for example, or starts distributing products through eBay or Shopify, it can drastically reduce the profits of franchisees.

>> Franchisees often don't have special legislation to protect them against franchisors, because only about half of the provinces to date have passed franchise statutes.

Finding a franchise

Franchises are available in just about any business area, from accounting and tax services to pet care to lawn services to senior care services. So the first step in finding a franchise is to decide on the kind of business you want to be in. We talk about choosing your business in Chapter 1.

After you decide on the kind of business you want to be in, find out whether any franchises exist in that kind of business, and if so, whether any franchises are being offered in the location you're interested in.

You can look for franchises that are available in Canada in a number of ways:

>> **Read franchise magazines:** A number of magazines are geared to people interested in buying a franchise, such as *Canadian Business Franchise Magazine* (www.franchiseinfo.ca), and *Franchise Canada Magazine* (http://franchisecanada.cfa.ca), the official publication of the Canadian Franchise Association (CFA). These magazines and resources contain general information and advice about franchising and contain ads for franchises for sale.

- » **Check a franchise directory:** The *Franchise Canada Directory*, published by the Canadian Franchise Association, lists available franchises.

- » **Search the Internet:** Many websites contain information about franchises for sale. The Canadian Franchise Association's website (www.cfa.ca) contains a "Find a Franchise" feature that allows you to browse franchises either by name or by category. Only CFA members in good standing are listed. You can also check BeTheBoss.ca (www.betheboss.ca) or Franchise Solutions (www.franchisesolutions.com).

- » **Visit franchise shows:** A number of franchise shows are held across Canada throughout the year, such as the National Franchise and Business Opportunities Show (www.franchiseshowinfo.com); and the Franchise Show, which is organized by the Canadian Franchise Association.

- » **Use a franchise advisor:** Some accounting firms, such as BDO Dunwoody or Grant Thornton, provide help in finding and evaluating potential franchises. You can also find business brokers who deal in the resale of existing franchises.

Evaluating the franchises you find

A franchise is a very expensive purchase. Many require an investment of at least $100,000. And when you buy a franchise, you're not just purchasing a product and walking away; you're entering into an ongoing relationship, somewhat like a partnership. So you should be confident that you want to go into business with the franchisor. Make a list of the franchises you find, and then investigate each of them thoroughly and carefully.

What information are you looking for?

TIP

You should know a number of things about a franchise opportunity before you buy. Form 5-1 also gives you this handy checklist of questions. (This book's Introduction provides instructions on how to access the free downloadable content.)

- » **How does the franchisor make most if its money?** Beware of a franchisor that makes most of its money from the sale of new franchises, rather than from the profits of ongoing franchises. That's an indication that the franchisor is far more interested in selling franchises than in supporting its existing franchisees. A franchisor that is interested in the ongoing success of its franchisees will be as cautious about selling to you as you are about buying, and will want extensive information not only about your financial status, but about your personal and business background.

>> **What is the franchisor's business record?** Is the franchisor well established and does it have a good business reputation? How successful is the franchisor? How successful are its franchisees?

>> **How much will the franchise cost, and does the franchisor offer any financing?** Up-front costs include the franchise fee paid to the franchisor and the cost of setting up the franchise premises (construction or leasehold improvements, equipment, and initial inventory). Also consider ongoing fees such as royalties and contributions to the franchisor's advertising and marketing program. These costs are in addition to the usual everyday costs of running the business. You may also have to pay a renewal fee at the end of the original term of your franchise agreement.

>> **How much can you expect to earn?** What income will the franchise generate? And is the income enough to cover your ongoing expenses, including finances, and to provide you with a reasonable profit?

>> **What is the term of the franchise agreement?** How long will your franchise rights last and is the term long enough for you to recoup your up-front investment?

>> **Where will your franchise be located?** Will the franchisor choose your location or help you to choose? Will you be given an exclusive territory in which the franchisor agrees not to locate another franchisee? You want an exclusive territory that is large enough to protect you from competitors within the franchise, while at the same time small enough to provide wide exposure of the franchise name in your area. If your premises are leased, is the lease term at least as long as the term of the franchise agreement?

>> **Will the franchisor train you?** Will you be given training before your franchise opens? What kind, and who pays for the training? Will you be given ongoing training and assistance after your franchise opens?

>> **What rights do you have to sell the franchise?** Does the franchisor place unreasonable limits on your right to sell the franchise if you decide you want out?

Where can you find it?

TIP

You can get your franchise information from several sources:

>> **The franchisor:** Alberta, New Brunswick, Ontario, Manitoba, British Columbia, and Prince Edward Island have franchise legislation or regulations that require a franchisor to give prospective franchisees a franchise disclosure document containing, among other things, the business backgrounds of the franchise and its directors, audited financial statements and credit reports, and copies

of all franchise agreements. If you live in another province, but the franchise operates in Alberta, Manitoba, British Columbia, New Brunswick, Ontario, or Prince Edward Island, ask to see the disclosure document required in those provinces. Canadian Franchise Association member franchises agree to abide by a code of ethics that requires full and accurate written disclosure to prospective franchisees. Ask the franchisor to provide you with the names and contact information of existing franchisees, and of financial institutions and suppliers willing to act as references. This is an important part of the franchise disclosure process. Be very suspicious if the franchisor is less than forthcoming about any of the information you request.

>> **Other franchisees:** Talk to several current and former franchisees either by phone or in person. How much did they have to invest? What were the hidden costs? How long have they been in business? How long did it take for the business to make a profit? Did they receive adequate training and ongoing support? Has the franchisor lived up to its side of the agreement? Would they advise you to purchase a franchise? Ask them if they would want to gain the rights to this franchise again if given the opportunity.

>> **The Internet:** Search the franchise on Google, Bing, and Yahoo!, and see what turns up.

>> **The Better Business Bureau and trade associations:** Check to see if any complaints have been filed against the company or its products with the Better Business Bureau in your area and the area where the franchisor's head office is located. Find out the franchisor's reputation within any industry trade association and within the Canadian Franchise Association and/or the International Franchise Association.

Doing due diligence before you sign

Get advice from your accountant and your lawyer:

>> Have your accountant review the franchisor's financial statements to see if they disclose any problems, and to tell you whether the financial projections are based on reasonable assumptions.

>> Have your lawyer, one experienced in franchise law, review the franchise agreement. At the very least, your lawyer should make sure that you under-stand the agreement fully. If appropriate, your lawyer should try to negotiate necessary changes to the agreement.

Chapter **6**

Ownership Issues

Before you can start your business, you need a vehicle for carrying on your business — a "form of business" or a "business organization." Only a few forms of business exist, and we take you around to each one of them and help you kick the tires. After you've looked at all of them and thought about your own business circumstances, you can decide which form of business is right for you.

Should You Go Alone or Take on a Co-Pilot?

You'll often get asked, "What's your business?" But right now, we ask, "Who's your business?" Is your business you and only you? Is it you and a pal? You and a group?

If your new business is a team effort, you can skip ahead to "Should You Incorporate?" now. If your new business is a one-person show, stick around and read this section.

Certainly, being the only owner of a business has its advantages. Here are just a few of them:

» The profits of the business will be yours alone. (When you've accumulated some profits you can sit on the floor and rub $50 bills all over your body, shouting "Mine, mine, all mine!" Obviously this kind of behaviour would be out of bounds if you had a co-owner.)

>> You have the only say in what the business does and you don't need anyone else's agreement to do what you want to do. So there.

>> Setting up a business with just one owner is usually easier, faster, and cheaper.

But here are reasons that you might want to, or have to, have a co-owner:

>> You may want someone else to share the financial risks of the business with you.

>> You may want company — being in business all by yourself can be lonely.

>> You may need someone else to provide skills or knowledge that you don't have.

>> You may want someone to share the workload.

If we've now got you considering sharing ownership of your business with someone else, you should consider these questions:

>> Are you capable of working well with a co-owner (and especially with any particular co-owner you have in mind)?

>> Is the business likely to be able to generate enough revenue to support two (or more) owners?

>> Does the business have roles for two (or more) owners to play?

>> Does your potential co-owner have skills and knowledge that will add to yours (instead of having no useful skills and knowledge, or having the same skills and knowledge as you)?

Ultimately, the reason you decide to go on alone or take a co-pilot with you should be that it will give your business a better chance of success.

Should You Incorporate?

"Should I incorporate?" is a very common first question that entrepreneurs ask, whether they're working alone or in a team. But it's not the right first question. It can't be answered in a vacuum. And before you even ask the question, you need to know about the alternatives to incorporation.

What are your options?

When you ask whether or not you should incorporate, what you're really asking is "What form of business organization should I choose?" You have choices, and the choices available to you depend on whether your business will have only one owner, or two or more owners.

If you will be the only owner of the business, your choices are

>> To operate as a sole proprietor

>> To operate as a corporation that is owned by you

If two or more people will own the business, your choices are

>> To operate as a partnership

>> To operate as a corporation that is owned by you and your co-owner(s)

What's the difference?

The main distinction between a business that's incorporated and one that's not is that an incorporated business is a legal being separate from the owner of the business. So if you incorporate your business, your personal assets (property owned by you personally) and the assets of the corporation (property owned by the business) are separate. Your personal debts (money owed by you personally) and the debts of the corporation (money owed by the business) are also separate. In theory, then, your personal assets can't be seized to pay the debts of the business.

What many people don't realize is that, in practice, keeping the business debts of your corporation away from your personal assets is not always possible. (We tell you more about this under the section "The Corporation — A Form of Business with a Life All Its Own") Many people are also unaware that you can protect your personal assets without incorporating your business. (For more about this, see the section "Protecting Your Assets without Incorporating.")

Here are two other main differences between an incorporated and an unincorporated business:

>> The profits of a corporation are taxed differently by the Canada Revenue Agency (CRA) than the profits of a business operated as a sole proprietorship or partnership.

>> The amount of paperwork increases greatly when you're setting up and running a corporation.

We talk about all these distinctions in more detail later in this chapter. Incorporation should not be an automatic step, because it may or may not make sense for you and your business.

The Corporation — A Form of Business with a Life All Its Own

A corporation is probably as close as most people will get to an alien life form, barring abduction by extraterrestrial beings for bizarre medical experiments. And we're not kidding when we call a corporation a "life form."

Understanding corporations

A *corporation* is a legal being that is created by the process of incorporation, and that has a separate legal identity from that of the individuals who create it and own it as shareholders.

Even though a corporation is not human, it has many of the legal powers, rights, and duties of a Canadian resident. But because it is not human, it must act through its human directors and officers.

Corporations can be public or private. A public corporation, or offering corporation, can sell its shares to the public. A private, or non-offering, corporation is very limited in its rights to sell its shares. Whether you know it or not, if you're thinking about incorporating a new business, you're thinking about a private corporation. When we talk about corporations in this chapter, we're talking about private corporations. In Chapter 18, we talk about the process, if you're curious, of taking a corporation public. Very few private corporations ever become public.

Who owns a corporation?

The shareholders of a corporation own the corporation through their ownership of shares in the corporation. The shareholders acquire their shares for a set price and they pay for them by giving money, goods, or services to the corporation. (The money and goods become the property of the corporation. Shareholders are not the legal owners of the corporation's property.) If the corporation is a failure, the shares will go down in value — maybe even down to zero — and the shareholders' investment will diminish and disappear. But the shareholders will not usually lose more than what they already gave in exchange for the shares, because they are not ordinarily responsible for paying any debts the corporation has.

A corporation can have several classes of shares, each of which has different rights. Common shares usually give a shareholder the right to elect directors, receive a portion of the corporation's profits in the form of dividends, and receive a share of the corporation's property if the corporation closes down. Preferred shares (also called preference or special shares) always have the right to receive dividends before the common shares do, and can have other special privileges attached to them.

Who runs a corporation?

Every private corporation must have at least one director, whose role it is to manage the corporation's affairs. No upper limit exists on the number of directors a corporation can have, but even big public corporations don't usually have more than 10 or 20. A director has a duty to be reasonably careful in running the corporation's affairs, to act in the corporation's best interests, and to carry out his or her duties honestly and in good faith. If a director doesn't fulfill these duties, the shareholders can take the director to court.

A director must be at least 18 years old, of sound mind, and not bankrupt. In federal corporations and in most provincial corporations, a majority of the directors must be Canadian citizens who reside in Canada; and in some provinces, at least one director must also be a resident of the province.

In many corporations, the director(s) and shareholder(s) will be the same people, so the people who own the corporation also run the corporation.

Setting up a corporation

You incorporate a business by filling out and filing incorporating documents with the government and paying government fees. You can incorporate your business as a federal corporation (in which case you file with the federal government) or as a provincial corporation (in which case you file with your provincial government). Incorporating documents vary a little, but they usually include the following:

- » **The name of the corporation:** For more about naming a corporation, have a look at Chapter 3.

- » **The address of the corporation:** Although the business does not actually have to be carried on at the registered address, a federally incorporated business must have a registered office somewhere in Canada, and a provincially incorporated business must have a registered office somewhere within that province.

- » **The number of shares the corporation can create:** (The maximum number of shares can be limited or unlimited.) Also, the rights and conditions different classes of shares will have, and any restrictions on the shareholders' rights to sell or give away their shares.

>> **The director(s) of the corporation:** A corporation must have at least one director.

>> **The type of business the corporation may carry on:** Federal and most provincial corporations can carry on any kind of business unless the incorporating document sets limits.

>> **The powers of the corporation:** Federal and most provincial corporations have the same legal powers as a human being, but limiting their powers is possible — for example, their power to borrow money.

TIP

In most provinces the incorporation forms are available on the government website, and the forms themselves look relatively simple to fill out. You don't legally need a lawyer to incorporate your business, but if you do it yourself you may make mistakes that will be difficult to correct later. We strongly suggest that you use a lawyer or at the very least a qualified paralegal.

After the documents are filed and the fees paid, the government will issue a certificate of incorporation or, in Prince Edward Island and Quebec, a charter by letters patent. This is the moment when your corporation is "born." Before it can actually start to carry on business, though, it has to have a first directors' meeting. At this meeting, the first directors pass the corporation's by-laws — the rules about how the corporation will be run — and make resolutions appointing officers of the corporation (such as the president, treasurer, and secretary, who will run the corporation day-to-day according to the directors' orders), among other things. You can buy standard printed by-laws and standard forms for the first directors' resolutions if you don't have a lawyer help you with the incorporation and this initial organization.

Running a corporation

You can't be spontaneous and freewheeling when you're running a corporation. You need to follow certain procedures and protocols for making decisions and keeping records and telling the government what you've been up to. For example, you must

>> Hold directors' meetings as necessary to make decisions, in the form of resolutions passed by a simple majority of the directors, about the affairs of the corporation — although meetings can be bypassed if all the directors agree in writing to a resolution. (A "simple majority" means 51 percent.)

>> Hold annual shareholders' meetings to elect directors, appoint (or dispense with) an auditor to examine the corporation's finances, and review the corporation's financial statements. Most shareholders' decisions are made by a simple majority vote. (Again, meetings can be bypassed if all the shareholders agree in writing to resolutions making the decisions.)

>> Keep complete corporate records, including the incorporating documents, corporate by-laws, minutes of (a written report about what happened at) directors' and shareholders' meetings, and resolutions in writing.

>> File required documents with the government, such as notices about changes that have occurred in the corporation. And if you don't file as required, the government can dissolve the corporation. (Watch in horror as your corporation disappears before your eyes and screams, "I'm melting, I'm melting!")

Reviewing the advantages of incorporation

Incorporation has a number of benefits. Some are undeniable, and others are a bit more theoretical. Here's the undeniable upside:

>> Your potential customers or clients may be more impressed by an incorporated business.

>> The shareholders of a corporation are not responsible for each other's acts in the course of business, so avoiding being held financially responsible for the acts of your business associates is a bit easier.

The two main — theoretical — advantages of incorporating a business are

>> Limited liability

>> Tax advantages

Limited liability

The main reason most people incorporate is to limit their personal liability to pay debts of the business, in case the business fails.

Here's how limited liability works in theory: The corporation is a separate legal being. If it borrows money and can't pay it back, the lender can sue only the corporation, not its directors and/or shareholders, and can collect on its debt by taking only the assets of the corporation, not the assets of its shareholders.

Similarly, if the corporation injures someone in carrying on its business, only the corporation can be sued.

Here's how limited liability works — or doesn't work — in real life: The corporation applies to a bank to borrow money. The bank realizes that the corporation doesn't have a lot of assets for the bank to take if the corporation doesn't pay back the loan. So the bank tells the corporation's directors that it won't lend money to the corporation unless the directors and/or shareholders give a personal guarantee to repay the loan if the corporation can't repay. If the corporation doesn't pay the loan, the bank can sue the directors and/or shareholders personally to recover the money it lent. Other businesses or suppliers, such as landlords, that enter into big contracts with the corporation may also require personal guarantees from the directors and/or shareholders.

REMEMBER

In other words, incorporating does not mean that you will escape personal liability for the debts of your business. You may not be liable as a shareholder, but you'll likely be liable as a guarantor.

Taxes

Corporations are taxed differently from human beings (who are known as "individuals" in tax jargon), and the taxes an incorporated business pays can be lower than those of an unincorporated business.

All taxpayers, whether individuals or corporations, pay both federal and provincial income taxes. Taxes are calculated as a percentage of income. Corporations are taxed on their profits at a flat rate — the percentage stays the same no matter how high the profits. The rate of tax an individual pays, however, goes up in steps as the person's taxable income goes up — the higher a person's income, the bigger the percentage paid in tax. The federal corporate and personal tax rates are the same throughout the country, but the provincial tax rates vary from province to province.

The highest flat rate for corporate taxes (provincial and federal combined) is between about 26.5 percent and 31 percent (depending on the province or territory). However, the federal Small Business Deduction for Canadian Controlled Private Corporations may reduce the tax rate to between about 11.5 percent and 16 percent on the first $450,000 to $600,000 of taxable income (known as *business limits* and depending on the province, with most provinces having a $500,000 limit).

The lowest personal tax rate (provincial and federal combined) is zero for a person whose taxable income is less than about $12,000. The highest combined personal tax rate is between about 43 percent and 54 percent on income over approximately $144,000 (depending on the province and the exact amount of income).

Check out the Government of Canada website (www.canada.ca/en/ services/taxes/income-tax) or the CRA website (www.canada.ca/en/revenue-agency) for exact and ever-changing corporate rates.

Let's put this all together: If you do not incorporate your business, all the profits of the business will be taxed in your hands personally, and the rate of tax will depend on your total taxable income, perhaps to as high as about 54 percent. On the other hand, if you do incorporate your business (assuming your business qualifies for the Small Business Deduction and has a taxable income of less than $450,000 to $600,000, depending on your province), the corporation will pay tax on its profits at between 11.5 percent and 16 percent. But that's not the whole picture! At this point, the money is sitting in the corporation's hands, not yours. When you take money out of the corporation, that money will be taxed in your hands.

If as an employee you are paid a salary by the corporation, the amount of the salary will be deducted from the corporation's taxable income (and the amount of taxes the corporation has to pay will be reduced), but the salary will be taxed in your hands at your personal rate. If as a shareholder you are paid a dividend from the profits of the corporation, the dividend is taxed in your hands at your personal tax rate. However, the dividend is taxed to a maximum of about 39 percent and often to a much lesser rate (again depending on your province, year, and tax bracket), because the profits were previously taxed in the hands of the corporation. Refer to the CRA website (www.canada.ca/en/revenue-agency) for the exact dividend tax rate maximums as well as the special "gross-up" rules that are beyond the scope of this book.

TIP

If your business makes only a small profit — which is what often happens in the first year or two of business — you may pay less tax if your business is not incorporated.

TIP

If your business loses money — which also often happens in the first year or two of business — you're almost certainly better off from a tax standpoint if your business is not incorporated, because you will be able to personally deduct the business's losses from any other income that you have. You don't get this deduction if your business is incorporated.

To decide whether incorporating your business offers you a tax advantage, you must compare the taxes you think you'd pay if your business were incorporated with the taxes you think you'd pay if your business were not incorporated. Tax planning for your business is extremely important and complex, and you should absolutely consult a Chartered Professional Accountant (CPA) and/or tax lawyer about whether it makes sense for you to incorporate.

Delving into the disadvantages of incorporation

As we discuss in the previous section, some of the "advantages" of incorporation can turn out to be disadvantages for your business. Incorporation also has its disadvantages:

>> Corporations are expensive to set up — the government fees alone are several hundred dollars, and if you use a lawyer you will have to pay his or her fees as well.

>> Corporations are expensive to run because of the requirements to maintain corporate records, hold meetings, and file documents with the government.

>> The residency requirements for directors can be a problem if a majority of the people who run the business are not Canadian, or if all the directors live outside the province.

Protecting Your Assets without Incorporating

Most people incorporate to protect their personal assets in case their business has debts that it can't pay — but that strategy doesn't always work. And incorporating may not be right for you in any event (see the previous section for more). But all is not lost, because you can protect your assets without incorporating.

The classic method for protecting personal assets from business debts is to put those assets in the name of a spouse or other family member who is not an owner of the business. That means

>> Legally registering the title to your home, cottage, or other real estate in the other person's name

>> Legally registering the ownership of your car, boat, or other vehicles in the other person's name

>> Changing your personal bank accounts or investment accounts so that they are in the other person's name only

TIP

For this method to work, you must change ownership *before* your business runs into trouble. If you wait until your business starts to encounter financial problems, transferring your property to another person is considered a form of fraud, and anyone trying to collect money from you is entitled to have the property transfer set aside.

WARNING

After you put property into someone else's name, the property belongs to that person. So this approach involves risk. If your marriage or relationship with your family member falls apart, your property may disappear with the relationship. You have to decide what you're more worried about financially — the failure of your business or the failure of your relationship.

You can also protect yourself from certain financial liabilities through business insurance. See Chapter 12 for more on that subject.

Your Choices If You're the Only Owner

In this section, we help you decide what form of business to choose if you're going it alone: sole proprietorship or solely owned corporation.

Sole proprietorship

If you decide to carry on business as a sole proprietor (your business is then called a sole proprietorship), no legal distinction between you and your business exists:

>> The property of the business belongs to you.

>> The debts and liabilities of the business belong to you — you can be forced to use your personal, non-business, assets to pay the debts of your business.

>> The profits of your business are personal income and are taxed at your personal tax rate, and many business losses can be deducted from your personal income.

Setting up a sole proprietorship

You don't have to do very much to set up a sole proprietorship. In fact, if you start doing business all by yourself right this very minute, without taking any further steps, you are a sole proprietor. Because it happens automatically, sole proprietorship is a very easy and inexpensive form of business to set up. You don't need the help of a lawyer. In most provinces you have to register your business name with the provincial government, but that's just about the only formal requirement you'll have. For more about business names, see Chapter 3.

Running a sole proprietorship

No formal requirements about how to run a sole proprietorship exist. You can make it up as you go along. However, your accountant will probably tell you to set up a separate business bank account and keep track of your business income and expenses separately from your personal income and expenses — even though there's legally no difference between your personal and business income and expenses. Separating the two will make it easier for you to prepare the statement of income and expenses that as a sole proprietor you have to file as part of your income tax return.

Reviewing the advantages and disadvantages of a sole proprietorship

The advantages of a sole proprietorship are

>> Simplicity of setting up and running the business.

>> Low cost of setting up and running the business.

>> A tax advantage if your business is losing money — you can deduct its losses from your other income.

>> A tax advantage if your business profits are low — the rate of tax you pay on your business income will also be low.

The disadvantages of a sole proprietorship are

>> The income of the business is taxable at personal rates, which go higher than corporate rates — if your business does really well, and your income is higher than $127,000, then the tax rate can be as high as 54 percent.

>> Your personal assets can be seized to pay the debts of your business, if the business can't pay them.

A solely owned corporation

If you decide to incorporate, you will be the only shareholder of the corporation and the only director. But a corporation with only one shareholder or director is still a corporation. You have to follow all the usual steps to incorporate, organize, and run your corporation.

Setting up a solely owned corporation

The incorporation process for a solely owned corporation is the same as for any corporation. You don't have to do anything extra, and you can't leave anything out, either.

Running a solely owned corporation

Even though your corporation is just you, you must still fulfill all the requirements for director's and shareholder's meetings and resolutions. You can either meet with yourself over drinks, or simply make all your director's and shareholder's resolutions in writing. Unless you're really conflicted, you shouldn't have any trouble getting unanimous approval for anything you propose.

Your Choices If the Business Has Multiple Owners

If you're going to be in business with an associate, your options, you may recall, lie between carrying on business as a partnership and as a multi-shareholder corporation.

Partnership

If you start to carry on business with another person and do not incorporate your business, you will automatically be partners under provincial law.

If your business is a partnership (just as with a sole proprietorship), no legal distinction exists between you and your business:

>> Your share of the partnership property belongs to you personally.

>> The debts and liabilities of the partnership belong to you personally — you can be forced to use your personal, non-business assets to pay the debts of the partnership.

>> Your share of the partnership profits is personal income and is taxed at your personal tax rate, and any losses of the partnership can be deducted from your other income.

You can let the relationship between you and your partners be defined by the statute law of your province, or you can define the relationship yourself in a partnership agreement. If you stick with provincial law, the following parameters apply in most provinces:

>> All partners have an equal say in management of the partnership business.

>> All partners are entitled to an equal share of partnership assets.

>> All partners share equally in the profits of the partnership.

>> All partners are equally responsible for the debts of the partnership.

>> If one partner dies, goes bankrupt, or withdraws from the partnership, the partnership is at an end, even if the partnership has more than two partners.

>> All existing partners must consent before a new partner can be admitted to the partnership.

You can and should enter into a partnership agreement with your partner(s) if you want to change any of these terms. You should know, however, that statute law sets two terms about partnership that you can't change through a partnership agreement — because they involve the responsibility of partners toward people and businesses outside the partnership:

>> All partners are themselves individually responsible for the wrongful acts (in the course of business) of the other partners. This is called *joint and several liability* for the partnership's obligations, where each individual partner may be held legally liable for the total amount of any partnership obligation or debt. If someone sues the partnership, he may go after one or all of the partners.

>> All partners are bound by contracts entered into by any partner in the ordinary course of business.

TIP

Most partnerships need a partnership agreement because the terms set by the provincial statutes usually do not reflect the way partners want their partnership to work. See the sidebar "You need a partnership agreement if . . ."

TIP

If you need a partnership agreement, you need a lawyer — in fact, you need more than one lawyer. Each partner should have his or her own lawyer to review the agreement. If you and your partners have agreed on a lawyer for the business, that lawyer can draft the agreement, but should direct each of you to other lawyers for independent legal advice.

WARNING

Don't try to draft a partnership agreement yourself. If you can't afford a lawyer, you'll most likely be safer living with the partnership terms set by your provincial statute. However, it's still best to find a lawyer or a very well-recommended and experienced paralegal if a lawyer is not an option.

YOU NEED A PARTNERSHIP AGREEMENT IF . . .

You need a partnership agreement if you want to

- Own the partnership property unequally.
- Define how the work will be divided among the partners.
- Define the partnership income.
- Divide the partnership profits unequally.
- Give yourself and your partner(s) the right to draw an advance (salary) against your share of the profits.
- Divide responsibility for partnership debts unequally among the partners.
- Have the partnership continue even if one partner leaves, goes bankrupt, or dies.
- Set up a method for buying back the partnership interest of a partner who leaves or dies.
- Give each partner the right to force the other partner(s) either to buy him or her out or sell their interests to him or her.
- Require life and/or disability insurance for the partners.

Setting up a partnership

In most provinces, you don't have to do much to set up a partnership. A partnership automatically exists under provincial law if you start to carry on business with someone else with a view to making a profit. You don't even have to prepare and sign a partnership agreement (although we strongly recommend that you do). About the only requirement is that you may have to register your partnership's business name with the provincial government, similar to a sole proprietorship.

Running a partnership

The partnership statute or your partnership agreement gives you some ideas about how to run your partnership — for example, either that every partner has an equal share in management — that's the statute — or that one partner will be the manager or that a sub-group of partners will form the management committee. Apart from the terms of the statute or agreement, make sure that you and your partner(s) have regular communication. Even with just two partners, schedule regular meetings to discuss the ongoing business of the partnership.

You must also keep track of the income and expenses of the partnership. At the end of each year, you (or the partnership's accountant) must prepare a partnership financial statement that sets out the income and expenses of the partnership and how the partnership's profit (or loss) for the year has been divided among the individual partners.

The partnership does not file a separate income tax return. Instead, you and your partners simply include your individual share of the partnership's profit or loss in your individual tax returns.

Looking at the advantages and disadvantages of a partnership

The advantages of a partnership are similar to those of a sole proprietorship. A partnership can be easy and inexpensive to set up (if you don't have a partnership agreement) and reasonably easy to run. Tax advantages may apply if your combined income from the partnership and other sources is low, or if the partnership loses money.

The disadvantages of a partnership are also similar to those of a sole proprietorship. If your combined income from the partnership and other sources is high, your tax rate may be high. At the other extreme, if your business goes down the tubes, you can be forced to use your personal assets to pay the partnership's debts. And you can be held personally financially responsible for the acts of the other partners performed in the course of partnership business (such as injuring a customer or entering into a contract that the partnership couldn't carry out).

Investigating limited liability partnership

In some provinces, members of a profession can set up their business in the form of a *limited liability partnership (LLP)*. Unlike a general partnership (which is the kind of partnership we discuss earlier in this chapter), in which the partners are liable for debts and liabilities arising from the acts of all partners, the partners in a limited liability partnership are not personally liable for the acts of another partner. However, assets belonging to the partnership can still be seized to pay debts.

A multi-shareholder corporation

If you and your co-owner(s) decide to incorporate your business, you will all be shareholders, and probably directors as well, of the corporation.

Setting up a multi-shareholder corporation

Earlier in this chapter, we tell you about the steps involved in setting up a corporation. In a multiple-shareholder corporation, you need to take another step in addition to the incorporation and initial organization of the corporation — the preparation of a shareholders' agreement. If you and your fellow shareholders are essentially partners, you should have an agreement that sets out your mutual rights and obligations. A shareholders' agreement can deal with matters similar to those in a partnership agreement (see the sidebar "You need a partnership agreement if . . .") as well as other matters, such as the right of a shareholder to be or to appoint a director and how to resolve voting deadlocks.

You need a lawyer to prepare a shareholders' agreement. This is not an area for do-it-yourselfers.

Shareholders' agreements are prepared separately from the incorporating documents and are not filed with the government.

Running a multi-shareholder corporation

The requirements for running a corporation include holding regular directors' meetings and annual shareholders' meetings.

If you have multiple directors, you will have to hold actual directors' meetings (which can include telephone or Skype meetings), unless you can get all the directors to agree to and sign written resolutions. The directors will have to meet as often as required to make decisions about the corporation's affairs. You need a quorum (a minimum number) of directors to hold a meeting. If your directors are all busy people, getting a quorum may be difficult at times.

If you have multiple shareholders, you'll have to hold actual shareholders' meetings to elect directors, to appoint or dispense with an auditor, and to review the corporation's financial statements — again, unless you can get all the shareholders to agree to and to sign the necessary resolutions. A quorum is required to hold a shareholders' meeting too (normally, the holders of a majority of the shares entitled to vote constitute a quorum), but a shareholder can be represented by a proxy, who doesn't have to be a shareholder himself or herself.

So How Do You Choose?

How do you choose between the three forms of business? Look at the advantages and disadvantages of each form of business organization, and think about how they relate to your particular business situation.

TIP

Get advice from a lawyer and an accountant (accredited CPA) to help you make an educated choice. After you choose, take the necessary steps to put your form of business into effect.

WARNING

Don't incorporate your business just because you think that's what everybody does. Don't let your business become a sole proprietorship or partnership simply by doing nothing. Choosing the wrong form of business can have a major financial impact.

Other Start-Up Issues

Other start-up concerns include interfering mothers-in-law, nosy neighbours, falling space debris, and rational and irrational fears of failure, disability, and dismemberment. However, we'll leave those to you to ponder alone. Instead, we talk about some incredibly boring topics like permits and licences, payroll taxes, getting a business number, and registering for GST/HST.

Investigating permits, licences, and other government requirements

The odds are very good that some regulatory scheme, either federal, provincial, or municipal (often more than one), applies to your type of business. If that's the case, you may have to get government permission in the form of a permit or licence to carry on your business. The process for getting that permission may be short and simple (and maybe even inexpensive), or it may be long and complicated (and very expensive). But if you need government permission and operate your business without it, you may face a fine or risk having your business shut down.

TIP

You can find out whether your business requires permission to operate by consulting a lawyer, a trade or industry association, or by contacting the different levels of government directly. You can start by using the permits and licences search feature on the Canada Business website (www.canadabusiness.ca).

Registering for payroll taxes and GST or HST

We tell you about taxes of all kinds in Chapter 16 (now isn't that something to look forward to!). But without going into all the gory details here, if your business will have employees, you will have to deduct and remit payroll taxes, and if your annual sales and revenues are more than $30,000, you will have to collect GST or HST from your customers and pay it to the government. In other words, for most small business owners, the requirement to charge/collect GST/HST doesn't apply until you've reached $30,000 in sales revenue.

Federal payroll taxes

Employers must withhold from their employees, and send to the federal government, a certain amount on account of the employees' income taxes as well as the employees' contributions for Canada Pension Plan and Employment Insurance. Employers must also make Canada Pension Plan and Employment Insurance contributions on behalf of their employees.

GST and HST

Briefly, the GST (Goods and Services Tax) is a tax charged by the federal government on almost all goods and services supplied in Canada. GST is charged to everyone along the production and sale chain from the supplier of the materials, through to the manufacturer, wholesaler, retailer, and consumer. (Credits and refunds are built into the system to make sure that the government keeps only the tax paid by the ultimate consumer.) Provinces that combine their provincial sales taxes with the GST charge a Harmonized Sales Tax (HST). Aside from Quebec, British Columbia, Manitoba, and Saskatchewan, all other provinces (except Alberta) levy the HST. The province of Alberta and the Northwest Territories, Nunavut, and the Yukon have no provincial sales tax so only GST is charged. The Government of Canada website (www.canadabusiness.ca) has links to the exact tax rates charged in each province.

Any business that provides GST-taxable goods or services and has annual sales and revenues of more than $30,000 must register for, collect, and send GST or HST to the federal government. If your business's annual sales and revenues are less than $30,000, you don't have to register and charge GST, but you may do so if you want. If you don't register, you can't claim a refund of any GST you pay. Even if you expect your sales to be less than $30,000 for the foreseeable future, you might want to register for the GST so that your customers don't know that your business income is so low.

Your business number

If your business will be collecting and remitting GST to the government and/or collecting and remitting federal payroll taxes, you must register the business with the CRA and get a business number. The CRA uses this number to keep track of you, and you'll put it on your invoices to show customers and clients that you are entitled to charge GST or HST (and aren't just pocketing the money).

Chapter **7**

Getting Your Gear Together

This chapter is essentially a list of the equipment you'll need for your business. If you love shopping, this is the chapter for you! If you hate shopping, this is also the chapter for you. For most businesses, equipment makes up most of the start-up costs, and we give you a good idea of how much it will cost to set up your business physically. Consider this more of a scouting expedition than a shopping one — you'll probably have to hold off on the actual purchases until after you get your financing in order (see Chapter 9).

Setting Up Your Business Office

You may start off running your business on a shoestring, but you probably can't continue to run it on a cast-off kitchen chair and your fingers. You're going to need something to sit on; some means of communicating with clients and suppliers; and some equipment to help you keep track of what's coming in and what's going out.

Choosing between functional and fancy

If you have a home office, you may never invite anyone there — you'll meet instead at clients' offices, suppliers' offices, or in restaurants, or in an office rented for the duration of a meeting. Then your office only has to be functional. Whatever you can live with is fine.

But if potential investors or clients or suppliers or business associates are going to see your office — whether it's a home office or an office in commercial space — you should consider your office an important part of your business image. Even if you can't afford to look Fortune 500, you still want to look respectable and clean and well-managed.

Keep in mind that if you look too down-market, clients will go to someone who looks more successful; and if you look too upscale, clients will fret that you're overcharging them and spending the money on luxuries for yourself.

Finding furniture

We'll leave it to you to decide on the quality of your office furniture. We'll also leave it to you to decide whether everyone in your office should have the same or similar furniture for a coordinated look. But whatever the quality or look, you'll need these basic items:

>> Desk and chair for working (They should not only be comfortable but also ergonomically correct, or you'll end up with injuries to your back or shoulders or arms or wrists — most businesses that supply office furniture can discuss ergonomics with you. Some desks also come with an electrical power mechanism to move a desk higher or lower to allow you to stand or sit.)

>> Table and chairs for spread-out work, group work, or meetings

>> Chairs and/or sofa for client entertaining; maybe a coffee table or end table as well

>> Lighting (Even if your office already has overhead lighting, you'll need "task lighting," like a desk lamp. If you try to work without proper lighting, you'll end up tired and cranky.)

>> Filing cabinets

>> Supply cupboard

>> Shelves or bookcases

>> Baskets or inboxes and outboxes to organize your paperwork

>> Wastebaskets and recycling boxes for non-confidential paper

TIP

If you're operating out of a very small space — say, the dining room or a bedroom of your home — you may not have room for even a few items of furniture. But help is at hand! You can get a hideaway office — a unit that folds up, when you're not using it, into something that looks like a cupboard. These units usually include a desk, storage space, and a desk extension so you've got room to work with or without a computer.

Many stores specialize in office furniture — they may provide mainly fancy furniture, or a range from functional to fancy. At some of these stores you can rent or lease furniture, as well as buy. Often these stores sell used and new furniture. Hunt for "office furniture and equipment" in your favourite search engine, or use the "Find a Business" feature on www.canada411.ca.

Large stores that sell business supplies in Canada (such as Staples) usually carry a certain amount of office furniture — often made of melamine or fibreboard, so it's more functional than fancy. Stores that sell furniture for homes may also sell furniture suitable for an office, such as desks and shelves; some large home furnishing stores such as IKEA sell home office furniture along with everything else.

Big stores such as Staples and IKEA publish catalogues and display their merchandise on their websites, so you don't have to trek to the store for a preliminary reconnaissance. However, you may find that the piece of furniture you're looking for isn't available on the showroom floor and has to be ordered.

TIP

You may be able to get office furniture at a low price or even for nothing from a business that is redecorating or closing down and wants to get rid of things. To find an opportunity like this, you usually have to keep tapped into your network of business acquaintances, although sometimes you'll come across an ad in the paper or on the Internet. You may also be able to find used and inexpensive office furniture through websites like Kijiji and Craigslist.

Finding furnishings

You may be spending a lot of time in your office, so make the place bearable. Paint it a colour that won't get on your nerves, and then add some touches that you find attractive, such as

» **Carpets, if they don't come with the territory:** If dreadful carpet comes with the territory, you can cover it (or some of it) with an area rug. If you have carpets, you'll also need chair mats to protect the carpets as chairs roll back and forth or get pushed in and out.

» **Pictures, posters, paintings, sculptures, or carvings:** You need something to look at other than the view from your window or the business documents strewn over your desk and floor. Posters are an inexpensive way of getting good art.

TIP

If you want real art but can't afford it, you may be able to borrow some. The Canada Council Art Bank, and some provincial and municipal and university art galleries, have corporate lending programs. (They've got art in storage and want to let it out for some fresh air.) In other words, you can rent a painting. Or you may be able to make a deal with a private art gallery or with an artist for the loan of a painting or sculpture, or several. If this fails, check out some Value Village or Salvation Army used item stores, which typically carry very decent and well-framed paintings and prints.

>> **Plants and flowers, real or artificial:** If you choose real plants, don't forget to water them; if you choose artificial plants because you have a black thumb or your office doesn't get much light, don't forget to dust them occasionally.

>> **An aquarium:** Fish are great if you'd like to see something alive in your office. But keep in mind that they're more work than plants.

>> **Newspapers and/or magazines:** Deciding on which ones to display can take a little thought. A daily newspaper is easy; so is a magazine or journal related to your business (you may be getting it anyway, so now you just put it out where anyone can read it). If you're setting out reading material mainly for clients or customers to look at while they're waiting for you, choose things your clients might like . . . within reason. Go middle of the road with things like news magazines (*Time, The Economist, Newsweek, Maclean's*) or business magazines.

Stocking survival equipment

After thinking about office furniture, you might as well go on concentrating on your physical comfort. Make provisions for the following items:

>> **Necessities of life:** These include microwave, fridge, water cooler, coffee-maker, kettle, teapot, toaster oven, plates and mugs or cups, cutlery, napkins. Even if you don't have a kitchen with a sink in your office (use the bathroom sink), you can fit small appliances into a corner of the office some-where . . . perhaps inside a cupboard.

REMEMBER

>> **Housekeeping supplies:** You don't want clients and customers to be disgusted by your dirty office, and even if you've made arrangements for cleaners to come regularly, they're not at your beck and call every time someone spills coffee or tramples cracker crumbs all over the floor. So keep on hand a vacuum (even a small one, like a Dustbuster or Dirt Devil Express); a mop or broom and dustpan; dishwashing liquid and a sponge or dishcloth; dishtowels; paper towels; and all-purpose cleaning fluid.

Getting low-tech hardware

You probably don't need much hardware, but you might want

>> **A sign or nameplate for your door:** Sign companies can provide all kinds of signage, from discreet brass nameplates to awnings to banners to illuminated signs to neon signs to billboards. If you're just looking for something very small and unambitious, you may be able to get it, or order it, from a hardware store.

>> **A postage meter:** This will come in handy if you expect to send a lot of mail.

>> **A fireproof safe:** They're inexpensive, and they're available at many hardware stores and at stores that specialize in business equipment (such as Staples). If you store valuable documents on your premises, you may find this a good investment.

Getting high-tech hardware

When your office is beautified, with a desk and chairs and pictures and plants and whatnot, you have to add the equipment that makes it useful.

A lot of sophisticated computer hardware is available that seems to be essential for an office. At least prices for these things have dropped considerably over the past decade, and many kinds of equipment have shrunk in size or combined with others so that they don't take up too much room.

If you're going to be on the road a lot, you may need two offices — a head office and a portable office. Some people find that they can get along pretty well with just the portable office, even when they're working in head office.

Head office

You can probably count on needing the following:

>> **A phone and phone line:** You can get phone service with a traditional telephone company such as Bell Canada. Alternately, if you have high-speed Internet service, you can sign up for VoIP (short for *Voice over Internet Protocol*) with a service provider such as Rogers or Vonage Canada.

Other VoIP services work through your computer, such as Skype (www.skype.com), which is owned by Microsoft. (Microsoft Teams will eventually replace Skype.) Skype and most other VoIP providers offer free computer-to-computer calling worldwide, and calls to regular telephones (landlines or mobiles), typically for a fee. For a list of VoIP providers, check out www.gonevoip.ca for a full directory.

If you're on the phone a lot, a hands-free headset is also a good idea.

>> **A fax machine or a fax program on your computer** (which saves money on paper and ink): You can have a separate fax line; or you can have automatic phone–fax switching (arranged through your telephone service provider with a special number and ring for the fax).

Don't use phone–fax switching that isn't automatic: It looks unprofessional.

>> **A combination copier/printer:** Single devices that photocopy, print, fax, and scan — also known as *all-in-one printers* — can be found at just about every major electronics and office supply retailer. They're available in wireless formats, and they generally use either laser printing technology or ink dispensing tanks. The cost of laser or ink cartridges can add up, so do the math carefully before buying. Also, check out providers of legitimate ink refill services to contain your printing costs. But if you want to be able to photocopy flat (books, magazines) or large items en masse, you may need a more expensive stand-alone photocopier, which can also be leased.

>> **A desktop personal computer (PC) or Apple (Mac) computer:** Whether you go with a PC or a Mac, get a big screen (at least a 17 to 19 inches) flat-screen monitor — it will be easier on your eyes. If your computer does not have a CD (and/or DVD) writer (known to computer geeks as a *CD burner*) for accessing software and backing up your data, don't worry. You can back up and edit your data on a USB flash drive or an external CD/DVD drive.

Better yet, you can back up your files in the cloud, which means that you can store and access your electronic data and programs over the Internet instead of your computer's hard drive or on a removable storage device. The cloud is really just the Internet.

You can also buy a docking station to connect with your laptop. A docking station allows you to connect your laptop to a separate monitor, and likewise lets you connect your mouse, keyboard, speakers, and even USB flash drives to your laptop but through one central location or conduit. A docking station essentially allows you to work as you would with a desktop, but with portability.

>> **A surge protector:** So your computer doesn't get fried in a power surge.

>> **A document shredder:** If you're throwing away documents that contain sensitive information (the kind of stuff you don't want scattered all over the street if a raccoon gets into your garbage . . . or scattered all over the newspaper if an investigative journalist gets into your garbage), you need to make it unreadable before you send it off. Burning papers in a wastebasket will probably cause a fire, and shredding paper by hand is inefficient and tiring (although it can be a satisfying alternative to grinding your teeth or pounding your fist on a desk). Opt for a cross-cut versus straight-cut shredder for a better shredding experience!

Portable office

With a portable office you can work from almost anywhere. The key to a portable office is wireless technology. With a wireless-enabled computer, you can get access to the Internet and pick up your email wherever a wireless network signal is available. You can purchase your own monthly wireless access to the Internet, or find a free Wi-Fi (short for wireless fidelity) hotspot. Personal hotspot technology (an Internet access option found in most cellular phone plans) will let you pick up email in places where no local network area (LAN) can be found. Even if no wireless network signal is available, you can use whatever Internet connection is available — cable, DSL, or dial-up — where you are staying.

For an up-to-date portable office you'll need

TIP

WARNING

>> **A laptop, notebook or netbook computer:** You can even use a laptop or notebook as your main computer at head office, and carry it around with you on your travels, though many people find the keyboard and mouse uncomfortable or the screen too small to use all the time. Laptops and notebooks can be heavy, so consider the weight before you buy one. Although *netbooks* (small computers designed primarily to access the Internet) are lighter, their screens, keyboards, and mouse pads are also smaller, and they usually lack the processing power to handle some applications.

Using a wireless mouse will help when you're on the road; if you want to travel really light, you can also connect your laptop to a wireless keyboard.

Keep in mind that a laptop is easy to steal, so be fanatical about backing up documents! And also keep in mind that someone who steals your computer will have access to your confidential information — so lock and protect your computer and files with passwords! A strong password is at least eight characters long and preferably includes special characters (not just letters and numbers). It should not be related to your birthday, your kids' names, or your anniversary. Also, don't use the same password for all your devices, and don't write down your passwords, if possible.

>> **A smartphone:** You can even use it as your only phone if you want to. Usually, you buy the smartphone itself from the service provider. Special discounts are available that make the phones relatively inexpensive, because the providers make their money on the service plan you buy.

If you get a smartphone, such as an iPhone or Android device, the phone will also serve as a personal digital assistant to keep track of

- Your schedule and your time — including alarm clock reminders
- Addresses and contact information
- To-do lists and memos
- Your email

Smartphones also let you connect to the Internet and feature applications ("apps") that can perform many specialized business functions, essentially turning the phone into a powerful and versatile mini-computer.

>> **GPS (Global Positioning System) device:** It could come in handy in case you get lost on a road trip and discover that you are no tracker, and can't figure out your location by looking at the stars or moss on the north side of trees. Many smartphones have a GPS function so this may not be a top priority unless you are located in or going to a more remote area with less robust cellular coverage.

Buying computer hardware

TIP

If your needs are more than very basic, consider consulting with a computer expert to find out what you require before you go on a buying spree. Although in some stores you may find very knowledgeable staff who will help you decide what's best and what's a good price, in other stores you may find staff who haven't even bothered to read what's written on the packages.

Nowadays you can find a computer store on every block, not to mention on the Internet. You probably want to buy at the best possible price, so shop around and compare prices on the same models and on similar models. You can start by checking the websites of some of the larger suppliers:

>> Apple (www.apple.com/ca)

>> Dell (www.dell.ca)

>> Staples (www.staples.ca)

>> Tiger Direct (www.tigerdirect.ca)

Don't try to scrimp on your computer purchase by buying low-end or second-hand or reconditioned equipment. A good recent-model computer is a good investment for your business that will make your business life easier.

Getting software and services

Your hardware won't work very well without some software and some services.

Software

Computers usually come loaded with basic software packages, but you may want to upgrade the standard package or buy additional software. Some software can actually almost replace employees or outside contract workers if you can't afford to hire help (such as a secretary or bookkeeper) yet. Here's some of the ordinary software you'll want (some of which we include online — turn to the Introduction for instructions on how to access this free material):

>> **Word processing:** The tools incorporated into the software can help you format business letters and print envelopes, among many other things. Most common is Microsoft Word.

>> **Desktop Publishing:** This software allows you to get a bit fancier than you can with word processing software in creating documents such as newsletters, brochures, business forms, letterhead, and business cards. Microsoft Publisher is an example.

>> **Spreadsheets:** These help you crunch numbers to your heart's content (Microsoft Excel, Google Sheets).

>> **An accounting package:** Check with your accountant (if you have one) before buying, to see which package he or she recommends. Most common are FreshBooks and QuickBooks.

>> **Security software:** To protect your computer system against viruses, spyware, spam, and hackers, such as Norton Internet Security, Avast, and AVG Internet Security.

>> **A customer relationship management (CRM) system:** To keep track of customer contacts and activity. ACT! is an example.

>> **Adobe:** You'll need Acrobat Reader to be able to read PDF files.

>> **Presentation software:** Microsoft PowerPoint is an example.

>> **Videoconferencing software:** Microsoft SharedView, for example, which allows you to set up a videoconference through your computer.

>> **Website software:** You can design and create your own website using software such as Visual Site Designer by CoffeeCup software and WebPlus by Serif. Also check out Shopify (www.shopify.ca), which helps you build online storefronts and is ideal for small businesses.

>> **WinZip:** To condense files so that you can store more in less space on your hard drive and to make emailing large files easier.

>> **Voice recognition software:** A little out of the ordinary, it will allow you to dictate to your computer instead of typing in text. However, it takes quite a while for the program to get used to your voice and to become accurate in taking down your remarks; and even then, the process is slower than typing if you can type at a reasonable speed. Check out Dragon Speech Recognition at www.nuance.com/dragon for an industry-leading solution.

Services

The kinds of services you'll need include the following:

TIP

» For your office phone:

- **Call forwarding or call answering:** You can arrange for call forwarding to your cellphone when you're out of the office; you can have call-answer service provided by your phone company. And call-waiting is also available, so you never miss a call.

  As a businessperson, use call-waiting very sparingly! No client likes to think he's less important than the totally unknown person who's beeping to get in.

  You may also wish to consider Caller ID, so you'll know who's calling (and then either pick up immediately or totally ignore the phone).

- **Special long-distance rate packages:** Or a toll-free phone number if you want customers to call from outside the local area or if you're going to make a lot of long-distance calls.

- **Interactive Voice Response (IVR) technology:** If you want your business to a have the telephone presence of a large (and some might say, irritating) organization, this may be for you. IVR technology is what is behind the automated telephone reception systems that route calls by having the caller press a number on a telephone keypad or, when coupled with speech recognition technology, by speaking simple answers in response to voice prompts. A number of companies provide this service off-site, so you don't have to purchase your own equipment and software. Check out Genesys (www.genesys.com) or Contact Automation (www.contactautomation.com), for example, or search for "interactive voice response" or "IVR" on the Internet.

» For your cellphone:

- **A voice plan:** You can get various voice plans from service providers — for a flat fee you can make calls for up to a specified number of minutes per month. Cellphone plans also usually include plain text message, picture, and video message options.

- **A data plan:** If you have a smartphone you can get various data plans that allow you to send and/or receive a certain volume of data each month for a flat fee. Cellular data is used for email, accessing web pages, streaming videos, downloading applications, and making software updates.

- **Special long-distance rate packages:** If you use your cellphone to make long-distance calls, see if your carrier has a deep long-distance package. All of Canada's large cellular networks provide reliable national coverage. Quality and pricing of the networks will be your key criteria.

» **For your computer(s):**

- **An Internet service provider (ISP) and connection:** In most parts of Canada you can get high-speed (or broadband) Internet access through your larger local and national providers such as Rogers, Telus, and Bell. In rural and remote areas that do not have access to wired broadband service, you can possibly get high-speed Internet via satellite through providers such as Telesat Canada (www.telesat.ca) or Galaxy Broadband Communications Inc. (www.galaxybroadband.ca). The website canadianisp.ca allows you to search for an ISP anywhere in Canada.

TIP

If you use your laptop, notebook, or netbook extensively, you should look into mobile Internet service as well.

- **Email:** You can use email to correspond with customers, suppliers, lenders, employees, and colleagues. You can enter into binding contracts via email — even contracts that are required by law to be in writing.

Unlike a phone call, email gives people a chance to look into a matter before answering you, and it provides a written record of what was said. You can also send email attachments such as word-processor and spreadsheet documents or image files.

Email can also be a very useful marketing tool for your business. We tell you more about that in Chapter 11.

TIP

Don't delete important email messages. Treat them like important letters. Print them and file them in hard copy, or else file them electronically.

To send and receive email you need an Internet email address. If you've already got Internet access, you probably also have one or more email addresses with your ISP, as part of your service. Also, a number of websites provide free email accounts, such as Microsoft Outlook (www.outlook.com) or Google's Gmail (www.gmail.com).

WARNING

Everyone knows these days which email addresses are free, and it looks kind of cheap and cheesy to be running a business on a free email address. Make the (not-so) big investment and get paid-for email; and better yet, get an email address that uses your own domain name (see "Domain name," later in this chapter, for more).

Unless you're using a web-based email address, you also need an email program to read, send, address, and file your emails. The most popular desktop email programs are Outlook, which is included for free as part of Microsoft Office, and Thunderbird, a free application from the makers (Mozilla) of the Firefox web browser. Email applications that reside on your laptop or desktop are considered to be more secure than those that reside

TIP

in the cloud like Gmail or Yahoo! Mail (http://mail.yahoo.com). That's because the cloud, which is essentially a network of remote servers hosted on the Internet to store, manage, and process data, is more visible and accessible to hackers than your personal computer or server.

As long as you have access to the Internet, you can read and send email from any computer. Just go to your ISP's website and you'll be put in touch with the email that's still on the server. With most ISPs, you have access to your email from anywhere in the world because your email sits on the ISP server until you download it to your computer.

- **Instant messaging:** Instant messaging (or IM) is an Internet service that allows you to create a private chat room and communicate in real time. It's like a telephone conversation except it's text-based instead of voice-based. IM is great for communicating confidentially with your colleagues and clients when you're in a boring meeting or a public place, or for communicating with your teenaged children. Seriously though, IM is becoming more popular in the business world, because it allows employees to have instant access to managers and co-workers in different offices without having to place phone calls.

  The most popular instant messaging applications are WhatsApp, Facebook Messenger, WeChat, Snapchat, and QQ Mobile. To learn more about them, just run these names through your favourite search engine.

- **Computer technical support:** You can get support through your software manufacturer (if you don't mind waiting on hold forever) or hardware manufacturer (if you don't mind returning the hardware for service). If you want in-home service, you may be able to arrange a service contract through the manufacturer or the retailer. Or if you live near a university or community college with a computer science department, enquire whether a student, or even a moonlighting technical employee, can be your tech support person.

- **Unified messaging:** You can get voice messages, faxes, and email all directed to a single point (a phone or computer).

- **A courier account:** Unless you have an account, the courier won't pick up from you. Set it up before you need it, or you'll find you don't have it exactly when you're desperate for it.

And while you're thinking about business service–providers, consider a cleaning service for your business if you're not going to do it yourself and it doesn't come with your leased premises. If you're going to generate a lot of garbage, also think about a private waste removal company.

EMAIL ETIQUETTE

When you're in business, your emails should be businesslike. We give you some pointers for using email for your business:

- **Clearly describe the subject matter of your email in the "subject" line.** People are inundated with email. A clear subject line helps the recipient distinguish your email from junk email and to relocate it quickly if it gets filed or stored.

- **Use salutations ("Dear Mr. Smith") and complimentary closings ("Yours sincerely") when you begin an email exchange.** Start off the email exchange with customers and clients with a certain amount of formality. Because an email exchange becomes more like a conversation than a letter as it goes on, these formalities become optional later on.

- **Organize your email.** Start with what you want the reader to know, and then give background information or an explanation if necessary. Use short, single-spaced paragraphs. Long paragraphs are hard to read on a computer screen.

- **Use proper spelling and grammar.** Also follow the standard rules of capitalization. Edit and proofread your email before you send it.

- **Use a businesslike and polite tone.** Don't be overly informal or familiar, sarcastic, or rude. Avoid capitalizing entire words because that's considered yelling in emailese. (An entire phrase, or worse an entire sentence, in capitals would come across as maniacal rage or a tantrum.) Follow this rule with email: Don't write anything in an email that you wouldn't want to read aloud in front of your mother . . . or a judge. If your mother is a judge, be doubly circumspect.

- **Use an electronic signature.** It sets out your name, your business's name, your position, telephone number, and fax number. You may also want to include your business mailing address.

- **Take care when using email for confidential correspondence.** Email can be misdirected and/or read by someone other than the intended recipient. Check your addresses once then twice before you hit the Send button, and be sure to include a confidentiality warning at the bottom of the email, like the one we offer in Chapter 12.

- **Don't be a spammer.** *Spam* is the term used to describe unsolicited mass emails, and they are a nuisance. If you send out mass emails, they are likely to be deleted without being read.

Establishing an online presence

Every small business is expected to have its own website. You don't have to do business through your website — but potential customers like to be able to look up information about you without having to call you during business hours. The first step is to get your own domain name, which is your Internet address.

Domain name

You can purchase a domain name through a web host company or Internet service provider that sells a monthly hosting package, or you can buy a name independently through an authorized domain name seller such as GoDaddy Canada (http://ca.godaddy.com). For more about choosing a domain name, go to Chapter 3 on using ideas in your business, and for more about purchasing a domain name, have a look at Chapter 11.

Website

After you have a domain name, you have to put some content at the web address. That's your website. The thought of creating your own website may be a little daunting, but getting help is easy. Earlier in this chapter, we mention that you can buy web site set-up packages that take you through the process step-by-step. Or you can use a business that will help you design and set up a website. For a basic website, expect to pay about $500. For recommendations, ask business acquaintances who did their websites.

TIP

As an alternative to doing it yourself or paying for professional assistance, you may be able to get a university computer science student, or a student from one of the many advertising and web design programs offered at community colleges to create a website for you. If you live near a university or community college with a computer science department, advertise for a student. Sometimes students are already running their own businesses as website designers. They'll be delighted to help you, they'll do good work (but ask to see some of their work before you hire them), and they won't charge much.

See Chapter 11 for a more complete discussion of websites.

Getting remote access to your data and colleagues

You can get access to your email almost wherever you are, but what if you have to get some information from your computer in your hometown and you're hundreds of kilometres away?

You can access your business computer from remote locations using a *virtual private network* (VPN) — a secure, encrypted connection over the Internet connecting a computer or network at one end with a personal computer at the other. You can purchase remote access software such as AnyDesk (www.anydesk.com), which costs about US$230 for a one-year licence. Subscribing to a VPN service provider such as AccessAnywhere will cost you about US$85 per month for six users (plus a one-time set-up fee).

You can also try "peer-to-peer" file sharing. With file sharing, the data isn't stored on a central server or website; instead it's placed in shared workspaces, copies of which exist on each of the computers. Whenever one user updates information in the shared workspace, the updates are copied to each of the other computers. A remote user can work off-line, but as soon as he or she logs onto the Internet, his or her updated files will be copied to all the other computers. This is the same type of software that your kids may use to share (hopefully not illegally) music over the Internet. Some examples of file-sharing software are Microsoft SharePoint (http://docs.microsoft.com/en-us/sharepoint), FileFlex (www.fileflex.com), and ShareDirect (https://web.laplink.com).

Specific Equipment for Your Business

Every business is individual and may need special equipment:

>> If you need to visit customers or make deliveries or transport supplies, you may need a car or van.

>> If you're a dentist, you'll need the chair and the drill and the instrument sterilizer and the X-ray machine and so on.

>> If you're a gardener, you'll need a lawn mower and a leaf-blower and a hedge-clipper.

>> If you're manufacturing something, you'll need a system for creating your product, and depending on what your business is, this could be anything from a set of chisels or a couple of sewing machines to a smelter or a laboratory.

>> If you're setting up a retail business, you'll probably need a cash register or other cash-tracking equipment, systems for accepting credit cards or debit cards, inventory-control systems to prevent shoplifting, and display stands, cases, and cupboards. You'll also need initial inventory (the stock you're going to sell).

We can't address all the possibilities for specific equipment here. Just don't forget to take your special equipment into account when you're making your shopping list for gear.

Buying Equipment versus Leasing Equipment

If you don't already have your business furniture, hardware, and other equipment lying about, you'll need to acquire it. You can usually acquire equipment in two ways (three if you include illegal activity) — buying and leasing. Each can have advantages and disadvantages.

TIP

Check with your professional accountant before you make a decision about buying versus leasing, because of possible tax implications for your business. The deductibility issues of purchases, lease payments, and loan payments are all different. We talk about taxes in Chapter 16.

Buying

You can make purchases in the following ways:

>> **Paying with your own cash:** Then you're the owner, no strings attached, as soon as you make the purchase.

>> **Paying with your own credit card:** Again, you're the owner, no strings attached, as soon as you make the purchase. (But remember you have to be able to pay off your credit card.)

WARNING

Interest rates for credit cards are much higher than interest rates if you borrow money from a bank. So if you need to borrow to buy equipment, borrowing from the credit card company isn't the best idea. The only advantage is that using a credit card is easier than filling out forms at a bank and waiting to be approved. If you think we've just insulted credit-card buyers by suggesting that they're irrational and addicted to instant gratification, you may be right. Credit-card buyers who are also masochistic can find additional abuse in Chapter 9.

>> **Paying with money borrowed from a bank or other outside lender:** If the purchase is for an expensive item (say, for several thousand dollars), the lender will want you to repay the loan according to a schedule and may also want you to give back a chattel mortgage as security for the loan. If you give a chattel mortgage, you're the owner of the item, but the lender has the right to seize it if you don't repay the loan on time.

>> **Paying with money borrowed from the seller (assuming the seller is willing to lend):** If you borrow from the seller, the seller will want to be repaid on a regular schedule and will also want security, just like an outside lender. (The seller will probably also want a down payment, so this isn't necessarily a

no-cash option.) The security will probably take the form of a conditional sales agreement. If you buy via a conditional sales agreement, you won't own the equipment until you make the final payment; until then the seller owns the equipment, and can seize it if you don't make your payments. However, it will be up to you to maintain and repair and insure the equipment from the time you get it.

Leasing

A *lease* allows you to commit less cash or equity to acquiring equipment.

If you lease, you become a *lessee*. The person or company that leases to you is called the *lessor*. The lessor owns the equipment throughout the term of the lease, and you make lease payments throughout the term of the lease.

Besides being required to insure the leased item, you may be required to enter into a separate maintenance contract, so you'll have to make regular payments for maintenance as well as for the equipment. But if you have problems with your leased equipment, you can't complain to the lessor. You have to complain to the manufacturer. And you have to make your lease payments whether the equipment works or not.

WARNING

If you don't make your lease payments, the lessor can usually take back (repossess) the item and then demand that you pay whatever balance is still owing under the lease to the end of the term, minus the amount that the lessor can get by selling the item or leasing it to someone else.

Two main types of lease are available:

» **Simple lease:** No down payment is required and the regularly scheduled, equal payments are usually calculated so that you've paid the full value of the item (plus interest) by the end of the lease. When the lease ends, the item has to be returned to the lessor. So you've paid for the item and the lessor gets it. But cheer up! In a simple lease the term usually lasts as long as the useful life of the item, and by the end of the lease the item has no value anymore. However, some leases make you guarantee that the item is worth a stated amount at the end of the term, and if the lessor sells it and gets less than the guaranteed amount, the difference comes out of your pocket.

» **Lease with an option to purchase:** A down payment may or may not be required, but regular equal payments are certainly required. (If you make a down payment, the regular payments will be lower.) When the lease ends you can return the item to the lessor, or you can choose to purchase it by paying an amount that's stated in the lease. If you decide to buy, the regular payments you've made plus the extra amount you've paid to buy are calculated to give the lessor the full value of the item (plus interest). So leasing and then purchasing is much the same thing as borrowing to purchase, at least in theory. That's because all leases have some small nuances you need to need to watch out for.

TIP

If you're thinking of taking a lease with an option to purchase, you should check to see if it would simply cost less just to borrow the money and buy the item. (But check with your accountant, too, to make sure you take into account the possible tax benefits of leasing.) However, periodic lease payments may be lower than each loan repayment, because leases often have longer terms than loans.

A lease with an option to purchase may make sense if you don't want to buy equipment because you expect that it will be obsolete in a short time. This is often the case with purchases of technology equipment. When the lease ends, instead of buying the equipment, you'll take out another lease on a new model of the equipment. But, as with some simple leases, you may be required to guarantee that the equipment has a stated value at the end of the term. If you don't buy and the lessor sells the equipment to someone else, you're required to pay the difference between the value you've guaranteed and the price the lessor actually gets. (But if the lessor gets more than you've guaranteed, you don't get a refund for taking such great care of the equipment.)

Looking for help?

On the Government of Canada site (under "Money and finances") you'll find a Vehicle Lease or Buy calculator (www.canada.ca/en/services/finance/tools). It can help you decide whether buying or leasing makes more financial sense. Equilease (www.equilease.com/lease-calculators) lets you do the same for equipment.

Getting Business Stationery and Printed Materials

REMEMBER

When you're not around to make a personal impression on potential customers, investors, suppliers, and media types, your materials are doing it for you. So you want to be sure that your materials are making the right impression. You might consider getting help from a graphic designer, who will help you create a logo and a look, and make sure that all your materials are consistent. Your printed materials include your

>> Letterhead

>> Envelopes

>> Business card

>> Brochure

>> Catalogue (if a brochure isn't enough)

>> Newsletter

>> Cover or presentation materials

>> Event or trade show signs and posters

>> Invoices, estimates, standard contracts, and purchase orders

What impression are you aiming for? No matter how conservative or how wacky your business's product or service, you want your business itself to project the image of being

>> Well-managed

>> Successful (or at least poised to be successful)

Well-managed

One way of creating an image of good management is to make sure that all your materials are consistent with each other. Brand consistency shows that someone's in charge, has a plan, and thinks through all the details.

Your materials should all send the same clear message about your business:

>> Your logo and slogan should give some idea about what your business does; they should be the same colour and style each time (although you can have versions of them, such as black on white, white on black, and colour on white).

>> Your stationery should all be the same colour and finish and quality of material; but the weight of the paper can differ between letterhead and business card.

>> Printing should all be in the same font (see "Letterhead" a bit later on).

Your materials include the following items, which should also be consistent with your printed materials:

>> Packaging materials, package labels

>> Business sign

>> Website and emails (Your website and emails will actually replace a lot of printed materials. Use the standard colours and logo of your business, and make sure your logo or business name appears on every page.)

>> Window displays and decoration of office or store

>> PowerPoint presentations, slides, and videos

>> Giveaways and specialty items, such as mugs, T-shirts or sweatshirts, baseball caps, pens

And don't forget these matters:

>> Letters should be in the same format whoever writes them, and should end with the same closing salutation.

>> Email signatures should be common on all communications (include the name of your business, slogan, "visit our website" and the website address, street address, phone number, and fax number).

>> The voice message on your phone should identify the business, sound professional (not too long or folksy), promise (truthfully) a quick return of the call, and not send callers into a voicemail jail of automated options. Change your message as needed, to give your clients useful information.

Successful

One way of looking successful is to have materials that are of good quality and are in good taste.

For paper, good quality is usually associated with a heavier weight, a raised finish on the paper, and a watermark. For a business card, you'll want paper of a heavier weight than for your letterhead and envelopes, but you can still have the same finish and colour.

Good taste in paper is associated with a conservative colour (white, ivory, cream, and pale grey are all pretty safe) and the absence of too much decoration. Yes, it's possible to get paper with rainbows or forest scenes printed on it . . . but don't. Most customers and investors will feel more comfortable if your paper is not exuberant.

Letterhead

All your business correspondence will be written on your letterhead. Look at other businesses' letterhead, and then experiment with your computer and printer to see what looks best, or hire a graphic designer for help.

Whether or not you come up with your own design, you may want to get your letterhead professionally printed, especially if you want to incorporate a logo your computer printer can't handle or you want to use colours other than black. Some printers offer graphic design services. If you have your letterhead professionally printed, make sure you get the template so that you can put it into your own computer. And don't order a huge amount of letterhead, because your business will probably undergo changes before you use it all up.

Your Page 1 letterhead should show two pieces of information:

» **Name of your business**

» **Contact information:** The street address, phone and fax numbers, email address, website address. Some people put all the information at the top, or all at the bottom. It can be split up between top and bottom, or it can even be put at the side.

Your Page 2 (and following) letterhead only needs to show the name of your business, and the name can be in a smaller font than on Page 1.

You should also have a fax form in the same style as your letterhead. Keep a template in your computer, and also keep some printed forms handy for scribbling quick fax messages.

The printing on your letterhead is also going to send a message about how successful you are or will be. A serif font looks more conservative than a sans serif font. (Sans serif fonts look more modern because they don't have extra little thingies — serifs — dangling from the letters.)

Your font should normally be 12 points, so that it can be read easily but doesn't shout at the reader.

Business card

Technically, you can print your own business cards with your computer and printer — but don't even think about it. The paper is of a light weight, so it ends up looking cheap and it isn't especially durable; plus, the perforations on the edge where the cards are separated from the sheet are visible. And you have very limited choices about the design of the card.

Your business card should be professionally printed on heavy paper, the same colour and finish as your letterhead. The ink on the card can be flat or it can be raised. The card should create a positive, interesting impression and should include

>> Your name and your business's name

>> Your logo and slogan, if any

>> Your contact information — street address, phone and fax numbers, cell-phone number, email address, and website address

Don't clutter up your business card with extra information. Its design rather than extra information should be what creates the good impression. You have a lot of freedom to design your own business card — although there are standard formats, you can ask your printer to do almost anything. Collect business cards and think about what design and format create the strongest (good) impression before you start working on your own. Your printer will also have a catalogue with lots of examples of cards that you can imitate or modify.

TIP

You can also have printing or a design on the back of your business card. If you decide to do that, be careful not to overwhelm the front of your card, or cancel out its impression.

TIP

Printing and graphic services can be quite expensive, so shop around. Some companies do offer lower-cost services. Search the Internet for "printing" or "graphic design" or "logos," because you may find it cheaper to use a service in a remote location. For example:

>> **GotLogos.com:** This company will design a logo for your business within four to five business days. The cost is US$25 for a format suitable for use on a website, and US$100 for a format that will allow you to print and use the logo on any media and at any size and resolution, such as letterhead, business cards, or signs.

>> **VistaPrint:** A high-volume printing company (www.vistaprint.ca) offers low-price printing and free graphic design services.

Putting It All Together

Take a look at Table 7-1 here (and reproduced online as Form 7-1 — turn back to the Introduction of this book for instructions on how to access the free online content). This table shows you how all the items we discuss in this chapter can be tallied up. Use it to calculate your costs as they occur and to keep a close eye on your spending. You'll use the total from this table in calculating your start-up expenses when you apply for a business loan (see Chapter 9).

TABLE 7-1

Start-Up Plan — Expenses for Equipment

List Individual Items (such as)	Cost of Individual Items
Furniture and furnishings	Total cost $
Desk	$
Chairs	$
Light fixtures, etc.	$
Computer hardware and software	**Total cost $**
	$
	$
Website design	**$**
Business stationery (graphic design, materials, and printing)	**$**
Special equipment for your business	**$**
Vehicles	$
Machinery	$
Cost of initial inventory (for a retail business)	**$**

Chapter **8**

Your Business Coordinates

I n the previous two chapters, we talk about choosing a form of business and deciding on the equipment you'll need to run the business. The next step is finding a location for your business. You need to know the cost of your location to determine the financing you'll need for your business, and you may have to hold off on your final decision until you see how much financing you can get (see Chapter 9).

When choosing your business premises, aim to spend as little as possible while making sure that your place of business satisfies the needs of your newly launched enterprise.

Working from Home

There's no doubt about it — working from home is the cheapest way to go. With computers, high-quality multifunction printers, email, fax, and voice mail, a home-based business doesn't have to look like an amateur operation. And the Internet allows even the smallest company to have worldwide exposure. You can project a big business image even if your head office is the kitchen table.

In addition to cost, working from home has other advantages, too:

TIP

>> You'll be able to claim an income tax deduction for a portion of the expenses of running your home, even though you would have to pay these expenses anyway (see the sidebar entitled "The home business deduction" for more details).

>> You won't have the cost, irritation, and wasted time involved in commuting to and from work.

>> You'll have more flexibility to deal with your children, aging parents, or pets.

Working from home does have some disadvantages as well, though:

>> You may have little, if any, room for expansion as your business grows.

>> You may find it hard to accommodate employees.

>> You may find that you need facilities and services that you can't have at home.

>> You may feel isolated from business associates.

>> You may find yourself not isolated enough from family and friends!

But you can overcome most of these disadvantages (see the section "Tips for working at home successfully"), and so our advice to you is to operate your business from home if at all possible, at least in the beginning.

Should you have a home-based business?

It may or may not be wise, or even possible, for you to run your business from home, depending on

>> The amount of space your business will need

>> The type of business you will be running

>> The legal restrictions you may face

>> The insurance you may need and your ability to get it

>> The demands of your family

>> The nature of your personality

Space considerations

In Chapter 7, we show you how to make a list of the equipment your business will need. How much space will the necessary equipment take up? Will you be able to fit your business into your home and still have a home to live in? If not, are you willing to let your business take over your home so that you're actually living in your office? If you need more space than you actually have to run your business, a home operation may not be possible for you.

Do you need to hire employees to help you run your business? If so, do your municipality's bylaws permit you to do so? And do you have enough room for employees and their equipment — not only enough to satisfy you, but enough to satisfy any provincial occupational health and safety requirements? Even if you go around with a measuring tape and determine that you physically have room for everyone, how will you feel about sharing your home with your employees?

THE HOME BUSINESS DEDUCTION

If you run your business out of your home, you will be allowed an income tax deduction for the business use of your home. For example, you will be able to deduct a business use percentage (based on how much of your home your business occupies) of the following home-related expenses:

- The interest portion of your mortgage payments (if you own your home) or your monthly rent (if you rent your home)
- Property taxes (if you own your home)
- Utilities — heat, water, and electricity
- Repairs and maintenance
- Home insurance

To calculate your deduction, start by adding up all these expenses. Then calculate what percentage of your home you use for your business by dividing either the number of rooms used by and dedicated to your business by the total number of rooms in your home, or better yet the number of square feet occupied by your business by the total number of square feet in your home. The latter yields a more precise calculation. Multiply the resulting percentage by your expenses. You will be allowed to deduct that amount of your home expenses as a business expense. As long as your calculation is performed on a reasonable basis, the CRA should leave you alone.

The nature of your business

Does the type of business you will be operating lend itself to a home-based location? The answer is probably no if

>> Your business requires a lot of heavy equipment, because your home probably lacks the necessary infrastructure, such as reinforced floors, special ventilation or electrical capacity, to run the equipment.

>> Your business is dangerous in any way, for example, if it produces toxic fumes or waste, or uses dangerous substances or equipment.

>> Your business relies on a walk-in trade — because let's face it, you're not going to have high-volume pedestrian traffic on a residential street or down the corridor of your apartment building.

>> Your business involves frequent meetings on the premises with clients who expect you to have professional office space. On the other hand, working out of your home is quite feasible if your business field is so informal that a home office meets your clients' expectations. A home office is also fine if your clients don't come to you at all — you call on them.

Legal restrictions

TIP

Before you decide to set up shop in your home, make sure that no legal reasons will make operating your business from home difficult or impossible:

>> If you live in rented premises, check to see whether your lease prohibits you from carrying on a business in your home.

>> If you live in a condominium, find out whether the condominium bylaws forbid home-based businesses.

>> Even if you own your own home, municipal bylaws may limit your ability to work from home. Investigate whether your municipality prohibits some or all kinds of business operations in your area; or prohibits employees; or requires a permit before you can run a business from your home.

Many landlords, condominiums, and municipalities turn a blind eye to in-home businesses unless someone complains. Maybe you can't imagine that anyone would complain, but your neighbours will get testy if your business brings extra traffic to the area, or creates noise or smells.

Insurance considerations

Don't assume that your home insurance policy will automatically cover your home business. You will almost certainly need to make changes to your insurance coverage and limits to adequately protect your business, so be sure to contact your insurance company or agent. You may even have to switch insurance companies, because some companies won't provide home insurance if a business is carried on in the home.

You may invalidate your home insurance policy if you don't advise your insurance company about your home-based business.

See Chapter 12 for a more detailed look at insuring your business.

Family considerations

Your family and friends may think that because you're working from home, you're not really working at all:

>> Your children may barge into your office at will, whether or not you're on the phone or meeting with clients. Or perhaps they'll be capable of understanding that you aren't to be interrupted while dealing with others, but won't allow you to complete so much as a thought if you appear to be alone.

>> Your spouse may believe that you can now deal with every home repair, school meeting, or children's medical appointment. Your siblings may believe that you can manage any crisis involving your aging parents. Your pets may believe that you're ready and willing to provide treats and entertainment all day long. After all, because you're at home, you must have lots of free time — in fact, you're probably looking for things to do so you won't be bored.

>> Your friends and relations and neighbours may think you're now available for babysitting, dog-sitting, and other neighbourly chores, or are free to chat on the phone at any time of the day.

Do you have the moral fibre to set boundaries? Will you be able to tell your family, friends, and neighbours — firmly — that your work is important and that you are not available to them during your working hours? (Unless it's an emergency. Or unless it's not an emergency but it's really important. Or unless it's not an emergency and it's not that important, but it's something that you'd like to hear about. Or that they'd really like to tell you about. Do you see what a slippery slope this can be?) They're more likely to go along with you if you don't work 24 hours a day.

If boundary-setting doesn't work too well and family, pets, and friends bother you no matter what you say to them (and how loudly you say it), do you have the discipline not to be distracted by the interruptions?

Personality considerations

Perhaps you don't need outside interruptions, because you can interrupt yourself without any help from others. Of course, a person with a tremendous talent for being distracted can be thrown off task even when working in a stern and quiet office with a boss hovering over you like a drone, but your home has so many more fun things to distract you — the television, the refrigerator, even cleaning the bathrooms if you're trying to avoid a particularly unpleasant piece of work. Getting on task and staying there takes discipline.

Or perhaps you are the opposite personality type. Getting down to work is not your problem, getting away from work is. You would stay at your desk 24 hours a day, 7 days a week, 365 days a year if you could. When you work in an office with other people, sooner or later they'll make you go home . . . if only to take a shower and change your clothes. When you're already home, no one will throw you out, so you must be able to limit your work hours on your own.

Even if you have the discipline to work by yourself without working yourself to death, think about how you will like working without having any colleagues around. Will you feel isolated? Are you likely to stay in your pajamas all day and stop combing your hair until you look like a poster-child for clinical depression? You'll have to make sure that you get out regularly and maintain contact with the outside world (see the "Tips for working at home successfully" section for some helpful hints). Still, you have to be able to stand a certain amount of solitude to work at home.

Tips for working at home successfully

Here are ten tips for working at home successfully.

Keep your business separate from your family

TIP

Have a space in your home that is dedicated to your business, whether it's the basement, the attic, a spare bedroom, or a corner of your dining room. Use it only for working. That way your family will know (and so will you) that when you're in your workspace you're no longer "home," you're at work.

If your workspace has a door, keep it closed when you're at work.

If your kids aren't old enough to be left alone, or disciplined enough to leave you alone, think about hiring a babysitter, at least part-time. Use that babysitter time to make your business phone calls.

Keep your business phone separate from your family phone

Unless you live alone, have a separate business telephone number if at all possible. That way your clients won't be plagued by busy signals while your spouse or children are chatting on the phone. And you won't have to worry about sullen teenagers rudely answering your business calls or taking messages that have about as much chance of reaching you as a message in a bottle tossed into the sea.

Get an answering machine, or better yet get the call-answer or voice mail service from the telephone company, to make sure that your clients can leave a message for you if you're not there. (Call-answer is better than an answering machine because it will also take messages if you are on another call. This is preferable to call-waiting, which is very annoying to the client whose call is interrupted.) Make sure that the outgoing message your clients will hear is professional in tone and updated daily. And be certain to pick up and return your messages promptly.

If you send or receive a lot of faxes, or are on the Internet constantly and don't have high-speed Internet service, consider getting at least one additional line, so that your clients can always get through to you on the phone. Call-answer is useful, but if you're in your office, clients will prefer to reach you in person.

Run your business like a business

Just because you're running your business from home doesn't mean it shouldn't be a professional operation:

>> Don't be lazy, cut corners, or take shortcuts. Make sure that you comply with all legal requirements for your business, that you have proper insurance and all the equipment you need.

>> Have appropriate stationery and business cards. Make sure that your business correspondence is neat, spelled properly, and grammatically correct.

>> Be organized. Keep track of your appointments and deadlines. Have a proper filing system so that you don't lose important documents.

>> Keep your work in the office and your food in your kitchen so that you don't have to worry about grease stains on your correspondence or coffee spills on your computer keyboard.

Have set work hours (even if they're odd hours)

One reason to work at home is so that you can be flexible in your work hours. But you should still have set hours. And if you're someone who tries to avoid working, setting fixed work hours will help you make sure that you actually do work. If you're a workaholic, setting fixed work hours will make sure that you don't work all the time.

Having regular business hours makes it easier for your clients to find you. If you must go out during your set hours, make sure that your answering machine or call-answer service is set to take messages, and that you check for and return your calls promptly when you get back.

To reinforce the sense that you are "at work," dress in your work clothes during your business day. And be sure to take normal breaks, including lunch.

Create a comfortable working environment

TIP

Don't run a sweatshop operation. Treat yourself as well as an employer would in creating your work environment. Get a comfortable chair. Make sure that you have a large enough work surface. If you use a computer, make sure that the keyboard is properly positioned so that you avoid wrist injuries, and that you have a computer monitor that is easy on your eyes. Make sure you have adequate lighting and proper ventilation. Have plants, put up pictures, and play pleasant music (unless, of course, you hate plants, pictures, and music).

Avoid social isolation

Take advantage of being at home to spend some time with your family during the working day. Make a point of going out for lunch with friends or colleagues or customers or clients at least once a week. Get out of the house for a bit every day, even if it's just for a walk.

TIP

A number of home business associations, many of them local, are out there. Join one, attend meetings, and take advantage of their information-sharing and networking opportunities.

Don't lose touch with your field

It's important to stay current in your field and to make and maintain professional connections. Join a trade association or professional organization. Also, consider joining a local business association or attending events sponsored by your local Chamber of Commerce or Board of Trade if you have one. Subscribe to at least one trade publication. Use the Internet to check in regularly on relevant websites. Stay current with developments in your field by attending trade shows, conventions, and conferences, and by taking professional development courses in your field.

Make use of outside business support services

TIP

Your business may need facilities and services that you can't have in your home, but that doesn't mean you can't have them at all. A wide variety of business support services are available, such as the following:

>> Printing and photocopying services

>> Couriers

>> Packing and shipping services

>> Research materials (at libraries or through the Internet)

>> "Corporate identity" services to answer your phone calls and give you a business mailing address on a major street while forwarding your mail to your actual location

>> Office centres that rent out office and/or meeting space on a part-time or occasional basis

>> Freelance help such as secretaries and bookkeepers who work from their own business premises

>> Virtual assistants who provide administrative, creative, and/or technical services on a contractual basis from their own business premises

Don't annoy your neighbours

Even if your municipality, landlord, or condominium corporation doesn't want you running a business out of your home, they're not likely to do anything about it unless someone complains. So don't give your neighbours any reason to complain. Don't make too much noise. Don't let litter escape from your premises. Don't stink up the neighbourhood. Make sure that your clients or customers don't arrive at your door at odd hours, or block your neighbours' driveways or park in their parking spots.

Know when it's time for your business to leave home

A home office is a great way to start your business. And depending on the nature of your business, it may grow in revenue without ever outgrowing the space you have in your home. But look for signs that it may be time for your business to leave home and get its own place.

Working from Real Business Premises

If you can't work from your home, you'll have to look for business premises elsewhere.

Premises available, apply within

Different types of premises are available, and the type you choose will primarily depend on the nature of your business and where your customers typically work and live:

>> **Retail:** If your business involves selling directly to the public, you need retail space. You can find retail space in a variety of locations, such as indoor shopping centres, outdoor strip malls, free-standing buildings, airports, train stations, hotel lobbies, office buildings, university campuses, and theatres. You may also be able to set up a retail operation in an industrial plaza (see the third point in this list).

>> **Office:** You can find office space in downtown or local office buildings, business parks, above stores on streets with retail character, or in suburban shopping malls.

>> **Industrial:** If your business involves manufacturing or large-scale distributing, you'll need industrial space for your manufacturing plant or warehouse facility. Industrial parks or plazas are zoned by municipalities to offer space designed for light manufacturing operations and for businesses that need showroom as well as manufacturing facilities.

Space-sharing arrangements

If you can't work from home, it doesn't mean that you have to rent and equip your own retail store, suite of offices, or industrial space. You have other options for premises that may be of modest size, and cheap to rent and equip, and that may be available on a short-term basis. One of these arrangements may be right for you:

>> If you need office space, you may be able to sublet a single office from another business, or rent an office in a business centre or executive suite — the landlord provides reception services and use of a boardroom and office equipment (as part of your monthly rent) and access to secretarial and other support services (usually for an additional fee).

>> If you need retail space, you may be able to operate from a booth or cart in a shopping mall or in a pedestrian area. If your goods are seasonal, this may allow you to operate on a seasonal basis. A booth is also a good way to test your product before investing in a traditional store.

>> If you need industrial space, you may be able to use a self-storage unit for your warehousing needs and maybe even for some light manufacturing or assembly of merchandise.

TIP

If you need space for your business, you should see if a business incubator is right for you. These mentoring facilities usually provide flexible rental space and flexible leases for start-up businesses accepted into their programs. See Chapter 2 for more information about business incubators and accelerators.

Form 8-1 is a checklist of questions (like the one we show here) to ask before entering into a space-sharing agreement. (Turn to the Introduction for instructions on how to access this book's free online content.)

POP-UP STORES

A *pop-up store* is exactly what it sounds like — a retail location that pops up out of nowhere. Pop-up stores are often used by retailers looking to extend their business lines and brands by introducing totally new or hybrid products or services and then battle-testing those new ideas and approaches at street level.

Pop-up retailers come in a variety of themes and sizes and can be found in the most unusual locations. These locations include traditional stores, as a store within a store, as a stand-alone kiosk, in a derelict and soon to be demolished building, or in a motorized vehicle. The pop-up industry today is valued at over $12 billion in sales in North America, so it's no small deal.

As a small business entrepreneur with perhaps a bit of a daring idea, you can take advantage of the more flexible lease agreements associated with these types of stores. This flexibility allows you to test your idea, and if it doesn't work out you can at least "fail fast" (which is less costly than suffering a slow business failure) and then learn from the experience. From there, you can either fine-tune your idea and move to a more permanent site, or abandon the enterprise altogether.

When you look for shared space, make sure that the premises meet the needs of your business. Find out the following information:

>> What the premises will cost up front — besides the first month's rent, will you have to pay last month's rent or a damage deposit?

>> What the premises will cost on an ongoing basis — will you be paying a flat monthly rental fee that includes all utilities and services, or will you pay extra charges for secretarial, reception, or cleaning services?

>> What access will you have to the space — will you be able to get into and out of your premises whenever you want to?

>> What limitations are placed on your use of the premises — will you be able to carry on all the necessary activities of your business?

>> What kind of security is available — will you be safe when you're on the premises and will your premises be safe against break-ins when you're not?

WARNING

After you finalize arrangements for the space, you will be entering into a contract. Make sure that the contract is in writing, that you understand it, and that it sets out all the terms that are important to you.

Renting Business Premises

Most small businesses that need permanent retail, office, or industrial space rent the space (rather than buy). You should consider a number of factors before you rent space.

Knowing what you're looking for

Before you start to look for rental premises, stop and think about your business needs:

>> What kind of space are you looking for — retail, office, or industrial?

>> What kind of image are you trying to project for your business — upscale, middle of the road, economy, grunge?

>> What location is most accessible to your potential clients or customers and employees?

>> What kind of parking do you need for yourself, your employees, and your clients or customers?

- » Is it best to locate near competing businesses or away from them?

- » How much space do you need now? How much are you likely to need in the future?

- » What kind of layout or floor plan do you need?

- » What are your electrical and plumbing requirements?

- » Will your suppliers need special access to make deliveries to you?

- » Are you willing to pay for improvements to the property you rent?

- » How long do you want to rent these premises for?

- » How much rent are you willing and able to pay?

Finding what you're looking for

TIP

To find commercial rental space, you can look at classified ads in the newspaper or on online classified websites such as Craigslist (www.craigslist.org) or Kijiji (www.kijiji.ca) under headings such as Commercial, Industrial Space, Office Space, or Stores for Rent. You can also search for those terms on the web, or you can drive around areas that seem suitable and look for For Rent signs. But your best bet is probably to use a real estate or leasing agent who specializes in industrial, commercial, and investment properties.

An agent will know what space is available and can save you time by weeding out properties that don't suit your needs or meet your budget, and by taking you to see only those properties that might be appropriate. If you find a property you're interested in, the agent can help you negotiate the deal.

Usually the real estate or leasing agent is paid a commission by the landlord if you enter into a lease. If the landlord's agent shows you a property, the agent is legally the landlord's agent, not yours. A landlord's agent still has a legal and ethical duty to answer your questions accurately and honestly, and can

- » Help you decide how much you can afford to spend

- » Help you screen and look at properties

- » Identify and estimate the costs involved in the transaction

- » Prepare offers or counter-offers on your instructions and present them to the landlord

However, a landlord's agent cannot

>> Recommend a price to you other than that set by the landlord

>> Negotiate on your behalf

>> Tell you the landlord's bottom-line price

>> Disclose any confidential information about the landlord

If you're working with the landlord's agent, you shouldn't tell him or her anything that you would not say directly to the landlord. If you'd rather work with an agent who represents only your interests, you can hire and pay for your own agent.

TIP

Look around before you choose your space, even if you think you know just the location you want or you've had your eye on some particular building for years. It may turn out that other premises actually suit your needs better or come at a better price.

Determining the cost of your space

The rent charged for business space varies widely based on the economy, the area of the country, the type of space, and the specific location, so looking around before choosing your space is important. A real estate or leasing agent can give you information about the costs of comparable space.

REMEMBER

If you're looking for office space, the cost will depend not only on the location of the building, but also on the "class" of the building. A new, tall, luxurious Class A skyscraper can cost quite a lot more than the perfectly respectable but older and smaller Class C building just across the street. Be sure to look at a range of buildings in several locations.

TIP

You may be able to find space in a building you're interested in at a lower rent than that offered by the landlord if you can find an existing tenant who wants to sublet the premises or assign the lease. You'll deal with the tenant rather than the landlord, and the tenant may have had a much better deal from the landlord than what the landlord would offer you as a new tenant.

If you're looking for retail space, the rent will vary by shopping area — so be sure to look at stores in a number of locations. You may be able to get the same type and volume of clientele in several different areas in town. When you find an area you like, be sure to compare the price of similar space in the same location.

Exploring commercial leases

REMEMBER

When you rent business space, you enter into a contractual relationship with the landlord called a commercial tenancy, and you'll sign a contract called a commercial lease. Commercial tenancies are very different from residential tenancies. Commercial tenants don't have the legal protection from their landlords that residential tenants have. In Chapter 20, we tell you about some of the trouble you can get into with your landlord (and what to do about it).

Finding the right premises

As you look at different premises, and before you start negotiating with a landlord, focus on the following matters:

>> **Size of the space:** What's the square footage of the space you're getting? This is important because the rent will probably be calculated by the square foot. Is all the space actually usable? Will you be able to rent additional space if your business expands?

>> **Cost of the space:** What is the basic or flat rent? In addition to basic rent, will you have to pay for anything else such as utilities, or a share of the landlord's taxes, or maintenance or operating costs? Make sure you know what the total cost is before you sign anything.

>> **Leasehold improvements:** What renovations or decorating are needed to get the premises into shape? Will the landlord pay anything for them, or will you have to pay for them yourself? Will the landlord require you to spend a minimum amount of money on renovations or decorating, even if you're happy with the space the way it is?

>> **Insurance coverage:** The landlord may have insurance coverage for some things and will certainly require you to provide coverage for other things. Sort out who's covering what, so that no insurance risk is missed . . . or covered twice at your expense.

>> **Term of the lease:** How long does the lease run? If the term is long, you could be in trouble if your business outgrows the premises and you want to move, or if the business fails and you don't need premises anywhere anymore. If the term is short, you may find yourself forced to move too soon from a location that has become key to your business's success. When the term ends, can the lease be renewed? If so, how will the new rent be determined?

>> **Your right to terminate the lease before the term is up:** If you have to or want to move before the lease ends, will you be able to get out of the lease, or will you be on the hook for the entire term of the lease? In most leases, it's the latter. Often the best you can do is get the right to assign (transfer) the lease to someone else or sublet the premises to someone else — but you'll almost certainly have to get the landlord's consent to do that.

>> **Date the premises will be available:** When do you want to be able to move in, and when does the landlord say the premises will be available? If they turn out not to be available on the date promised, what will the landlord do for you (offer temporary space elsewhere, offer a reduction in the first month's rent, agree to terminate the lease so you can find something else)?

>> **Use of the space:** Can the space be used for all the activities your business needs to carry out?

>> **Protection against competition:** If you're leasing retail premises, will the landlord agree to prevent other tenants from competing with you?

>> **Hours of business:** Will you be able to get access to the premises whenever you need to (and have heat or air-conditioning and electricity when you're there)? If it's retail space, will you be forced to be open during hours (such as the evening) or on days (such as Sunday and holidays) that you'd rather be closed?

>> **Facilities:** Does the building have elevators, and security, cleaning, and other services?

>> **Unforeseen problems with the premises:** What happens if the building suffers major damage or undergoes extensive repairs? Will you be expected to go on paying rent at the usual rate, or to stay open for business? Or will the landlord reduce your rent and/or let you close up shop either temporarily or permanently?

Form 8-2 is a checklist of the questions you need to have answered before you begin negotiating a lease. This book's Introduction provides instructions on how to access this material.

Negotiating a lease

When you've found premises that you'd like to take, you will negotiate the terms of the lease with the landlord by discussing some or all of the matters set out in the previous section. You may negotiate with the landlord directly or through a leasing agent, and you may negotiate with or without help from a lawyer. When you and the landlord reach an agreement in principle, you will be asked to sign one or more legal documents.

You may be given a standard form lease to sign right away, or the landlord may ask you to sign a written offer in which you agree to sign the landlord's standard form lease at a later time.

WARNING

Don't sign an offer agreeing to sign the landlord's standard form lease unless you have seen the lease itself and are in fact willing to sign it and be bound by its terms. Once you sign the offer, you're legally obligated to go through with signing the lease.

The landlord's standard form lease will be long, difficult to understand, and written to benefit the landlord. Most commercial landlords are not willing to make many, if any, changes to their standard form lease.

TIP

Because commercial leases are so long and complicated, you should have a lawyer look at the lease and explain it to you before you sign it. But don't spend a lot of money to have the lawyer try to negotiate changes for you, because the landlord is likely to tell you and your lawyer to "take it or leave it."

TIP

You should also go over the lease with your insurance agent or broker before you sign it so you're sure about the coverage you'll need and what it will cost.

The lease itself

Commercial leases fall into different categories based on how the rent is calculated. Here are common leases:

» **Gross lease:** Sets out a fixed amount of rent, and nothing is added to it.

» **Base year lease:** Sets out a fixed amount of rent for the first year of the lease. In the following year(s), in addition to the fixed rent the tenant also pays a share of any year-over-year increase in the landlord's operating costs.

» **Net lease:** Sets out a fixed amount of rent plus additional rent to cover the tenant's share of all the landlord's operating costs for the coming year (based on the landlord's estimate of what those expenses will be). At the end of the year the landlord gives the tenant a statement of the actual operating costs. If the additional rent payments did not cover the tenant's share of the actual costs, the tenant has to make up the difference.

Some retail leases may also include a requirement to pay the landlord a percentage of the business's sales or profits.

Commercial lease documents are l-o-n-g — they can be 50 pages or more. Most commercial leases deal with all the matters we list in "Finding the right premises" . . . only at considerably greater length and in language you won't understand, even if you could keep your eyes open long enough to read a page or two.

Buying Business Premises

Buying a home is a much bigger decision than renting an apartment, and likewise buying business premises is a much bigger decision than renting space.

REMEMBER

If you buy property you will have to come up with a down payment and then continue to make the mortgage payments and pay for property taxes, utilities, insurance, maintenance, and repairs. Most start-up businesses can't afford to buy their premises, especially in the context of today's high commercial, retail, and industrial real estate prices. Compare the cost of ownership with the cost of renting before you decide to buy business premises.

TIP

The choice between buying and renting has tax implications, so speak to a qualified and experienced accountant before you make up your mind.

Aside from cost, buying business premises isn't usually a good idea for a start-up business (unless buying is absolutely necessary for the type of business you'll be operating — for example, a bed-and-breakfast), because you have less flexibility to walk away if your business outgrows the premises . . . or fails.

If you're thinking about buying, you should look at business properties with the help of a real estate agent who specializes in industrial, commercial, or investment properties.

TIP

If you find something you want to buy, you will have to make an offer to purchase the property. You definitely should have a lawyer review any offer you make before you submit it to the seller, because if the seller accepts the offer, you will have a legally binding agreement and you'll have to go through with the purchase. You need a lawyer to act for you to complete the deal, anyway.

TIP

Tell your lawyer how you intend to use the property. The lawyer will make sure that the offer promises that the property is appropriately zoned to allow the use you have in mind, and then will check with the municipality to make sure that the zoning bylaws permit that use.

Chapter **9**

Figuring Out Finances

I f you're starting a business, you need money. Maybe just a little bit, and maybe you already have it; maybe a lot, and you have to scout around for more. In any case, you need to know exactly how much money to hunt for, where to hunt for it, what you're going to have to do to bag it, and what risks you may have to take.

Your Business Needs Capital

You'll have to spend money so your business can begin operating. These are *start-up expenses* or *capital expenses*. In previous chapters, we help you come up with a list of the things you need to do and items you need to acquire . . . and very few of them are free. For example, you'll need money to

» Acquire or protect the right to use an idea in your business (see Chapter 3).

» Identify the nature of your business — researching and developing your product, and doing market research (see Chapter 4). You'll also need money for your initial promotional activities (see Chapter 11).

» Set up your business as a legal entity (see Chapter 6):

  • And while we're hanging out at the lawyer's, you'll need money for any additional work your lawyer does for you, such as preparing standard documents for your business to use (see, for example, Chapters 13 and 14).

- Not to favour lawyers over accountants, you'll also need money for initial advice and assistance from a certified accountant about the form of your business you choose and how best to structure it to keep accounting difficulties and taxes to a minimum (see Chapters 16 and 17).

>> Buy equipment for your business (see Chapter 7).

>> Locate your business in its own premises (see Chapter 8).

>> Buy an existing business (see Chapter 5).

At the end of Chapter 7, we help you to create a table of your start-up expenses, which focuses on equipment.

Table 9-1 helps you to add up the cost of everything related to start-up. We also include this table online (as Form 9-1) for you to print out and fill in. (This book's Introduction has instructions on how to access this free online content.)

TABLE 9-1

Start-Up Expenses for a Custom-Built Business

Your Initial Capital (the money you already have for your business enterprise)	$
Fees for licensing a product to manufacture or use or sell, or patenting your own invention (Chapter 3)	$
Research and development of your product or service (Chapter 4)	$
Initial promotional activities (Chapter 11)	$
Legal and accounting fees for business set-up (Chapters 6, 16, and 17)	$
Purchase of equipment (the total figure you arrive at by filling out the table in Chapter 7)	$
Purchase price and legal fees if you intend to buy property for your business premises (Chapter 8)	$
Leasehold improvements and legal fees to review the lease, if you intend to rent business premises; or renovation costs if you set up a home office (Chapter 8)	$
Total New Capital (add up Initial Capital plus the costs you've listed)	$
Total Capital Required (subtract Initial Capital from Total New Capital): This amount is how much you need but don't have at the moment.	$

If you're buying a business instead of building your own, your table of start-up expenses will look like Table 9-2. (This table is online, too, as Form 9-2.)

TABLE 9-2   ## Start-Up Expenses If You Buy an Existing Business

Your Initial Capital (the money you already have to buy a business)	$
Purchase price of the business	$
Professional fees (lawyer, accountant, broker, valuator, and so on) associated with the purchase	$
Total New Capital (add up Initial Capital plus the price of the business plus professional fees)	$
Total Capital Required (subtract Initial Capital from Total New Capital) This amount is how much you need but don't have at the moment.	$

Forecasting How Much Your Business Will Need to Operate

After you figure out the capital requirements of your business, you're still not ready to carry on business . . . at least not for very long. You also have to work out how much money you'll need to run the business on a day-to-day basis (actually a month-to-month basis). These are called *operating expenses*. After your business is generating a steady income, your revenues will cover all or most of your operating expenses. But until then, you'll need to borrow money to pay for such things as

>> Salaries

>> Lease or mortgage payments

>> Utilities such as hydro, and water

>> Telephone, fax, and Internet fees

>> Insurance premiums

>> Property taxes, if you own your business premises rather than rent them

>> Ongoing professional fees (legal, accounting, advertising, publicity)

>> Cost of running any vehicles

Projecting your expenses and revenues

For some of your operating expenses, you'll be able to write down a fairly accurate estimate from a supplier (such as a landlord or accountant or insurance agent). For others (such as utilities, and maybe salaries) you'll just have to guess.

After estimating your expenses, you have to estimate how much revenue you'll bring in to cover your expenses. This step will give you a better grasp of how much money you really need to borrow for monthly operations.

Projecting your expenses is easier than projecting your revenues. But you can make a guess at your revenues by making some assumptions. The usual assumptions are

>> The number of customers or clients you'll get

>> The average amount of each sale or transaction

Multiply these two figures together to estimate sales. (Make a note to yourself about how you chose the figures you're using. You'll need to add that information as a footnote to your forecast of projected revenue and expenses.)

Preparing a forecast of revenue and expenses

The figures we discuss in the previous section get plugged into a forecast or projection of revenue and expenses. Take a look at Table 9-3, which is also online, as Form 9-3 (see the Introduction for guidance on accessing this book's online content).

TABLE 9-3

Forecast of Revenue and Expenses (for the first year of operation)

Revenue		
Sales or revenues	$	
Other	$	
Total revenue		$
Expenses		
Salary of owner	$	
Salary of employee(s)	$	
Lease payments	$	
Advertising	$	
Insurance	$	
Utilities	$	

Revenue		
Telephone, fax, and Internet	$	
Legal costs	$	
Accounting services	$	
Vehicle operation and maintenance	$	
Other	$	
Total Expenses		$
Net Profit or Loss (deduct Total Expenses from Total Revenue)		$

Filling out this table gives you a reasonable idea of what your operating expenses will be for your first year of business, and whether you can expect that, by the end of the year, your revenues will cover your expenses, or that you'll be in the hole (and how deep the hole is).

Projected cash flow

Knowing how much money you need to operate your business isn't enough — you also have to know when you need the money. Revenue and expenses rarely match each other exactly, so you can't necessarily expect to be able to pay your expenses out of the revenue you're making. Your revenue may come in a lump once a year or a few times a year, whereas your expenses are likely to be fairly steady on a month-by-month basis. By preparing a *cash flow statement* — a statement that shows the money going into and out of your business over time — you'll know when you may need bridge financing to keep the business afloat. This information is especially important during the first year or so of your business's existence, before revenue is steady or before you've been able to put aside some profits to operate the business between infusions of revenue.

Many of your expenses won't change from month to month (lease or mortgage payments, for example), and others may be predictable even though they change during the course of the year (a snow removal contract during the winter months, or salaries for extra staff during a busy season). But if you had trouble estimating your total annual revenue, you'll have even more trouble estimating how it will come in month by month. Give it a shot, though, taking into consideration that your monthly revenue will probably increase over the course of the first year as your business gets established. Your business may have seasonal highs and lows, too. An accountant, for example, can probably expect a high just after income tax returns are filed and the bills go out for tax preparation; a business that sells cards and gifts can probably expect highs just before Christmas, Valentine's Day, and Mother's Day.

In Table 9-4, we didn't have room for all 12 months plus an annual total, so we use some representative months. (Fill in all 12 months when you prepare your cash flow statement. On the version of this form online, which is Form 9-4, every month is present and accounted for.)

TABLE 9-4

Projected Cash Flow Statement

	Jan.	Feb.	...	Nov.	Dec.	Year
Revenue:						
Cash sales						
Receivables						
Total Revenue						
Expenses:						
Salaries						
Lease						
Advertising						
Insurance						
Utilities						
Telephone						
Professional						
Total Expenses						
Cash Flow:						

(Subtract monthly expenses from monthly revenue. If the result is a negative number, put brackets around the number.)

Cumulative Cash Flow						

(Move from left to right adding the previous month's cash flow to the following month. For January you will have the same number as for the January cash flow, but for February you will add the cash flow numbers for January and February together; for March you will add January, February, and March together; and so on. Again, put brackets around negative numbers.)

Filling out this table gives you some idea of how many months of the first year you'll need a loan to pay your operating expenses (from the Cash Flow line), and at what point your revenues will start reducing your need for a loan (from the Cumulative Cash Flow line).

Locating Sources of Financing for a Start-Up Operation

The previous sections help you to know, more or less, how much money you need to start up and run your business for the first year. So where are you going to find that money? Generations of businesspeople have wondered the same thing, so you can turn to a standard list of sources of money. The sources include

>> Personal assets

>> Money from family and friends

>> Borrowed money:

- Mortgage on home or vacation property

- Commercial loans (capital and operating)

- Micro-credit loans

>> Credit:

- Suppliers

- Customers

>> Sale of accounts receivable

>> Grants and loans from government

>> Investment from external sources:

- Angel investor

- Venture capital company

That's a respectable-looking list — somewhere among all these possibilities you should be able to find a buck or two.

TIP

The federal Innovation, Science, and Economic Development Canada website (www.ic.gc.ca) maintains a financing page that provides information on finding sources of funding and financial assistance. Click the Business Grants and Financing tab to learn about various financing options including government grants and loans.

Mix-and-match financing

Most businesses need a combination of financing. For example, besides using personal assets and funds from family and friends to get started:

>> To get equipment, a business might need

  - A capital loan

  - A conditional sales agreement

  - A lease

>> To get operating funds, a business might need

  - A line of credit

  - Payment in advance from customers and clients

  - Credit from suppliers

>> To make leasehold improvements, a business might need a capital loan

So you'll likely be dealing with several sources of financing. We recommend that you read all the following sections carefully.

Personal assets

Most entrepreneurs start off using at least some of their own money. Look around and see what money you have handy — or what property you could turn into cash — to finance your business start-up. Keep in mind that you still need money to live on while you're getting your business off the ground. You're not going to be a very effective CEO if you're starving or sleeping on the street.

Personal assets include

>> Money in bank accounts

>> Bonds

>> Stocks (But if they've increased in value since you acquired them, you'll have to declare a capital gain on your next income tax return and could end up taking a tax hit — see Chapter 16 for more about capital gains.)

>> RRSPs (But remember that you'll have to pay withholding taxes to the tax man and also add any amount you withdraw to your income for the year, which may attract more taxes.)

>> Personal property or real property (Property you can sell, such as vehicles, jewellery, collectibles, art, a vacation home . . . or even your real home. If property other than your real home — your principal residence — has increased in value since you acquired it, you'll have to declare a capital gain on your income tax return and may have to pay tax.)

Money from family and friends

Family and friends may be willing to lend money to you, or they may be willing to give it to you flat out. Think very carefully, however, before asking relatives and friends for money. If your business tanks and you can't repay them, they'll probably stop speaking to you. Then not only will you have no business, but no one to give you sympathy, either.

If you do go ahead, make a formal arrangement with the lenders, for two reasons — first, so that they can get something back if you're successful or if you go bust (a document will provide the evidence they need to make a claim against your business as a creditor); and second, so that they can't demand their money back just when you desperately need it. Awkward moments aside, if the money or property is a gift, the giver should sign a document stating that the money or property is a gift and is yours absolutely to do with what you like. If the money is a loan, you should have a contract (a promissory note) with the lender setting out

>> The amount of the loan

>> The rate of interest payable on the loan (if any)

>> The amount of each payment and the payment dates (a schedule of payments)

>> The nature of the security, if any, the lender wants for the loan (*Security* is something the lender can take in exchange if the loan isn't repaid. It could include a mortgage against your home, or the taking of shares in your corporation, or a guarantee from someone else associated with you or the business that he or she will repay the loan if you don't.)

Money borrowed from commercial lenders

Commercial lenders are banks, trust companies, credit unions, *caisses populaires*, finance companies, and insurance companies. They've got lots of money . . . if you can just get your hands on it.

Many commercial lenders can also help you get access to funds from the Business Development Bank of Canada (visit its website at www.bdc.ca for more information about its lending activities) and from the federal government's Canada Small Business Financing (CSBF) program (www.ic.gc.ca/eic/site/csbfp-pfpec.nsf/eng/Home). Most small businesses starting up or operating in Canada are eligible for CSBF loans, as long as their estimated annual gross revenues do not exceed $5 million during the fiscal year in which they apply for a loan. As for the Business Development Bank of Canada, it does market itself as "the only bank exclusively devoted to entrepreneurs." Hold the bank to it!

Credit cards

If you need to borrow from a bank, your first thought may be to use your credit cards. It's easy — no application forms to fill out, no waiting, no business plan to prepare, no intimidating interview with a bank manager. You may even have a high enough limit on your card(s) to get as much money as you need.

Absolutely don't use your credit cards! The interest rate on credit cards is astronomical compared to the interest rate you'll pay if you borrow in a more business-like fashion — probably at least double and maybe triple. We have better suggestions here.

Mortgage on your home or vacation property

If you own real property and it isn't already mortgaged to the hilt, you can borrow against that property by taking out a mortgage. If you're thinking of mortgaging property, consider these factors:

>> **What's the property worth?** Will mortgaging it get you as much money as you need? You probably won't be able to borrow its full unmortgaged value.

>> **Is the property already mortgaged?** If it is, you may not have enough equity (unmortgaged value) in the property to get as big a loan as you need.

>> **Do you need someone else's legal consent to mortgage the property?** You do if you have a co-owner. Even if you're the only owner, if you're married, in most provinces your spouse will have to give consent to the transaction before you'll get any money (sometimes even if it's not your family home that you're borrowing against).

>> **Can you afford to lose the property if your business fails?** If you default on your loan (don't pay it back on time), the lender has the right to take the property — and either keep it or sell it to cover your unpaid loan. Don't kid yourself for a second. Banks can be ruthless and will sell your property from under you in a second. (If it's sold, you'll get the excess over the outstanding amount of the loan plus legal fees.)

Business loans

If you're borrowing because you need money to purchase capital assets for your business, you'll apply for a *capital loan*. If you're borrowing because you need money to cover the ongoing costs of running your business, you'll apply for an *operating loan*. You can get either kind of loan from a commercial lender. But choose a branch that regularly handles small business clients, if you can find one — if the branch staff are only used to making deposits and withdrawals, they won't know what to do with you . . . and they might show you the door.

Banks, most credit unions, and many trust, loan, and insurance companies can make a loan under the Canada Small Business Financing (CSBF) program for capital expenses, including the purchase or improvement of real property, leasehold improvements, and the purchase or improvement of equipment. The federal government partially guarantees CSBF loans, so lenders are more willing to lend, and owners don't have to provide personal assets as security (see the section "Non-repayment of the loan," a bit later).

The chances are good that at some point you'll want a business loan, so we tell you about loans in detail.

PRINCIPAL AND INTEREST

The amount of money the lender gives is called the *principal* or *principal amount* of the loan. The amount the borrower pays for the use of the money is called *interest*. (You're not going to find an interest-free loan if you deal with anyone other than your mother.) Interest is calculated as a percentage of the principal. If you're charged *simple interest* on the loan, you pay interest only on the principal you've borrowed. So if you borrowed $100,000 at 10 percent, you'd owe $10,000 in interest per year.

But commercial lenders charge *compound interest* on a loan if the terms of repayment stretch past the time the interest is actually due. Compound interest is interest on the principal and on the interest owing. When you're charged compound interest, you end up with a higher interest rate (the *effective interest rate*) than the rate you're quoted (the *nominal interest rate*). And the more often the interest is *compounded* or *calculated*, the higher the real interest rate.

WARNING

Interest can be compounded on any basis the lender chooses — daily, weekly, monthly, semi-annually, or annually. If you borrowed $100,000 at 10 percent compounded monthly, your real interest rate would actually be 10.47 percent. And in commercial loans, unlike consumer loans, the lender doesn't have to tell the borrower the total amount of interest payable over the life of the loan (the cost of borrowing).

REPAYMENT OF THE LOAN

You'll likely take out either a *term loan* or a *line of credit*. Capital loans are usually term loans. Operating loans usually come in the form of a line of credit. If you have a term loan, the lender sets a schedule for regular repayment of principal and interest.

If you have a line of credit, also known as *overdraft protection*, the lender (which is normally your bank) tops up your business account if you don't have enough in the account to cover a cheque. Then when you make a deposit to your business account, the money is automatically applied to pay down the loan. You may also be required to make regular payments or make a deposit to the account within a fixed period of time to cover the overdraft.

A line of credit is usually a *demand loan*, which means that the lender can demand payment in full at any time, not just after you've missed a payment. However, if you make your payments on time, demand will not be made — unless you do something to lead the lender to believe that your business is in trouble. The lender also usually requires you to sign blank promissory notes, which it fills in as the line of credit goes up. The promissory note provides evidence of what you owe, and the lender can also sue you on the note if you don't pay the loan.

NON-REPAYMENT OF THE LOAN

Lenders don't take for granted that borrowers will pay up on schedule — or ever. They know they could sue the borrower for failing to pay, but they also know that suing someone is expensive and time-consuming, and even if they win the lawsuit, collecting the money is often difficult. So to make life easier for themselves, lenders usually require borrowers to give *security* or *collateral*. When a borrower gives security, he legally gives the lender the right to take specified property from the borrower if the borrower doesn't make his payments. The lender usually sells the property to pay off the loan. Typically, lenders take security on such property as

>> **Real estate:** Security will take the form of a *collateral mortgage* or *charge* or, in Quebec, a *hypothec*.

>> **Equipment and other non-land assets:** Security may take the form of a *chattel mortgage*, known in some provinces as a *specific security agreement*.

>> **Accounts receivable, also known as *book debts*, which is money that customers or clients owe the borrower:** Security can take the form of an *assignment of accounts receivable*, which gives the lender the right to collect debts owing to you if you default on your loan.

>> **Inventory:** The lender may be able to take security under *s. 427* of the federal *Bank Act* if you are borrowing from a chartered bank.

If you have a capital loan, the lender will probably want security over the capital property (real estate or equipment) you're buying. If you have a line of credit or overdraft protection, the lender may want security over your business's accounts receivable and inventory.

Other forms of security that a lender might ask for include

>> **A general security agreement:** This gives a lender security over almost all the borrower's existing and future assets (usually excluding real property, but including equipment, vehicles, machinery, inventory, and accounts receivable).

>> **A debenture:** This is much like a general security agreement, except that only a corporation can give a debenture as security for a loan, and a debenture usually includes real property as well as other assets.

>> **A pledge of shares (or of bonds or debentures) that are the personal property of the borrower or a guarantor:** For example, if the borrower is a corporation, the lender may want a pledge of shares of the corporation from the shareholders who have guaranteed the loan. Then, if the borrower does not repay the loan, the lender can take control of the corporation.

And lenders don't always stop at taking security. Sometimes they want (instead of or in addition to security) a *guarantee*. A guarantee is a promise by someone other than the borrower that if the borrower doesn't pay up, the *guarantor* (the person or business giving the guarantee) will repay the loan. For example, if the borrower is a corporation — especially a corporation that doesn't have much by way of assets — the lender might ask for a guarantee from the individuals associated with the corporation, such as the shareholders or the directors. A bank can also ask for security from the guarantor, such as a *collateral mortgage* on the guarantor's home.

If the borrower does not meet the lender's criteria to receive a loan, the lender may be willing to go ahead with the loan if someone who does meet the criteria agrees to co-sign the loan. Unlike a guarantor, a *co-signor* can be required to repay the loan even if the borrower is capable of repaying the loan himself.

Micro-credit funds

Micro-credit is a small loan (usually only a few thousand dollars), available to individuals with a low income, to help them start up a very small business. (They're often targeted toward young people, or women, or new immigrants, or people with disabilities; and/or they may be targeted toward a restricted geographical area.) Micro-credit can be used for capital investment or operating funds. Micro-credit may be made available by an independent operation, as part of an integrated community economic development program, or by a micro-finance program of a commercial lender. They often offer, besides money, business courses and networking opportunities.

Credit from suppliers and clients

Maybe you didn't realize you could put your customers and suppliers to work for you as lenders.

Suppliers

If you're buying equipment or machinery, you may be able to finance the purchase through a loan from the vendor, a conditional sales agreement, or a lease. (See Chapter 7 for more about equipment, and Chapter 14 for more about suppliers.) The vendor will probably want a down payment and security (for example, a chattel mortgage if the vendor is loaning you the money), and will want to be repaid on a regular schedule, as would a commercial lender.

If you're buying inventory or supplies, you may be able to get financing through a credit arrangement. Suppliers may offer 30, 60, or 90 days to pay, with a discount if payment is made within a shorter time. (Two problems exist here: First, because you're a start-up without a credit history, suppliers might not want to extend credit and might instead want cash on delivery from you. Second, the effective interest rate you pay on the money you're "borrowing" by not taking the discount is high — in the range of 20 to 30 percent or more.) Suppliers might also sometimes offer a loan, or else a sale on *consignment* (you don't pay the supplier until a customer purchases a consigned item). If you buy inventory on credit, the supplier may want to take security in the form of a *purchase money security interest* (in other words, the supplier takes security on the items purchased on credit).

Customers

You may well be able to get your clients or customers to finance the work you do for them by getting them to pay a deposit or *retainer* (that's what professionals call a deposit) and/or instalment payments as you do the work (instead of waiting to be paid when everything's finished). See Chapter 13 for more about dealing with customers.

Sale of accounts receivable

You can sell your recent accounts receivable at a discount for instant cash. This is called *factoring* and it's more expensive than borrowing — it can be a lot more expensive — but you don't have to show that your business has revenue and you don't have to put up security. The factor pays you a percentage of the value of your receivables immediately, collects the receivables, deducts fees, and sends you the balance. (Depending on your arrangement with the factor, your customers needn't know they're dealing with a factor instead of with your business.)

The initial percentage you get from the factor will depend on things like the value of the receivables, number of customers and credit-worthiness of the customers — it can run anywhere from about 90 percent down to 30 percent. In "recourse" factoring, the factor can look to you to cover any bad debts, while in "non-recourse" factoring (which is, naturally, more expensive) bad debts are the factor's risk. Factoring is available from factoring companies, finance companies, and some banks. It's traditionally used in the apparel, textile, carpet, and furniture industries, but it's not restricted to those industries.

Government loans and grants

TIP

You, too, may be able to snarf up some money from the public trough to start and run your business! You can find lots of government assistance programs — to browse, go to the Innovation, Science, and Economic Development Canada site (www.ic.gc.ca) and click the Business Grants and Financing tab for information on government grants and loans. You can search for financing available throughout Canada, or restrict your search to financing available in your province.

For example, these sources may provide you with some repayable or even non-repayable money for your business:

>> The Industrial Research Assistance Program (IRAP) of the National Research Council (www.nrc-cnrc.gc.ca/eng/irap), if you need to research and develop a new technological product or service

>> Canada Council for the Arts (www.canadacouncil.ca), if your business involves artistic creation (like writing, painting, music, performance)

>> Industry Canada (www.ic.gc.ca), which may provide grants or loans for various business initiatives

Arm's-length investment

For some businesses, a start-up loan isn't much use. If you take out a loan, you have to pay it back — usually beginning right away — and your business, even though it has fantastic prospects over the next few years, won't be able to generate cash revenues for some time *and* it needs a cash infusion (perhaps a big one) to get started at all.

So maybe what you need is seed *financing* or *seed capital* from an angel investor or a venture capital firm, rather than a loan from a lender.

Seed capital provides money for business activities such as the following:

>> Proving that an idea or invention actually works in practice as well as it does in theory (*proof of concept*)

>> Protecting intellectual property (usually through a patent — see Chapter 3)

>> Completing a prototype (*working model*) of a product or invention

>> Doing market research

>> Creating strategic partnerships with other businesses or with potential customers

>> Hiring experienced managers for the business

>> Creating a business plan

>> Hunting down even more capital that's required to start the business operating

The great majority of start-up businesses don't need seed capital for these kinds of things. And even start-ups that do aren't that likely to get outside investment in the business. Most requests for investment get rejected either because the business has limited financial prospects or because the managers of the business don't have the necessary skills to run the business successfully. But we'll go on and briefly tell you about outside investors anyway.

Angel investors

If you go around talking about angel investors, chances are most people will think you've been out in the sun too long. You'll get the same kind of reaction as if you mentioned that aliens are broadcasting messages to you through the fillings in your teeth.

Angel investors actually do exist, however. They are individuals, often successful businesspeople, who want to invest their own money in promising new businesses, usually in the same field the angel comes from (many or most come from a high-technology background), and usually in businesses in their own geographic area.

WHAT ANGELS OFFER

Angels usually invest an amount in the range of $10,000 to $150,000, although some may go as high as $500,000 or more if they've got the money and they really like the business's prospects. Besides providing money, angel investors also take an interest in the running of the business. Because they're experienced, they may be able to proactively help you find customers and sell your product, put you in touch with suppliers and professional advisors, and prepare you and your business to hunt for the next round of financing.

WHAT ANGELS ARE LOOKING FOR

Angels are looking for a good return on their investment in your business — typically 30 percent compound annual returns. Not many business owners even plan for their business to grow that aggressively, much less are capable of making it happen. Angels are also looking for *equity* in (a share in the value of) your business and the right to be involved in major decisions and to get frequent status reports.

WHERE TO FIND AN ANGEL

TIP

Heaven? Sure, but maybe closer than that. Network in your own business community and ask around about angel investors. Ask your lawyer or accountant. Some business incubators help to connect client companies with angel investors. Or you can try the National Angel Capital Organization (www.angelinvestor.ca). The website has a page that lists angel investor groups in Canada, organized by region.

If you find an angel, he or she won't necessarily be interested in investing in your kind of business. Learn as much as you can about an angel before approaching him or her, and customize your pitch to match the angel's interests.

Venture capital

Venture capital is money that's available for risky investments with a good chance of getting a high return on the investment. Over $12 billion in venture capital is floating around in the Canadian economy at the moment, and in the past few years venture capitalists have poured about $2 billion per year into businesses, mostly in the technology, life sciences, clean tech, and agricultural sectors. However, that doesn't mean that you'll be able to get any of it. Venture capitalists (VCs) are ridiculously fussy about whom they give their money to.

WHAT KIND OF BUSINESS OPPORTUNITIES IS A VC LOOKING FOR?

Venture capitalists are typically looking for three things:

>> **A large market opportunity** — one that will provide very high returns within a fairly short time, about five to seven years

>> **Good managers** — or at least one good and committed manager who will be able to recruit a strong management team

>> **A strategic plan about building the business** — one that includes a lucrative exit strategy (see "What a VC wants in return") for the venture capitalists

WHAT A VC CAN OFFER

Like angel investors, venture capitalists offer money, management expertise, and connections — to other money, to professional advisors like lawyers and accountants, and to suppliers and potential customers.

WHAT A VC WANTS IN RETURN

To put this section into perspective, we'll tell you that venture capitalists are also known, affectionately of course, as vulture capitalists. What they usually want is

>> At least a 25 percent return on investment — and they're really thrilled at the prospect of getting a 300 to 500 percent return (a *home run*).

>> Significant ownership of the business — they usually want 20 percent or more of the business's equity, plus their own director(s) on the board of directors.

>> A lucrative exit strategy within five to seven years. Exit strategies include the following:

- An *initial public offering* (IPO — see Chapter 18)

- Sale of the business to another corporation (see Chapter 21)

- A company buy-back (the business or business owners buy back the VC's share of the corporation)

- A write-off of the investment (as lost money) . . . although clearly this is not "lucrative"

WHERE TO FIND A VC

TIP

Venture capital firms are very easy to find. You can get a list of them by going to the Canadian Venture Capital and Private Equity Association website (www.cvca.ca), and from there you can link to the home website of each association member. You can get contact information, as well as some information about the interests and expectations of each member, from their website. Finding venture capitalists, of course, does not necessarily mean getting money from them.

Crowdfunding

You've likely heard about crowdfunding, and you may be wondering what it's all about, whether it's right for your business idea, and its legality. *Crowdfunding* occurs when a person or organization raises money over the Internet by soliciting a group of people for individual contributions. There are various forms of crowdfunding, but the main ones simply seek donations. Crowdfunding is also used by companies and non-profit organizations to raise capital. If you see crowdfunding as an option to explore and you want to actually pursue this avenue, you need to provide investors with some information such as an offering document, financial statements, and periodic updates about how the money you raised is being used. It requires time, thought, and effort. Regulators will be watching, too, so it's important to know whether your province allows crowdfunding and, if so, what the rules are.

Crowdfunding in Canada is mostly regulated at the provincial level. An in-depth discussion of this emerging form of financing is beyond the scope of this book, but you can check out an excellent source of information at www.crowdfundontario.ca, which is geared more toward Ontario investors but offers an excellent overview of the industry as a whole. From there, check out the links to the Ontario Security Commission's pronouncements and requirements over businesses engaged in crowdfunding. Another great site, geared toward businesses exploring crowdfunding options in British Columbia, is www.bcsc.bc.ca/For_Companies/Private_Placements/Crowdfunding. This website has useful guides as well as links to *funding portals* — the online platforms actually used to make your case and raise and collect money. Just Google the term *crowdfunding* and the name of your province to learn more.

WARNING

Check with security regulator websites such as www.osc.gov.on.ca to stay on top of rapidly changing regulations over crowdfunding. There are risks and penalties involved if you run afoul of these regulations — all geared toward protect investors. Be sure to check with your legal counsel before proceeding with this route.

Applying for Money

REMEMBER

Be aware that before you approach a commercial lender, a government granting agency, an angel investor, or a venture capital firm (and maybe even members of your family whom you're tapping for love money), you'll have to show what you plan to do with any money you get, and why you should be trusted with it. The more money you want, the more work you'll have to do when you apply for it. The most work you'll be asked to do is prepare a business plan. But for a loan that's not too large (say, under $35,000 to $50,000), and assuming that over the years you've built a good credit rating, you'll probably just be asked to fill out an application form provided by the lender. For more about the application process, see Chapter 10.

Chapter **10**

Writing a Business Plan That Gets You Money

S ometimes preparing an application to get money involves filling out a form created by the lender, and sometimes it involves preparing a business plan. Most of this chapter focuses on a formal business plan because preparing a business plan is a lot more difficult than filling out an application form. If you want a more in-depth look at what goes into a business plan, check out the current edition of the popular *Business Plans For Canadians For Dummies* by Paul Tiffany, Steven D. Peterson, and Nada Wagner (Wiley).

Don't Panic!

Preparing a business plan can seem thoroughly intimidating. However, to get you off on the right foot, we start by telling you why you shouldn't panic at the thought of reading this chapter — or having to prepare an actual business plan.

First reason not to panic

You don't always have to prepare a formal business plan to get money. When you're looking for money, the first thing you should do (after identifying a source of money) is contact the source and find out what documentation they want in order to consider your request. Especially for smaller amounts of money (say, under $35,000 to $50,000), the source may want only a limited amount of information about your business. (See the section "Filling Out an Application Form.") Or the source may not need a full-strength business plan and instead be willing to settle for a mini business plan (see the section "Checking Out What Goes into a Business Plan").

Second reason not to panic

Most business books put the business plan chapter almost at the very beginning, where it's especially unnerving. Who knows how many people have decided not to go into business because they couldn't face writing a business plan as the first step in starting a business? And individuals aren't able to put together a description of their business and an analysis of the marketplace, and financial statements, before they've even thought about their product or service (refer to Chapter 4), their business organization (check out Chapter 6), what equipment they'll need (dig into Chapter 7), where they'll be located (explore Chapter 8), and what sources of funding are available to them (look at Chapter 9).

We put the business plan way in the middle for a reason. If you are working through this book chapter-by-chapter, by the time you get here, you've done a lot of the work needed to create a business plan — and you didn't even know you were doing it. Besides that, after going through Chapter 9 you're much more motivated to work to get some money.

Third reason not to panic

Even if you have to prepare a business plan, you don't have to prepare the business plan on your own. Help is available in the form of software, templates, and consultants. See "Getting Help with Your Business Plan" at the end of the chapter for more information.

First Step

REMEMBER

Before you write down a word or add up two numbers, contact the source of financing you're interested in. Tell the source how much you want to borrow and in what form, and then ask about the application process. If you just have to fill out a form, get the form. If you have to prepare a business plan, ask about any guidelines or forms you can have to show what the source wants to see in the business plan. If the source doesn't offer guidelines, you have to prepare the business plan yourself — but in this chapter, we offer a lot of help about the form and content of a business plan.

Filling Out an Application Form

You may only need to fill out quite a short, simple application form to apply for the money you need. Typically, an application form will ask you to give information about how much money you want and what you're planning to use it for, and also about

>> The business's primary financial institution (it might or might not be the institution you're requesting the loan from)

>> The name, trade name, and address of your business

>> The form of your business (sole proprietorship, partnership, or corporation — refer to Chapter 6)

>> The nature of your business

>> The length of time the business has been established, and the number of employees it has

>> The financial problems and setbacks your business has experienced (if any), such as claims from creditors and lawsuits, and whether the business has ever been in receivership or declared bankruptcy

The application form will also ask for a summary of financial information about your business, including

>> Total gross annual sales or revenues for the preceding fiscal year (if you've been in business for more than a year) or as projected for the year ahead (if you're a start-up)

>> Net after-tax profit or loss (for the preceding fiscal year if you've been in business for more than a year, or as projected for the year ahead if you're a start-up)

Be prepared to provide the financial statements themselves. For information about preparing financial statements, see Chapter 17.

Finally, the application form will ask for information about the owner(s) of the business, including

>> Names and addresses

>> Income in the preceding year (as reported on the owner's tax return)

>> A list of each owner's assets and debts (Later, in the "Preparing a Business Plan" section, we have a personal balance sheet to show you the kind of information the lender has in mind.)

For a start-up business, the decision whether to lend will be based as much on the owner's personal financial status as on the business's, because start-up businesses normally don't have much in the way of assets.

REMEMBER

If the owner has no assets, the lender will be very reluctant to lend the business any money. Probably the best indicator of whether you'll get the loan is if you own a home (one that's not 100 percent mortgaged already). The lender will feel much more comfortable giving you money if it can take back a mortgage as security. (See Chapter 9 for more about security for a loan.)

Preparing a Business Plan

Sometimes you have no choice . . . if you want money you have to prepare a business plan to submit to the lender.

A business plan sets out how much money you want and what you're going to do with it, describes your business, places it within the context of the industry it belongs to, examines the marketplace and competition and sets out a strategy for competing in the marketplace, and provides detailed financial information about your business.

A lender or investor looks at a business plan to see whether it's safe to put money into your business. If your business is well thought out, it's more likely to be successful, generate a profit, and be able to repay the lender or investor.

When you show someone a business plan, you're revealing a lot of important information (important to you, at least) about your business. If you want to impress on the potential lender or investor that this information shouldn't be broadcast around Canada, you may want to ask the lender or investor to sign a confidential disclosure agreement before looking at the business plan. You'll find a sample of this document online as Form 3-1. (Turn to this book's Introduction for instructions on how to access the free online content.)

Checking Out What Goes into a Business Plan

Books and even chapters about business plans are often incredibly detailed and seem to be written for existing businesses that are looking to expand and need huge amounts of money. They're intimidating, and by the time you get to the end of the book or chapter you feel like writing a business plan is pointless because you don't have an MBA and you don't understand the marketing and accounting jargon.

Don't twist yourself into knots about writing a business plan. Although almost every book or article you read about creating a business plan will tell you a somewhat different way to set up the plan, all business plans contain the same — quite understandable — basic information.

A full-scale business plan

If a lender is looking for the whole shebang, business-plan-wise, here's the core information required:

>> The amount of money you want from the person who's reading the business plan and what you're going to do with it.

>> A description of what your business does, and a description of the industry your business is part of.

>> An explanation about why your business can compete successfully, and your strategy for competing (that is, for marketing your product or service).

>> A description of how your business runs or will run on a day-to-day basis, including information about the business's managers.

>> The financial information about your business, including projections about revenue and expenses (as a start-up you won't have much financial history), and also about your personal financial status and individual financial commitment to the enterprise — so the lender or investor can decide whether investing is safe. A lender or investor will expect to be paid back out of profits of the business or (if the business doesn't generate enough profits) out of the sale of what the business owns . . . and/or what you own.

The rest of the chapter goes through these sections at much greater length.

A mini business plan

If the lender doesn't want to know every last detail about your business (and who can say whether the lenders who do want to know every detail actually read the business plan from cover to cover?), you need to prepare only a short version. A mini business plan would cover any given topic more briefly, and it might include only the following information:

>> The amount of money you want from the lender and what you'll do with it

>> The name and address of the business, form of business, and how long it's been established

>> The nature of your business, and what its goals are (essentially the 5 Ws: who, what, when, where, and why)

>> A basic analysis of your market and competition

>> The financial statements (also including a *pro forma* projected balance sheet, income statement, and statement of cash flows with assumptions)

Stating How Much You Want (Your Objective)

You should say right up front how much money you want and what you're going to do with it. You should also say right up front how this money will increase the profits or value of the business so that the loan can be repaid or the investment can provide a return.

REMEMBER

No, you're not being rude or pushy by saying what you want. You'll save your potential lender or investor time and annoyance. No one with money wants to plod through pages of information without knowing beforehand why they're plodding. They'll want to assess what you want against what you have — and against what they have to offer — from the very beginning of your plan.

Describing Your Business

Next the plan describes your business, and how your business fits into the larger industry it's part of.

Your product or service

Start with what your business does — what product it manufactures or sells or what service it provides.

For example, if you're firing up a bakery operation, you'll describe the baked goods you're going to produce and your potential customers. If you're setting up a bookkeeping practice, you'll describe the services you plan to offer and to whom.

If your business has an intellectual property component — for example, if you're

>> Manufacturing a product that's patented or whose design is registered as an industrial design

>> Distributing or selling a product under a licence agreement or marketing a product under a trademark

then your plan should describe the status of protection of the product or service. For instance, if your product or method is patented, say so and mention its patent number, or if a patent has been applied for, say that a patent application is pending; if you're distributing a patented product, talk briefly about the licence agreement you have. For more about intellectual property and its protection, refer to Chapter 3.

For a business that needs money to start manufacturing a product, you should be prepared to show a potential lender or investor working drawings and designs of the product.

The goals of your business

While your immediate goal is to get your business set up, you presumably also have other goals on the way to success. An investor would like to know where you're headed. So your plan should outline

>> Your short-term goals

>> Your long-term plans

In the case of the bakery, for example, your short-term goal might be to produce ten dozen loaves of bread per day within a month of starting the operation and distribute them through five local independent food stores. A longer-term goal might be to produce 100 dozen loaves per day and distribute them through a grocery chain with stores around your city. Your ultimate goal (for the moment) might be to expand your baking operation to the point that it supplies bread for the grocery chain throughout the province; or it might be to franchise your bakery and sell franchises across the country.

If you think your business might attract a lot of interest from the world at large (and not just from your doting family and satisfied customers) and will need a large amount of invested money to expand and function properly, your long-term goal might be to become a publicly traded company. Publicly traded companies are able to raise money by offering their shares to the public through a stock exchange. (For more about going public, see Chapter 18.)

If you think your business is likely to be of great interest to one or more large corporations in the industry, and that a large corporation would show its interest via a nice fat offer to buy you out, your long-term goal might be to sell your business to a larger business. (For more about selling out, see Chapter 21.)

Your business within the industry

Your business won't be operating in isolation. Even if you haven't thought about it that way, it's part of some fairly large-scale industry. Your bakery is part of the baked goods industry, your bookkeeping practice is in a small corner of the accounting industry, your computer program for hunting down certain kinds of information on the Internet is part of the computer software industry. The lender or investor you approach may not know much about the industry at all and will need background information to make a decision.

TIP

So you need to write a short profile of the industry. To do this you'll have to conduct some research by contacting industry associations, or reading industry publications, or searching for newspaper and magazine articles, or going through Statistics Canada data at www.statcan.gc.ca/eng. Chapter 2 gives you some ideas about doing your research.

Include some of the following information in your profile:

>> **The size of businesses in the industry:** Some businesses are mainly made up of large multinational corporations, like the pharmaceutical industry; some are mainly made up of national corporations, like the Canadian banking industry . . . although you're probably not thinking of starting up a bank; others may have a mix of large and small businesses, like the legal and accounting industries; and some mostly consist of small businesses, like the personal services industry.

>> **The total volume of sales in the industry and the total value of sales:** You're just going to have a small piece of the pie to start with, but do show that the pie is nice and big.

>> **Any legislation, regulations, and standards that apply to the industry's products or services:** For example, the manufacture of food and drugs is heavily regulated by the federal government; travel agencies are regulated by

provincial governments; cafés are regulated and inspected by municipal governments.

>> **Trends in the industry:** It might be growing, or shrinking, or shifting its focus from certain products or services to others; or it might be facing stricter government regulation, or it might be about to be deregulated.

>> **The main challenges and problems the industry faces:** Is it being forced to compete globally instead of nationally? Is it losing customers because it isn't meeting changing customer needs? Has it priced its goods or services out of the larger marketplace? Is it sluggish because it hasn't upgraded old infrastructure?

>> **The future of the industry:** Will it stay much as it is but expand — or contract? Will it change significantly in response to consumer demand or new legislation?

By the way, don't make this stuff up. Making it up is easier and more fun, true, but it's a bad move. You'll look light-minded and untrustworthy if anyone finds out.

And because you're not making it up, you should footnote facts and opinions that you state to show their source. If a lender or investor wants more information about the industry, he, she, or it should be able to locate your references.

After you've finished your industry profile, you have to discuss how your business fits into the industry. Are you going to create a product that will revolutionize the industry . . . or even make it obsolete? Are you going to take advantage of a gap and expand your business to become a major player? Are you going to quietly but competently fill a little niche? How will industry trends affect your business's chance of success? How will your business meet the industry's challenges? How will your business fit into the industry's future that you've projected? This section gives you quite a mental workout! But preparing it makes you reflect on a lot of points that are important to your business success.

Why your business can compete successfully

After you describe your business world, you have to show that you can survive in it by competing successfully. In trying to figure out how well you'll be able to compete, you have to consider both the market for your product or your service, and your competition in the marketplace. In Chapter 4, we take you through the process of developing a product or service and researching its market and its competition.

Your market

You need to know a reasonable amount about the market for your product or service so that you can

>> Identify your target market for the product or service.

>> Identify your portion of the total target market — probably not the total market, at least not to begin with.

>> Identify marketing strategies (covering things such as prices, distribution, and business promotion).

Your target market

You can determine your target market in different ways. One is geography. Your target market may be the people (or businesses) within a geographic area. For example, if you run a retail business, you may see your target market as the people who live within walking distance or a short driving distance of your store. If you're distributing a product, you may have a distribution agreement with the manufacturer that allows you to distribute the product within your province or within a region (for example, the Maritime provinces, or the Vancouver area, or specified towns in northern Ontario). If you're the sole manufacturer of a product that's in demand (say, a hula-hoop during a hula-hoop craze) your geographic market might be the entire country or the entire continent.

Another way of determining your target market is by the characteristics of your customers or clients — for example, sex, age, interests, needs, and/or income level if your customers or clients are individuals; the kind of business and/or annual sales if your customers are other businesses.

Yet another way to view the market is in terms of its behaviour. Behavioural market segmentation is a human-centered approach that segments your target market based on what your customers or clients actually do. For example, this form of segmentation considers how your customer base purchases certain types of products or services. Do they prefer online or bricks-and-mortar storefronts? Are customers repeat customers? At what time of day do they prefer to shop? This type of market analysis uses available data, observation, and focus groups to distinguish a market by its behaviour.

Your share of the target market

Besides figuring out who or what your target market is, you have to try to estimate what share of the target market your competitors hold and what share you can capture. This is guesswork unless you've got very few competitors. As an example, if you open a convenience store in a residential area where no other stores are located, you've got a good chance of getting a very big share of the target market (which is the inhabitants of the residential area). But — to take an example from the opposite end of the spectrum — if you're planning to sell T-shirts over the Internet (a huge total market), you may never be able to estimate your market share or a competitor's with anything approaching accuracy because many businesses are competing in a fickle market.

TIP

If you're looking for a large sum of money, consider having a professional marketing study done to examine in detail the size of the market, the existing competitors in the market, and the market share your business might expect to capture.

Marketing strategy

A lot of details go into identifying a marketing strategy. These details include

>> **Your planned method(s) of selling and/or distributing your product or service:** Are you going to sell directly to the end user, or are you going to go through a third party (such as a manufacturer's agent or a distributor or a retailer, if you're a manufacturer)? If you already have contracts or partnerships with individuals or businesses or governments who are going to buy or distribute your product or service, mention them here.

>> **Your location (if it affects marketing):** Your location is important if, for example, you're a retail store or service relying on walk-in customers, or if you provide a product that can be shipped only short distances to customers, or if you need to project an image to customers that can be achieved in only a certain area. Canadian wine coming from the Niagara region would be an example of the latter. Location isn't particularly important if you provide a service or product without needing face-to-face contact with your customers or clients. For example, running a call-centre operation from an industrial plaza in the middle of nowhere is fine . . . as long as you can get workers to go there.

>> **Your strategy for promoting the product:** This covers things like

- **Your business image:** How are you going to present your business? Are you going to package it around a logo or trademark? Are you going to build it around a concept (such as one-stop errand running if you're starting up a personal assistant business) or a special product? Are you going to promote it as an essential for your target market (such as a business-district spa for businesswomen)?

- **Your advertising message:** What's your message, and your method and budget for getting the message out? Methods might include TV and radio spots; social media and other sites like Facebook, Twitter, blogs, and podcasts; newspaper ads; billboards and signs; flyers distributed around neighbourhoods or to local businesses — or even just word of mouth. The method should be appropriate to the target market and to the image you want your business to project.

- **Your public relations plan, if any:** Do you have a plan for approaching the media (in the hope that they'll write about you or interview you on TV news or a business program or a lifestyle show) and organizing events to attract media and/or customer attention? Media approaches might include press releases, contacts with acquaintances or friends-of-friends, or cold calls.

- **Your sales strategy:** How are you going to set your basic price? (Generally speaking, it should be high enough to cover your costs of providing the product or service and earn you a profit, and low enough that your competitors are not underpricing you. Refer to Chapter 4 for more about pricing your product or service.) What other pricing procedures are you going to use to attract customers and clients? (Possibilities include gifts, coupons or two-for-one offers; special sales to groups; or special rates for large purchases.)

- **Finding and keeping customers:** What's your plan for coming up with leads to find new customers and clients? (Tried and true methods include advertising, arranging for other individuals and businesses to refer clients to you, and buying customer lists.) Are you going to make presentations to prospective clients or customers? (What will the content of the presentation be, and how will you jazz it up to give it impact?) How are you going to satisfy the customers you do get? (Think about a returns policy, guarantees, and product service provided on the premises.)

Your competitors

You need to know your market, but you also need to know your competitors. If you can't beat them at their own game, that will be the end of you.

In this part of your business plan you'll

- » **Fearlessly and transparently name your competitors.** Remember, though, you're talking about your competitors in your target market and not all the competitors in the total market. If you're starting a dog-walking business, your competitors aren't every personal-service provider in the province, or even every dog-walker in the city, just the dog-walkers in the neighbourhood you plan to service.

- » **Describe the similar products or services available from the competitors.** What are the strong points about the competing products or services, and what are the weak points? What do they do better than anyone else to distinguish themselves? What problems or vulnerabilities exist with the competition's product or services?

>> **Explain why customers will buy the product or service from you instead of something similar from the competition.** Describe the strengths of your product or service.

Strong points of either the competitors' businesses or your business might include:

>> Higher quality of services or product

>> Innovative nature of the product or service (being the first to provide a product or service can give the provider a competitive edge — but keep in mind that the first provider isn't necessarily the best provider)

>> Lower cost of services or product

>> Better distribution system

>> Better management

>> Better customer service — efficient, fast, friendly

>> Better service guarantees that accompany the product or service

>> A more convenient location

>> Established base of loyal customers or clients

>> Loyalty of customers or clients to a particular brand

>> Access to a client/customer base that hasn't been tapped yet

Weaknesses are the flip side of these matters — such as higher cost of the product, poorer quality of the service, less convenient location, and so on.

WARNING

Don't overdo describing your competitors' strengths or your own weaknesses. You don't want to deep-six your business proposal by presenting the competition as unbeatable or you as a lost sheep among the coyotes. But you do want your potential investor to know that you've taken an objective look at the market and your chances of turning a good profit.

Explaining How Your Business Runs

Investors are amazingly curious about how you will run your business. Some even go so far as to say that they care less about the product or service the business provides than they do about who's in charge. Poor management can destroy even a great idea, while good management can nurture a less-than-fantastic idea along the path to success.

Business info and history

You can start with the easy stuff about your business:

>> The address, phone and fax numbers, and the email address

>> A statement about the form of your business (sole proprietorship, partnership, or corporation — refer to Chapter 6 for forms of business organization)

>> A description or picture of any business logo, design, trademark, or trade name you're using

>> A brief history of the business, including the date of business start-up

Business managers

Then you get down to the nitty-gritty: Who's running this show? Here you list key people (it may be a short list) and their titles, if any:

>> **The owner(s) of the business:** The sole proprietor of a sole proprietorship, the shareholders of a corporation, the partners in a partnership.

>> **The manager(s) of the business:** For example, the managing partner of a partnership, or the CEO (chief executive officer) of a corporation — and the compensation the manager is to receive. Each manager's CV (*curriculum vitae, or resume*) should accompany the business plan and show that the manager has relevant business experience. If you're a novice at running a business, your CV should at least show that you've got related work experience and/or that you've attended some courses or workshops on setting up and managing a business. If you're starting a complex business or one that requires a lot of money (hundreds of thousands or millions of dollars) at the outset, don't fool around playing CEO if you're not a seasoned professional. Investors won't look at your business unless you've got a professional with a track record in place.

>> **The key employees of the business:** For example, the person responsible for sales and marketing or the person in charge of research and development.

>> **The inventor(s) or creator(s) of the idea on which the business is based (if any):** For example, the inventor of a drug or medical device, or the designer of a product that the business is going to manufacture. If at all possible, you want the creative brain behind the business to come along with the business. Have an inventor or creator provide a CV to attach to the business plan.

>> **The professional advisors of the business:** The lawyer, accountant, publicist, advertising firm.

>> **The investors already on board:** These could be you (via your bank account, investments, sale of property, and so on) and your family and friends who loaned you cash or contributed equipment; or your bank that gave you a start-up loan, or some other arm's-length investor. Getting a credible person or well-respected third-party organization to endorse your product or service would be an added benefit if you could add this name to your list.

Business operations

If it's relevant to your business — for example, if you're a manufacturer or if you service products — you should also provide information about

>> Your facilities or physical plant or infrastructure

>> Your equipment, and methods of operation

>> Your materials and supplies, and their sources

Supplying Financial Information

In the finance section of your business plan you're going to crunch the numbers to show that you've got a good chance of making a profit, or at least of paying back the loan or generating a return on the investment. This is a spot where lenders or investors will become eagle–eyed because they want to be pretty sure that they'll get their money back someday.

You do this part of the business plan through spreadsheets (financial tables) rather than written text.

Specifically, investors will want to know

>> **How much money the business needs to get up and running** (or to expand, if this isn't a start-up operation) — in other words, what the present *capital requirements* of the business are.

>> **How many assets the business already has and how many liabilities it has** — how much property it owns, such as money, real estate, equipment, valuable contracts such as licence agreements and leases; how much it owes, such as mortgages, loans, and accounts payable. This is the *balance sheet*.

>> **What the projected profit of the business is** — how much the business will earn and how much it will cost the business to earn that amount. Or to put it another way, what the income and operating expenses will be (this is a *statement of income and expenses*). You may also have to show when the income comes in and when payment of expenses goes out, with a *cash-flow statement*.

>> **What assets and liabilities the principals of the business have** — this means preparing a *personal balance sheet* for each owner of the business. A loan for your business will actually be a personal loan if your business is a sole proprietorship or a partnership. And even if your business is a corporation, you'll likely be asked to guarantee a business loan personally if your business doesn't generate enough profit and doesn't have enough assets to sell to repay the loan. If you're not a good loan risk personally, the whole deal may very well fall through.

If your business has been in operation for two or three years and isn't a start-up, you'll also be expected to provide *balance sheets* for the preceding years and *income* (or *profit and loss*) statements. See Chapter 17 for more about these statements.

Capital requirements of your business

We talk about calculating the capital requirements of your business in Chapter 9, which includes a table to help you to prepare a statement of your start-up capital needs.

Assets and liabilities of your business

The assets and liabilities of your business are set out in a balance sheet. In Chapter 17, we explain balance sheets and how to prepare them.

Projected revenue and expenses of your business

We talk about preparing a forecast of revenue and expenses in Chapter 9, where we also provide a table to help you work out your forecast of revenue and expenses for the first year of business.

Your personal capital

The lender or investor may well be looking to you to pay up if your business can't. If so, you'll be asked to provide a *personal balance sheet*, often called a *statement of net worth*, listing your own assets and liabilities. This provides a snapshot of the "financial you."

TIP

Table 10-1 shows an example of a personal balance sheet. You can download Form 10-1, which is a copy of this spreadsheet that you can fill in and print out. (Turn to this book's Introduction for instructions on how to access this free online content.)

TABLE 10-1

Personal Balance Sheet

Assets		
Cash	$	
Investments	$	
Cash-value life insurance	$	
Real estate (home, cottage)	$	
Vehicles	$	
Personal property	$	
Personal loans	$	
Other	$	
Total Assets		$
Liabilities		
Mortgages		
Personal loans		
Credit card balances		
Other personal debts (for example, unpaid property taxes, unpaid income taxes, outstanding bills, child support)		
Monthly bills		
Total Liabilities		$
Net Worth (total assets minus total liabilities)		$

Providing References

You're exhausted, but you're not finished. As a final touch, a lender or investor might like to know more about your business reputation (or if you don't have a business reputation yet, your personal reputation) — but not from you. So be prepared to provide, if asked, the names of two or three people the lender or investor could speak to — for example, your bank branch manager if you've dealt with him or her for some time, or other business people you've dealt with over the years (probably best not to name your competitors here . . . or your mother). If you've never been in business for yourself before, you could name an employer or a customer or client you worked with. Ask your references for permission before you give their names. At the very least, you don't want them to be taken by surprise when a lender calls up for a chat about you.

If your business venture revolves around marketing a new technology (say, new computer software or hardware), a lender or investor would probably like to have the names of a couple of people who know the field and who can give an opinion about the commercial potential of your technology. Again, avoid giving the name of a competitor.

Pulling the Final Product Together

After you've put together a first draft of your business plan, ask someone with business experience whose judgment you trust to read the plan and comment on it. Then you revise the plan and polish up the prose. Your final version of the plan will include the following:

>> Cover

>> Title page

>> Table of contents

>> Executive summary

>> The plan itself

>> Financial statements

Cover

Don't get carried away with something expensive, or covered with decorations. Just buy a plain paper cover — preferably in a conservative colour.

Executive summary

TIP

If your plan is more than three or four pages long (excluding financial charts), you need to provide an executive summary at the beginning of the plan so that the reader can decide even more quickly whether to talk to you or simply toss your plan in the circular file. The summary should

>> State the amount of money required and what you will do with it.

>> Briefly describe the business (including the five Ws: *who, what, when, where,* and *why*).

>> Describe the business's product or service.

>> Summarize income projections.

Getting Help with Your Business Plan

This chapter shows just how much hard work goes into a business plan, and we wouldn't blame you if you want some help. Well, help is out there — some of it free, some of it for a price.

You can purchase business plan software, such as Business Plan Pro (www. palalto.com), and you can access over 500 sample business plans online at www. bplans.com.

You can also get free templates, writing guides, and sample business plans from the websites of various business organizations:

>> The Business Development Bank of Canada (www.bdc.ca) provides business plan templates.

>> Scotiabank (www.scotiabank.com) has the Scotia Plan Writer — an interactive business planning tool.

>> Community Business Development Corporations (www.cbdc.ca) has an online business plan.

>> Futurpreneur Canada (www.futurpreneur.ca/en) supports aspiring business owners ages 18 to 39 and has an interactive business plan writer.

And if you don't feel like doing this all by yourself — just you and the software — you can go to your accountant. Your accountant can, at a minimum, put together the financials for your business plan after talking to you about your business and what you're planning to do with it.

You can also hire a consultant who can write a business plan for you — but expect to drop several thousand dollars for this service. You'll want to use a consultant who specializes in your business field.

TIP

You can find consultants (you can likely find consultants galore!) by asking your business acquaintances, or approaching your provincial, municipal, or regional economic development office for suggestions. You can also get in touch with a university business school — MBA students run assistance programs and will work with you on a business plan for a modest fee.

IN THIS CHAPTER

» **Knowing exactly what marketing involves**

» **Finding customers or clients**

» **Getting your own website**

» **Marketing with email**

» **Employing online surveys**

» **Using popular social media sites in your business**

Chapter **11**

Making a Marketing Buzz

Marketing is about creating — and then keeping — a relationship with your customers or clients. Whether you use traditional marketing methods or web-based marketing methods — and you should use both — marketing is about locating potential customers or clients or helping them to locate you, and then selling your product or service to them.

We're taking just one chapter in this book to look at marketing, but entire books have been written on the subject. We encourage you to find out more by reading some of those books. *Small Business Marketing Kit For Dummies*, 3rd Edition, by Barbara Findlay Schenk, and *Marketing Kit For Dummies*, 3rd Edition, by Alexander Hiam (both published by Wiley), focus on traditional marketing methods. For more information about web-based marketing check out *Web Marketing All-in-One For Dummies*, 2nd Edition, by John Arnold, Ian Lurie, Marty Dickinson, Elizabeth Marsten, and Michael Becker (also published by Wiley).

Finding Customers or Clients

In Chapter 4, we tell you how to develop a product or service and settle on a price. After doing that, you'd like to find someone who'll pay the price you've set for your product or service! So the next step is to locate potential customers and clients and tell them that you're open for business.

You can announce your presence in three different ways:

>> Promotion

>> Advertising

>> Publicity

REMEMBER

A successful marketing strategy will mix and match promotion, advertising, and publicity, using both traditional and web-based methods.

Promotion

In business, the word *promotion* gets tossed around quite a bit and can mean various things. We use it to mean activities that say "I'm here!" but that are neither paid advertising nor media-provided publicity. Promotion is sometimes considered a form of free advertising, but it isn't really "free" — everything has a cost . . . at a minimum, your time and a new tie.

You can promote your business in lots of different ways. Whatever way you choose, although you may not look as if you're soliciting business, finding customers or clients is your aim.

Here are some promotional activities:

>> **Networking:** Getting out and meeting people who may become customers or clients or who may refer customers or clients to you. You can network practically anywhere, but typical places to network include business meetings; social, professional, or trade events; clubs; groups associated with your church, synagogue, mosque, or temple or with your ethnic or cultural roots; conventions; conferences; trade shows; neighbourhood events; and school reunions.

>> **Providing useful information in a public forum:** Teaching a course, giving a talk or presentation to a community group or at a conference, writing a column or article for a newspaper or magazine, writing a book, creating a podcast, publishing content on YouTube, putting out your own print or email

newsletter for potential and existing customers or clients, creating your own informative website or blog, contributing to someone else's website or blog, and posting on social networking sites such as Facebook, LinkedIn, or Twitter.

TIP

Whenever you engage in a promotional activity, provide your contact information: your address, telephone number, email address, website address, and details of or links to the social media sites you use. Consider sponsoring an event. If you engage in an in-person promotional activity, include that information in a "take-away" such as a business card or brochure.

Advertising

You can advertise in many different ways (and they all cost money — some more than others). After you figure out what message you want to send about your business, you can send it via

>> Direct mail — mailing, faxing, or emailing a brochure or flyer to the unsuspecting public. However, be mindful of the fact that many potential customers dislike direct mail.

>> Print ads — in local, regional, or national newspapers or magazines

>> Ads on websites — pop-up ads or banner ads (web surfers are pretty good at ignoring traditional ads, but Facebook, Twitter, and Instagram offer social ads that can be targeted to users based on demographics, interests, and keywords in their profiles). You can also buy ads that will appear on search engines when readers enter certain search terms related to your business.

>> Flyers, handbills (delivered by hand or by Canada Post's direct mail service), and street posters, or posters in other businesses' stores or offices (if they'll let you put them up)

>> Business cards or brochures left on display at other businesses, community centres, and so on, if they don't mind

>> Billboards and bus boards

>> Radio

>> TV

>> Podcasts and videocasts (vlogs) online

>> Product placement in a movie or on a TV show

As with promotion, make sure your ad contains contact information for your business.

Publicity

We're all looking for our 15 minutes of fame, but publicity is harder to come by than promotion or advertising because you have no real control over it. You can't force the media to be interested in you — okay, so you can probably grab the media's attention if you do something extreme like rob a bank and hand out your business card to the terrified tellers and customers as you depart, or if you announce that you're going to be the area's first nude retail store — but that would be getting carried away. Try to keep a cool business head when you're seeking publicity.

REMEMBER

To pique media interest, you don't need to do something that will be front-page news tomorrow morning. You do need to do something that's unusual or innovative, or that is of local interest (to a local paper or TV station) or of human interest. This is your "hook" for the media. Here are some things to try:

>> Issue a press release about the opening of your (interesting and innovative) business or about some significant activity you're undertaking or some event you're planning.

>> Contact an appropriate editor or journalist and issue an invitation to an event you're staging, or ask if they're interested in writing about something you're doing (the answer is probably no . . .).

>> Contact an appropriate editor or journalist to let him or her know you're available to be interviewed as an expert on a particular subject (if you are). When a story breaks, newspapers and TV stations often hunt down experts for quotable comments.

Unless it's a slow news day or you and your business are absolutely fascinating, don't expect too much from a publicity initiative. And certainly don't expect constant publicity if you do happen to get a nibble or two.

Professional help

You can find individuals (freelancers) or firms who will help you with promotion, advertising, and publicity. They're advertising agencies, publicists, marketing agencies, and public relations firms. If you want this kind of help, investigate before you hire. Watch for ads you like or PR you are impressed by, and then contact the firm or individual responsible for creating it. Ask for a detailed explanation about what the freelancer or firm can do for you, and how much it will cost.

Don't get discouraged

In some cases, you'll have to cast your net far and wide to accumulate customers or clients. Don't expect to acquire a large number of clients from every activity you undertake (maybe not right away, maybe never). General contact methods such as the ones we've described above often have a pretty low success rate — if your "I'm here!" announcement reaches 100 people, you may get a response from as few as 10 people or only 1 person (or even nobody at all). Try different methods, and definitely track the results, and see if one seems to work for your particular business.

If nothing works, it could mean that you came up with a bad business idea . . . but we hope you figured that out at the evaluation stage.

Establishing a Web Presence for Your Business

More and more consumers are searching for local products and services on the web. According to Internet World Stats, just over 90 percent of the Canadian population uses the Internet. Today, there are more than four billion Internet users around the world. According to Quora, the top broad search categories in order of frequency are news, products and services, and businesses. Obviously, the last two are key to any small business owner seeking to leverage the Internet for promotional and other business purposes. Every small business must establish a web presence!

Establishing a web presence involves

>> Getting a website

>> Marketing with email

>> Blogging

>> Using social media sites

>> Monitoring the web

We tell you about each of these topics in the following sections.

REMEMBER

As you establish your web presence, remember to maintain a consistent brand across the different web-based mediums, by always using the same name, logo, and colours. (They should be the same as what you're using in your printed materials.) We tell you more about brand consistency in Chapter 7.

Getting a Website of Your Own

Entire books have been written about business websites, and we only touch on some of the main points in this chapter. For more information, we recommend the popular *Starting an Online Business For Dummies* by Greg Holden (published by Wiley).

Understanding the importance of a website

Should your business have a website? In a word — yes! Setting up your business website is the first step in establishing and maintaining a presence on the web.

Your business should have a website because

>> **It lends credibility for your business.** People expect certain things of a business — to have a phone number, email address, fax number, and maybe even a street address. And more and more, people expect a business to have a website; if it doesn't, potential customers may wonder whether you really are serious about being in business!

>> **It lets the world know you're there.** You don't have to do business through your website, but potential customers like to be able to look up information without having to call you during business hours. Virtually all Canadians are now connected to the Internet or have ready access to it, and many of them begin their research about businesses not in the Yellow Pages, but on the web. A website is a great way to describe your products and/or services, hours of business, location (including directions and a map if you'd like), and contact information such as phone and fax numbers and your email address. All kinds of other tools called *widgets* can be added on as well. Widgets are special apps that can be added to a website to provide extra functionality, including booking calendars, advertisements, weather information, or links to your social media pages. To make sure that your website appears prominently on search results, check out Google's advertising tools at `https://ads.google.com`.

>> **It provides service to your existing customers.** You can post answers to your customers' or clients' most frequently asked questions (FAQs), allowing them to get answers on their own whenever they want. An online FAQ can save you time in dealing with simple, repetitive questions. Your website can also provide a point of email contact for your customers, especially if, for some reason, you don't want to give out your email address to every passing stranger. You can have a "contact us" section on the email that allows customers to write to you without you actually having to show your email address. Thus you can avoid being spammed by everyone.

>> **It allows you to carry on your business.** You can use your website to actually sell your goods and services to the world, 24 hours a day, seven days a week.

Deciding between a server of your own or a web host

No one will be able to find your website unless you have a *web server*, a computer that is connected to the Internet all of the time and delivers (or serves up) web pages. Any computer can be turned into a web server by installing server software. The web server stores all of the files needed to display the pages of your website when someone connects to your site using a web browser.

Many web server software applications are available, such as Internet Information Services (IIS), available for purchase from Microsoft (`www.microsoft.com`), and Apache HTTP Server, available free of charge from the Apache Software Foundation (`www.apache.org`). Of course, you'll still need an Internet service provider (ISP) to connect your web server to the Internet.

Does all of this sound too technical for you? If you don't have the technical expertise, and don't want your own web server, you can use a *web host,* a business that provides space on its server. You can check with your ISP like Rogers, Shaw, Bell, Videotron, and many others to see if it offers an appropriate monthly hosting package (you'll likely be entitled to some free web space as part of your existing Internet package). You can also find web hosting services by searching on the web for "web hosting." Your choice of web host will affect which software you use to create your web pages, and may affect your web address and the appearance of your site.

TIP

One of Canada's technology success stories is Shopify (`www.shopify.ca`). Shopify is an end-to-end online e-commerce platform that lets you start, grow, and run a business. With it you can create an online store or an online representation of your physical store. You can sell in multiple marketing channels, including web, social media, online marketplaces, mobile devices, and physical shops. The platform has functionality to let you manage products, inventory, payments, and shipping. Shopify is completely cloud-based and hosted, so you don't need to maintaining software or computer servers.

Claiming your domain name

The first step to setting up a website is to register your own domain name or uniform resource locator (URL). When you register a domain name, you're inserting an entry into a directory of all the domain names and their corresponding computers on the Internet.

Understanding domain names

TECHNICAL
STUFF

A domain name has two parts. The first part identifies the site's name, and comes before the dot. The second part, which comes after the dot, is the top-level domain — one of the primary categories into which Internet addresses are divided. The most common top-level domain name is .com. In Canada, a website may use the country code top-level domain name .ca.

TECHNICAL
STUFF

The Internet's Domain Name System (DNS) allows a website to use a domain name instead of a long, complicated string of numbers (which is what an Internet Protocol [IP] address is). The DNS is administered by the Internet Corporation for Assigned Names and Numbers (ICANN), an internationally organized, non-profit corporation that oversees the distribution of domain names.

You have to be a little more special to register a domain name ending with .ca than with .com. You must meet certain Canadian presence requirements. For example you must be

>> A Canadian citizen

>> A permanent resident of Canada

>> A legally recognized Canadian organization

>> A foreign resident of Canada who holds a registered Canadian trademark

Choosing a domain name

You have to come up with a unique domain name — if possible, your domain name should be the same as the name of your business. Check initially whether your name is going to be the same as, or confusingly similar to, another business's trademark or name or trade name by entering your potential domain name as a web search.

If someone is already using the domain name you want, you may be able to buy it from the owner. Check for contact information on the owner's website or try to contact the owner by typing in the domain name in the WHOIS Lookup at www. register.com or https://cira.ca/ca-domains/whois. You can also find websites where people offer to sell their domain names (www.sedo.com or www. register.com).

Registering your domain name

Once you decide on a domain name, you register your name by buying it through a registrar. Check the ICANN website (www.icann.org) for a list of ICANN accredited registrars and their web addresses, or, if you're interested in a name ending in .ca, the CIRA website (www.cira.ca) for a CIRA certified registrar. You can also arrange to buy a domain name through a web-hosting company or an Internet service provider that provides hosting services. The transaction is completed online and will include a search to ensure that the name you want is available to buy.

WARNING

When you buy a domain name, you're actually getting a subscription to use that name for a set period of time, usually from one to ten years. Your domain registrar will send you a reminder 30 to 45 days before the subscription runs out, but if you don't renew it within 60 days, the name may be released to the public.

TIP

Make sure that your domain registrar has your most up-to-date email contact address so that the renewal notice doesn't disappear into cyberspace.

Putting content on your website

After you have a domain name, you have to put some content at the web address — and that becomes your website.

Content

No matter what your business, every business website should contain certain things:

>> A description of your products and/or services, including your background and areas of expertise

>> Your hours of business and, if you have a physical business and want people to come to it in person, your location (including directions and a Google Map)

>> Contact information such as your address (you may want to include a Google Map with directions to your location), phone and fax numbers, and email address (or if not an email address, a contact form)

>> Information that new and existing customers will find useful and that adds value to your website and your business, such as

- Frequently asked questions about your business or service or products (and of course some intelligent answers)

- A blog (we give you more information about blogs later in this chapter)

- Informative and/or how-to articles

- Links to other helpful websites and to your Facebook and Twitter pages (we tell you a lot more about these later in this chapter, too)

>> A link to allow visitors to your website to sign up for your email newsletter (we give you more information about email newsletters later in this chapter)

>> A Terms of Use Agreement containing

- A website information disclaimer regarding the accuracy of the information contained on your site (see the sidebar about disclaimers)

- A copyright notice claiming copyright in the content of the website. In Canada, a copyright notice isn't actually necessary to obtain copyright protection, but it might make web surfers think twice before pilfering your frequently given answers and informative articles (see Chapter 3 for more about copyright)

- Your privacy policy, if your site collects any personal information from your customers (see Chapter 13)

- A hyperlink disclaimer, if your site contains links to other websites, stating that you don't guarantee or endorse the linked sites (see the sidebar "Sample disclaimers" for more about disclaimers)

If you sell goods or services on your website, your Terms of Use Agreement should set out the terms of your usual contract for the sale of goods or provision of services, as the case may be (see Chapter 13).

SAMPLE DISCLAIMERS

Here are two sample disclaimers. You can download these as Form 11-1 and Form 11-2 online. Turn to this book's Introduction to get instructions on how to access this free content.

Accuracy of content disclaimer

The website and all content are provided as is. By accessing and using the website you acknowledge and agree that use of the website and the content is entirely at your own risk. We make no representations or warranties regarding the website and the content, including, without limitation, no representation or warranty (1) that the website and/or content will be accurate, complete, reliable, suitable, or timely; (2) that any content, including, without limitation, any information, data, software, product, or service contained in or made available through the website will be of merchantable quality or fit for a particular purpose; (3) that the operation of the website will be uninterrupted or error free; (4) that defects or errors in the website will be corrected; (5) that the website will be free from viruses or harmful components; and (6) that communications to or from the website will be secure or not intercepted.

Design

After you know what you want to say on your website, make sure to say it. You may find the prospect of designing your own website a bit overwhelming, but getting help is easy. WYSIWYG (what you see is what you get) website creation software takes you through the process step-by-step without your having to know HTML coding. One example is WebPlus by Serif, which costs about US$100.

You can also find businesses that will help you design and set up a website. For a basic website, you can expect to pay from $500 to $1,500. Search the web to find a web designer whose portfolio (and price range) appeals to you, or get business acquaintances to recommend their website designers.

TIP

Many ISPs offer help with the entire process from domain name selection through web hosting (check out Hostpapa at www.hostpapa.ca) to website creation (which firms like GoDaddy Canada at http://ca.godaddy.com can help you with as well).

The design of your website should suit your business. If you're setting up an accounting firm, you want your site to look conservative to show you're responsible with other people's money. If you're running a rent-a-clown business, you might want to have a little more lively splash and colour. Whatever the look of your site, it should be

>> **Fast:** Your web pages should load quickly, so keep the bandwidth-hungry bells and whistles to a minimum.

>> **Legible:** Use easy-to-read fonts and make sure that your text and background are in contrasting colours. For example, don't use navy blue text on a black background, or pale pink text on a white background.

>> **Understandable:** Your written content should be clear and concise.

>> **Secure:** If your site collects any personal information from your customers, especially credit card information, your site must use technology that encrypts (or encodes) your customers' information. Secure Socket Layer (SSL) or Transport Layer Security (TLS) technology are the most commonly used. You must also comply with the privacy provisions of Canada's *Personal Information Protection and Electronic Documents Act* (PIPEDA). See Chapter 13 for more information about this very important piece of legislation you must know about.

Attracting visitors

Many of your potential customers will do a web search to find businesses that offer products or services such as yours. Make sure that your business will show up in the search results of the major search engines such as Google, Yahoo!, and Bing.

TIP

Getting your website listed with a search engine is only a start. You also want to try to get it ranked as highly as possible in the search engine results — this is called *search engine optimization*. Do this by identifying the keywords that people will most likely use in a web search for your type of business, and repeat those words frequently on your home page. You can also use a paid search engine optimization service such as Search Engine People (www.searchenginepeople.com) or AddMe (www.addme.com). We recommend you check out *Search Engine Optimization For Dummies* by Peter Kent (Wiley) for more.

You can list your website with individual search engines by going to the search engine's website. You will be asked to submit your URL — your domain name — and information about your business. If you don't want to do the work yourself, you can use a free submission service such as Add Me (www.addme.com).

Marketing with Email

Email is a very important business marketing tool. Email marketing, if done properly, helps you build strong relationships with your customers by staying in regular touch with them in a professional, cost-effective way.

An effective email strategy involves

>> Developing and maintaining a permission-based list of email subscribers

>> Maximizing the deliverability of your emails

>> Coming up with valuable content for your customers, so that they will keep opening your emails when they receive them, because after all, content really is king

TIP

Email marketing works best when used in combination with other marketing methods. As we tell you in the previous section, your website should encourage visitors to sign up for your emails. You can also use traditional marketing methods — such as signage or print advertising — to attract customers to your brick-and-mortar location; then collect email contact details from the customers who respond to your initial marketing, for example, by giving a free sample to a customer in return for his or her email address and information about his or her particular areas of interest in your product or service. Use this information to send an email newsletter to your contacts targeted to their interests.

Developing and maintaining a permission-based email list

You need a list of contacts and — more importantly — their email addresses so that you have somewhere to send your emails.

WARNING

In the United States, sending commercial email — email containing an advertisement, promotion, or content from a business's website — is illegal without permission. Canada's anti-spam legislation (CASL) came into effect in 2014 to protect Canadians while ensuring that businesses can continue to compete in the national and even global marketplace. For details about what businesses can and cannot do with spam check out the Government of Canada's website at `http://fightspam.gc.ca`. That means that every person on your email list must provide consent that you can send him or her emails. In addition, CASL and its consent requirement applies to emails, text, and instant messages, and any similar messages sent to electronic addresses. CASL does not apply to promotional information you post online in places like blogs or social media. If one of your email contacts asks to be removed from your email list, you must do so within ten days.

A permission-based email list is a good idea in any event, because you know that the people you email are interested in your business and want to hear from you.

You can collect contact information in a number of ways:

>> Include a sign-up link on your website, in your email signature, on your Facebook page, on your blog, and in any online advertising.

>> Collect email addresses at your place of business with a sign-up form or guest book or by requesting this information (and permission to send emails) from customers when they make purchases.

>> Include email sign-up information in your direct mail or print advertising.

TIP

You can try to collect not only email addresses, but information about your customers' particular areas of interest in your product or service. You can then use that information to create specialized contact lists based on their interests and send email messages targeted to those interests.

Maximizing deliverability of your emails

Your emails will not necessarily reach everyone on your contact list even though you send them only to contacts who have given you permission to email them.

>> **Your email may be returned because the contact's email address contains an error or has changed:** You can check the returned message for spelling errors, although most of the time you won't be able to tell whether the email address is misspelled or has simply changed. Try to keep up with email address changes by sending your contacts a subscription reminder every two or three months asking them to let you know if their email address changes.

>> **Your email may be blocked and returned by an email firewall:** An *email firewall* is software designed to return emails that appear untrustworthy. A potential solution is to ask your contacts to add your email address to their address book, contact list, or friends list when they sign up.

>> **Your email may be directed to a junk or spam folder by an email filter:** An *email filter* is software that scans the content of emails to look for unwanted content. The solution here is to draft your emails so that they don't look like spam. See the sidebar, "If it looks like spam and it quacks like spam . . .".

Even if your emails make it into your contact's inbox, you're not home free. Some of your contacts, even though they have given you permission to send emails, may still report your emails as spam to their ISPs. And, if too many of your emails are marked as spam, ISPs may block your email server from sending emails to any of their customers. To reduce spam complaints, try the following:

IF IT LOOKS LIKE SPAM AND IT QUACKS LIKE SPAM . . .

Spam filters — software that screens incoming emails and blocks unwanted emails from reaching the user's inbox — usually look for spam-like content. To keep your emails from looking like spam, try the following:

- Don't use your contact's first name in the subject line of your email.
- Always identify your business in the From line of the email; otherwise phishing (hacking) prevention software will kick your email into your recipient's spam folder.
- Don't use strings of exclamation points or dollar signs or other excessive punctuation.
- Don't send attachments.
- Don't write in all capital letters.

>> Make your email content valuable to your contacts so that they want to receive your emails. (See the section, "Creating an email newsletter," later in this chapter, for more.)

>> Make it easy for your contacts to identify the source of your emails by clearly identifying your business in your From line and by using your business logo.

>> Don't send out emails more often than is relevant and valuable to your contacts.

Creating an email newsletter

An email newsletter is a terrific way to keep in contact with your customers. Because email newsletters are less expensive to print and distribute than paper ones, you can send them out more frequently. In the previous two sections we tell you about getting your emails delivered. In this section we tell you how to make sure that people actually read your emails!

REMEMBER

The trick is to provide your contacts with relevant and valuable information, rather than simply a sales pitch, and to do so in a format that is eye-catching and consistent with your business's brand. (See Chapter 7 for tips about brand consistency.)

Your newsletter might pass on some of your own business or professional knowledge. For example:

>> A gift store can give Christmas gift-giving ideas.

>> A pet store can provide tips on protecting pets from the heat.

>> An accountant can discuss recent changes in tax legislation.

>> A real estate agent can give advice on making a house ready for sale.

You can also use content prepared by others, such as:

>> **Articles relevant to your area of business that you find on the web.** Summarize the article, say why you think it's interesting, and provide a link to it. (Be sure to check that the website's reprint policy allows linking.)

>> **Articles written by experts available for reprint without charge.** Check websites such as www.ezinearticles.com and www.ideamarketers.com. These articles must be reprinted in full and include the author's name. Check the terms of use on each site.

Make sure that your email contains design elements such as images, colours, borders, fonts, and effective layout. Also don't forget to add an email disclaimer. You can download this as Form 11-3 online. Turn to this book's Introduction to get instructions on how to access this free content.

Getting help

If all of this sounds like a lot of work, that's because it is! But professional help is available from email marketing service providers (ESPs) such as ConstantContact (www.constantcontact.com), AWeber (www.aweber.com), or MailChimp (www.mailchimp.com) who will, for a monthly fee, help you with the following:

>> Design your email newsletters using email templates

>> Create email content that helps you build your brand

>> Automate your email delivery

>> Create and manage a permission-based email list that includes an "unsubscribe" function or link to avoid alienating email readers

>> Improve your email deliverability effectiveness by adding subscribers 24/7

>> Track and analyze the performance of your email marketing communications

These services also provide advice and consulting, and their websites contain a lot of helpful information in the form of PDF documents and instructional videos.

For more detailed information on this topic, we recommend *E-Mail Marketing For Dummies* by John Arnold (published by Wiley).

Blogging

A *blog* is a continually updated news or content section of a website, with the most recent entry at the top of the page. A *blogger* is a person who maintains a blog, and *blogging* is the act of maintaining a blog. Search engines love blogs because they're updated regularly and often delve into a variety of topics readily caught by these search tools. It makes sense to consider them to help you tell your business story.

Blogging begins with a sound strategy. Possessing and executing a good blogging strategy means developing a company blog policy, selecting a blog platform and bloggers, allocating time, using compelling content that drives search engine traffic to you, promoting your blog, and measuring your success. Next, we further highlight why you should blog and we provide some suggestions about content.

TIP

We can only begin to touch on the subject of blogging in this chapter. For more information on the subject, we recommend *Corporate Blogging For Dummies* by Douglas Karr and Chantelle Flannery (published by Wiley).

Understanding the importance of blogging

The content of your blog can provide potential customers and clients with information about you and your product and service and help to demonstrate your knowledge and expertise in your field.

Having a blog on your website will increase traffic to your site. A blog also helps you convert that traffic into leads. Blogs help you become an authority in your business field, and also drive results over the long term. In other words, any quality effort put into blogging yesterday can turn into many ongoing leads in the future. Finally, many studies show that small businesses that blogged consistently received many more visitors to their websites than businesses that did not blog.

Each time you post an entry in your blog, you're adding a new page to your website, thereby increasing your web presence and helping your search engine optimization (particularly if you write your blog entries with *keywords* — words that search tools really love — in mind). Finally, because a blog is regularly updated with new content, it gives your website visitors a reason to come back to your site. And the more contact you have with consumers, the more likely they are to buy your product or use your service. This is the essence of customer engagement, and blogs promote engagement.

Adding a blog to your website

You need two things to begin your blog: a place on the Internet to put your blog and software that can run a blog. If you already have a website, you have the place, as long as your web host meets the minimum technical requirements of your software.

Two of the top blogging software packages are WordPress and TypePad. WordPress is free open-source blogging software available for download from `http://en-ca.wordpress.org/download`. TypePad is available at a monthly cost of between US$9 and US$50 per month, depending on the features you choose. A free 14-day trial is available on TypePad's website at `www.typepad.com`. Your web host may offer a set-up guide for adding a blog to your website that will automatically install WordPress for you.

Putting content on your blog

Your blog should have a theme or focus. Think about who your audience will be and what information they will find useful and interesting. Don't use your blog to make a sales pitch — a blog is far more valuable for demonstrating your business's insight and expertise. For some advice on topics and sources of material for your blog, have a look at what we tell you about content for your email newsletter earlier in this chapter under the section "Creating an email newsletter."

Whatever you choose to write about, keep in mind that you'll have to update your content regularly, so write about things that you know about and that you find interesting.

WARNING

Decide whether or not you want to allow readers to post their comments on your blog. Keep in mind that the comments will not all be flattering or constructive. If you do allow comments on your blog, you will have to monitor the comments regularly and respond to them as appropriate.

Using Social Media to Market Your Business

The term *social media* is used to describe online media that allows readers or viewers to participate in the creation or development of the content — in contrast with traditional media, which merely delivers content. Traffic on social networking sites such as Facebook, Twitter, and LinkedIn has grown dramatically over the last decade. A Pew Internet report called "Global Digital Report 2018" found that at the end of that year, the number of Internet users worldwide was 4.021 billion, up 7 percent year over year, and that the number of social media users worldwide in the same year was 3.196 billion, up an even greater 13 percent year over year and accounting for a huge share of Internet usage. This was in large part empowered by the 5.1 billion mobile phone users who drove much of the overall Internet and social media traffic.

Given this increased traffic, should you be using social media to market your business? Proponents of social media marketing say yes. Some studies suggest that consumers are more likely to buy from businesses they come into contact with through social networking sites.

On the other hand, opposing studies suggest that social media are not as highly effective as marketing tools as many people may think. Detractors blame the influx of fake news and *trolls* (crusty people who only post negative comments) over the last few years. Many entrepreneurs surveyed in these studies found that social media marketing required more effort than they anticipated.

In the following sections, we tell you a bit about some of the top social networking sites, to help you decide whether social media marketing is for you. If you're truly interested in this topic, check out *Social Media Marketing For Dummies*, by Shiv Singh and Stephanie Diamond (Wiley).

Getting to know the major social media sites

In 2019, the top three social networking sites in the United States and Canada were Facebook, Twitter, and LinkedIn, according to Small Business TRENDS (`www.smallbiztrends.com`) as well as many other Internet analytics companies. You probably don't have to time to participate in all of them, and even the most ardent supporters of social media marketing recommend that you limit yourself to two or three sites — but which ones? You want to use the sites your customers use, so ask your customers which social media sites they frequent and join those.

In this section, we look at the major social media sites that will be the most useful to you as a small business owner.

Facebook

Founded in 2004, Facebook has more than 1.5 billion monthly active users. This makes it one of the best forums for connecting people with your business. Start using Facebook by creating a Fan Page for your business. Unlike a personal Facebook profile, fan pages can be seen by everybody on the Internet. You can do this free of charge by going to www.facebook.com. Facebook's extensive Help Center (www.facebook.com/help) provides general information about using Facebook and as well as information about business solutions.

Any Facebook user who visits your Fan Page will see the information you post. Facebook users can choose to become fans of your page by clicking the "Like" button on your page. Then, any time you post content on your Fan Page, the content will also show up on your fans' pages, where, in turn, their Facebook friends will see it.

TIP

Encourage customers, clients, and colleagues — even family and friends — to become fans of your page. You should also promote your page on your website, in your email newsletters, and on your print materials.

After you have your page, you can use it to post information, photos, and videos, as well as links to other websites. Like your blog, your Facebook page requires new content on an ongoing basis.

TIP

For some ideas on content, search on Facebook for the Fan Pages of your competitors and have a look at them to see what they're doing. For more advice on topics and sources of material for your Facebook page, check out the section "Creating an email newsletter," earlier in this chapter.

Unlike a blog, where you have the choice of whether or not to allow comments by your readers, the essence of Facebook is community and participation. So at least some of your posts should encourage discussion among your fans.

REMEMBER

A Facebook page is an ongoing commitment. You have to monitor the discussions and come up with new content on a regular basis.

For more information about using Facebook, check out *Facebook Marketing For Dummies* by Stephanie Diamond and John Haydon (Wiley).

Twitter

Twitter was founded in 2006 and has more than 320 million active monthly users. Many users use the 280-character limit to pass on information. Businesses can use Twitter to interact with potential clients, answer customer questions, release the latest product news, and use targeted advertising with specific audiences.

As you likely already know, Twitter is a micro-blog platform that allows its members to post short messages — *Tweets* — containing no more than 280 characters. As long as a member's Twitter account is set to public status, anyone, member or non-member, can view that person's Twitter page. Members can choose to "follow" other members on Twitter. Whenever a member posts on Twitter, his or her Tweets automatically go out to all of his or her followers.

You can sign up for a Twitter account free of charge at twitter.com. Be sure to sign up in the name of your business. After you sign up, visit the Help Centre and have a look at the Twitter Basics section. Search to see if your competitors have Twitter accounts, and if so, check to see how they're using Twitter in their businesses. Do this by using the Find People link on your home page. Twitter also has a search function (`http://search.twitter.com`) that you can use to search your business name to see if you appear in anyone's Tweets. And if so, you should consider responding. Do this by starting your Tweet with the person's username preceded by the @ symbol.

Encourage your customers, clients, colleagues, family, and friends to follow you on Twitter. Promote your Twitter account on your website, in your email newsletters, and in any of your printed materials.

What will you Tweet about? You can, for example, Tweet

>> Links to stories about your business

>> That you've updated your blog, and provide a link to your blog

>> About sales, events, or loyalty programs

REMEMBER

Remember to check your Twitter account regularly to see if your customers or clients have Tweeted you. If they have, be sure to respond.

TIP

Twitter can also be a great tool for finding potential customers. Use the Twitter search function (`http://search.twitter.com`) to search keywords that describe your product or search. Perhaps someone out there is looking for the very product or service you have to offer!

For more information about Twitter, we recommend *Twitter Marketing For Dummies* by Kyle Lacy (published by Wiley).

LinkedIn

Launched in 2003, LinkedIn is the most popular social media site for professional individual networking. The website is available in more than 25 languages and has well over 400 million registered users. LinkedIn is ideal for people looking to connect with other people in the same industries or sectors, networking with local professionals, and displaying business-related information and statistics. LinkedIn is more business-oriented than most other social networking sites. LinkedIn's motto is "Relationships Matter" and its stated mission is "to connect the world's professionals to make them more productive and successful."

Join LinkedIn for free at www.linkedin.com. A Learning Center is available (http://learn.linkedin.com) where you can find a link to a New User Guide, and the Customer Support Center (www.linkedin.com/help) provides answers to frequently asked questions.

You can join LinkedIn as an individual and create a profile summarizing your own accomplishments and areas of expertise. As a member, you can then develop and maintain a list of people you know and trust in business — called "connections." LinkedIn members can connect only through "invitations." You have to invite the other person, who must then accept the invitation. If the person you invite to connect is not already on LinkedIn, he or she will have to join in order to accept your invitation.

Your business can also have its own profile. After you establish a business profile, people searching for businesses in specific fields can find it. You can ask other members to give you a "recommendation" that you can include in your profile.

TIP

After you join LinkedIn, search for customers and suppliers and connect with them. You should also search for your competitors to see if and how they're using the service. And search to see if any "groups" — smaller networks based on type of connection or area of interest — exist that are relevant to your business and expertise, and ask to join. You can then participate in the groups' discussions and demonstrate your knowledge and expertise to other group members.

For more information about LinkedIn, check out *LinkedIn For Dummies* by Joel Elad (Wiley).

Telling your business story with Instagram

In this section, we tell you about Instagram, a Facebook-owned company. Hundreds of millions of people are using Instagram, so for that reason, as well as the reality that a picture really is worth a thousand words, you should consider leveraging this unique platform for your business. Instagram is suited for any size of business, and it can make your business come to life in the minds and eyes of potential and existing customers. Like Twitter and Facebook, you can partner with influencers and use creative hashtags that can increase your visibility and better engage with customers and clients. Instagram is ideally suited to mobile devices, so that makes it a particularly stable and convenient platform to use in business. In the following sections, we highlight some of the more important aspects of Instagram that you need to be mindful of. We begin with the obvious: the setup.

Setting up an Instagram account

When you've decided to use Instagram, and as you begin to set up an Instagram for Business account, make sure that your username on Instagram matches the username of your other business social media profiles. It sounds obvious, but many businesses fail to do this and miss out on the ability to *go viral* (have a friend tell another friend about your product, service, or idea, and so on). Aside from this element, the only other information that appears on your public Instagram profile is your website address — which you can readily update to promote campaigns or new pieces of content on a new page — and a short bio.

TIP

Instagram is all about images and image, so your Instagram profile photo should be your company's business logo to make it more discoverable. Discoverability is also enhanced because people who follow you on Twitter or Facebook will more readily recognize your brand.

After you've set things up, kick off your Instagram presence by following a bunch of users. Think about customers, significant influencers in your industry sector, and other people in the ecosystem of your business. Add your Instagram handle to your website, as well as other social media profiles for cross-promotion.

Aligning Instagram content with your business strategy

Your marketing and communication strategy, to the extent that it's also using Instagram, should address what your business hopes to achieve by using Instagram. For example, a new business will want to efficiently and economically attract customers and build brand awareness and value, resulting in increased sales and raw traffic to your website. Instagram is well suited to enhancing this type of initial and ongoing engagement. It can help you generate these and other attractive business outcomes.

Developing a content strategy

Your marketing and communication strategy should be underpinned by pictorial content that makes sense. Wedding photos may be perfect for a post that stays posted for, say, a decade! But for a fast-moving and ever-changing business, you need to constantly refresh your images. Ideally, a posting schedule that makes the most sense is one that considers variety and freshness but stays clear of daily carpet bombings of your followers with endless images.

Be sure to keep your content style consistent as you proceed with updated posts and even a variety of business themes. However, as much as possible use the same colour filter or hue for every post in order to create a unique style that will be recognized by your followers. Be careful how and when your business engages on Instagram with other accounts on Instagram — this includes everything from liking and commenting on other people's photos to professionally and personally dealing with the incoming comments on your own account. Also, consider the best way to use nonvisual text elements within your Instagram posts. For example, it's best to use common language or style for captions, and a brand-oriented hashtag descriptive of your business.

TIP

Check out mobile photo-editing apps like Enhance or VSCO for filtering and editing your images and importing them into Instagram.

Getting creative

A golden rule of marketing is to grab some positive attention. One way to do this is to combine a reasonably sized and mixed collection of photos and videos (Instagram currently allows up to ten per post). Remember that captions are critical — they present an excellent opportunity for you to tell a story about your business. Captions let you expand on the image and give it some context. Also, Instagram Stories, a feature on Instagram where you can capture and post related images and videos in a slideshow format along with text and drawings, has more than 240 million average daily users. Need we say more? It can pay to get to know Instagram's extra features.

Getting even more fancy and technical

Instagram has recently launched special tools for business users. These tools include new business profiles, analytics, and the ability to create ads from posts directly within the Instagram app.

If you have a business profile you can choose how you want your customers get in touch with you. They can call, email, or text your business with a tap of a contact button, and they can get directions to your location as well.

Insights on Instagram is a feature that provides businesses with useful information about who their followers are and which posts are more effective than others. This feature lets you identify top posts, reach, and the extent of user engagement around posts, as well as privacy-respecting data on your followers like gender, age, and location. Learning about the behaviour and demographics of your target market is always a good idea. Instagram also lets you convert well-performing posts into ads right within the Instagram app. To create and run an ad, you'll be able to identify your most popular and existing posts on Instagram and then add a button or icon to encourage potential customers to take action.

TIP

If you want to get into more gory detail about using the Instagram app, growing your target audience, and boosting your brand with creative stories, pictures, and even live video, check out *Instagram For Business For Dummies* by Jenn Herman, Eric Butow, and Corey Walker (Wiley).

Managing your social media marketing time

So now you're pumped and ready to use social media to market your business and you've decided to use Facebook, Twitter, LinkedIn, and Instagram. Hmmm. How long will this all take? Log in and post on Facebook. Log in and post on Twitter. Log in and post on LinkedIn. Assuming you're also maintaining a blog on your website and creating and distributing email newsletters, how will you have any time to carry on your business — even if you recycle your content? Help is available. Check out HootSuite, a for-fee service (available at www.hootsuite.com). It supports anywhere from 10 to 35 social media profiles. A final point about social media is that you don't need to leverage this marketing and outreach channel if your existing or potential customers don't use social media. However, trends are definitely in your favour if you do leverage it because more and more Canadian small businesses and individuals are jumping on this online bandwagon.

Monitoring the Web

The final piece (and yes, we promise it is the final piece) in establishing a web presence is to monitor any mention of your business on the web. You need to know what is being said about your business and you need to respond as appropriate. Track any mention of your business's name by

» Signing up for Google Alerts (at www.google.com/alerts) to receive email updates of the latest relevant Google results (web, news, blogs, and so on) based on your choice of query or topic

» Searching Twitter, from your Twitter home page, if you're logged in, or at http://search.twitter.com

>> Searching Facebook by using the Search bar at the top any Facebook page, and then clicking on "Posts by Everyone"

You should also become familiar with any websites that review businesses like yours in your area. Search on Google, Yahoo!, or Bing for your business category, reviews, and your city.

Now Get Out There and Sell!

As a result of all your marketing efforts, you've attracted a potential customer or client who wants to know more about your product or service. (It's pleasant but a little unusual for someone just to walk in to your premises or call you up and say, "Gimme a dozen of those, here's my cash.") How do you get from the enquiry to the sale?

TIP

Here are some tips for landing your customer or client:

>> **Know your product or service inside out.** And make sure your associates or employees do, too, so that all of you can answer any question about it, such as the following:

- What is it?

- How much does it cost?

- What if I buy it and it doesn't work? (What support do you provide, and what warranties or guarantees are provided?)

- What do you know about it? (That is, what expertise does your business have?)

- Does anybody else like it? (Can you provide references from people who've dealt with you?)

- How will you get it to me, and when? (What's your delivery method and timing?)

>> **Know the customer or client.** This may mean doing some research (for example, on a potential business customer's website) and/or simply listening to the customer you're dealing with to find out what he or she really wants (or needs — the two may be different). So don't spend your precious customer contact time doing all the talking. You won't learn anything about the customer with your mouth open and your ears shut.

You also have to figure out your potential customer or client's business style and needs so that you can adapt to meet it. For example, you'll know more about how to keep the potential customer interested in buying if you can find out whether the customer

- Is most interested in low price or high quality or reliability or speed . . . or (commonly but unrealistically) in all four

- Wants to close a deal quickly or needs time to think privately and consult with others

- Wants a prepackaged product or wants to pick and choose the components

- Prefers you to take charge or simply wants you as support for his or her own decision

» **Make a presentation geared toward the potential customer's needs and business style.** This doesn't have to be a massive undertaking — and it can start as simply as, "May I show you our product/tell you about our service?"

» **Make a proposal for a deal that you think will suit the potential customer.** For example, "Would you like to buy one of these to try?" If the potential customer starts to wiggle and squirm, he or she may not be really interested right now, or maybe you need to go back to point two: Know the customer or client.

» **Close the deal if the customer is willing.** Closing may take a few tries, even with an interested customer.

» **Keep the door open if the closing doesn't happen.** Suggest reasons for you to contact the potential customer within a short time. ("Shall I find out if we can order it in another colour, and call you?" "Shall I call you on Tuesday to see if we can arrange another meeting?")

» **Get feedback — from customers who close and from customers who don't.** You don't need to do much work to give people the chance to tell you if they're unhappy. (If you have a website and contact email, encourage users to let you know what they think about your business.)

» **Act on the feedback.** Unless it seems totally loony.

3

Operating Your Small Business

Chapter **12**

Managing Risk

Any business can be a risky business. Although you may have a risk-taking personality and an instinct to seize a small business opportunity (you wouldn't be going into business for yourself if you didn't), you don't want your business to run any risks that aren't identified, evaluated, and managed well. You do want to run your small business in a risk-aware way. In this chapter, we show you how.

A good place to start is to first define what we mean by risk. The technical version reads something like "risk is the effect of uncertainty on objectives." That's a bit boring, and we wouldn't be writing a *For Dummies* book if we didn't break things down a bit in a way that sane people can relate to. To that effect, think of risk as a two-sided coin. The first side defines risk as something that stands in the way of a business objective. This objective or goal can be your strategic plan, desired profit, and or sales volume target. The other side of the coin defines risk as an objective that is not seized when the available indicators point to a truly compelling opportunity. Apple seized an opportunity to build super-cool and multifunctional smartphones that were inspired by early-day cellphones and pagers — the same kind of pagers and cellphones developed by a company that used to be called Research in Motion and is now called BlackBerry. The big difference is that Research in Motion failed to seize an opportunity to innovate — a deadly mistake when operating in the world of high technology. The folks at BlackBerry are still busy wiping away their tears to this day.

You would be correct to think that steering clear of risks seems to be counterintuitive to the fact that you're considering seizing an opportunity, which essentially means you're a risk taker. But the reason the two are *not* mutually exclusive is because all we ask is that if you do seize the opportunity, you do so in a risk-aware way. This means being aware of the brand-new set of risks you'll face when you start a small business and, therefore, seize an opportunity. So don't ignore risks. We dedicate this chapter to showing you how not to ignore them!

Risk awareness, to be clear, means actively managing risks you identified as being inherent in and pertinent to your business, assessing their likelihood and impact, finding ways to *mitigate* (reduce, eliminate, or transfer) those risks, and seeing if the *residual risk* left over (risk after mitigations are considered) is acceptable to your personal tolerance or appetite for risk. To be sure, this is extra work, just as many aspects of running your own business involve extra effort. But rest assured that most businesses that fail do so because of significant risks that were not identified and managed, and this oversight resulted in severe or catastrophic outcomes. We're talking bankruptcy and insolvency here. Ouch. So if you want to stay out of trouble's way, engage in and take very seriously this discipline that almost all successful businesses perform: *risk management.*

To recap and simplify, risk management is a process that involves the following:

>> Figuring out what kind of trouble your business can run into by identifying what can go wrong

>> Deciding how serious the risks are (both how frequently a risk may occur and how severe the damage would be if the risk materializes) to determine how bad it can get

>> Making your risks as small as possible and figuring out what you can do about it

A useful acronym is RIM, short for "risk, impact, and mitigation," which answers the questions "What can go wrong?" "How bad can it get?" and "What are we doing about it?"

What Kind of Risks Does a Business Face?

Operating a small business is no bed of roses. Your business might encounter a lot of risks, which fall broadly into several fundamental categories and subcategories.

Strategic risk

The main and initial risk you face when you start a small business is *strategic risk.* Strategic risk includes selecting a business strategy that won't work in the current economic, competitive, or demographic environment. It also represents your inability to execute your strategy and/or an inability to implement your strategy in a timely way. Getting this risk wrong by failing to manage strategic design, execution, timing, and monitoring means that your business will not perform as well as it could have, and at worst it can threaten the ability of your small business to continue as a going concern.

You can manage strategic risk by mitigating it. For all risks, *mitigation* means developing plans and taking actions to reduce threats and unwanted outcomes that adversely impact business objectives. It also means finding ways to enhance opportunities that help your objectives. Recall the two-sided "risk versus opportunity" coin we mention earlier. One example of a way to mitigate strategic risk is to identify the key drivers that provide you with a competitive advantage. Examples of drivers include your expertise and reputation. Rank the drivers you identify in order of priority. Usually there are a handful of critical drivers that, if not managed, executed, or leveraged well, can result in business failure. For example, if you're running a technology-oriented company, then staying up-to-date with technology trends, and perhaps even leading the charge on those trends, will help you to sustain your competitive advantage and minimize strategy execution risk.

WARNING

Managing strategic risk is more difficult than other risks because other risks have the benefit of standards against which to be measured. On the other hand, there are no real standards or basic qualifications that are required to develop strategy. Evaluating a good strategy versus a poor one is not an easy thing to do until you actually experience the execution of the strategy. Many strategies are also backed by very few facts and mostly unsubstantiated data. This is true for most companies, so don't feel bad if you don't think you got the strategic risk management thing right!

Starting and running a small business is full of uncertainty, but it can also be exhilarating and exciting. All we say to you again is to run your business in a risk-aware way! *Remember:* Strategy is the compass by which your ship will sail. Navigate it with eyes wide open.

Growth and expansion risks

In Chapter 18, we give you some pointers on what to do when your business is growing. Business growth may include, among other scenarios, buying another small business to merge with your own business. If you're facing and enjoying rapid business growth, be aware of certain risks pertinent to this.

The main risk associated with buying or merging with another small business is if the other business you transacted with fails to meet your expectations and does not create the value you thought it would. Acquisitions are always risky because they are inherently complex and uncertain and have a lot of integrated and fast-moving parts.

Growth and expansion risks also present a different face if, for instance, the new business that you just acquired does not align with your small business's overall strategy. Yet another face appears if you didn't do your proper due diligence, or if there are differences in corporate culture or leadership styles in a company you acquired. Other aspects of this risk include overvaluation of the business you acquired or financing that is costlier than you expected.

TIP

To mitigate business expansion-related risk, do your homework before transacting. Tour the facilities and meet with staff and management of the small business. Ask for certified (audited) financial statements and seek the advice of a Chartered Business Valuator. In Chapter 2, we point you to the types of professionals who can help you out here.

Financial risk

Financial risk is an umbrella term covering a range of risks, from the liquidity aspect of financing to availability of capital to the nature of the *capital structure* (mix of debt and equity capital you and others contributed) of your small business.

Liquidity risk is one aspect or subset of financial risk. It refers to a company's ability to generate enough internal cash flow of its own to keep operations going. Problems of liquidity usually occur when your small business has sustained ongoing losses, when you're undergoing a major purchase, or when you face unexpected expenses that may not be insured and are now required.

A risk that is also related is the availability of capital. Small businesses typically seek debt financing at the outset, often right after the business owner injects his or her personal capital into the business. In the case of really large companies, the issuance of share capital is how money is primarily raised. Your access to debt or equity capital may be restricted from time to time or be outright unavailable. A catch-22 situation to keep in mind is that sometimes, later on, money is not easily available when difficult economic times arise, and that is exactly the time when many small businesses require money most.

The way your capital is structured also poses risks. For instance, if your small business has a large amount of debt, that alone can create a going concern. If your business is highly underpinned by debt, any mismatch of short- and long-term debt with ability to repay, perhaps combined with poor sequencing and timing of payments and/or a large amount of repayment, can also severely complicate things for you and your small business.

Foreign exchange risk is yet another subset of financial risk. It occurs when your small business buys or sells goods to other countries, resulting in foreign exchange losses. On the flip side, you can also view this as an opportunity to make foreign exchange gains!

In addition, the movement of interest rates in the wrong direction will also hurt your business financially, especially when your debt load is high and loans come due for renewal. As with foreign exchange, the reverse is also true.

TIP

The best way to manage these subsets of financial risk is to make sure that your bank is providing you with the best possible advisory service and products. Also, keep your eye on the financial news to see how the economy is doing and which way interest rates are going.

Organizational risk

Organizational risk includes things like management leadership; quality of key staff, supervisors, and managers; your ability to retain good staff; running your organization with an eye on value for money; and the "corporate" culture within your small business.

With a small business, you're likely the leader. However, you'll likely have other staff members to whom you delegate the authority to make important decisions. Failure to delegate authority to the right people and right levels poses a big risk. The risk of underperformance of your senior or key staff is best managed by making the right hiring decisions and making sure that your key staff are qualified. Check references and speak with past employers. Failure to manage this risk can do a lot of damage. You and your most trusted staff and leadership team have to be able to execute the strategy that you've developed. This is true whether your small business can afford only one senior staff member whom you trust to make decisions when you're away or you've hired a whole team of people.

You can mitigate organizational risk by watching for high voluntary turnover or other unusual patterns that may be indicators of a bigger organizational problem. Keep pace with the changing requirements of attracting, managing, rewarding, and retaining the best performers and leaders. Know what the leading human resource practices are. Have a succession plan in place, and make sure that poor performers are performance-managed appropriately and quickly. These universal concepts apply to any size of business, big or small!

Operational risk

Operational risks come in a wide variety of flavours or subsets. But three common subsets are people, processes, and technology. Having the wrong people can result in failure to have the best quality of the product or service your small business offers. An example of process risk that impacts operational effectiveness is where demand is high but you may not have the capacity to meet that demand. Process risks include business continuity issues like information technology failures, disruptions in electricity, or damage to buildings, all of which can cause operations to be disrupted. Economic dependence on one customer or reliance on one supplier is also an operational risk. Operational risk usually has more to do with failure to execute as opposed to the selection of a bad strategy. We examine these kinds of operational risks in more detail in the sections that follow.

People

You have to have the right front-line employees in place with the skills you need to compete, innovate, or grow. It's no wonder that for most small businesses, finding the right front-line people is a key success factor. If you don't provide interesting work, young employees will leave for a better opportunity the first chance they get. If you utilize an older workforce for front-line or clerical positions in your small business, just keep in mind that Canada has an aging workforce, so the pickings may be slim.

To mitigate the risk of not having the right people (skilled and motivated) in the right positions at the right time (by finding the sweet spot between overstaffing and understaffing), perform some serious workforce planning. If your business is really small, such planning is minimal. But as you grow, you need to take planning seriously and do the following:

» Create job specifications and compensate staff appropriately, taking into account labour supply and the skills required for a position.

» Create a basic code of conduct to deal with the risk of unethical behaviour that can damage your ability to attract customers or even new employees.

» Align your hiring with your business strategy and annual business plan and take into account the time it takes to train new staff.

» If your small business is big enough to afford one, hire a staff member that has experience with human resource matters. That will help you deal with other business matters and not leave all human resource duties to you.

Processes and business resilience

Errors or oversights caused by staff can result in inferior or failed processes. For example, if a stock clerk incorrectly enters an order from your customer, the order may be filled at the wrong price or quantity, potentially resulting in a significant loss if not caught later in the sales process. You can reduce the risk of human error by designing processes that are human-friendly and are underpinned by process maps or manuals. Breakdowns of equipment or computer devices can also disrupt processes such as manufacturing or supply chain operations.

Business continuity risks are present for all businesses, big or small. This is a risk area that needs to be planned for. Property and infrastructure outages such as failure of basic communication channels can trigger process failures. In many cases, it's the poor quality of a process itself that can lead to failure. For example, a customer service process may work under normal conditions, but it may crash and burn when sales enquiries and sales volumes spike. You can mitigate this risk by identifying the business continuity risks such as power outages, IT network disruptions, fires, floods, and so on. Identify your critical processes — the ones you need up and running fastest — and create a basic *business continuity plan* (the documented steps by which you will re-establish the critical processes) and consider the plan's reasonability in your mind. If you want, it's always a good idea to test it.

Technology

In the past, cyber or data breaches were typically things that only very large businesses had to worry about. Not anymore. Some of the most valuable intellectual property resides in small businesses. Is the success of your business based on information like a client list with sensitive personal information, or a secret recipe that you don't want other restaurant or cannabusiness competitors to know? If so, you need to protect it.

The risk of technology errors or data security breaches can halt operations — big or small — instantly. A breach can mean many things, but it's essentially the intentional or unintentional release of secure or private and confidential business or personal information or intellectual property into an untrusted environment. In plain and simple terms, someone stole your stuff! This risk is often caused by vulnerabilities in third-party or in-house processes or controls, or the theft or loss of computing equipment. Mitigate these risks by using common sense. This includes everything from using secure passwords and offsite backups of key documents, all the way up to hiring an IT security expert if your business is technology heavy and has lots of intellectual property.

External risk

An *external risk* is something that cannot be controlled by you or your small business. Examples include floods, fires, earthquakes, pandemics, environmental hazards like pollution, vandalism, and even terrorism. We discuss some of these in the "Processes and business resilience" section, earlier in this chapter, where we explain that the best way to manage these uncontrollable risks is to watch out for them and plan ahead with a basic business continuity plan.

Other types of uncontrollable external risks do not necessarily disrupt your business but instead impair it over a longer period of time. A big example is the risk of unfavourable macro-economic changes. Economic downturns are always difficult to anticipate. When they do occur, they tend to hit small businesses faster and harder than larger businesses. That's because most small businesses are not as well capitalized to withstand a long downturn.

TIP

Be watchful of the economy. You can plan by making sure that your small business can withstand a downturn by avoiding too much debt, keeping your workforce lean, and keeping an eye on sales volume and revenue. Your small business will likely work in a defined industry, so watch for the cyclicality of the industry. Sometimes the structure of the industry will change, so keep watch over that as well. Examples include automation, foreign involvement in the industry, offshoring of production, changes in the nature and extent of research and development, the use of technology, and competition.

Reputational risk

Reputation can take years to build but minutes to impair. Manage this risk well. It seems hardly a day goes by without another company or individual with a high public profile hitting the headlines for all the wrong reasons. Your business needs to nurture a culture where ethical behaviour is expected and doing the right thing is paramount. Any reputational damage could not only harm your sales but also negatively impact your ability to recruit and retain top talent. Start with a basic employee manual that includes a code of conduct, and keep a constant eye out for any unusual patterns that may indicate an ethical breach. It's worth noting that reputational risk is not so much a risk as it is an outcome of other risks having turned into issues that need to be managed. For example, if your business manages organizational risks poorly because you hire the wrong people, you may have adverse reputational outcomes when word of this gets out to your customer base.

Recognizing the Risk of Not Seizing Opportunities

Risks and rewards are two sides of the same coin. Generally speaking, the higher the risks, the higher the rewards. For your neighbour, a situation may appear to be posing more risks than the rewards, while for you, the reverse is likely true simply by virtue of the fact that you're reading a book about small business!

Assessment of risk and opportunities is, at the end of the day, a rational process that plays out in everyone's mind differently, depending on personality attributes and the context that a risk or opportunity operates in.

REMEMBER

Stay open to new ideas, adapt to new situations, learn from the experiences of others, and see if the opportunity is worth the risk. Just remember that when you seize an opportunity, it creates a whole new set of negative risks as well. When Apple seized the smartphone innovation opportunity that Research in Motion failed to seize, it faced supply risk, financial risk, and the risk that the market would not be responsive. We all know how well that story ended (for Apple, at least)!

Paying Extra Attention to Legal and Regulatory Risks

The risks that your small business will face don't end with the ones we note earlier in this chapter. Other very important risks you will need to manage include the fact that:

>> Your business may cause injury to others.

>> Your business itself may be injured.

>> You and your business associates and employees may be injured.

TIP

You need to review your business (or business-to-be) to identify all your risks and then decide which ones you need to guard against. Some risks involve a small amount of damage but are likely to occur frequently, so worrying about them is worthwhile. (For example, shoplifting and pilferage if you run a retail business. Even though each incident might not involve a significant financial loss to your business, the total loss can be significant over time.) Some risks involve a lot of damage and are reasonably likely to occur (earthquakes on the West Coast) — worrying about those risks is also worthwhile. Some risks involve a large amount of damage but are unlikely to occur (for example, earthquakes in most parts of Canada), so don't worry too much about those risks.

Injury to others

WARNING

If your business causes injury to someone outside the business (the injury could be physical harm, damage to property, or damage to financial interests), your business is exposed to a lawsuit. Most lawsuits claim money damages to compensate the injured person or business. If your business loses the lawsuit and is ordered by a court to pay a large amount of money, you could end up losing your business — and if you're a sole proprietor or partner, you could end up losing your personal property as well, because the law doesn't distinguish between you personally and your business (see Chapter 6). Here are the main ways a business can harm others. Your business could

>> Harm customers or clients or suppliers or even total strangers (and their property) by causing them to have an accident on your business premises (this is an area of law called *occupier's liability*). For example, a customer might fall while inside your store, or a passing pedestrian might be knocked over by your outdoor signboard on a windy day.

>> Harm customers or clients because you or a person associated with your business gives careless advice or uses poor judgment in carrying out a business action (this is an area of law called *negligence*). For example, you or an employee might cause a motor vehicle accident while on delivery, your business might manufacture a product that is defective (such as food that makes someone sick), or you or an employee might recommend the wrong product for a customer's needs.

>> Harm customers or clients or suppliers or passing strangers through a deliberate wrongful act (this could be either a civil wrong, called a *tort*, or a *crime* — or it could be both). For example, an employee might steal from a client, or you or an employee might detain a person you incorrectly believe had shoplifted.

>> Harm customers or clients or suppliers because your business fails to fulfill all its promises under a contract. For example, your business might not deliver a promised product to a customer on time, or might refuse to accept a product ordered from a supplier.

Injury to your business

Your troubles may not involve injury to an outsider but injury to your business itself. Here are the usual ways your business can be harmed:

>> Business premises can be damaged by fire, flood, windstorm, and other natural and unnatural disasters.

>> Property belonging to the business (office equipment, inventory, and so on) can be lost in the same sort of disaster that damages the premises. Or it can be stolen . . . or just mysteriously vanish.

>> Records and valuable information can be lost, especially electronic records when a computer breakdown or hacking occurs.

>> Accounts receivable (money owed to you by customers and clients) may not be paid, and you can't get anything even if you sue because the client or customer has gone bankrupt or disappeared.

>> Business activities may be interrupted because of

- Damage to your own premises or equipment (such as computer failure, loss of power or heat, fire or flood)

- Damage to neighbouring premises (such as fire in another tenant's office or store that leads to the building being closed for days or weeks)

- Outside activities (such as the municipality tearing up the street outside your store, or a bomb threat leading to evacuation of your entire office building)

>> The business may lose important personnel because of ill health or accident or death.

Injury to you and your business associates

In a small business, no one's expendable. Especially you. If you're injured or become ill, who's going to run the business to earn income for you? And what if you're sued personally for giving bad advice or making careless decisions? This can happen if you're a professional who is either a sole proprietor of a business or a partner in a business, or if you're a director or officer of a corporation. And don't forget your employees. What if they're injured on the job?

Minimizing Your Legal, Regulatory, and Similar Risks

You can't make all legal, regulatory, and similar risks associated with your business vanish, but you can try to cut them down to size.

Injury to others due to safety, legal, and contractual issues

To avoid lawsuits against your business by people or other businesses that have been injured . . . don't let anyone get injured in the first place! That's not as tall an order as it sounds. You can take sensible precautions so that your business doesn't pose too much (unintended) danger to others.

Preventing physical injuries and damage

WARNING

If you own or lease business premises, take a tour of them and look for problem areas. Here are some of the most common problems and some suggestions for avoiding them.

To prevent slip-and-fall or trip-and-fall incidents:

>> Clean up spills of any kind as soon as you discover them.

>> Regularly check for and mop up water and slush that accumulates inside entrances when it's raining or snowing; put mats down at entrances to soak up the water; put out "Caution: Slippery Floor" signs.

>> Level off uneven flooring.

>> Make sure carpets and mats can't bunch up and turn into a trip hazard.

>> Close off areas where you're doing repairs or renovations.

>> Clear snow and ice off sidewalks outside your premises, and keep walkways and parking areas free of snow and ice and wet leaves.

>> Fill in any holes in walkways or parking areas, and call the municipality to have uneven sidewalks repaired.

>> Don't leave things lying around where people will walk into them, whether inside your premises, or on the sidewalk or walkways, or in the parking area.

>> Install handrails on stairs with three or more steps; make sure handrails on any staircase are sturdy; mark the edges of the steps to make them more visible.

>> Make sure ramps aren't too steep and that they have rails if necessary; put non-slip material on the ramp and mark the ramp edges.

>> Keep your premises well lit, inside and outside; replace any burnt-out lights immediately.

To prevent people from getting whacked or felled by doors, windows, signs, and so on:

>> Mark glass doors and other large areas of glass so that people won't try to walk through them. (The alternative is to never clean glass . . . that makes it visible all right, but it doesn't do much for your business's image.)

>> Check that outdoor seating (such as benches and chairs) is stable.

>> Make sure that awnings and outdoor signs are securely fastened to the building or to some other firm anchorage.

>> Trim back overhanging tree branches, especially low or rotting ones.

>> Check the roof and flashing to make sure that nothing is loose and might fall off.

To prevent injuries involving business equipment and business vehicles:

>> Maintain all your equipment and vehicles properly.

>> Make sure that anyone who is operating business equipment or a business vehicle is properly trained and licensed, and that they understand that safety comes first.

>> Don't serve alcohol to your associates or employees (even at parties) and don't allow anyone to drink or use cannabis or cannabis-based products while at work, even if that's what your small business is all about!

To prevent injuries caused by manufacturing or selling defective products:

>> If you're manufacturing a product, know all safety measures required and best manufacturing practices — and follow them; have quality assurance professionals review the product for potential defects that could cause injury.

>> If you're manufacturing or selling a product, make sure that it's licensed or approved for distribution and sale by the proper government authorities.

>> Keep informed about the potential dangers of any product you manufacture or sell, and put warning labels about the dangers on the product in accordance with provincial occupational health and safety-related legislation and national laws (do a Google search by province); notify in writing any customers who have already bought the product (you need to keep good records to do that).

To prevent deliberate injury or damage to customers or clients, hire carefully if employees are going to enter customers' or clients' homes or handle valuable property (including pets) or work with children. (As part of the interview process you may want a candidate to produce proof that he or she has no criminal record, and you certainly want to check references thoroughly.) For more on hiring, see Chapter 15.

Preventing damage caused by giving careless advice

WARNING

Sometimes just opening your mouth can pose a danger to others. So before anyone in your business says a word, consider the following advice:

>> Make sure that you and your associates and employees are properly educated and/or trained and/or licensed to give advice or recommendations in any particular area.

- » Stay current in your field. Go to (or send employees to) continuing education seminars or industry-sponsored training sessions, and read newsletters and other materials that are meant to keep you up-to-date.

- » Use care when you give advice. Make sure you know the facts before you form an opinion. Don't make assumptions. Don't be lazy. And don't let yourself or your associates be hurried into giving advice.

- » Include disclaimers of liability in the documents you provide to customers and clients. A disclaimer says that you won't be responsible for certain kinds of damage (or even for all damage) that results from your carelessness. Disclaimers aren't always successful in providing protection, but they're worth a try. For more about disclaimers, see Chapter 13.

- » Keep detailed documents showing exactly what information your clients or customers have provided, what advice you have given, and what work you have done.

Preventing damage caused by not fulfilling a contract

WARNING

Contracts are the daily stuff of business. Take your contracts seriously.

- » Read and understand every contract you enter into — before you enter into it! That's not easy if you're not a lawyer (and even lawyers don't always understand contracts, especially if the contracts are in an unfamiliar field or if they're badly written). Don't just sign a contract and assume everything will be all right. Get advice from a knowledgeable lawyer about the contract's meaning and its consequences for you.

- » Make careful note of all the things you're required to do under the contract, so that you don't accidentally fall short of the requirements.

- » Set up a "tickler" system to remind you in plenty of time about contract deadlines, so that you don't miss them. (For more about tickler systems see Chapter 18.)

- » If you think you may not be able to fulfill a contract, speak to your lawyer right away. It may be possible to build a bridge, legally speaking, to keep you from falling into a pit.

Mitigating physical, financial, information technology, and business resilience risks

If your business is damaged through someone else's fault, you may be able to sue for financial compensation. But that could be a long time coming — so protecting your business is better than counting on getting paid for any trouble you suffer. And anyway, the damage might be inflicted by you, or by someone you can't sue.

Damage to premises

You can take several steps to safeguard your premises against damage.

Here's how to prevent fire:

>> Install approved fire alarms and fire extinguishers, and maybe even sprinkler systems and emergency lighting.

>> Be a good housekeeper:

- Keep premises clear of paper, packing materials, and other litter; empty wastebaskets daily.

- Unplug appliances when not in use.

- Label hazardous materials and store them safely.

- Dispose of hazardous waste properly.

- Consider a no-smoking-on-the-premises policy.

>> Check out building maintenance:

- See that heating and electrical systems are in good condition and are properly maintained. (While you're at it, investigate the plumbing system, as well. You don't want fires, but you don't want floods, either.)

Here's how to prevent vandalism, robbery, and theft:

>> Lock or fasten securely all doors and windows; you may even need bars or shatter-resistant glass on windows and doors.

>> Install burglar alarms.

>> Cut down trees and shrubs that grow around entrances and windows and could provide cover for someone who wants to break in.

>> Keep the premises well lit outside at night; you may also want to leave interior lights on so that police patrols can see inside.

>> Fence the premises if necessary.

>> Consider hiring a security guard.

>> Keep vehicles in a secure area, with doors locked. Don't leave valuable equipment inside vehicles unless absolutely necessary.

Register your business with your local police and fire department so that they know whom to call in an emergency.

Non-payment of accounts receivable

As a businessperson, what you'd like best is to be paid in advance for your work, or have an absolute guarantee of payment. That way you don't have to worry about clients and customers who ignore your bills.

>> If you're a professional such as a lawyer or accountant, you can ask clients for a *retainer*, an advance payment that is put into a trust account. (Although you have the money safely in hand, you cannot legally touch it until the work has been done and a bill has been sent to the client.)

>> In any business you can ask for partial payment in advance for the work you're going to do. If a job can be divided into stages, you can ask for payment in advance for each stage.

>> In any retail business you can insist on payment in full before delivering the item you're selling.

But if you have to deal with people who can't or won't pay in advance, here are some ways to avoid being left holding the bag:

>> Don't extend credit yourself. Make arrangements to accept certain credit cards and tell clients they can use those cards.

>> Make sure customers and clients understand, before you do the work or supply the product, how much it's going to cost. (If they're not taken by surprise, they're more likely to pay the bill quietly.)

>> Do your work properly; supply good products; provide guarantees. Clients balk at paying bills if they're unsatisfied.

>> Bill regularly if you're supplying a product or doing work on an ongoing basis. If one month's bill isn't paid, consider not doing any more work or providing any more supplies until it is. That way you'll limit the damage to your business.

>> Send regular reminders of unpaid bills, and start collection proceedings (small claims court, or handing the matter over to a collection agency) within a reasonable time.

For more on getting paid, see Chapter 13.

Theft and embezzlement

To prevent theft and embezzlement by employees or associates, you need to have management control systems for handling cash and cheques. (For example, require that all cheques bear your own signature, or the signatures of two people. Don't keep large sums of cash on the premises. Separate the cash handling, recording, and authorization duties behind cash transactions with three different people.) You also need to hire carefully in the first place, and not allow employees (or associates) to handle money unless you're sure you trust them.

To prevent shoplifting:

>> Keep valuable items in an area where only staff have access (such as locked glass cupboards).

>> Install a security system that sets off an alarm if goods that haven't been deactivated are taken past the exit.

>> Have enough salespeople on the job and make sure they stay alert (nobody can effectively prevent shoplifting while chatting with pals).

Loss of paper records

To avoid losing your important paper records — even temporarily — take these precautions to keep paper records safe:

>> Store written records in fireproof filing cabinets.

>> Store valuable written documents in a safety deposit box in a bank or in a fireproof safe on your premises.

>> Keep photocopies of your most valuable paper documents off-site.

>> Scan paper documents into your computer and store them off-site on a DVD, removable mass storage device, thumb drive, or cloud service provider (like Amazon Web Services or Microsoft Azure).

Computer and Internet hazards

To avoid losing or sending astray electronic data, take the following precautions:

>> Maintain your computer equipment properly, and protect it from harm — with surge protectors and humidity control, for example. Remember that computers need to be well ventilated, so don't stick yours right up against a wall or cover it with papers, boxes, and so forth. Computers collect dust and need to be vacuumed every now and then — but by a computer professional, not by you with your Hoover! If you eat while you work (like most small business owners do, because a day only has 24 hours), be careful not to spill liquids on your keyboard.

>> Protect against sudden power failures by installing a UPS (uninterrupted power supply — a battery backup system). The system will give you a grace period if the power goes off — your computer will go on running normally long enough for you to shut down without losing unsaved data.

>> Don't let untrained or unauthorized people mess around with your computer systems. If you can't keep your computer in a locked room, you can password protect it. However, the ability to password protect depends on your operating system plus the specific programs you're using. Be aware that some operating systems or programs claim to have password protection . . . but for practical purposes they really don't, because any kid with ten spare minutes on his or her hands may be able to crack the password.

TIP

If you need password security for your computer, ask a computer professional for advice.

>> Take extra precautions with your laptop, notebook, or netbook computer. These portable computers require more security than desktop computers, because someone has to break into your office or home to steal your desktop. Notebooks are already out in public, just waiting to be put down for an unguarded moment in an airport or left behind in a coffee shop. So you really want to be sure that your notebook computer has proper password protection.

>> Guard against viruses and worms and whatever else hackers can come up with: Start with a good security package for your computer (Norton and McAfee are probably the best known, but others are available). Security products are constantly changing, and what worked best last year may not be as good as something else this year. So don't become emotionally locked in to your security system. When your annual renewal notice appears on the computer screen, ask for your computer professional's advice, or take time to comparison shop — check Internet chat sites to find out what people are saying about their experiences with different products.

>> Don't leave your computer (or one of your networked computers) running and hooked up to the Internet 24 hours a day unless you have to — it gives hackers who are fishing for a computer more opportunity to find *yours*. If you're using your computer as a server with constant Internet access, maybe you should consider going to a third-party provider that will look after the security issues better than you can.

>> Don't download programs from the Internet, especially screensavers, which are known to be loaded with malicious content such as viruses, Trojan horses, spyware, back doors, and keyloggers. Don't allow programs to be installed without verifying what they are — automatic updates to your software should be okay, but otherwise take care and don't download anything from websites you aren't sure are safe.

>> Don't open emails from sources you don't know, and especially be careful about opening attachments (which may be gateways to *phishing*, which is the fraudulent practice of sending emails pretending to be from reputable companies in order to trick people into revealing sensitive and personal information, such as passwords and credit card numbers). Your security program may give you warnings about major new viruses circulating via email, and sometimes the morning news even runs an alert.

>> Back up your computer files frequently, and store a copy of the backup on an encrypted and password-protected flash drive in a fireproof safe in your office, or in a safe place off-site. The primary offsite alternative used by most businesses today is electronic file transmission and storage in the cloud, with services like Amazon Web Services (`https://aws.amazon.com/canada`) or Microsoft Azure (`https://azure.microsoft.com/en-ca/solutions`). You can get a computer backup program as well. Backing up your data is a nuisance, but you should do it once a day if you can. Check your backup copies regularly to make sure that they don't contain corrupt data. (Or even no data at all . . . one author religiously backed up data using a well-known product and discovered after several years that no data had ever reached her backup disks!)

>> Stop and think before you hit the Send button on your email: Check and then recheck the addressee(s). Unfortunately, you can easily send an email, even one containing confidential information, to the wrong person or (oh-oh!) a total stranger. As a second-line of precaution, if your email contains any sensitive information, either in the body of the email or in an attachment, add a confidentiality notice below your signature, letting recipients know that if the email is not intended for them they should not read it. See the sidebar "For their eyes only" for some wording for a confidentiality notice.

Business interruption by outside forces of evil

It may be tough to second-guess what others are up to that will interfere with your business. But you can give it shot. Take the following precautions before you lease or buy business premises:

>> Check what other tenants in the building or businesses in neighbouring buildings are doing. Avoid doing silly things like sharing premises with a fireworks manufacturer or locating next door to an abandoned industrial site (toxic materials may well be on the site, which could cause a fire or pollute neighbouring properties).

>> Check what plans the landlord has for the building or the municipality has for the street. The landlord may be about to start a major renovation that will put off walk-in customers; or the municipality may be planning to spend several months digging up the street and installing new sewer lines, so that traffic will be restricted or banned.

FOR THEIR EYES ONLY

We recommend adding this postscript to your emails:

NOTICE: This communication is intended only for the use of the person(s) to whom it is addressed. As its content, including any attachment, may be confidential, any distribution, copying, or other use by anyone else is prohibited. If you have received this communication in error, please notify the sender immediately and delete the copy you received without reading, copying, or forwarding it to anyone.

And after you're in your premises, keep an eye on others in your building and on your neighbours, and be prepared to complain to the landlord or even to the police or fire department if you think they're creating a fire or any other hazard.

Outside forces of evil can include foreign governments as well as municipal. If your business involves doing something that is illegal under the laws of another country, be very careful about travelling to that country! You could find yourself arrested and detained at the border or airport. You don't even need to be selling marijuana over the Internet or running a terrorist training camp to get into trouble this way; you could be doing something perfectly legal in Canada, such as trading with Cuba (which is illegal in the United States). In the recent past the United States has taken issue with Canadian citizens residing in Canada who were violating U.S. federal law — and don't assume that the United States is the only country that might act this way.

Death or departure of a key person

If you're the one who dies or leaves, you may not care that much about what happens to the business. But if it's a partner or business associate who dies or leaves, that's a different matter. How are you going to get along without them — especially if they were storing important information in their heads? And what if the person (if he or she is alive) or the person's family (if he or she is dead) is demanding the return of an investment in the business?

If you want to keep key personnel healthy and happy in the first place, make sure everyone takes care of himself or herself. Hard work is necessary, but so is time off. Take vacations and get others to do the same. Encourage your associates to take things easier if they're turning grey and getting dark circles under the eyes, or becoming fat and wheezy.

Don't let any one person be the only person with access to essential business information. Make sure important information is written down and stored carefully. Have key personnel "cross-train" so that two or more people have at least some familiarity with essential operations. Or have an associate or employee act as an "understudy" for each key person. Take your cue from high-ranking politicians (like prime ministers and deputy prime ministers, or presidents and vice-presidents), and have key personnel travel in different cars and airplanes.

If you want to avoid destroying the business when someone leaves or dies and a big payment is demanded, start a fund that can be used to buy out a partner's or shareholder's interest. Add to the fund yearly.

Transferring Your Risks to Somebody Else

You can't eliminate every possible risk, even if you try. So you also need to pass at least some of your risks off to somebody else. Who's going to be stupid enough to take over your risks? In case you hadn't already guessed — an insurance company.

Most people think insurance is boring. But it's really quite fascinating. Once you start thinking of all the dreadful things that can happen to your business and you and the people you deal with, you'll feel as though you're living in an adventure serial! You'll realize that you're constantly surrounded by danger, and that a wily mind and constant vigilance are your only protection. Although you likely already know how the insurance process works, the fundamental point is that when you take out an insurance policy, you're in effect transferring the risk of financial loss or other horrible outcome (like the time and money cost of a lawsuit) to another entity. You are not transferring the pain and anger of going through a fire or flood or, worse, loss of life. In the world of risk management, insurance is a key mitigation and it's so crucial that we discuss it separately. If nothing happens, the insurance company gets to keep its money — the premium that you paid to buy the policy. This is the best outcome!

Have you already got insurance?

You may think you've already got enough insurance to cover your business, but you probably don't. For example, if you're going to run your business out of your home, your home insurance probably doesn't cover your business. Most home insurance policies exclude or limit coverage for business activities. If you're going to use your car as a business delivery vehicle, your existing car insurance probably doesn't cover that kind of business use. Key people in your business may already have life insurance — but the beneficiary is unlikely to be your business: It's probably their family members or their estate.

Do you really need insurance?

Some businesses need certain kinds of insurance, whether they want it or not, because they're required to be insured under legislation governing their field, or under a contract they've entered into. (Commercial leases typically require the tenant to have insurance.)

But if you don't have to have insurance, do you need to have insurance? You don't need insurance against every risk. But insuring against certain risks makes a lot of sense. Take these examples:

>> If your business involves giving advice, you should have insurance against giving bad advice.

>> If your business involves manufacturing a product, you should have insurance against defective products.

>> If your business involves having customers or clients come onto your premises, you should have insurance against injuries that occur there.

Having insurance protects you from going out of business if you're sued and the court rules against you. And it also ensures that anyone you injure receives compensation for the damage you've caused.

For risks that are unlikely to materialize or that won't cause big losses, you can consider self-insuring. That means bearing the risk yourself. Sometimes a risk is so remote, or the loss is so small, that you're throwing away money taking out insurance against it. You're also self-insuring in a way if you choose a high insurance deductible. Until your loss is higher than the deductible amount of your policy, you can't make a claim. (A higher deductible means a lower premium.)

You need to talk to an insurance agent or broker (agents work for just one company, brokers deal with several companies) about your business's needs. An agent or broker will help you evaluate the risks in your business and suggest what insurance coverage you need and in what amount. It is critical that you begin by knowing what perils (risks) you and your business face and, after that, which ones are insurable and to what extent.

Choose someone who is knowledgeable about your kind of business. Ask business associates for recommendations, and then make an appointment to talk to two or three of the agents or brokers recommended, before choosing one who seems best able to give you advice and find the coverage you need. Make sure the one you choose has errors and omissions insurance, as well as directors and officers insurance if you have a duly constituted board of directors. (In Chapter 6, we discuss incorporation issues, which include board of director responsibilities.) Errors and omissions insurance protects you if you make a costly mistake and damages result. Directors and officers insurance provides coverage for defence costs and damages (awards and settlements) stemming from wrongful act allegations and lawsuits against a board of directors and/or its officers. Then, if the agent or broker makes a mistake in getting the right coverage, you'll be able to recover compensation for any damage you suffer as a result.

REMEMBER

You may need different insurance from year to year, so you should review your coverage annually with your agent or broker.

Examining Different Insurance Policies

Various kinds of insurance policies are available. You can often get a package policy geared to your particular kind of business. For a home-based business you may be able to get a home business insurance package that provides coverage for things such as your business property (inventory, samples, supplies, filing cabinets, computers and software, tools, customers' goods) on and off the premises, loss of cash, business interruption if your home is uninhabitable, and legal liability (for products or services, or business-related accidents on the premises). Alternatively, you may be able to get an extension of your existing home insurance policy to cover your business. You may also be able to find packages for retail businesses, skilled trades, manufacturing, day care, or office-based businesses.

In the next few sections, we discuss the separate kinds of coverage that come in packages or that can be purchased on their own.

Insurance in case your business causes damage

Here are the standard forms of insurance protection for damage by your business to others.

Liability insurance

Liability insurance, also called general liability insurance, covers your business if the *negligence* (carelessness) of a person in the business causes injury to a customer, client or consumer, or innocent bystander. This kind of insurance will pay the cost of defending a lawsuit brought against your business and will pay the judgment awarded by a court or the settlement negotiated with the injured party. You may be used to thinking of insurance as a fund that pays something to you if you run into trouble. The usual rule with liability insurance, however, is that payments go to the injured party, not to you or your business.

Commercial general liability insurance can provide coverage for a range of problems — for example, physical injury, property damage, and financial loss and liability under a contract. Some policies may also cover civil wrongs (torts) like libel and slander (collectively known as defamation) and false imprisonment. A commercial insurance package might also cover some of the following things, or you might have to arrange separate coverage for each:

>> **Product liability insurance** — which covers third parties who are injured or suffer a loss because of a defect in a product you manufacture.

>> **Errors and omissions insurance** — which covers third parties who suffer loss and injury caused by your careless advice or careless work.

>> **Boiler insurance** — which covers ancillary damages caused by pressure vessel (pipe) explosions or malfunctions.

>> **Tenant's liability** — which covers loss and injury caused by your business to other tenants of the building your business is in. If you rent commercial premises, be sure to show the lease to your agent or broker, to make sure you get all the coverage you're required to have under the terms of the lease.

>> **Limited pollution liability** — which covers loss and injury to third parties caused by an unexpected or unintentional discharge of pollutants from your business.

WARNING

Automobile insurance covers loss and injury to third parties caused by your business's vehicles. This is not normally included in general commercial policies and has to be arranged separately.

Surety bonds, performance bonds, and guarantee bonds

Instead of getting insurance for liability you might have under a contract, you might be able to take out (through an insurance company) a bond that will be paid to the other party to the contract if you don't perform your obligations under the contract. (Bonds are commonly used in the construction industry.)

Fidelity bonds

You may want to have employees bonded (through an insurance company or a bonding company) if your business involves handling valuable property or working in other people's homes. If a bonded employee steals from a customer who makes a legal claim against the business, the bonding company compensates the business if the claim is successful. (A fidelity bond will also compensate the business if the employee steals from the business itself.)

Insurance against damage to your business, staff, and data

Here's insurance that makes a payment to your business if the business suffers damage.

Property insurance

Property insurance usually covers damage to or loss of

>> The building, if you own the building where your business is located

>> Leasehold improvements (tenant's renovations), if you rent space for your business

>> Contents such as equipment, furniture, and inventory

>> Business property (such as business tools, like a notebook computer, but not usually vehicles or cellphones or mobile phones) that isn't on the premises

>> Employees' personal property that is on the premises

>> Accounts receivable (money owing by customers and clients)

>> Valuable papers, but not money or cheques for more than a few hundred dollars, or documents that prove ownership (like the title documents to a property) or debt (like an IOU)

You can insure against only a few risks or against a wide range of risks. The full range of risks includes fire, lightning, gas explosion, smoke, wind, vandalism, some kinds of water damage, impact by a vehicle, burglary, and theft. If you buy an all risks policy, you get paid if any of the risks listed here occur and you suffer damage as a result; if you buy fire and extended coverage, you're covered for most of the risks except burglary and theft, and most kinds of water damage; if you buy just fire coverage, you're covered only against fire, lightning, and gas explosion.

WARNING

Even all risks policies usually refuse to cover you against damage caused by (among other things) water seepage and leaks, mechanical or electrical breakdown, changes in temperature and humidity, wear and tear, defects in purchased equipment or products, and war.

TECHNICAL STUFF

You can pay extra to get a rider to your property insurance policy to cover your business if it suffers damage as a result of rather boring perils like the cost of complying with municipal building bylaws passed since the building was originally constructed, if the building has to be rebuilt or repaired . . . or of quite exciting perils like explosion of boilers, floods, earthquakes, and pollution of your property by others.

Business interruption insurance

Business interruption insurance pays you money if you cannot carry on your business and lose income because your business premises are damaged as a result of a risk against which you're insured. The risks you can insure against are usually the same ones you can insure your property against (see the previous section, "Property insurance"), and in fact business interruption insurance is sometimes provided as an extension of property insurance coverage. You'll get paid by your insurance company until your business reopens (but only for up to a year, as a rule) for loss of earnings, loss of profits, and extra expenses incurred in order to keep customers. Business interruption insurance often also covers you if you lose business not because your own business was damaged, but because another business in your building was damaged. Business interruption insurance also covers the costs of a data breach that disrupts operations, as long as an *endorsement* (policy add-on) is taken out for this type of peril.

Cyber insurance

Not a week seems to go by without hearing about hacking and data breaches. If your small business deals with intellectual property, you need to explore this coverage. Cyber insurance protects you against different risks.

One risk area is regulatory defense, where if you lose client and customer data (a situation that is highly regulated by government and comes with hefty fines) you're covered. Another coverage is for extortion, where hackers manage to obtain sensitive information and hold it against you, threatening you with public shame if you don't pay up. Also, if you get a "phishing" email from an unknown sender and accidentally open it, your entire computer network is vulnerable to hacking and losses associated with it. When the worst happens you'll need rather expensive public relations and crisis management help because your business reputation is on the line. In addition, if you're facing a data breach, you'll have to notify those who are affected, by law. These types of coverages will all help cover much of the costs of letting your stakeholders know about the event and otherwise deal with a cyber security event.

WARNING

Property insurance doesn't always cover or fully cover computers and data processing equipment and the valuable information they contain. Cyber insurance may cover only data-related costs and not the equipment. Just be aware of this potential coverage gap and ask your insurance broker how best to cover your actual computer equipment.

Crime or theft insurance

Crime or theft insurance covers losses to a business that are caused by employee dishonesty, forgery of cheques, loss of money on the business premises, robbery, burglary, and break-and-enter.

Credit insurance

Credit insurance protects accounts receivable if a customer goes bankrupt or refuses for a long time (or ever) to pay an account. It's often used by importers and exporters. (It can also cover against changes in import/export regulations, and war.)

Tenant's legal liability insurance

Tenant's legal liability insurance covers the tenant if the tenant's own premises are damaged and the landlord's insurer refuses to pay to repair the tenant's premises, on the grounds that the damage was caused by the tenant's negligence.

Overhead expense insurance or disability insurance

Either overhead expense insurance or disability insurance can cover the fixed expenses of your business if you get sick or are injured and can't work for a time.

Business life insurance and disability insurance

Some insurance policies can help your business deal with the loss (due to death or ill-health) of a partner or shareholder and the resulting demand from the former associate or the associate's family for return of the investment made in the business.

The business can take out life insurance, under various names such as *key person insurance*, *partnership insurance*, *business continuity insurance*, or *buy-sell insurance*. They all do the same thing — if the partner or shareholder dies, the insured business can use the insurance proceeds to buy the deceased person's partnership interest or shares from his or her estate. A business may also be able to take out *disability insurance* or *critical illness insurance* on a partner or shareholder. The insurance payment would let the business buy out the partnership interest or shares if the partner or shareholder were unable to come back to the business.

Insurance to protect the people working in your business

Insurance to protect the people in your business may be payable to the individual, or may be payable to a person harmed by the individual.

Errors and omissions insurance

Professionals who give advice to customers or clients need errors and omissions insurance or professional negligence insurance. (In some cases, the insurance can be purchased through a commercial general liability policy, but professionals sometimes have to be insured through a specific insurer. Most medical doctors, for example, are insured through the Canadian Medical Protective Association; lawyers are insured through their provincial law society or an affiliated insurer.) The insurance will pay the cost of defending a lawsuit if a claim is brought by a client or customer, and will pay the injured person if a court makes an award or if a settlement can be negotiated between the parties.

Directors' and officers' liability

Directors and officers of corporations can be sued by the shareholders, creditors, and employees of the corporation, or by members of the general public, if they've been harmed by a director's or officer's carelessness (but not dishonesty) in making decisions about what a corporation should do. A corporation can buy directors' and officers' (*D&O*) insurance that will pay the director's or officer's costs of defending a lawsuit and of paying an award ordered by a court judgment or negotiated in an out-of-court settlement. Alternatively, if the corporation has an arrangement to pay back (*indemnify*) directors and officers if they're sued, the policy can pay back the corporation for payments it makes to a director or officer.

Disability insurance

If you can't work, you won't have any money. But you can take out some income replacement insurance (*disability insurance* or *critical illness insurance*) to help you financially while you're out of commission.

Workers' compensation

Workers' compensation is insurance coverage provided by your provincial government, for employees who are injured on the job.

WARNING

If you've got employees (in some provinces, if you have no employees but you've incorporated), workers' compensation insurance may be mandatory in your province (check the website for your provincial Workers' Compensation Board or Workplace Safety and Insurance Board in the case of Ontario). You have to register your business with the provincial Workers' Compensation Board and you have to pay insurance premiums. Workers' Comp pays the medical bills and replaces income while the worker is off the job. Under this plan, employees lose the right to sue the employer for job-related injuries.

Employers' liability

Employers' liability insurance covers injury to employees caused by your business and its employees. Coverage is restricted to injuries not covered by workers' compensation.

Chapter **13**

Working with Customers and Clients

I f you're in business, you're going to have to deal with customers or clients to provide your product or service. Customers and clients need special handling. On the one hand, you have to satisfy them — by providing good quality products or services and by treating them well. On the other hand, you have to get them to satisfy you — principally by paying you in full and in good time.

In this chapter, we talk about managing your relationship with your customers or clients so that you'll both be satisfied.

Recognizing What You Want from Your Customers or Clients

Creating knowledge of and interest in your product or service is called *marketing*. We tell you about marketing in Chapter 11.

Your potential customers must know that you exist, what you have to offer, and where to find you. They must also be interested enough in you and your product or service to seek you out — in person, by telephone, or on your website — or (if you have to seek them out instead) to sit through your sales pitch. But making contact is just the beginning. When you have your customers' attention, you want them to do several key things:

» Take the plunge and actually agree to buy your product or service.

» Allow you to make a profit by paying a reasonable price for your goods or services (including delivery).

» Pay you promptly.

» Come back for more and refer other customers to you. (If you can get repeat customers and referrals, you won't have to go to the trouble and expense of rounding up new customers all the time.)

Reviewing What Happens in the Usual Business Transaction

After you know what you want from your customers, you have to think about how to get it. Your business transactions should be designed with this in mind. Here's what you want to happen:

» You make contact with the customer and make your pitch.

» You close the deal.

» You document your agreement.

» You perform your work and/or deliver your product.

» You invoice (bill) your customer.

» You get paid.

» Your customer comes back again and/or refers other customers.

Making the Sale

WARNING

Don't make the mistake of thinking that if a customer is interested in you and your product or service, you've already made the sale. You've still got some work to do.

The pitch and the close

We talk about the actual process of making a sale in Chapter 11. Briefly, here's what you or your staff should do:

>> Know your product or service thoroughly so that you're prepared to answer all questions about it and not have to give lame answers like "That's a good question," or "I can look that up for you."

>> Listen to the customer or client so you know what he or she really wants, and gear your sales pitch to the customer's needs.

>> Propose a deal that you think will meet the customer's needs (and yours too, of course), and close the deal if the customer is willing to accept the offered terms and you're able to deliver on your commitment. (And try again if the customer isn't willing.)

When your customer agrees to buy the product or service you're offering, you have entered into a contract. After you have a contract, you have a legal obligation to deliver your product or service, and your customer has a legal obligation to pay you for it.

First impressions

Customer service is an important part of any business and of every stage of contact with your customers or clients. (For more about customer service than we can cover in this chapter, check out the latest edition of *Customer Service For Dummies*, written by Karen Leland and Keith Bailey and published by Wiley.)

TIP

Your customers will get the first taste of your customer service when they make contact with your business and while you're making your pitch. Treat them properly. Don't keep them waiting. Greet them politely and then pay attention to them. They do not want to be ignored in favour of other customers or, even worse, your personal business. Listen to their concerns and show that you're interested in solving their problems rather than in simply making a sale. If customers or clients come to your place of business, make sure your premises are always clean, organized, and well maintained.

Customer service doesn't end after the customer agrees to buy your product or service. You may still lose the sale if you take your customer for granted while processing the sale — for example, by taking too long to complete the paperwork or by failing to be attentive to the customer while he or she is waiting.

Documenting Your Agreement

One of the keys to good customer relations is to make sure that both you and your customer or client have a clear understanding of exactly what each of you is expected to do. What goods or services must you provide and when? What is the customer to pay? Does the customer have to do anything to enable you to do your work and/or deliver your product (for example, remove the old kitchen cabinets so that you can install the new ones, or provide certain documents for you to review), or does he just sit back until it's time to pay you?

TIP

The way to ensure clear expectations on both sides is to have a contract that both of you understand and are reasonably happy with. A contract doesn't have to be a pages-long document filled with small print and incomprehensible language. Contract documents and their contents vary from business to business. (In fact, a contract doesn't have to be in writing at all.) In this section, we tell you about the things you should be aware of, no matter what form your contracts take.

Contracts for the sale of goods

You may be a manufacturer who sells your goods to wholesale or retail businesses, or you may have a retail business in which you sell goods to other businesses or directly to consumers. Every time you make a sale, you and your customer are entering into a contract for the sale of goods.

The terms of the contract

When you and your customer enter into a contract, you come to terms on many matters. All contracts for the sale of goods involve agreement about the following points, whether or not the contract is put in writing:

>> **The parties to the contract:** One party (you) agrees to provide the goods; the other party (your customer) agrees to pay for the goods. Your customer may be an individual, a partnership, or a corporation. If it's a partnership or a corporation, make sure you're dealing with a person who has the legal

authority to contract on behalf of the partnership or corporation. Be suspicious of someone who wants to sign but is not an officer of the corporation (for example, vice-president is a much more comforting title than administrative assistant), and ask for confirmation from a corporate officer that the person has delegated authority to bind the corporation.

>> **The goods being sold:** Include quantity, brand name, and model number, or any other important details.

>> **The price the buyer is to pay for the goods:** Any amounts for GST and PST, or HST, should also be identified, but separately from the basic purchase price.

>> **The date(s) payment(s) is to be made:** If your contract doesn't address this question, provincial sale of goods legislation says that the buyer must pay at the time of delivery. If you agree to accept payment after delivery of the goods, your contract should set out the amount and date of each payment, and the interest rate being charged.

>> **The quality of the goods:** If your contract says nothing about the quality of the goods, provincial sale of goods legislation implies a promise on your part that the goods are of reasonable quality. If the goods turn out not to be of reasonable quality, the customer can return them and get his money back. If you want to limit your responsibility and the customer's right to return the goods, your contract needs to say so. For example, the contract might say that you will replace or repair the goods free of charge within 90 days after the sale if a defect in materials or workmanship exists. Or (if you are not the manufacturer) the contract might state that the buyer must deal with the manufacturer rather than you if anything is wrong with the goods.

Note that if you are selling goods to a consumer (rather than to another business), provincial consumer protection legislation will not allow you to limit your responsibility for the quality of your goods.

>> **The place and date that the goods are to be delivered:** If your contract doesn't address the place, provincial sale of goods legislation says that your customer must pick up the goods at your place of business. If your contract addresses the place but not the date, the legislation says that the goods must be delivered within a reasonable period of time.

>> **The right of the buyer to return the goods:** In the absence of a problem with the quality of the goods, a buyer has no right to return the goods unless the seller agrees to give that right. Your business should have a returns policy set out clearly in the contract — for example, no returns; or returns for exchange or credit only; or full returns, no questions asked.

If your goods will be shipped to your customer, your agreement must also deal with

>> How the goods are shipped

>> Who pays for shipping

>> Who bears the risk of damage or loss to the goods during shipping

TIP

Consider the customer relations aspects of your contracts:

>> Think about how your customers will feel about your contract terms before you finally decide on them. (For example, having a strict no-returns policy may cost you business.)

>> Make sure that your customers are aware of your contract terms (whatever they are) when they enter into the contract. (You may lose repeat business from a customer who doesn't notice that you don't take returns until the customer is standing in your store asking for his or her money back.)

Visible contracts

If your business involves selling products to other businesses, you will probably have a written contract of some type:

>> **A sales order form or invoice created by you:** If your customer orders your products by phone or over the Internet and doesn't set any terms for the contract, the terms will be governed by the wording on the invoice or sales order form you include with the shipment.

>> **A purchase order form created by your customer:** If your customer orders goods by sending you a purchase order form setting out the terms on which the customer is willing to buy your goods, and you fill the purchase order, then the purchase order will govern the terms of your contract.

>> **A formal written contract signed by both parties:** If the contract involves a large amount of money, or a custom-made item, you and the buyer may have to negotiate a contract that deals specifically with this transaction.

Invisible contracts

If you own a retail store, you'll be entering into a contract for the sale of goods every time you ring up a sale at the cash register. You won't have a written document for these sales — you may have nothing more than a cash register receipt. But you've still got a contract. If you don't say or do anything to change the terms imposed by provincial law, the basic terms of the contract will generally be

>> The customer must pay for the goods in full on or before delivery.

>> The customer must take the goods away with him or her.

>> You are responsible to the customer if the goods are not of reasonable quality.

>> Unless a problem exists with the quality of the goods, the customer has no right to return or exchange the goods.

TIP

You can change or narrow these terms by printing different terms on your sales receipts, or by placing signs at your cash register, or by telling your customers at the time of sale — in fact, you'd probably be wise to use all three methods. (Remember that if you're dealing with consumers, you can't change the term that you're responsible for the quality of the goods.) For example, you might want to inform customers that you don't accept personal cheques as a method of payment, or that you will allow returns but only within ten days.

Contracts for services

If your business is providing services to other businesses or consumers, you will be entering into a contract every time you agree to do work for your client.

Written contracts

TIP

All your contracts should be in writing, and the more complicated the deal, the more detail you will want in the contract. By putting the contract in writing, you and your client are forced to define the details of your agreement — and that's how you'll be sure that you really are in agreement. As you perform your services, your agreement will serve as a checklist of the work you are supposed to do. And, if a dispute occurs later on, a detailed written contract serves as evidence of what was in fact agreed to.

WARNING

Make sure each party has an original signed contract. (Especially make sure that *you* have an original signed contract and that you keep it in a safe place. A client may lose his or her copy and then come up with all kinds of wild fantasies about what was in the contract in the first place.)

The terms of the contract

Whatever kind of services you are providing, your contracts with your clients should always deal with the following terms:

>> **Who the parties to the contract are:** One party (you) agrees to provide the services; the other party (your client) agrees to pay for the services. Your client

may be an individual, a partnership, or a corporation. If it's a partnership or a corporation, make sure you're dealing with a person who has the legal authority to contract on behalf of the partnership or corporation.

>> **What services are to be performed:** The contract should state in detail the nature of the services and (if appropriate) the standard of quality they must meet.

>> **What the services will cost:** The cost could be fixed, or based on the amount of time you spend doing the work. Have the contract show any amounts for GST and PST, or HST, but separately from the basic price for the services.

>> **How payment is to be made:** Will you be paid in full at the beginning, or paid in full at the end, or paid in instalments as you do your work or after you complete the work? If you will be paid in instalments as you provide the services, try to schedule the payments so that your costs are covered as you incur them and you are paid some of your profit as you go. If you agree to accept payment over time after you've finished providing the services, the contract should set out the amount and date of the payments, and the interest rate being charged.

>> **When the services are to be performed:** The contract should give a starting date, and perhaps an end date — especially if the customer needs you to finish by a certain date.

>> **What rights the parties have to change or end the contract:** You may want to give yourself the right to end the contract for certain reasons, and you may want to limit the customer's right to end the contract due to some sort of wrongdoing on your part. You may also want to give yourself the right to change the contract in certain circumstances — for example, the right to raise the agreed price if the cost of materials rises.

>> **What happens if you don't perform the services properly:** You may want to offer a *warranty*, under which you agree to remedy problems for a fixed period of time after your service has been performed. And/or you may want to limit what you have to do if a problem occurs — for example, reduce the agreed payment by a fixed maximum amount.

>> **What happens if you cause injury to someone or cause damage to property:** You may want to include in your contract an exemption or *exculpatory clause* that limits your liability if you cause damage or injury. (With or without an exemption clause, you should make sure that you have proper insurance in place — see Chapter 12.)

Speak to your lawyer

Before you open for business, have your lawyer prepare your standard documents, such as sales order forms and invoices, and standard form contracts.

TIP

If a customer presents you with a purchase order form or standard form contract that you don't understand clearly and agree with fully, have your lawyer review it before you fill the order. Ditto if a customer wants to make a change to your standard sales order form or standard form contract. If the terms of the customer or client are unfavourable to you, you may be able to negotiate changes.

You may also want to consult your lawyer if you are negotiating a contract that involves a lot of money or a long-term commitment.

Doing the Work

After you enter into a contract with a customer, you have to do what the contract says you will do. If you don't carry out your promises, even if you don't get sued, you won't stay in business very long.

Happy customers

The first step in keeping your customers happy is to do what you agreed to do.

TIP

However, just doing the work isn't enough if you want to be paid promptly and get repeat business and referrals from your customers. You must also keep an eye on customer service:

>> **Don't make promises you can't keep:** Don't promise to do something unless you are sure you can do it. Don't promise that you will have an item in stock by a specific date unless you know for certain that it will have been delivered to you by then.

>> **Keep the promises you make:** This is the corollary of "Don't make promises you can't keep." If you say you'll order in a particular product, order it. If you say you'll be finished the work on the 30th, be finished on the 30th. (If you're serious about making your business a success, you just have to ignore anything that gets in your way on the 28th and 29th and fulfill your promise.)

>> **Document all changes:** If your customer asks for changes to your original contract, write down the changes and make sure that both parties sign to show that they are aware of and agree to the changes. That way you will both be clear about what now has to be done, and what the additional cost, if any, will be.

>> **Communicate:** Make sure your customer knows what is going on. If she ordered a product that is not available, tell her when it will be available. If the

product doesn't arrive when you expect it, call her to let her know you're experiencing a delay. Call her again when the product finally comes in.

If your customer can't see the work as you are doing it, keep him or her advised of your progress. Don't wait for your customer to call to ask you how you're doing and when you'll be finished. Provide progress reports, either by phone or email or letter.

>> **If you make a mistake or miss a deadline, deal with it:** Say you are sorry, fix the problem, and do something to try to make it up to the customer. For example, send a small gift or offer a discount on future products or services, give a free product or service, or promise preferred service in the future. Be careful about admitting that you did something wrong. Try saying, "Sorry for the inconvenience," instead of "Sorry that we screwed up and didn't do your work on time."

WARNING

Especially don't admit in writing that you did something wrong. Your words could come back to haunt you if you get taken to court over the mistake.

Unhappy customers

Under the previous heading we tell you how to keep customers happy. Under this heading, we tell you what to do with customers who are unhappy or who may be downright difficult.

Even if you do everything right, you're still going to encounter unhappy customers. Sometimes things go wrong, and sometimes it's not even your fault. Sometimes you'll have a customer who is simply impossible to please. But you must be able to deal with complaints, whether or not they're justified.

TIP

Here are the keys to dealing with a difficult customer:

>> **Listen to what the customer has to say:** That's the only way that you'll learn what the problem is. Also, your customer may not be able to think about any kind of solution to his problem until he's had a chance to let off some steam.

>> **Show that you understand the customer's problem:** Say things like

- I understand.
- This must be very upsetting.
- I can see how frustrating this must be.
- I can sympathize with the way you feel.
- I'm sorry.

>> **Try to solve the customer's problem:** Before you come up with a solution, ask the customer what solution he or she would propose. See if you can reasonably do what the customer wants. If it involves performing an unnatural physical act on yourself, politely ask the customer for a different solution.

In this type of scenario, where customers are unhappy, it's helpful to remember the three As: acknowledge, apologize, and assure. As we mention earlier, make sure that you listen well to their concern and that you acknowledge what they said and understand their frustration. This extra step lets them know you empathize with them. Then apologize for what happened. When you show that you're truly sorry, acknowledge the concern, and apologize, the situation tends to defuse itself. Then you can proceed to solve the problem and protect your reputation.

TIP

Even if you decide that you never want to have anything to do with a particular customer again, and you doubt that the customer will ever refer any business to you, try not to send the customer away angry. You don't want him or her bad-mouthing you to potential customers.

Getting Paid

REMEMBER

Often you won't get paid until after you do your work or deliver your goods, but that doesn't mean that you should put off thinking about payment until then. In fact, it's essential to lay the groundwork at the time you and your customer make your deal.

Planning to get paid

TIP

The best way to make sure that you get paid is to avoid situations in which you risk not getting paid.

>> **Turn some customers away:** No, our brains aren't addled by overwork. If you don't have the time or ability to do a job well, you're better off referring the customer elsewhere. If you can't do the job, you not only risk not getting paid, you also run the risk of gaining a bad reputation or getting sued. You run the same risk with a customer who has unrealistic expectations about what you can do. You should also avoid doing work for a customer who can't really afford to pay for your services, because he or she probably won't.

>> **Make sure your agreements are fair to your customers:** You shouldn't enter into a contract that's totally one-sided in your favour, even if you have the bargaining power to do it. A customer who feels he has been treated

unfairly is far less likely to pay than a customer who is happy with the deal he has made.

>> **Get paid up front if you can:** Try to structure your deals so that you get paid before you deliver any goods or provide any services. Having customers pay for goods before delivery is reasonably common. Having customers pay in advance for services is less common. If your customers won't agree to pay you in full before you deliver your services, unless you're 100 percent positive you'll get paid after you deliver, you should structure your deal so that you're paid in instalments as you go.

>> **Don't be sneaky when you bill customers:** Your bill (or any part of it) should not come as a surprise to your customers. Don't include any charge you haven't discussed with a customer beforehand — your customer will think you're a sleazebag, and possibly dishonest.

>> **Don't extend credit:** If your customers are consumers (rather than other businesses), don't extend credit. Ask them to use a credit card instead. Although extending credit to business customers is customary in some industries, don't do so lightly.

>> **Protect yourself if you do extend credit:** If you're planning to enter into a long-term relationship with a customer and the customer would like a credit arrangement as part of the relationship, have your customer apply for credit as he would apply for a loan at the bank. Design a credit application form (get one from one of your suppliers to use as a sample). Check your customer's credit history (to see if he has a history of non-payment of debts) and credit references (to find out whether other businesses consider him a good credit risk). If your customer is a business, think about asking for audited (if available) financial statements as part of the application process. If unaudited statements are the only type available, then review them carefully. The financial statements will tell you what assets the customer owns, what liabilities it already has, and what its revenues are. (See Chapter 17 for more about financial statements.)

TIP

You may want your accountant to help you assess the creditworthiness of a customer.

In the credit agreement, make sure that you establish terms for payment, including the amount and date of the payments, and the interest rate being charged.

If you are extending credit to a corporation that does not have significant assets, think about asking for *personal guarantees* from the shareholders and/ or directors. That way, if the corporation doesn't pay you, you can demand payment from the guarantors. See Chapter 9 for information about guarantees.

TIP

If you decide to ask for a guarantee, get your lawyer to prepare the document.

If you are selling goods on credit, think about taking a security interest in the goods until they are fully paid for (for example, sell the goods under a conditional sales contract). A *security interest* allows you to take back and sell the goods if you are not paid. (See Chapter 9 for more about security.) If you take a security interest, you will have to register it under your province's *Personal Property Security Act*. This legislative act is the name given to each of the statutes and regulations passed by all common-law provinces, as well as the territories of Canada. They regulate the creation and registration of security interests in all personal property within their respective jurisdictions. If you take security, get your lawyer to prepare the documents and register the interest in accordance with legislation.

>> **Do what you promised to do:** A satisfied customer is far more likely to pay for your goods and services than a dissatisfied one.

Collecting your accounts receivable

Your accounts receivable are money owed to you by your customers. It's often necessary to make a concerted effort to collect them. Nobody's keen on paying bills.

TIP

You (or your bookkeeper) have to establish a method for keeping track of and collecting what your business is owed. That includes the following:

>> Your outstanding receivables should be *aged* at least once a month. Calculate the number of days that every unpaid invoice has been outstanding (typically 30, 60, 90, or 120 days).

>> Have a policy about what to do with unpaid accounts when they have been outstanding for periods of time — for example, add interest after 30 days (if your contract doesn't prevent that); send a reminder invoice requesting immediate payment (with interest) after 30 and 60 days; write a polite letter and make a follow-up phone call after 90 days; threaten legal proceedings after 120 days.

>> Cut off customers who don't pay within a certain time. Do not continue to ship goods or provide services to a customer who has not paid a bill already owing, or else insist on payment before delivery.

If you are assertive in collecting an account, you may lose the customer. But keep in mind that a customer who doesn't pay is not the kind of customer you want.

Getting Paid Online

If you'll be selling goods through your website, you should have a way to get paid before you process your customer's order. You can either set up a credit card merchant account with a credit card company, or you can use a third-party credit card processing company.

Merchant account

Setting up a merchant account valid for accepting online credit card payments can be very expensive, because the risk of fraud is higher when you process credit card payments without seeing either the credit card or the purchaser. The application fee alone can be several hundred dollars. In addition, you'll have to pay a monthly charge *and* a percentage commission on each transaction. You can get information about setting up a merchant account with Visa at `www.visa.ca/en_CA/run-your-business/accept-visa-payments.html`, and with MasterCard at `www.mastercard.ca/en-ca/merchants.html`. You can also Google the word Visa or MasterCard followed by the word *merchant* to take you to these same landing pages.

Third-party processor

When you use a *third-party processor,* your customer is directed to the processor's website to complete his or her payment. In return, you pay a transaction fee plus a commission to the processor for each payment processed.

PayPal (`www.paypal.com`) is one of the most popular third-party processors for small businesses. You might also want to investigate Canadian-based third-party processors such as Payment Services Interactive Gateway Corp. (`www.psigate.com`) based in Toronto, Ontario; and Bambora (`www.bambora.com/en/ca`) based in Victoria, British Columbia.

REMEMBER

If you use a third-party processor, you are not responsible for the security of your customers' credit card information, but you must still comply with the privacy provisions of PIPEDA, by making sure via a written contract that the third-party processor complies with PIPEDA. For more information about PIPEDA, see the section "Addressing Customer Privacy."

Apple Pay

Customers who use Apple products like iPhones can pay you in a really cool way. They can use their fingerprint or passcode or even face ID to confirm payment within the Wallet app on their iPhone 6 or above (and iPhone 10 and above for face ID), iPad Air 2, iPad mini 4, and iPad Pro to complete purchases protected by robust technology. In Canada, Apple Pay works with Visa, Mastercard, American Express, Interac, and other card providers.

Accepting Apple Pay is faster than traditional credit and debit card payment methods. Your customers can check out with a single touch or glance. Accepting Apple Pay is also more secure for your small business than accepting traditional cards because every transaction requires your customer's face ID, touch ID, or a passcode. In addition, you don't receive your customer's actual card numbers, so you aren't handling actual credit or debit card numbers in your systems, which protects you (and your customers) in the unlikely event that you get hacked.

If your small business is a store, you need to have a contactless payment–capable point-of-sale terminal to enable and accept Apple Pay. The full technical, financial, and other details are found at `http://support.apple.com/en-ca/HT204274`.

Addressing Customer Privacy

In the good old days, you could keep extensive files about your customers' birthdays, wedding anniversaries, and tastes in scotch. You could harass your customers by cold-calling their homes at dinner time, sell your customer lists to another business so *it* could harass your customers at dinner time, and much more — all without asking your customers' permission or risking more than a telephone receiver being slammed down. Alas, the good old days ended on January 1, 2004, which was the date that the federal *Personal Information Protection and Electronic Documents Act (PIPEDA)* came into force across Canada for all commercial activities. What with all the weekly news we hear about data breaches by hackers, it's no wonder that this important piece of legislation is gaining in prominence, and in enforcement! This is another important section with yet another important message.

REMEMBER

If you want to collect, and keep and use or disclose any personal (factual or subjective) information about an identifiable individual, you have to get that individual's consent beforehand, and even then you can use the information only for the purpose for which consent was given. And *even then* you can collect, use, or disclose the information only for purposes that a reasonable person would consider appropriate in the circumstances. The customer can call the Privacy Commissioner of Canada on you if you violate PIPEDA. (However, the Commish isn't necessarily a heavy by nature; he or she will work toward finding a solution to privacy problems and complaints, rather than immediately throwing you in jail . . . even if you probably should be thrown in jail. Having said that, the Commish is beginning to lose patience with the growing number of scofflaws, so beware!)

Personal information includes

>> Name, address, phone numbers, identification numbers (like a social insurance number or a driver's licence number)

>> Age, social status, ethnic origin, medical information and records

>> Income, or credit or loan records

>> Existence of a dispute between a customer and a business

>> Opinions, intentions, and comments (even the printable ones)

(We'll throw you a crumb here — personal information does not include the name, title, business address, or business telephone number of an employee of an organization.)

Individuals have a right to look at the personal information that your business holds about them, and to correct any inaccuracies.

And it doesn't end here! A whole pile of responsibilities goes with PIPEDA. To give you a quick summary, Schedule 1 says that you have to observe ten principles about personal information:

1. **Be accountable:** Protect the information you collect (see principle 7). Develop and implement PIPEDA-compliant policies and practices for your business, and appoint someone to be responsible for your business's compliance with PIPEDA. If not, engage a lawyer to help you stay current and to advise you of your obligations.

2. **Identify your purposes:** Before or at the time you collect personal information, for example at the cash register, or in application forms, questionnaires, or surveys, explain why you're collecting and how you will use the information (and if your reasons later change, go back to the client and explain how they have changed).

3. **Get consent:** Get the individual's consent to collect and use his or her personal information before or at the time of collection, and get consent again if you come up with a new use for the information.

4. **Limit your collection:** Don't go around collecting personal information without good reason, and don't mislead an individual about why you're collecting his or her information.

5. **Limit your use, disclosure, and retention:** Use or disclose personal information only for the purpose for which the individual agreed it could be used or disclosed, and keep the information only as long as necessary to satisfy that purpose. Create guidelines and procedures for keeping and for destroying the information (that includes keeping information used to make a decision for a

reasonable time, so that the individual involved can get the information from you), and destroy or erase or make anonymous any information no longer required for the purpose (unless you're required by law to keep it).

6. **Be accurate:** Do your best to make sure that the information is correct, whenever you make a decision based on it or disclose it outside your business.

7. **Use safeguards:** Protect the information against loss, theft, unauthorized access, copying, modification, and disclosure outside your business. For example, don't bring up personal information on a computer screen that's in public view and then wander away from the computer. Use password protection and encryption software, and make sure your employees don't do anything silly like posting sensitive personal information on social media!

8. **Be open:** Tell your customers and clients about the policies and practices you created (see principle 5), and make them available and easy to understand. (Don't forget to tell your employees that you have policies and practices, and that the customers are entitled to know about them!)

9. **Provide answers and access:** If customers ask, tell them what personal information you're keeping about them (let them see it if they want to, and give them a copy of it; and correct anything in it that customers say is inaccurate).

10. **Provide recourse:** Develop easy-to-use complaint procedures, and let your customers know about them and about other available complaint procedures — such as those of the Privacy Commissioner, industry or professional associations, or regulatory authorities. Investigate any complaint promptly, and correct your own practices and f they seem to be falling short.

Note that if PIPEDA doesn't apply in your province — don't jump for joy yet. There's a stinger in the tail here: if the province has enacted legislation that the federal government has deemed "substantially similar" to PIPEDA. (In other words, this means that you may not have to comply with PIPEDA itself . . . just with PIPEDA under another name . . . .)

For quite a lot of useful information about privacy in the commercial sector, and how a business goes about complying with PIPEDA, go to the Privacy Commissioner of Canada's website at www.priv.gc.ca. Or you can call 1-800-282-1376. And no, this is not the Privacy Commissioner's home phone number.

Getting Repeat Business and Referrals

If you want your customer to use your business again and refer other customers to you, first of all you've got to do your work right. But your relationship with your customers isn't over just because you've done your work and you've been paid. You have to go on paying attention to your customers.

CUSTOMER SATISFACTION SURVEY

If you think that you won't find out what customers really think about your business just by chatting with them, then offer them a customer satisfaction survey to fill out. Below is a survey that can be used for pretty well any business (it's available online, too, as Form 13-1 — check out this book's Introduction for instruction on how to download this free online content) — or you can adapt the survey for your own business. Be sure to explain on the form that you will use the survey only internally for the purpose of improving service, and that you will not retain the forms once the anonymous answers have been added to your survey tabulation. (You may also want to check out www. zoomerang.com and www.surveymonkey.com, two excellent sites that enable you to run online surveys.)

1. If you called our company, were you happy with the way your call was handled?

☐ YES   ☐ NO

Comments:

_____

2. If you've visited our place of business, did you find the premises pleasant?

☐ YES   ☐ NO

Comments:

_____

3. When you dealt with our staff, did you find them courteous, knowledgeable, and helpful?

☐ YES   ☐ NO

Comments:

_____

4. Are you satisfied with the quality of the product/service we have provided to you?

☐ YES   ☐ NO

Comments:

_____

5. If you've had any complaints or questions, have they been handled quickly and properly?

☐ YES   ☐ NO

Comments:

_____

6. Do you plan to deal with our business again in the future?

☐ YES   ☐ NO

Comments:

_____

7. Would you recommend our business to others?

☐ YES   ☐ NO

Comments:

_____

Your customers may have questions or problems that come up days or weeks after you've provided the product or service, and even at that point it's still important to give them good service. If your customers think that you don't care about them once you've got their money, they're less likely to deal with you again or refer other customers to you.

TIP

And if your customer doesn't contact you, you should contact him or her. After delivering a product or performing a service, call to say thank you for the business and to ask whether he or she is happy with your work or product. As time goes by, contact your customers about new products or developments in your field that may be of interest to them. (Of course, you can do all of this only if you have permission to use a customer's contact information for these purposes!) Send holiday greeting cards, and, depending on how personal your relationship with your customers or clients is, perhaps birthday and anniversary cards as well (but only if you have collected birth dates and anniversary dates with consent, naturally).

When Peaceful Coexistence Is Shattered

Your relationship with your customers and clients will not be undiluted sweetness and light. In particular, two nasty things could happen:

» You could be fired, without having done anything wrong.

» You could totally screw up (and very likely get fired).

This is the end of the business relationship. But it may not be the end of the entire relationship — you could run into the customer or client again . . . in court.

If you get fired for no good reason

It's one thing never to get any repeat business or referrals from an unhappy customer. But it's another to be told you're through while you're in the process of providing services or goods. No doubt the customer or client has reasons for booting you off the job. Some may have something to do with you, and others may not have a thing to do with you (the client's nephew's girlfriend just set up a competing business and the client wants to patronize it instead).

If your agreement with the customer or client gives him or her the right to terminate the agreement for no reason (usually on a few days' or weeks' notice), then you just have to put up with this injustice.

If your agreement doesn't give the customer or client the right to terminate for no reason (or for the reason that the client has stated), then you may be entitled to sue the customer or client for the full amount that's still outstanding under the contract. If the outstanding amount is a large sum, you may look upon this as an attractive idea. On the other hand, you may be concerned about what suing a customer or client will do to your business's image and reputation.

TIP

Talk the situation over with your lawyer before you make a decision to sue or not to sue. For more about deciding to sue, see Chapter 20.

If you really screw up

It's always desirable, but it's not always possible, to avoid making mistakes. Sometimes fixing a mistake can inspire as much customer loyalty as doing it right in the first place. But that's not the kind of mistake we're talking about here. We're talking about a situation where a simple apology and a small gift are not going to get you off the hook. You've got an excellent chance of being fired and a pretty good chance of being sued.

WARNING

You can be sued if

>> **You don't finish your work (on time or at all), or you do the work poorly.** You can be sued for the return of money that was paid for work that was not done or not done properly, and for the extra costs of having someone else finish or redo the work. In addition, you can be sued for any loss the customer or client suffers because the work wasn't done, including a business opportunity the customer or client lost.

>> **You don't deliver the goods, or deliver the goods late.** If you don't deliver the goods you won't get paid, and if you've already been paid you can be sued for return of the money. You could also be sued for any loss the buyer suffers

because the goods weren't delivered. If you deliver the goods late, in most cases you can still insist on being paid (but you can be sued for losses caused by late delivery).

>> **You provide damaged or defective goods.** You won't get paid, or you can be sued for return of money already paid, and you can be sued for any extra loss the customer suffers because of the condition of the goods.

>> **You injure someone or damage their property, either directly or by providing defective goods.** If you injure someone, you can be sued for (among other things) the cost of their medical treatment, their pain and suffering, any wages they lost while they couldn't work, and for income they'll lose in the future if the injury affects their ability to work. If you damage property, you can be sued for the cost of repairing or replacing the property, and also for costs that result from the property damage (for example, lost business if the damage causes the business's premises to close for a few days).

Don't screw up in the first place

TIP

It's a little late to tell you not to make the mistake, but we're going to do it anyway. This is our way of saying "I told you so." If you don't want to make mistakes that could end up being very costly,

>> **Do your work . . . on time.** Don't take on a job that you don't have time to do, and make sure that you structure payments so that you can afford to finish the job.

>> **Do the work well.** Don't take on a job that you can't do properly, and focus on the work once you start it.

>> **Deliver the goods . . . on time.** Don't promise to deliver goods that you don't already have in your possession or that you're not sure of getting.

>> **Don't deliver goods that are damaged or defective.** If you're the manufacturer, inspect goods before they leave your premises. If you're a retailer, inspect goods before you pass them on to customers, if possible. If you receive a warning from the manufacturer or a government authority that one of your products is dangerous, stop selling it immediately, until you can be sure that any problem has been corrected. If you're shipping goods, pack them carefully and use a careful shipper.

>> **Don't let anyone get injured, or anyone's property get damaged.** This is kind of a tall order. Read Chapter 12 about risk management strategies.

Anticipate screwing up — and protect yourself beforehand

If it's too late to tell you not to screw up, it's also too late to tell you to protect yourself. But you've seen that we're not to be deterred.

TIP

One way of protecting yourself is to put an exemption or exculpatory clause in your contract. (We talked about this earlier in the chapter. An exemption clause may work with business customers, but may not work with consumers.) This clause limits your responsibility if you do a bad job. You could have a clause, for example, that says that

>> You are not responsible at all (for a particular kind of loss such as non-delivery, or for any kind of loss, period).

>> You're responsible only for correcting the mistake, or repairing or replacing the goods.

>> You're responsible only to the extent of reducing the contract price by a fixed maximum amount, or of refunding the amount the customer or client paid.

The most important way of protecting yourself is to have third-party liability insurance. Your insurance company will defend the lawsuit and pay any compensation you are required to pay. (See Chapter 12 for more about insurance.) You can't insure against deliberate screw-ups, only careless screw-ups.

But if you aren't protected . . .

So. You couldn't or didn't prevent the screw-up from happening. And you either didn't get insurance for this kind of risk, or you can't get insurance for this kind of risk.

But all is not lost. Just because you screwed up doesn't mean you'll get sued. The larger the amount of money involved or the madder the client or customer, the more likely it is that you'll get sued. If the customer hasn't suffered a big financial loss because of your mistake, it probably won't be worth his or her while to sue you.

Suppose, though, that you do get sued. If you have insurance coverage, your insurer will defend the lawsuit on your behalf, and will pay compensation on your behalf. It's very important that you notify your insurer as soon as you realize you have a problem (even before you get served with legal documents, if possible). They'll let you know whether you're covered, but if you wait too long to notify them, you may forfeit that coverage.

Keep in mind that if you make a claim against your insurance, your premiums will rise.

If you don't have insurance coverage, speak to your lawyer right away so you can take the proper steps to defend the lawsuit.

And just because you get sued doesn't mean you'll have to pay a lot of money, or even any money . . . even if you have no insurance. The person who suffered the loss has to prove the loss and has to *mitigate damages* (take reasonable steps to reduce the loss). Sometimes people mitigate their damages right out of existence. For example, if you failed to deliver a computer system that a customer had ordered, but the customer was able to get a very similar one from another business immediately and for less money, the customer may not have suffered any damages at all. And if the customer didn't bother to try to get a computer system to replace the one you didn't deliver but just let her business go to pot, a court won't award her compensation to cover all the losses she suffered — it will order compensation only for the loss she would have suffered if she had bought a computer system from someone else.

In addition, even if you get sued there may be someone who's more responsible than you. For example, if as a retailer you sold defective goods, you can sue the manufacturer in your turn. You may not have to pay any money or may get reimbursed for the money that the court orders you to pay.

IN THIS CHAPTER

» **Figuring out what goods and services you will need**

» **Finding and choosing suppliers**

» **Establishing credit with your suppliers**

» **Entering into contracts with suppliers**

» **Building a good relationship with suppliers**

» **Handling problems with suppliers**

» **Working with professional advisors**

Chapter **14**

Dealing with Suppliers and Advisors

In Chapter 13, we tell you how to deal with your customers when you're providing your goods or services. But your own business needs goods and services too. So in this chapter, we tell you how to be a customer, and get the most out of your relationship with your suppliers.

As you'd guess, this chapter goes over a lot of matters that we cover in Chapter 13, only this time from the opposite point of view. We take you into the mirror-image universe of suppliers. But don't be alarmed. If you can handle customers, then you can handle suppliers. Stick with us and we tell you how.

So Now You're the Customer

If you read Chapter 13 you may think that customers and clients aren't all that much fun to deal with, although they are admittedly essential to your business. But now the tables are turned — you're somebody else's customer!

Unfortunately, when you're in business, being a customer doesn't automatically give you a licence to be demanding, snarky, and unreasonable (even if you see these as the defining characteristics of your own customers). Although you can indulge yourself occasionally, for the most part you're going to want to concentrate on building good relationships with your suppliers. Most businesses need suppliers as much as they need customers.

In this section, we ease you into the supplier universe. We talk about deciding what products or services you need from providers, how to make up a list of providers of those products or services, and how to choose a suitable provider from your list.

Determining what goods and services you need

Some of the purchases you make for your business simply support your business — for example, furniture for your office, computer peripheral devices, or office supplies or courier services. When you buy these goods and services you're essentially a consumer, and you'll make your purchases the way you'd make any consumer purchase — such as groceries or an oil change — by looking for a supplier with the best combination of price, selection, quality, service, and convenience. If you're not happy with the supplier, just go to someone else the next time you need to make a similar purchase.

But your business may (also) need specialized products, and their providers may be choosy about the businesses they deal with or the terms on which they deal with them. They may also not be easy to find.

Reviewing essential goods and services

Goods and services that don't just support your business but almost are your business are

>> The things you sell, called *inventory*, such as shoes for a shoe store, greeting cards and wrapping paper for a card store, ready-made desserts for a food shop

>> Parts and materials you use to make your product, such as the leather for making shoes if you're a shoe manufacturer, the paper for printing cards if you run a printing shop, fresh fruit and baking supplies if you have a dessert bakery

>> Ongoing services you need for your business operations, such as an Internet service provider for a web-based business, a pest-control service for a restaurant, or a window display service for an upscale clothing store

Determining what you need

TIP

Before you decide on what your particular business needs, do some research to find out what businesses in your field generally need. You can get help from the following sources:

>> **Trade associations:** Find the trade association for your industry using Innovation, Science, and Economic Development Canada (www.ic.gc.ca) or use a search engine such as Google (www.google.com), Yahoo! (www.yahoo.com), or Bing (www.bing.com) to locate the association's website. The website may have useful information or contact information if you want to speak directly to someone at the association. Many trade associations hold seminars and workshops. Contact the association to find out if they have seminars on necessary supplies and services.

>> **Trade publications:** Many trade associations publish journals and/or newsletters with current information about the industry. These publications contain advertisements for equipment and supplies used by businesses in the field, and may contain articles from time to time about useful products and services.

>> **Trade shows:** Most trade associations hold an industry-wide trade show at least once a year. They are a good place to make contacts in the industry and learn about the latest trends in the field.

See Chapter 2 for more about researching your business online. The website of Innovation, Science, and Economic Development Canada (www.ic.gc.ca) contains information on a wide variety of businesses organized by sector. The Government of Canada website has common and similar links to similar online resources (www.canada.ca). Each type of business has its own page with links to major trade associations, trade shows, research, new regulations, and publications in the field.

Finding suppliers

After you have an idea of what goods and services you need, you have to find a business that offers them.

TIP

You can locate suppliers in a number of ways:

>> **Speak to colleagues in your field.** Ask for the names of the suppliers they use and would recommend. (You may discover that your colleagues don't want to share their suppliers with you, though, because a good supplier gives a business a competitive advantage.)

>> **Contact your trade association.** Ask for a directory of industry suppliers.

>> **Read trade publications.** They contain advertisements for suppliers who provide products and services to the industry, and may contain articles discussing and recommending suppliers.

>> **Go to trade shows and conventions.** Look for displays by suppliers of products and services. Speak to their representatives and pick up their catalogues and other sales information.

>> **Use a searchable Internet database.** For example, Thomas is an industrial search engine that brings together industrial buyers and suppliers and provides a single source for finding the products, services, or suppliers you're looking for (www.thomasnet.com). The database includes more than 500,000 suppliers, more than 300,000 articles, and more than 6 million products.

>> **Search the Internet with a search engine.** The websites of major suppliers have online catalogues setting out details of various types of supplies and equipment, including pricing and shipping information.

>> **Search Alibaba.com.** Alibaba, based in China, is one of the world's largest suppliers of products for businesses. The advantages of dealing with this behemoth include lower costs, a huge number of suppliers, many product offerings to select from, and ease of navigation and purchasing from suppliers. Disadvantages include perceived lower product quality and labor standards, a language barrier, difficulty in verifying or visiting the manufacturer, much longer shipping time, cultural differences in business practices, customs clearance to overcome, and a lower level of payment security and recourse. A subsidiary of Alibaba, called AliExpress (www.aliexpress.com), exists to cater to individual consumers and may also be worth checking out for smaller non-bulk purchases of consumer (not industrial) goods.

>> **Look in the Yellow Pages.** Or search on www.yellowpages.ca to find the locations and phone numbers of suppliers in your local area.

Gather the names of a number of suppliers and make a list.

Choosing a supplier

After you figure out what you need and see who's selling it, you have to narrow your list of suppliers down to the supplier who's right for you. Take care, because this is a supplier with whom you'll be dealing on a regular basis and on whom you'll depend to keep your business in business.

If you rely on a single supplier for any of your important needs, you can run into serious problems if deliveries are interrupted for any reason. Sometimes you may have no choice about whom you deal with because only one supplier has what you need. Other times, you may be seduced into committing to a supplier because you're offered very good terms if you agree to deal with that supplier exclusively.

If you do deal with just one supplier, try to stay informed about other available suppliers, just in case you need them.

Inventory and parts suppliers

When you're deciding on a supplier of inventory or parts for your business, be sure to consider all of the following:

>> Does the supplier have the full range and selection of products that you need?

>> How competitive are the supplier's prices? Does the supplier ever offer any specials? Do large or standing orders receive discounts?

>> How reliable is the supplier? What is the supplier's track record for filling orders completely and on time?

>> Does the supplier have a robust and modern online e-commerce platform with electronic payment capabilities, and a decent web presence that includes multiple contact and communication channels? Does the supplier have an online catalogue you can conveniently browse? Does it take protection of your digital payment and personal information seriously?

>> What is the supplier's delivery time from the date an order is received until the date it's shipped? How are goods shipped? Who pays for shipping?

>> Will you be able to return or exchange defective, damaged, non-selling, or overstocked merchandise? If so, who pays for shipping, and will you have to pay a restocking charge?

>> Does the supplier provide good customer service? Will the supplier give reliable advice about what you should purchase? If you're buying complicated equipment, either for your own use or for resale to your own customers, does the supplier offer training in the operation of the equipment to you and your employees or to the customer? Does the supplier have a good reputation for responding to customer complaints?

>> Does the supplier extend credit? What do you have to do to establish credit? When you're granted credit, can you get a discount for cash payments on delivery or for early payment?

>> If you're buying goods for resale, does the supplier offer any advertising support?

Ask potential suppliers for names of customers you can contact for references.

Service suppliers

With some service suppliers you may have a close working relationship — that might be the case with a pest control company or a security firm or a window dresser. But some of your service suppliers may almost end up living in your back pocket — they'll be more like employees of your business than independent businesses themselves. If you hire a business that provides secretarial or book-keeping services or provides support for your hardware and software, you may be dealing with your supplier almost every day.

Take special care in choosing a supplier who will become an integral part of your business.

TIP

To avoid unpleasantness, when you're deciding on a supplier of services for your business, consider the following:

>> **Does the supplier offer the services that you need?** Is the supplier able to provide services of the quality you want? Does the supplier have the necessary qualifications or licence to provide the services?

>> **How competitive are the supplier's prices?** Check around and compare prices with those of the supplier's competitors.

>> **How reliable is the supplier?** What's the supplier's record for doing good work on time and on budget?

>> **Does the supplier stand behind his or her work?** How well does the supplier deal with customer complaints?

>> **Will it always be the same individuals performing the work?** Will the principals of the business do the work, or will they delegate the work to less skillful employees? If the service providers are going to be on your premises a lot or in constant communication with you, do you feel comfortable working with them? Or do they make your hair stand on end?

>> **Does the supplier extend credit?** What do you have to do to establish credit? Can you get discounts for cash payments on delivery or for early payment?

Ask for names of customers you can contact for references.

Establishing Credit with Your Suppliers

Most businesses like to have some flexibility when it comes to paying their bills. When you're the supplier, cash on delivery is very nice. But when you're the customer, you'd much rather have time to make your payments. You may need the time to collect your own accounts receivable so that you'll have money in the bank when the supplier cashes your cheque.

As a new customer, you may not be able to get credit from a supplier immediately. You may have to put up with being a COD (cash on delivery . . . and you already knew that, so stop making fish noises) customer until the supplier has had a chance to look you over and decide that you won't take the goods or services and then skip town without paying. After the supplier stops being suspicious of you, you may be granted a line of credit so you no longer have to pay on delivery. The supplier may first ask for financial statements and credit references. (If your business is just starting, you'll show your supplier your projected statements and you'll offer personal credit references instead of references for your business.)

After you've got credit, the supplier will still invoice you for the product when it's delivered or for the services when they are provided. But you'll be allowed a grace period (usually 30 days) in which to pay the bill without interest being charged. If you pay the bill before the 30 days are up, you may be given a discount. Suppliers commonly give a discount of 2 percent if a customer pays within ten days.

TIP

When you first get your credit, make sure that you pay your bills on time. (Just like when you first get the keys to your parents' car, make sure that you don't crash it.) Then you'll be able to use the supplier as a credit reference for new suppliers. Over time, you'll acquire a good credit rating and suppliers will be able to get credit information about you from credit rating agencies instead of from your suppliers.

Entering into Contracts with Your Suppliers

Every time you agree to buy goods or get services from a supplier, you are entering into a contract. In theory at least, your contracts with your suppliers will be the product of give and take on both sides, so that you negotiate an agreement that both of you are equally happy with. (In actual fact, however, you may not have a great deal of negotiating power, especially when your business is new and small and your suppliers are large and powerful.)

WARNING

After both sides have agreed to the contract (whether or not they're blissfully happy with it), both sides have to do what the contract says. Both you and your supplier must understand clearly what you are to do. If one party doesn't do what the contract says, the other party may have the right to sue and/or end the contract.

Contracts for goods

Unless you're making a purchase at a retail store, you should have some form of written contract with a supplier of goods. The contract may be

>> **A sales order form or invoice created by your supplier:** If you order your products by telephone and don't set any terms for the contract, the terms will be governed by the wording on the invoice or sales order form that your supplier includes with the shipment. Have the supplier fax or email you a copy of the invoice *before* you place your order.

>> **A purchase order form created by you:** If you order goods by sending a purchase order form setting out the terms on which you're willing to buy the goods and your supplier fills the purchase order, the terms of the purchase order will determine the terms of the contract.

>> **A formal written contract signed by both parties:** If the contract involves a large sale, or a custom-made item, you and the supplier may have to negotiate a contract that deals specifically with this transaction.

Whatever the form of your contract, it will involve agreement about the following terms:

>> **The parties to the contract:** The supplier agrees to provide the goods and you agree to pay for the goods.

If your business is a corporation, you should be sure it's clearly stated in the contract that you're signing only as an officer of the corporation and not personally — so your signature will go over your name, plus your corporate title and the name of your corporation.

>> **The goods being sold:** Include quantity, brand name, model number, and any other important information.

>> **The quality of the goods:** If the contract doesn't say anything about the quality of the goods, provincial sale of goods legislation implies certain promises that the goods are of reasonable quality. Your supplier will probably try to limit its responsibility or state that it has no responsibility at all. If the contract you sign limits the supplier's responsibility, as a business customer you will not be entitled to any protection under provincial consumer protection legislation — so you'll have no one to complain to about the goods.

>> **The cost of the goods:** GST and PST, or HST, should be shown too. Shipping and insurance costs should also be noted if you're paying for them. If you're responsible for the cost of shipping, find out what the cost will be — before you make the purchase — because the shipping costs can be quite substantial. You may want to request a less expensive method of shipping, or ask if your supplier will cover all or part of the shipping cost if you place an order over a minimum dollar amount.

>> **The date you must pay for the goods:** If your contract does not specify the date, by provincial sale of goods legislation you must pay at the time of delivery of the goods. If your supplier agrees to accept payment sometime after the date of delivery, the contract should set out the terms for payment, including the amount and date of the payments, and the interest rate being charged.

>> **The date and place that the goods are to be delivered:** If your contract does not address these matters, provincial sale of goods legislation says that you must pick up the goods from the supplier, and that the goods must be available within a reasonable period of time. If you have other plans, the contract should state where the goods are to be delivered and when. If the goods are to be shipped to you, the contract should state how they are to be shipped, who is to pay for the shipping, and who is responsible for the loss if the goods are damaged, destroyed, lost, or stolen during shipping.

>> **Your right to return the goods:** Unless you find a problem with the quality of the goods (and the supplier has not refused to accept responsibility for quality), you have no right to return the goods unless the supplier agrees to give you that right. So if you need or want to be able to return the goods even if nothing is physically wrong with them, try to get a clause to that effect in the contract — for example, that you have the right to return them (unused) within ten days.

Contracts for services

REMEMBER

Any time you get services for your business you should have a written contract. The more complex the arrangement for services, the more details the contract should include. By putting the contract in writing, you and your supplier are forced to define the details of your agreement, and that's how you'll be sure that you really are in agreement. As the supplier performs its services, your contract will serve as a checklist of the work your supplier is supposed to do. And, if a dispute occurs later on, a detailed written contract also serves as evidence of what was actually agreed to.

Whatever kind of services you're getting, the contract with your supplier should always deal with the following:

>> **Who the parties to the contract are:** The supplier agrees to provide the services and you agree to pay for them. (Again, if your business is a corporation, clearly indicate that you're contracting as an officer and not personally.)

If you want a specific individual to do the work, the contract should name the individual. Otherwise the supplier's representative who deals with you or signs the contract doesn't have to do the actual work — the supplier can assign the work to an employee or even delegate the work to another business (unless the supplier is an individual himself or herself and this is a contract for personal services). However, the supplier who is the party to the contract is still responsible for making sure that the work is done and done properly.

>> **What services are to be performed:** The contract should very clearly set out in detail the nature of the services, and state the standard of quality the services must meet. This detail is sometimes codified in a separate attachment to a contract and is referred to as a *statement of work* for services, used mostly in the case of larger consulting engagements.

>> **When the services are to be performed:** The contract should state a starting date, and perhaps an end date if you want to be sure that the services are fully performed by a certain time.

>> **What the services will cost:** Is the cost fixed or is it based on time spent?

If you're paying by the hour, you can protect yourself from having to pay more than you expect. Set a ceiling on the number of hours that your supplier can spend on the job or get a firm estimate of how many hours the supplier plans to spend. That way, if the job takes longer than expected, you'll be entitled to a reasonable explanation before you have to pay anything extra.

>> **How payment is to be made:** Will you have to pay in full at the beginning? At the end? Or will you pay in instalments as your supplier does the work?

If you'll be paying in instalments, try to match the amount of the instalments to the value of the work performed. That way the supplier is discouraged from quitting in the middle of the job because he or she has already been fully paid.

>> **What rights the parties have to end the contract or extend the contract:** One of the parties may want to end the contract before the services have all been performed, or to extend the contract to include additional services. If you have a contract for the supplier to provide regular services over a period of time, you may want to provide for early termination in case you're not happy with the services. Or you may want to include a right to renew the contract if you're happy with the services.

>> **What licences and/or permits are required:** If your supplier is required by law to be properly qualified or licensed, the contract should state that the supplier has the necessary qualifications or licence. If a permit is required for the particular job, the contract should state who will get and pay for the permit.

>> **What happens if the services are not performed properly:** The contract should say what your rights are if the quality of the work is unsatisfactory. The supplier may offer a *warranty* — promising, for example, that it will remedy any problems for a fixed period of time after the service has been performed.

>> **What happens if your supplier causes injury to you or causes damage to your property:** Your supplier may want an *exemption* or *exculpatory clause* in the contract that limits the supplier's liability for causing damage or injury, and you may have trouble getting your supplier to take the clause out. You may want the supplier to agree to maintain insurance in case it causes any damage or injury. (You should have insurance too, in case someone is injured while working on your business premises. See Chapter 12 for more about insurance, or, better yet, contact your insurance agent or broker.)

We've included a sample contract for the provision of services online — just look for Form 14-1. (Turn to this book's Introduction for instructions on how to access this free online content.)

Speak to your lawyer

TIP

You should get advice from your lawyer about the contracts you enter into with suppliers.

>> Have your lawyer prepare a standard purchase order form for you to use if you regularly order goods.

>> Have your lawyer review invoices or contracts for goods before you agree to them if you don't understand them and the supplier cannot explain them to your satisfaction. If different terms need to be negotiated, your lawyer may be able to do a better job at negotiations than you can. (See the heading "Using Suppliers of Professional Services.")

>> Consult a lawyer if you're negotiating a contract that involves a lot of money or a long-term commitment.

Establishing a Good Relationship with Your Suppliers

TIP

When you find suppliers you're happy with, you want to make sure that you do what you can to establish a good working relationship. Here are some tips:

>> Be clear about what you need and when you need it every time you place an order. Confirm that the supplier has or can get what you're ordering and can deliver on your schedule.

>> Communicate with your supplier. If you have a minor problem, let your supplier know. Don't wait until you accumulate many minor problems or until a minor problem becomes a major problem. Let your supplier know sooner rather than later, because doing so gives the supplier a better chance to correct the problem.

>> Don't squabble over every invoice, or try to get price reductions on everything you buy. Your supplier will quickly get tired of you, and call you unpleasant names behind your back, and won't be in a big hurry to offer you discounts or other freebies that come along. The supplier may even fire you!

>> Pay your bills promptly. If you know that you're going to have a problem paying on time, let your supplier know, especially if it's a temporary problem that you'll be able to fix.

>> Treat the supplier's sales and service representatives courteously, even if you have a complaint.

>> Ask for special service only when you need it. Don't ask for last-minute deliveries or extra goods or services unless you're in an unusual situation.

In return, you expect quality goods or services, reliably delivered. Over time, as a valued customer you should expect some extra service. You would like your supplier to

>> Tell you about new products that become available

>> Tell you about discounts, rebates, or special deals on products you often buy, or that might be of interest to you

>> Advise you of any possible delays in delivery before they happen

>> Help you out if you occasionally need extra inventory or immediate delivery

>> Be flexible if you have an occasional problem paying a bill on time

As a new, and perhaps small and rather insignificant, customer, you can't immediately expect the same kind of service a long-standing customer would get. Building that kind of relationship takes time, so be patient.

You may also want to keep in mind that your Canadian suppliers are required to follow personal privacy legislation (the *Personal Information Protection and Electronic Documents Act* — PIPEDA) just like you are. Go to Chapter 13 for a look at PIPEDA from the other side of the coin. That means your suppliers cannot collect personal information about you and your staff without explaining why they're doing it, getting your consent, and then going through the same whole rigmarole about protecting your information and showing it to you on request and so on. So although you can still expect mail and phone calls and faxes to come to your business address and numbers, you don't have to put up with any more personal communication from a supplier that you haven't agreed to beforehand.

TIP

If a supplier does not meet your expectations of quality, price, service, and reliability, don't fume, don't fight . . . just find another supplier. It's important from a business continuity perspective to keep your bases covered — even if things are going well with your suppliers, try to stay informed about other suppliers in case you need them one day. It just makes good business sense to do so.

TIP

If you ditch a supplier with whom you've had a long-term or important relationship, show good business etiquette and inform the supplier that you're moving on.

Problems with Suppliers

When you're the supplier, you run into problems with your customers. So as a customer, you'll likely run into problems with your suppliers.

Avoiding problems in the first place

TIP

The best way to deal with problems is not to have them in the first place. So may we suggest you take the following steps:

>> **Choose your suppliers wisely.** Your best protection against problems is to deal with a supplier with a good (and deserved) reputation.

>> **If you're buying goods, choose the product carefully.** Even if you're in the process of building a long-term relationship with one supplier, compare the price and quality of goods available from other suppliers. If your supplier is offering an inferior product or higher prices on the same product available elsewhere, bring that to the supplier's attention. You may be able to negotiate

a better deal with your supplier . . . or you may decide to go elsewhere (as long as your contract doesn't prohibit you from playing the field).

>> **Don't automatically accept your supplier's contract terms.** You may be presented with a pre-printed, standard form contract. If you're dealing with a large company and you're a small customer, your supplier will probably refuse to make any changes. But you may be able to get changes if you're dealing with a smaller supplier and you're giving it a lot of business.

>> **Try to arrive at an agreement that's fair to both sides (even if you're the one with the bargaining muscle).** If you enter into a deal that is totally one-sided in your favour, your supplier may simply walk away from the contract, figuring it's no worse financially to be sued by you than to perform the contract. Or the supplier may perform the contract, but never want to deal with you again.

>> **Put your deal in writing.** Unless you're making a purchase from a retail store, the key terms of your agreement should be in writing.

>> **See a lawyer if you need to.** Have a lawyer draft or review contracts that involve a lot of money or a long-term commitment, or that you don't understand fully.

Considering some problems that can arise

Even if you do everything right, problems can still arise. Here are some typical problems, and some solutions.

Contracts for services

>> **The supplier doesn't finish the work.** You'll have to find someone else to finish the work. Before you hire someone else, notify the first provider in writing that you consider your contract to be at an end. If you've arranged to pay when the work is done, or in instalments as it's performed and you've calculated your instalments properly, you won't have paid more than the value of the work, so you won't lose too much money. If you've overpaid for the work that was done, you'll probably have to sue to get the overpayment back. (Good luck on collecting any money a judge awards you!)

>> **The supplier does the work badly.** If you realize that the work isn't satisfactory as the services are being provided, ask the service provider to correct the problems. If the supplier does not correct the problems, you may have the right to end the contract and refuse to pay (speak to a lawyer before you do anything, though). If you've already paid something, you'll probably have to sue to get it back. If the supplier really messed up, you may want to sue for additional compensation to cover losses you've suffered as a result.

>> **The supplier injures you (or your associate or employee) or damages your property.** The injured person or the property owner can sue for compensation for personal injury or property damage. If the supplier has third-party liability insurance, the insurance should cover the damages. If the supplier doesn't have insurance, it may not have much property either, and you'll be out of luck when it comes to collecting any money a court awards you.

Contracts for goods

>> **The supplier doesn't deliver the goods.** Don't pay for goods that are not delivered. To protect yourself, try to keep the amount you pay before delivery as low as possible. This way you have some measure of leverage. If you have already paid some or all of the purchase price, you'll probably have to sue to get it back. You can also sue the supplier for compensation for any loss you suffer because of non-delivery, such as profits you lost because you didn't receive the goods.

>> **The supplier delivers the goods late.** Unless your contract states that "time is of the essence," you have to accept late delivery and pay for the goods in full. You may, however, be able to sue the supplier for compensation for any loss you suffer because the goods were not delivered on time.

>> **The supplier delivers the wrong goods or damaged goods.** You do not have to accept or pay for wrong or damaged goods. Inspect your shipments upon receipt and refuse to accept them if you spot a problem. You may also be able to sue for compensation for any loss you suffer because of defective goods. However, the supplier may have limited its responsibility by an exculpatory clause in the contract. Then you're out of luck again.

Knowing what to do if you suffer loss or damage because of your supplier

If your supplier breaches its contract with you (doesn't perform the contract as promised — for example, by not delivering the goods you ordered), you can sue the supplier for damages, which we've been referring to as "compensation" for losses you've suffered. If you win your lawsuit, the court will order the supplier to pay you money for your losses. The amount you receive in damages is supposed to put you in the position you would have been in if your supplier had performed the contract properly (and your business affairs had therefore sailed on smoothly).

WARNING

If you suffer loss or damage, you can't just sit back and let your losses pile up. You have a legal obligation to *mitigate* your damages — that is, to take all reasonable steps to keep your losses as low as possible. For example, if a supplier fails to deliver parts that you need to manufacture your product, you have to try to find an alternative supply of the parts. If you don't take steps to mitigate your damages, the court will not give you an award for your total loss, only for what you would have lost if you had made an effort to reduce your losses.

TIP

Consult a lawyer immediately if your supplier doesn't do what it promised under the contract and you suffer a loss as a result. Your lawyer can give you advice about steps you should take immediately to improve your chances of recovering damages from the supplier.

Using Suppliers of Professional Services

Suppliers of professional services — that is, professional advisors — are somewhat different than other suppliers. So you have to approach them a bit differently.

In the way of professional advisors, you'll need a lawyer, an accountant, and an insurance agent or broker. Depending on the nature of your business, you may also want help from one or more of the following individuals:

>> **A publicist or media relations expert** — to help you get publicity for your business

>> **A marketing consultant** — to help you identify the market for your product or services and determine how best to reach that market

>> **An interior designer** — to help you set up your business premises

>> **A graphic designer** — to help you design a business logo and the look of your business cards and letterhead

>> **A computer systems consultant** — to help you choose and set up your computer equipment and choose and install your software

>> **A management consultant** — if you need help with management skills

>> **A human resources specialist (also known as a head hunter)** — to help you hire staff

>> **Business coaches** — to help you with things such as management skills, presentation skills, dress code, and social skills

Finding professional help

TIP

You'll be looking for professional advisors with experience in small business matters, with whom you'll feel comfortable working, and who will charge you a reasonable fee. In hiring any kind of professional help, you should

>> **Get recommendations.** Ask your friends, relatives, or business associates for the names of lawyers, accountants, insurance brokers, and other consultants who have done similar work for them.

>> **Do some investigating.** Call the lawyer, accountant, or other business professional to find out more about his or her area of expertise. Ask how you'll be charged for his or her services. Ask if the professional will see you at your place of business. (If you'll have to go to the professional's office — as you normally will for a lawyer — you'll probably want an advisor who's in a convenient location.)

>> **Interview the best candidates.** Take the top two or three candidates and set up an appointment to meet with each one in person. You not only want information about the candidate, you also want to see how you react to him or her personally. Ask about his or her experience working with small businesses, what his or her fees will likely be, and whether your work will be handled by the professional personally or by someone else in his or her office.

Entering into contracts with professional advisors

You should have a contract in writing with your professional advisors, as you would with any other service provider.

Consultants

If you're using the services of most professionals other than a lawyer or accountant, your contract should cover the matters we talked about under the heading "Contracts for services." When you're dealing with an insurance agent or broker, you probably won't have a contract and the agent or broker will be paid a commission out of your insurance premium.

Earlier, we mention the importance of detailing in writing the nature of the services expected, as well as the standard of quality expected. A statement of work is a separate contract section or attachment that can be used to specify in detail the nature, extent, and timing of consulting services.

Lawyers and accountants

If you're using the services of a lawyer or a Chartered Professional Accountant (CPA), you should have a written contract. Lawyers call their contracts *retainer agreements*, and accountants call their contracts *engagement letters*. The form of these agreements is a little different from a consultant's contract. The agreement or letter should include

>> A description of the work the lawyer or accountant has been retained or engaged to do.

>> The name of the lawyer(s) or accountant(s) who will do the work.

>> The way in which you will be charged for the work — by the hour or a flat fee are common methods of billing lawyers' and accountants' services.

>> An estimate of the fee — this is easy if you're being charged a flat fee. If you're being billed at an hourly rate, the lawyer or accountant can still give an estimate of what the total fee will be, plus a promise to tell you before doing work that will take the charge beyond the estimate.

>> The frequency with which you'll be billed by the lawyer or accountant. You actually want to receive bills at least monthly, so you can keep track of what the lawyer or accountant is doing and how much you owe. Every bill should include a detailed account of the work done.

You needn't set out the standard of quality of the work or deal with licensing issues or insurance. That's because lawyers and professional accountants must belong to a government-recognized, self-regulating body and are bound by professional standards and a code of ethics. The regulating body can discipline its members for doing poor work or treating a client badly. These professionals are also required to have errors and omissions insurance, which will compensate a client if the lawyer or accountant makes a mistake.

Working with professional advisors

Whether you're dealing with a lawyer, accountant, or consultant, you should expect your professional service provider to do the following:

>> Perform his or her services competently and promptly.

>> Act honestly, and not behave in a sneaky way either with you or with the people he or she is dealing with on your behalf.

>> Keep confidential any information you share with him or her about your business (or personal life, for that matter, because PIPEDA applies to these advisors too).

- » Avoid any conflicts of interest (for example, not take your direct competitor on as a client).

- » Keep you thoroughly and regularly advised of all work being done for you.

- » Act only on your instructions, and not make his or her own decisions about what's best for you and then carry them out without your permission.

Dealing with problems with professional advisors

If you've chosen your lawyer, accountant, or consultant carefully, you shouldn't run into too many problems, but here are some pointers in case you do.

If you're generally pleased with the work being done by your advisor, discuss problems as they come up. Perhaps your lawyer doesn't return your phone calls soon enough, or your accountant has sent you a bill that you don't understand. So don't work yourself into a lather — give the lawyer or accountant a call, or send a letter or email, and explain your concern. You'll probably get a courteous explanation and an apology. Don't be completely stunned if you also get a bill for the time spent explaining and apologizing. That's just how professional advisors are, sometimes.

SERVICE, PLEASE!

When you're dealing with a professional advisor, you should expect good customer service. After all, professional advisors are in the service industry. Your advisor should

- Return your phone calls within 24 hours (you'll have to allow longer for replies to email messages).

- Treat you with courtesy and respect.

And your advisor should not

- Keep you waiting for appointments.

- Take phone calls or allow other interruptions during your appointments.

- Charge you for time spent on personal chit-chat with you, if it was the advisor who started the conversation.

If you've lost confidence in your lawyer, accountant, or consultant, or no longer feel comfortable working with him or her, you should end your relationship. If you're going to be replacing your advisor, you may want to hire a new one before you fire the old one. The new lawyer, accountant, or consultant should be able to smooth over transitional matters.

If you don't think much of the treatment you're receiving from your advisor, look for another one.

If you have more serious concerns, such as extremely careless work that was done or behaviour that was offensive to you, contact the provincial regulatory body (if any) that governs the advisor's profession. It may have the power to discipline the advisor for unbecoming conduct, or to start you on your way to making a claim against the advisor's professional liability insurance.

Chapter **15**

Beam Up the Crew

As your business grows and becomes more successful, you'll have more and more work to do. Sooner or later, you're going to need help. You may start off using computer software and contractors who provide services, but the time will come when you need another body around on a full-time basis. In this chapter, we tell you how to go about hiring an employee and being an employer. (Eventually we even tell you how to terminate an employee, which is also very unfortunate but important knowledge.)

In reality, human resource management also includes the realm of training employees, performance managing them, retaining the best employees, and continuously developing them. We touch on some of these matters in Chapter 12, which discusses the management of human resource risk. But we leave out this other technical HR stuff for other books and stick with the human resource fundamentals that more directly relate to starting a small business!

TIP

If you're interested in digging deeper into HR, check out *Human Resources Kit For Dummies*, 3rd Edition, by Max Messmer (Wiley).

What Are You Getting Yourself Into?

Hiring an employee is not like ordering in a pizza. Before you decide to take on an employee, you'd better have some idea of what will happen when you do. As an employer, you give birth to a whole new array of responsibilities that include the following human resource-related ones:

- ›› Pay the employee.
- ›› Give the employee time off . . . with pay!
- ›› Make regular payments to the federal and provincial governments on behalf of your employee and your business.
- ›› Provide a workplace that's safe, and free from discrimination, violence, and harassment.
- ›› Take legal and financial responsibility for your employee's actions.

Paying wages

When you have an employee, you have to pay the employee's wages — every pay-day, whether business is good or bad. Your employee gets paid before you do. (In some small businesses, especially in the start-up phase, the employees make a lot more than the owner — the owner just gets whatever's left after payroll and other expenses have been met.) You may even have to borrow money to pay your employee.

WARNING

You have more than an obligation to pay wages; you have to pay reasonable wages. All provinces have employment standards laws that set a minimum wage (depending on the province or territory) for most workers. Of course, if you're looking for an employee with skills, you'll have to pay a lot more than minimum wage to interest someone in the job.

Provincial legislation also requires you to pay your employees overtime (usually at the rate of one-and-a-half times their usual pay) if they work over a fixed maximum number of hours per week (between 40 and 48 hours, depending on the province or territory) or a fixed maximum number of hours per day (usually 8).

Providing paid vacation and statutory holidays

Not only do you have to pay your employees when they're at work, sometimes you also have to pay them when they're not at work.

Provincial employment standards laws set public holidays (between six and ten days per year, depending on the province or territory), and employees who have worked a set minimum amount of time prior to the holiday in question are entitled to be paid their usual wages while taking these days off. An employee cannot be required to work on a public holiday without being paid overtime.

REMEMBER

In addition, employees in every province and territory are entitled to a paid two-week vacation (in Saskatchewan it's three weeks) after completing one full year of employment. In most provinces, the length of the paid vacation goes up by an additional week for longer-term employees. Check out the website of RISE (www.risepeople.com/blog/guide-statutory-holiday-pay) for an excellent province-by-province summary of statutory holidays including key dates, eligibility criteria, and other important details. You can also search the Government of Canada website at www.canada.ca for similar information.

You'll be pleased to know that, in most provinces, you're not required by law to pay your employees when they're off sick (in Prince Edward Island you must provide one paid sick day per year for employees after five years of service). You decide whether to allow your employees a certain number of paid sick days per year. If you don't offer sick days, employees use up their paid vacation days to miss work; and after they use up their vacation days, you don't have to pay them for days they don't work.

Paying taxes

You're required by law to deduct income taxes, Canada Pension Plan (CPP) contributions, and Employment Insurance (EI) contributions from your employees' wages, and to remit them (send them directly) to the Canada Revenue Agency (CRA). You must also remit your business's contribution toward your employees' EI and CPP.

In addition, you may have to pay premiums to your provincial workers' compensation board for coverage for your employees in case they're injured on the job. In some provinces or territories, you may also be required to pay premiums for your employees' provincial health insurance coverage.

WARNING

If you don't make these required payments, you have to pay hefty interest and penalties (as well as be treated with scorn by government representatives).

Providing a safe workplace

As an employer, you have a duty under provincial occupational health and safety or other labour legislation to take reasonable steps to provide a safe and healthy workplace for your employees. If you don't, your employees can complain about you to the provincial government — and get you inspected, fined, and even shut down.

You also have a duty under human rights legislation to provide a workplace that is free from discrimination, violence, and harassment (see the sidebar "Don't discriminate" for details). This means that you can't discriminate against or harass any employee, and you can't allow your employees to harass or discriminate against other employees.

Taking responsibility for your employees' actions

WARNING

If your employee causes injury to a person or damage to property while performing his or her job, you are financially responsible for your employee's acts. That means that the injured person has the right to sue you the employer (that may be you personally), and you the employer are responsible for paying any sum of money a court awards the injured person.

In addition, if part of your employee's job is to enter into contracts on behalf of your business, then you'll have to carry out whatever contracts your employee makes for your business — even if they stink.

WARNING

DON'T DISCRIMINATE

The federal government and every provincial government have human rights laws that prohibit discrimination on a number of grounds. The grounds vary from province to province, but usually include the following:

- Race, colour, ancestry, ethnic origin, place of origin, and citizenship

- Religion

- Sex (male or female) or sexual orientation (straight, gay, bisexual, and so on)

- Age (Although, strangely, sometimes you can discriminate against the young — under the age of majority. Go figure.)

- Marital status (whether a person is married) or family status (whether a person has children or is pregnant)

- Physical or mental disability, including such things as alcoholism and drug addiction

- Political beliefs

- A criminal record for a provincial offence, or for a *Criminal Code* offence for which the person has been pardoned (*Criminal Code* offences are more serious than provincial offences.)

Hiring an Employee

When you hire an employee, you want someone with the right combination of skills and personality to do the job properly and get along with you and your customers. To find this paragon, go through the following steps:

1. Draft a job description and qualifications.

2. Figure out how you'll pay the employee.

3. Find candidates for the job.

4. Review the job applications.

5. Interview the most promising candidates.

6. Check the candidates out.

7. Make a job offer to the most likely candidate.

Drafting a job description and qualifications

What exactly do you want the employee to do? The answer to that question is what goes in the job description. Write it all down and be as detailed as possible. Include

» Duties to be performed.

» Days of the week to be worked.

» Hours of the day to be worked (start and end times).

» Whether the employee will be expected to work overtime.

» Whether the employee will be required to travel and be away overnight.

» Whether the employee needs to be bonded, because the employee will be handling valuable property — belonging to your business or to your customers or clients. (A *bond* is a kind of insurance policy that pays if the bonded person commits a dishonest act. Refer to Chapter 12.)

» Special physical demands, if any, such as heavy lifting, standing for long periods of time, or performing repetitive tasks like keyboarding.

TIP

You'll use the job description to find a qualified employee, to train your employee, to do employee performance reviews, and, at some point, to decide whether to give the employee a raise in pay.

After preparing the job description, think about what qualifications an employee needs to be able to do the job well. Consider the following qualifications:

>> Level of education

>> Courses or training programs required

>> Licences necessary for the job

>> Ability to operate particular equipment

>> Ability to speak English, or French, or any other language, well

Also consider how much previous work experience you would like the employee to have.

REMEMBER

Although hiring someone with experience may cost you more, you'll have less training and supervising to do. And you probably don't want to add "teacher and supervisor" to your own job description.

Write down all the qualifications you think are necessary for the job. You'll use this information to screen and interview candidates.

TIP

Writing down a detailed job description and set of job qualifications can protect you from false accusations of discriminatory hiring practices. If an applicant complains that you were discriminating when you did not hire him or her, you can use the job description and qualifications to show that you refused to hire the applicant because he or she didn't satisfy legitimate job requirements, not because you were discriminating against someone who was female/a recent immigrant/transgendered/paraplegic, and so on.

Did that last tip make you a little nervous? If this chapter's tips and warnings eventually psych you out, forget about hiring an employee and go back to using software and service contractors.

Funding an employee

Mostly, your employee's wages are going to come out of the revenues of your business, or out of business loans if you don't have enough revenues, or (worst-case scenario) out of your own personal funds. But you may be able to get government money to hire people from certain specified groups (youth, people with disabilities, and so on).

TIP

You can find information about some of these government programs for wage relief (such as wage subsidies, funding, and tax credits) from the Government of Canada website. The direct link as of this writing is `www.ic.gc.ca/app/scr/innovation/list-liste/813a940133f14492`, but if that doesn't work, go to `www.ic.gc.ca`, click the Business tab, click Hiring and Managing Employees, and click Wage Subsidies and Other Assistance Programs. The website is quite intuitive and well organized, but if you can't find the resource you're looking for, just use the search tool.

Finding job candidates

Start your quest for an employee by talking to people you know. Sometimes this is the easiest way to find qualified candidates. Speak to business colleagues, sports or hobby buddies, friends, and relatives.

If you're interested in hiring a recent graduate from a program that's relevant to your business, you can contact the career placement office of universities, community colleges, provincial technology institutes, private career colleges, or private vocational schools. Don't be afraid that you'll be sent only applicants with no previous work experience. Many students work the whole time they're in school or are returning to school after working full time.

TIP

Most schools have a career placement office, but don't stop there. Try to speak to the program coordinator who runs the course whose graduates interest you. He or she will have more personal knowledge of the students and may be able to recommend a particular person to you.

You can also find potential job candidates by

>> Placing newspaper ads

>> Posting ads on Internet job sites such as Workopolis (`www.workopolis.com`) or Monster (`www.monster.ca`)

>> Posting a sign in your window

>> Advertising on a community bulletin board

>> Contacting employment agencies

>> Posting your job with Government of Canada's Job Bank at `www.jobbank.gc.ca`

WARNING

If you place an advertisement or post a job notice, don't draft your ad or notice in a way that excludes potential applicants on the basis of any of the prohibited grounds of discrimination (have another look at the sidebar "Don't discriminate."). "Seeking straight white male under 35, no children or pets, no drug problems, to perform routine office duties" is definitely out.

TIP

When you place your ad, use your job description to provide the ad content. Instead of the "Seeking straight white male" ad, try "Seeking well-organized, reliable, and energetic individual with good computer skills and general office experience."

Reviewing the job applications

Ask job applicants to complete an application form you provide and/or to give you a resume setting out their qualifications and education and employment history. (By the way, make sure the application form doesn't contain any questions like "Where were you born?" "How old are you?" "Are you married?" "Do you have children?" "Do you have a criminal record?" Revisit the sidebar "Don't discriminate.")

Review the applications and/or resumes, and choose several applicants whose qualifications best match the qualifications you set out in your job qualifications. Arrange to interview them. Interviews normally take place at the employer's business premises.

Send a polite letter to all applicants you do not plan to interview, telling them that you cannot offer them an interview at this time. If you're soft-hearted, you can add that you'll keep the applicant's resume on file.

Interviewing the most promising candidates

When you interview a job candidate, you're trying to find out if the person has the skills and abilities to do the job and is someone with whom you can work well. So design your interview questions to give you information about the candidate's abilities and some insight into his or her personality.

Learning from a resume or application form

Don't ask questions that the candidate's resume or application have already answered, such as, "Where did you go to school?" and "What was your last job?" Instead, focus on getting answers to questions that you had after reading the resume or application. For example, you might want to ask the candidate

» Why he or she left each prior job

» Why he or she has changed jobs so often (if that's the case), or is thinking about leaving a current employer

- » What he or she was doing during any period of time that is unaccounted for in the resume

- » Why his or her references don't include someone from a past job (if that's the case)

- » Whom you can call for a reference at each of the candidate's past jobs

- » How and where the candidate acquired a specific skill that is mentioned in the resume

- » Why he or she is interested in a job for which he or she appears to be overqualified (if that's the case)

Asking about strengths and weaknesses

Don't waste a lot of time asking questions that allow the job candidates to give you canned answers about how wonderful they are. Any candidate who's taken Job Interviews 101 can go on at great length in answer to the question "What are your strengths?" But a candidate's assertion that he or she has stellar problem-solving skills or out-of-this-world conflict resolution abilities doesn't prove a thing. So put the candidate to the test. Come up with situations that you encounter in your business and ask the candidate how he or she would handle them. For example, ask, "We have a lot of elderly customers. What would you do if a customer fell and couldn't get up?"

On the other hand, you should ask a candidate about his or her weaknesses. Everybody has weaknesses, and a strong candidate will be willing to admit his or hers, while a weak candidate may not. Likewise ask the candidate about past mistakes and what he or she learned from them.

Getting a sense of personality

Throughout the interview, keep in mind that you're trying to get a sense of the candidate's personality. Therefore, pose your questions so that the candidate does most of the talking. Keep an eye out for traits that are important to you, such as a good sense of humour, an ability to maintain eye contact, a strong, clear speaking voice, relaxed body language. (Or whatever. Your preferred candidate may be totally humourless, be afraid to meet your eyes, have a barely audible voice, and be as nervous as a cat.) Feel free to ask questions that relate directly to personality issues such as:

- » **What drives you nuts about other people?** If you're always setting wet glasses and mugs down on the furniture and the candidate says, "I once took an axe to someone who left a coffee ring on my table," this would be a good time to end the interview, escort the candidate out, and bolt the door shut.

>> **What's your most productive time of day?** If you're a morning person and the candidate doesn't speak to anyone before noon, your productive time together will be considerably shortened.

>> **What are your favourite TV shows?** Newspapers and magazines? Movies? Sports teams? A *Survivor* junkie and a *Masterpiece Theatre* devotee may not just have trouble making small talk, they may have such different personalities that they can't get along at all.

>> **Do you keep a neat desk or a messy desk?** Neat desk people and messy desk people tend to think that people of the opposite persuasion aren't doing their work.

Being aware of human rights considerations

WARNING

Human rights legislation prohibits you from asking certain questions during an interview. The legislation is designed to keep you from making assumptions about how capable or reliable an employee is based solely on factors like family status, age, race, disability, or religion. (You might as well memorize the sidebar "Don't discriminate.")

Before you go into a sulk, ask yourself why you would want to ask these questions in the first place. You probably don't have anything against women with young children or men over 50 or people who use wheelchairs. In fact, some of your best friends may be women with young children or men over 50 or people who use wheelchairs. More likely, your concern is that the candidate might not be able to do the job — and that is a perfectly legitimate concern.

You can ask questions about what you're really concerned about — whether or not the candidate can actually do the job and work the hours required. See the sidebar "Don't ask" for examples of how to ask the questions you really want answers to.

WARNING

If you wrongfully refuse to hire a job applicant on one of the prohibited grounds, he or she can file a complaint with the human rights commission, which will investigate the complaint. In the most extreme case, you could be ordered to pay damages to the applicant and to hire him or her and to pay wages from the date you rejected him or her.

Checking out the candidates

After you finish your interviews, you may find one or more candidates who look good enough to hire. But looks can be deceiving. Just because a job candidate puts something in a resume or says something during an interview does not mean that it's true. Delve a little further into the candidate's qualifications and employment history before you make your decision.

DON'T ASK

To avoid getting into trouble over human rights issues when you're interviewing a job candidate, keep in mind that your real concern is whether the candidate can do the job, and not whether the candidate is green, tri-sexual, or possessed of a record for the provincial offence of parking a bicycle in a snow removal zone in January. So ask questions that address your actual concerns. Here are some examples:

If you need someone to open your business every morning . . .

Ask: Would anything prevent you from arriving at work every morning by 8:00 a.m.?

Don't ask: Do you have children? What are your day care arrangements?

If you need someone to travel out of town . . .

Ask: Are you able to travel out of town and be away overnight?

Don't ask: Are you married?

If the job involves standing all day . . .

Ask: Would anything prevent you from standing for long periods of time?

Don't ask: Do you have problems with your back or legs?

If you need someone who can be bonded to handle valuable goods . . .

Ask: Would anything prevent you from being bonded?

Don't ask: Have you ever been convicted of an offence?

If you need someone who can drive . . .

Ask: Do you have a driver's licence?

Don't ask: Can I see your driver's licence? (It contains information about age and disability that you're not entitled to know.)

Confirming education and qualifications

You can confirm a job candidate's educational background in two ways. One is to ask to see his or her diploma or degree and/or transcripts (although people have been known to forge these documents). Another is to contact the school and ask for confirmation of the candidate's diploma or degree and grades.

TIP

If you want to get confirmation from a school, you will probably need the candidate's written permission to the school to release the information to you.

If a job candidate claims to have a licence or to be a member of a professional or trade association, contact the licensing agency or governing body for confirmation. You typically won't need the candidate's permission to get confirmation because this information is a matter of public record.

Checking references

You should ask every job candidate for the names of two or three people you can contact as references. But don't feel limited to contacting only those people whose names you're given. In fact, a head hunter we know doesn't bother to contact the references he's given, because he knows they'll have only nice things to say about the candidate. Instead, he contacts some or all of the candidate's past employers. Past employment behaviour is a pretty good predictor of future employment behaviour, and that's what you're most interested in.

As a matter of courtesy, don't ever call a candidate's current employer without the candidate's permission. The employer may not know that the candidate is looking for another job.

TIP

If you're calling a large business, ask to speak to the human resources department or personnel director. If you're calling a small business, ask the receptionist who would know about the candidate's past employment. A large business will probably have a record of the candidate's employment even if it was some time ago. A small business, on the other hand, may have no recollection of a person who worked there many years ago.

WARNING

Most Canadians are neurotically polite (some would say mealy-mouthed) or so nervous about saying anything negative that they're unwilling to say anything nasty about another person. As a result, you may find it hard to get any dirt about your candidates. For help in coming up with some questions to ask a candidate's references or past employers, see the sidebar "Don't despair."

Making an offer

After you go through all this work, we hope you find at least one person you'd like to hire. When you do, offer him or her a job. Here are some things to keep in mind about making a job offer.

DON'T DESPAIR

When you speak to a former employer of a candidate, you have to work around their desire not to say anything negative (or, in some cases, anything at all). Here are some questions that may get you some information without causing the employer to shut up like a clam:

- How long was the candidate an employee? What position did he/she hold? What were his/her duties? (These questions confirm what's in the candidate's resume or application.)
- Did the candidate perform his/her duties well?
- Did the candidate show up every day and on time?
- Did the candidate get along well with his/her managers, fellow employees, customers, or clients?
- Did the candidate have a positive attitude, and was he/she well motivated?
- Was the candidate honest?
- Why did the candidate leave the job?
- What were the candidate's strengths?
- What were the candidate's weaknesses?
- Would you hire the candidate again?

Compare the answers to what the candidate said in his or her resume or application and at the interview. Listen to what's not being said as well as to what is being said. Even if the person you're speaking to is determined not to talk, the accumulated answers (or lack of answers) to these questions will tell you a certain amount about the candidate.

Always hire on a trial basis

Even someone who has a good resume, a great interview, and glowing references may not be the right person for you. And as we tell you later in this chapter, firing a permanent employee isn't easy.

TIP

Begin by hiring any employee on either a probationary or contract basis. If you hire an employee for a probationary period of a few months (six months is common, although three-month terms are sometimes used as well) and the employee doesn't work out, you can let the employee go at any time during or at the end of the probation period without any problem. Likewise, if you hire an employee on a short-term contract, you can decide at the end of the contract whether or not to renew the contract on either a temporary or permanent basis.

Have a written contract

After you hire an employee, you and the employee have a contract — even if you don't put anything down in writing — with rights and duties toward each other. Some of these rights and duties are imposed by law and can't be changed. Others can be changed by agreement. (See the section "Being an Employer" for more about employment rights and duties.) Most employers and employees don't have a written contract, just an oral one that addresses only a few of the terms of employment.

TIP

Have a written employment contract to make sure that both employer and employee are clear about the job title and description, wages, hours of work, and amount of vacation. A written contract is a must if you want to change any of the rights and duties imposed by law, or if you want to deal with matters that the law doesn't cover.

A written employment contract should include

>> The job title

>> The employee's work duties

>> The date the job starts and how long it lasts

>> The employee's hours of work

>> The employee's rate of pay

>> The employee's right to paid vacation days and statutory holidays

>> The employee's right (if any) to paid sick days

>> Any employee benefits you're providing (such as extended health care or dental care or group life insurance)

>> A selected period of probation

>> Any rights of the employer to discipline the employee (for example, to dock pay or suspend the employee — without this, the employer has no rights to discipline)

>> A promise by the employee to devote his or her full time and attention to the employer's business

>> A promise by the employee not to reveal trade secrets (refer to Chapter 3 for more about trade secrets) or other confidential information obtained during the course of employment

>> An agreement by the employee not to compete with the employer for a period of time after termination of employment

Plus, if the nature of the job requires or suggests it,

>> Any important representations the employee has made about his or her qualifications (for example, that he or she has a particular degree or diploma, or is licensed to do certain kinds of work)

>> Any unusual equipment the employer has to provide (such as a car) or unusual action the employer has to take (such as pay professional or trade association fees) for the employee to be able to perform the job

>> A statement of the employer's right to ownership of anything invented or created by the employee in the course of business

REMEMBER

If you're going to have a written employment contract, have it prepared, or at least reviewed, by your lawyer . . . before anyone signs it.

Contacting the unsuccessful candidates

Contact all the job candidates whom you interviewed, but did not hire, to let them know that you have hired another candidate. Sound regretful that you aren't able to offer them a job. You may find yourself hunting up an unsuccessful candidate's phone number in a month or two if your chosen candidate doesn't work out.

Being an Employer

Hiring an employee is just the beginning. After you become an employer, you must

>> Be a human resources manager

>> Comply with government requirements

>> Maintain secure records about your employees and protect the privacy of this information

>> Establish fair and reasonable policies for dealing with your employees

Being a manager

If you have an employee, you have to give him or her work to do. That involves

>> Knowing what you want done and defining the role

>> Instructing, training, and developing the employee in how to do it

>> Providing and maintaining any tools and equipment the employee needs

>> Motivating the employee to do the work with financial and non-financial incentives and rewards

>> Giving constructive feedback to manage performance

This stuff can be harder to do than you think, especially if you're used to doing everything yourself. It may take longer in the beginning to explain the work and to supervise its execution than to do the work yourself. But remember, you're hiring an employee because you can't do all the work by yourself. Your time spent in instructing, motivating, and constructively criticizing your employee is an investment that will pay off in time saved in the future.

Complying with government requirements

We tell you about some of your legal responsibilities as an employer under the heading "What Are You Getting Yourself Into?" Here's a little more detail for you.

Federal requirements

As we tell you earlier in this chapter, you will have to withhold from your employees, and remit to the federal government, a certain amount for the employees' income taxes, as well as the employees' and employer's contributions to the Canada Pension Plan and Employment Insurance.

You can calculate the remittance using the payroll deduction booklets, tables by province, and formulas that the Canada Revenue Agency (CRA) provides to employers (available online through the CRA website, www.cra-arc.gc.ca). Just enter the words "payroll deductions" or associated terminology into the CRA website's search tool to readily obtain this information. The CRA's website can also help you determine payroll deductions with an online calculator. It not only helps you figure out federal, provincial (except for Quebec), and territorial payroll deductions, but it will also confirm the deductions to include on your statement of earnings filing. Just remember that if you go this self-service route, you assume the risks associated with not using this calculator properly.

WARNING

The CRA's payroll deduction online calculator utilizes one certain proprietary method of calculating payroll deductions. However, there are other equally acceptable methods that you as an employer and/or payroll service provider may use. This could result in slightly different calculations. To be safe, try to avoid the manual do-it-yourself route for your statement of earnings. Instead, consider software like QuickBooks, which includes a payroll function that takes the guesswork out and reduces the risk of making a mistake. There are also many payroll processing businesses more than willing to charge you a fee to do this task for you. To make your remittances after they're calculated, you must be registered with the CRA and have obtained a business number, which you'll mention whenever you make your payments. You can get a business number online, by telephone, mail, or fax. See the CRA website for details.

Provincial and territorial requirements

REMEMBER

You have to comply with all provincial or territorial requirements, as well as federal requirements, for employers. The provinces and territories make up the rules about employment standards and workers' comp and health insurance and so on, so you must find out

>> What your province's or territory's employment standards are regarding minimum wage, overtime pay, statutory holidays, and vacation pay

>> What you must do to register for and make contributions to your province's or territory's workers' compensation (or safety and insurance) board

>> Whether you have to make provincial or territorial health insurance contributions on behalf of your employees

>> What you must do to satisfy your province's or territory's occupational health and safety legislation

>> What you must do to comply with your province's or territory's human rights legislation

You can get this information from your provincial or territorial government, or through the Government of Canada's website (www.canada.ca).

Maintaining records

You're required by Canadian tax laws and provincial or territorial employment standards legislation to keep records for each employee. Records should be secured from unauthorized access, be kept private, and include in most cases the following:

>> **Information about the employee** — such as name, address, social insurance number, date of birth, sex, and number of dependants (yeah, now that the government wants the information instead of you, you're allowed to ask about "prohibited grounds")

>> **Information about the job** — such as job title, the date employment commenced, and the date employment ended

>> **Information related to pay** — such as number of hours worked per day and week, including overtime, rate of pay, actual wages paid, deductions from wages, vacations and vacation pay, statutory holidays taken, and information on pregnancy or parental leave, or sick leave

You must keep *tax* records for six years after the end of the taxation year, and in some provinces you must keep *employment* records for up to five years after the employment ends. However, the general rule is that employers must keep payroll and other employment records for at least 36 months.

TIP

For the gory details on employment record retention requirements, do a Google search for *Section 24 of the Canada Labour Standards Regulations.* These regulations identify in excruciating detail the required records to be kept on file and for how long. Alternately, a treasure trove of legislation can be accessed at the Government of Canada's Justice Laws website (www.laws-lois.justice.gc.ca/eng).

TIP

While you're in the record-keeping mood, you should also set up a password-protected and securely stored file for each employee that contains a record of the employee's history on the job, starting with your job description and qualifications and the employee's job application. Keep notes on your employee such as:

>> The employee's attendance and punctuality

>> Any changes in responsibility or pay

>> Any complaints about or praise for the employee (from other employees, or from customers or suppliers)

>> Performance evaluations

You'll use this information when deciding to promote an employee, or give him or her a raise . . . or fire the employee.

Establishing policies

Maybe "establishing policies" is too highfalutin a term. But you shouldn't be making up rules for your employees as you go along. (This is especially true if you have more than one employee, because you have to treat all your employees the same way.) You need policies on issues such as:

>> **Performance evaluations:** On what basis will an employee be evaluated for his or her work?

>> **Wage increases:** How frequently will you review your employee's wages and what criteria will you use to decide whether or not he or she should receive a raise?

>> **Vacations:** How long will vacations be and how will vacations be scheduled?

>> **Sick days:** Are any sick days with pay allowed?

>> **Overtime:** How will overtime work be assigned?

>> **Ongoing training:** What kind of training is required, and how will it be provided?

If this sounds time-consuming, don't worry. Now that you've got an employee to help with the work, you've freed up some of your own time to write policies! (As well as to find out about and comply with laws and regulations, train and supervise the employee, evaluate the employee's performance . . . oh, well.)

Firing an Employee

What if your business doesn't do as well as you hoped and you can no longer afford to keep your employee? Or what if the needs of your business change, and your employee's skills don't? Or what if your employee becomes a complete pain to work with?

Well, we have good news and bad news. The good news is that you almost always have the right to get rid of an employee. The bad news is that you may have to give the employee notice or pay the employee money first.

Firing for just cause

You can fire an employee without having to give notice or having to pay any money instead of giving notice if you have *just cause* — a reason that the law recognizes as a good one. Some examples of just cause are

>> Dishonesty toward your business

>> Insubordination or disobedience toward you as employer

>> Continued bad behaviour toward other employees, customers, or suppliers

>> Drunkenness or drug abuse that affects the employee's work (but see the next section for a consideration of human rights concerns)

>> Repeated absences or lateness without a reasonable medical or personal excuse

>> Incompetence or carelessness in the performance of the job that continues in spite of warnings

>> A conflict of interest with your business

In most of these situations, you must give the employee a warning about the behaviour and an opportunity to correct it before you can fire him or her. But if you catch an employee with her hand in the till, or whacking a customer over the head with a chair, you can show the employee the door immediately.

TIP

If you start to have problems with an employee, make detailed notes about the problems in the employee's file. If you decide to fire the employee, the file will help you prove in court or before a human rights tribunal (you may have fired a militant employee) that you had just cause.

Firing without just cause

You can fire an employee even if you don't have just cause — for example, if you just can't afford to pay the employee any longer, or you can't stand being in the same office with the creature. However, you must give him or her reasonable notice in writing of the termination of employment ("Your job will end in X weeks") or pay in lieu of notice ("Your job ends today. Here's a cheque for X weeks' pay.").

What is "reasonable" notice? Employment standards legislation in each province or territory sets out the minimum notice that you must give to an employee. Generally speaking, an employee who has worked for less than a given period of time (one to six months, depending on the province or territory) is not entitled to any notice. An employee who has worked at least that period of time is entitled to one or two weeks' notice (depending on the province or territory) during the first year, and then, in most provinces and territories, one week's notice for each additional year worked, up to a maximum of between two and eight weeks (again depending on the province or territory).

Courts have decided that some employees are entitled to more than the minimum notice periods set by legislation, depending on factors such as position held, salary, level of responsibility, number of years of employment, age of the employee, and the employee's chances of finding another job.

If you don't want your employee hanging around during a notice period (wreaking who knows what havoc after being told that it's all over), you can pay the employee the full wages and benefits he or she would have earned during the notice period and walk him or her off the premises.

WARNING

Consult a lawyer before you fire an employee. If you fire an employee without just cause, or without reasonable notice or pay in lieu of notice, the firing is a wrongful dismissal.

Examining wrongful dismissal

An employee you have wrongfully dismissed can sue you for compensation, which will be an amount equal to the wages and benefits the employee would have earned during a reasonable notice period. The employee must, however, *mitigate damages* — take all reasonable steps to reduce his or her losses — by looking for other work and accepting any reasonable offer of employment.

WARNING

An employee may also be entitled to compensation for mental distress if you fired him or her in a humiliating or embarrassing way, or for damage to the employee's reputation if you make untrue statements about him or her to other employees, customers, or business associates.

Addressing human rights concerns

WARNING

Oh, no! Not again! Yes, afraid so. Human rights legislation has an impact on your right to fire an employee. You're not allowed to fire an employee on any of the prohibited grounds we tell you about in the sidebar "Don't discriminate."

You may not think you're firing your employee on one of those grounds. You may think you're firing him or her for persistent lateness or absenteeism or for an inability to do the job. However, if the underlying reason for the lateness, absenteeism, or inability to do the job is in fact one of those prohibited grounds, you must first take steps to accommodate the person. For example, an employee with young children might not be able to start work at 9:00 a.m., but could get to work by 9:30 a.m. Unless being at work by 9:00 a.m. is essential to the employee's job, you must try to accommodate the employee by allowing her to start work later and make up the half hour later in the day. And how's this for a catch-22? Alcohol or drug abuse that affects the employee's work is a just cause for firing. But, if your employee is an alcoholic or drug addict, the addiction is considered a physical or mental disability, which you must first take steps to accommodate. You don't have to make accommodations that cause undue hardship to your business, but it would be up to you to prove to human rights officials that a particular accommodation would cause you more hardship than you should have to endure. (You can argue factors such as the size of your business, the cost of the accommodation, any safety risks involved, and the effect of the accommodation on the morale of other employees.)

If an employee believes that he or she was fired on one of the prohibited grounds, the employee can complain to the provincial human rights commission, which will investigate the complaint. In the most extreme case, you might be ordered to rehire the employee, pay wages from the original date of firing, and also pay compensation to the employee. This type of outcome, if it gets out in the public domain, could cause you significant reputational harm, as well as the legal consequences we mention.

When Your Employee Is Gone

You must do certain things when an employee leaves, whether he or she quit, is fired, or reaches the end of the term of a contract for employment:

TIP

>> You must complete a Record of Employment (ROE) form (so that the employee can apply for Employment Insurance benefits) and mail or electronically transmit it to the government (Service Canada) within five days after the last day of employment. (Service Canada offers help in completing the form on its website at www1.canada.ca/en/esdc/service-canada.html).

You can complete the ROE form online using Service Canada's ROE web service, available at Service Canada's website. Look for the Records of Employment (ROE) link.

>> You must pay, in addition to any payment in lieu of notice, any outstanding wages and vacation pay.

>> If you agreed to continue providing benefits such as health insurance for a time, contact the benefit provider to make sure that coverage continues.

You may be contacted about the employee by a potential employer. Many ex-employers are worried that they will be sued for defamation (slander) if they say anything negative about a former employee, but you probably can't be successfully sued as long as

>> You honestly believe that what you're saying is true.

>> You have reasonable grounds to believe what you're saying.

>> You're not saying something negative for an improper motive, such as revenge or to prevent the employee from getting another job.

Keep in mind, however, that privacy legislation prohibits you from disclosing any of your former employee's personal information without his or her consent. So be careful not to disclose personal information, such as the employee's home address or any information about his or her health. For more information about what you can't disclose, see Chapter 13 where we discuss the *Personal Information Protection and Electronic Documents Act (PIPEDA)*.

Chapter **16**

Tax Attacks!

O ne of the unpleasant realities of being in business is that you are expected to pay taxes. Lots of taxes. Every level of government — federal, provincial, and municipal — wants a piece of the action. You will have to pay

» **Income taxes** — to the federal and provincial governments

» **Sales taxes** — to the federal and provincial governments

» **Payroll taxes** — to the federal and provincial governments

» **Business taxes** — possibly to the federal and provincial governments, and more likely to your municipal government

Taxes are not only hard to dodge, they are also complicated and difficult to understand. Explaining taxes fully in just one chapter would be impossible. In fact, you can still be pretty muddled (not to mention shell-shocked and bored within an inch of death) after reading whole books about taxes. So in this chapter, we give you just enough fundamental information to let you know the kinds of taxes you have to pay and when you have to pay them, and we throw in a bit of advice about keeping your income tax to a minimum. Where necessary, we also point you to online resources or experts that can help you navigate through some of the more complex tax stuff.

Choosing Your Tax Tactics

Before we focus on the other side, let's take a look at your side. Are you planning to fight this battle heroically alone, or are you thinking that you could use some support?

Doing your own taxes

If you're strong and brave, you may believe that you can face up to the enemy all by yourself. Well, don't forget that no matter how strong and brave you are, governments are bigger than you — the fight is hardly fair. So even if you've always done your own personal income tax return, now that you're in business, doing your taxes yourself is no longer a good idea.

TIP

But if you insist on going out on a solo mission, make sure that you know what to do.

>> Read annual guides on tax. We recommend the current tax guides offered by all the big accounting firms like KPMG (www.kpmg.ca), PwC (www.pwc.com/ca), EY (www.ey.com/ca), and Deloitte (www.deloitte.ca). To find these guides, just click the Tax link under the Services section on each of these websites.

>> Visit the Canada Revenue Agency (CRA) website at www.cra-arc.gc.ca. You can download forms, schedules, guides, pamphlets, and Interpretation Bulletins (technical and detailed statements of the CRA's position on a variety of specific subjects). Or contact your local Tax Services Office in person or by phone to ask questions.

>> Visit non-government websites that specialize in current tax issues such as TaxTips.ca (www.taxtips.ca). This site excels at providing the most current tax rates and advice under different scenarios and situations.

>> Visit the website of your provincial department or ministry of finance for information about provincial taxes on business.

>> Contact your municipality for information about municipal business taxes, or visit its website.

WARNING

The CRA is good for general information, but don't expect them to give you advice on how to save taxes. The CRA is primarily an administrative and enforcement function, not an advisory one. And provincial and municipal websites may be more interested in encouraging businesses to set up than in providing up-front details about taxes.

Enlisting cyber help

A number of software programs are available to help you prepare your own personal and corporate income tax returns, such as TurboTax Canada (http://turbotax.intuit.ca), TaxTron (www.taxtron.ca), Cantax (www.cantax.com), and UFile (www.ufile.ca).

When you use a computer program, you put in the numbers and your computer does all the calculations for you. If you forget something or have to make a change, the computer will recalculate your totals. Some programs offer online help and include tax-saving suggestions.

WARNING

No tax program will tell you whether your claims are reasonable or correct. You need personal advice for that kind of input. And software concentrates on income taxes, not on all the different taxes you may be required to pay.

Recruiting a Certified Public Accountant

TIP

Now that you're in business, your best bet is to hire a professional accountant with experience in small business taxation to help you with your taxes. An accountant can give you advice about a wide variety of matters relating to your tax obligations. We tell you about hiring and working with an accountant in Chapter 17.

Income Taxes

After you consider how to approach taxes, move on to an analysis of the enemy's movements. Income taxes are the main battlefront. Here you'll find the massed strength.

Individuals and corporations must pay taxes on income to both the federal and provincial governments. The Canada Revenue Agency collects both federal and provincial income tax from individuals (human beings, that is) in every province except Quebec, and from corporations in all provinces except Alberta and Quebec, where the provincial governments collect their own corporate income taxes.

TECHNICAL
STUFF

A business can also be taxed on its *capital gains*. A capital gain is the profit made on the sale or other disposition of *capital property*. Capital property is property acquired to be held onto rather than resold right away. Examples of capital property could include commercial real estate bought for use in a business, or shares in a corporation. A start-up business isn't likely to have capital gains while it's a going concern, so we don't talk about capital gains in this chapter. But a business may have capital gains or capital losses when the business is sold or is wound up, so we do talk about capital gains and losses in Chapter 21.

Understanding what income a business is taxed on

You will be pleased to know that you're not taxed on every cent your business earns. Your income taxes are calculated only on the *profit* your business makes. Your business's profit is its *gross income* (or *revenue* — the money the business takes in) minus its legitimate expenses (the money spent or expenses incurred in order to earn the income). This last point about money spent to generate income is a critical tax principle regarding the deductibility of expenses in the eyes of the CRA.

The lower your business's profit, the less tax you will have to pay. So the question is how legally to keep your profits as low as possible for tax purposes. There are only two ways to have low profits (and therefore low taxes). One is to keep your business revenues as low as possible and the other is to make your legitimate business expenses as high as possible. You want to avoid taxes — not evade them!

You are required by law to report everything your business earns. So the only way to reduce your profits and your tax payable legally is to maximize your legitimate deductible business expenses. Over the next few pages, we tell you what is considered to be business revenue and what is considered to be a legitimate business expense. It's not an exhaustive list, but it does cover the items most small business owners can expect to see.

WARNING

Everyone wants to pay as little tax as possible. Again, it bears repeating that tax *avoidance* is paying as little tax as is legally possible. Tax *evasion*, on the other hand, is failing to pay taxes that are legally owing — and it's a serious crime. Income tax laws are complicated and change constantly, so you need expert tax advice from an accountant and/or tax lawyer to make sure that you avoid as much tax as you can without evading any tax. You also need professional advice to make sure that any tax-avoidance scheme you come up with will actually work.

Defining business income

According to the CRA, *business income* includes money earned or valuable property received from any activity you engage in as part of your business. Business income includes

>> Fees charged to your clients for services you provide, excluding any sales tax you charged

>> The purchase price charged to your customers for goods you sell, excluding any sales tax you charged

We give you intelligence concerning sales taxes later in this chapter.

You are required to report to the CRA all income earned by your business during the taxation year.

Discovering what legitimate business expenses are

The CRA allows you to deduct from business income most reasonable expenses you pay in order to earn that income. Because the only legal way to reduce your profits — and therefore your taxes — is to maximize your legitimate business expenses, knowing what your legitimate business expenses are is very important. They include

>> Mortgage interest and property taxes on real property you own and use for your business (see the heading "Home office expenses" if you run your business out of a home you own)

>> Rent if you lease your business premises (see "Home office expenses" if you run your business out of your rented home)

>> The cost of labour and materials for any minor repairs or maintenance done to property you use to earn income

>> The cost of leasing equipment used in your business

>> The cost of buying or manufacturing the goods you sold during the year

>> Delivery, freight, and transportation expenses

>> Insurance premiums you pay to insure any buildings, machinery, and equipment you use in your business

>> Utilities such as telephone, electricity, heat, and water

>> The cost of office expenses and supplies — small items such as laser or ink printer cartridges, stationery, pens, pencils, paper clips, and stamps

>> Some of the expenses of running a motor vehicle that you use to earn business income (for more information see the heading "Car expenses")

>> Interest you pay on money that you borrow to run your business

>> Annual licence fees and levies (such as municipal business taxes) to run your business

>> Annual dues or fees for membership in a trade or commercial association (but not if the main purpose of the club is dining, recreation, or sporting activities)

>> Legal, accounting, and other professional fees

>> Management and administration fees to operate your business, including bank charges

>> Expenses for advertising your product or service

>> Travel expenses to earn business income

>> Fifty percent of business meals, beverages, and entertainment

>> Salaries and benefits you pay to employees, as well as your portion of Canada Pension Plan (CPP) and Employment Insurance (EI) premiums (see the heading "Employee salaries" for more information)

REMEMBER

The CRA's tax forms that deal with deductible business expenses, or the tax software we mention earlier, will have an exhaustive but well-organized list of the types of expenses you can deduct (or cannot deduct), along with special rules that some of these items carry with them, such as the 50 percent provision for meal allowances.

You may have noticed that in this list we mention only leased equipment, and purchased office supplies of a minor kind such as pens and paper. More important items that you purchase (rather than lease) such as a computer, phone system, fax machine or other office equipment, furniture, and larger items such as buildings or vehicles, can't be fully claimed in the year of *purchase* as a business expense. That's because these items, which are capital property, will continue to be useful to your business for more than one taxation year. However, since these items *depreciate* (wear out or lose their usefulness over time, except land), you can claim a percentage of the cost as a business expense each year over a period of several years until the entire cost has been claimed. The amount you are allowed to claim on *depreciable capital property* each year as an expense is called *capital cost allowance* (CCA), and the income tax form has a special place for calculating the exact amount of capital cost allowance you can claim in a given year. Each type of eligible depreciable capital property (excluding land) is placed into a special "class," and each class has its own depreciation rate. This deduction is subject to limits (you cannot deduct depreciation to reduce taxable income below zero), but it's still a very significant tax break.

Using computer equipment and the software that runs it as examples of costly assets that almost all businesses have, you can claim a portion (as prescribed by the CRA and further subject to special half-year rules that are beyond the scope of this book to explain) and deduct it from your income. In the case of computers and software, the classes, rates, and inclusions are as follows:

>> Class 8 assets such as photocopiers and communications equipment like fax machines, telephone equipment, and cellphones depreciate at a rate of 20 percent.

>> Class 12 assets have 100 percent full depreciation and are also subject to the half-year rule. It includes computer application software (not systems software) such as word processors, spreadsheets, accounting software, and database programs. Microsoft Office 360 is an example of computer application software.

>> Class 46 has 30 percent depreciation and includes data network equipment that underpins advanced telecommunication applications. This class includes hubs, routers, and domain name servers that are used to control, transfer, modulate, and direct data.

>> Class 50 has 55 percent depreciation and includes general purpose computer equipment and systems software used for that equipment. This class includes computers, servers, storage devices, monitors, disk drives, cables, and printers as well as pre-installed system software that operates these devices. Systems software is core software such as that used for Windows and Mac OS X.

As you can see, when you get to deduct against taxable income (hopefully) what in some cases is a very large fraction of the total cost of critical business equipment, you can keep taxes on that income at bay. At least for a while!

WARNING

Many of your business expenses are clearly only for your business, such as the cost of an ad in the newspaper or lease payments on machinery used to create the product you sell. But you may use other items both for your business and personally — for example, a cellphone, a computer, or your car. When you calculate your business expenses, you are not allowed to claim any part of the expense that relates to your personal use of the item. You can deduct only the portion of the expense that relates to your business use. For example, if you use half of your monthly airtime on your cellphone for business calls and half for personal calls, you can claim as a business expense only the amount paid for the business calls. The forms that the CRA or tax software provide help you make this calculation.

Home office expenses

If you operate your business from your home, you are allowed to deduct expenses for the business use of your home. This allows you to get a tax deduction for a portion of your home expenses (which you would have to pay anyway).

REMEMBER

For the costs to be deductible, your home office must either

>> Be your principal place of business

>> If it's not your main place of business, be used exclusively for business purposes and be used on a regular basis for meeting clients or customers in connection with the business

If your home office meets one of these two conditions, you can deduct a percentage of the following costs:

>> Mortgage interest and property taxes (if you own) or rental payments (if you rent)

>> Utilities such as heat, electricity, and water

>> Maintenance costs or condo fees

>> Home insurance

>> Allowable portion (a limited amount) of CCA

To figure out the percentage you're allowed to deduct, calculate what percentage of your home you use for your business. Divide the area of your office by the total area of your home. So, for example, if your home is 1,500 square feet in area, and the room you use exclusively for business is 300 square feet in area, then you can deduct 20 percent of your home costs. Or you may divide the number of rooms occupied by your business by the total number of rooms in your home. For example, if you have four rooms in your apartment and you use one of those rooms exclusively for business, then you can deduct 25 percent of your home costs.

WARNING

You can use the home office deduction to bring your business income down to zero, but not to put your business into a loss position, or to increase a loss that already exists. After you reach zero, any home office expenses that are left over can be applied against business income in future years.

Car expenses

You are allowed to deduct the expenses of running a motor vehicle that you use to earn business income. These expenses include

>> Fuel and oil

>> Maintenance and repairs

>> Insurance

>> Licence and registration fees

>> Leasing costs or interest paid on money borrowed to buy the vehicle (but note that if your vehicle is a passenger car, you are allowed to claim only a limited amount)

>> Capital cost allowance, if you own the motor vehicle (again, if your vehicle is a passenger car, you are allowed to claim only a limited amount)

If you use your car for both business and personal purposes, only the portion of your car expenses that relate to your business activities is a legitimate business expense. Use the following formula:

(Total car expenses @ts kilometres driven for business purposes) ÷
Total kilometers driven = Allowable business expense

Employee salaries

You can deduct the salaries you pay to your employees, as well as the portion that you pay of their CPP and EI contributions. You can also deduct the cost of any benefits you provide to your employees, such as health insurance and life insurance. (For more on these matters, refer to Chapter 15.)

WARNING

In the past, hiring a family member was a good way to reduce your business income taxes. By paying your spouse or child or parent a legitimate (as defined by the CRA) salary, you were able to reduce profits and, therefore, taxes payable. Your family member will have paid tax on the salary, but less tax than you or your business would have, as long as his or her tax rate was lower. At the time of this writing, legislation was passed to curtail the use of this "income splitting" strategy. You need to consult a qualified tax advisor to help you navigate this complex change if you want to avoid CRA scrutiny in the future.

WARNING

If you are a sole proprietor or a partner, you or your partners are not employees of the business, so you cannot deduct any salary or draw taken. In order to be employees and run the business, you have to incorporate. However, being a sole proprietor or partner has other tax advantages, so don't go rushing off to incorporate (see Chapter 6).

Assessing how much tax you will pay

The amount of tax you will pay depends on the form of your business (see Chapter 6). That's because sole proprietorships and partnerships are taxed differently than corporations.

If your business is a sole proprietorship or partnership

If you carry on business as a sole proprietor, from the tax point of view the business's income is considered to be your personal income. If you carry on business in a partnership, your share of the business's income is also considered to be your personal income.

You report your (or your share of the) business's profits or loss in your personal income tax return. (See the heading "Determining when and how you have to pay" for more.) Your business does not file a separate tax return.

If your business has made a profit, the profit (or your share of the profit) is included in your personal income and is taxed as personal income. If your business has suffered a loss, the loss (or your share of the loss) is subtracted from your personal income from other sources for the year. That means that a business loss reduces your total income.

TIP

If you have a business loss but you have no other income for the year, or if the loss from your business is greater than your income from other sources, you can carry the loss back and apply it against income you earned in the past three years, or you can carry it forward and apply it against income you earn in the next ten years. There are exceptions beyond the scope of this book, but check out the "Tax" tab at www.canada.ca to see what those nuances are, or consult your tax advisor.

Your federal and provincial income tax is calculated as a percentage of your total personal income, including your business profits or loss. Your tax rate depends on your total income — as your income goes up, so does the percentage at which it is taxed.

TECHNICAL STUFF

Federal tax rates are the same across the country, but provincial tax rates vary from province to province. As a result, the combined rates of federal and provincial tax vary across the country. You can find exact information about the combined federal and provincial tax for your province at TaxTips.ca (www.taxtips.ca), but in the meantime we can give you a very rough idea of what you'll have to pay. In the 2019 taxation year, depending on the province and the exact amount earned, taxpayers earning

>> Less than approximately $12,000 pay no tax

>> Between approximately $12,000 and $43,000 pay between about 20 percent and 31 percent on the amount over 12,000

>> Between approximately $43,000 and $88,000 pay between about 25 percent and 47 percent on the amount over $43,000

>> Between approximately $88,000 and $148,000 pay between about 31 percent and 49 percent on the amount over $88,000

>> Over approximately $148,000 pay between about 43 percent and 53 percent on the amount over $148,000

Again, these are very rough estimates for illustration purposes. For more precise brackets in a particular year, check out TaxTips.ca (www.taxtips.ca) or Google the tax guides offered by the big accounting firms like KPMG (www.kpmg.ca), PwC (www.pwc.com/ca), or Deloitte (www.deloitte.ca). For exact rates, go to the CRA website in the year you file.

If your business is a corporation

If your business is incorporated, the corporation is a taxpayer and has to file its own income tax return (see the heading "Determining when and how you have to pay" for more about how this is done) and pay tax on its profits.

Unlike individuals, whose tax rate increases in steps or brackets with the amount of income earned, corporations are taxed at a flat rate. The basic rate of Part I tax is 38 percent of your taxable income, 28 percent after a federal tax abatement, which is beyond the scope of this book to discuss. After the general tax reduction, also beyond scope, the net tax rate is 15 percent. For Canadian-controlled private corporations claiming the small business deduction, and with recent changes to legislation regarding small businesses, the net tax rate can drop all the way to 9 percent. (A *Canadian-controlled private corporation* is exactly what it sounds like — a private corporation controlled by Canadian shareholders.)

Depending on the province, the combined federal and provincial tax rate will probably hover in the mid to high 20 percent range. The average corporate tax rate in Canada stands at about 27 percent. Again, depending on a multitude of variables, including the nature and location of business operations, these are just illustrative figures.

REMEMBER

The federal small business deduction reduces the tax rate to between 11.5 percent and 16 percent on the first $450,000 to $600,000 (depending on the province, but most attract the $500,000 limit) of taxable income earned by a Canadian-controlled private corporation. This gives new corporations a good shot at keeping a good portion of what they earn away from the tax man.

WARNING

The small business deduction generally does not apply to a corporation's income from interest, dividends, rents, or royalties.

TIP

If your corporation suffers a loss, the loss can be carried back and applied against profits made in the past three years, or carried forward and applied against profits made in the next ten years. (The corporation's loss cannot be applied to reduce your personal income for tax purposes.)

The tax authorities aren't finished with you after they tax your corporation. If you receive any money from the corporation in the form of salary, benefits, a bonus, or dividends, you have to report that money as income on your personal income tax return and pay tax on what you receive. (See the heading "If your business is a sole proprietorship or partnership," for tax rates.) Salary, bonus, or benefits are taxed at your personal tax rate. Dividends are also taxed at your personal tax rate, but come with a dividend tax credit (after a gross up adjustment) that limits taxes to a rate that is less than the rate used for other forms of income such as salary or interest income. The dividend tax credit recognizes the fact that eligible dividends are a distribution of corporate profits on which the corporation has already paid taxes. As the federal corporate tax rate is reduced, these rates are likely to increase.

Determining when and how you have to pay

Every Canadian taxpayer is required to file an income tax return each year and pay whatever taxes are owing. The type of return you file, your deadline for filing it, and the deadline for paying your taxes depend on your form of business organization.

If your business is a sole proprietorship or partnership

If you carry on business as a sole proprietor or in a partnership, your profit from the business is considered to be your personal income and is reported in your personal tax return — the standard T1-General Form. Your business does not file a separate tax return. Instead you complete a Form T2125, Statement of Business or Professional Activities, and include it as part of your personal tax return. The form gives details of your business's income and expenses. You include the business's profit (or loss) as part of your income.

Individual taxpayers must file their personal income tax returns and pay any taxes owing by April 30 of the year following the taxation year. (That means, for example, filing your income tax return for 2019 by April 30, 2020.) If you are self-employed and are a sole proprietor or a partner, your tax return is not due until June 15 following the end of your business's fiscal period or taxation year (which for most partnerships and sole proprietorships must be the same as the calendar year). However, your taxes must still be paid by April 30. So even if you're not ready to prepare your income tax return, you have to estimate how much tax is owing and send that amount in by April 30 with a letter setting out your social insurance number and what the payment is for. (If you estimate wrong, you'll have to pay interest from April 30 on the amount you didn't pay but should have.)

WARNING

Don't for a minute think that just because you are self-employed and not receiving a paycheque, the CRA will sit back and wait to be paid all the taxes you owe on April 30. Self-employed taxpayers are required to pay their tax by quarterly instalments (due March 15, June 15, September 15, and December 15). After your first year of making a profit on which you have to pay at least $3,000 in tax ($1,800 in Quebec), the CRA will send you an instalment notice telling you that you have to start paying taxes on a quarterly basis, and thereafter it will send you quarterly reminders to pay up. The CRA calculates your instalment payments, but you don't have to pay those amounts. You can estimate your income for the year and pay one-fourth each quarter. But if you underestimate the amount of tax you owe, you will have to pay interest on the amount by which your instalments fall short.

If you have to make quarterly instalment payments, salt away in a special bank account the amount you'll owe at the end of each quarter, so that you don't accidentally spend it.

In the first year that your sole proprietorship or partnership makes a profit, don't forget that you're a taxpayer even though you don't have to pay taxes until April 30 of the following year! Estimate (generously) how much money you'll owe in taxes on each month's income, and put that amount into an interest-earning bank account or into treasury bills or GICs so that you'll have it ready to pay on April 30 and you'll have earned some interest income on it. We know, rates are low. But some interest is better than no interest, and these financial vehicles force you to save.

If your business is a partnership with six or more partners, the partnership must also file a partnership information return — Form T5013. (An information return is not a tax return. It is not used to calculate how much tax is payable, but rather to give the CRA information to ensure that tax information for the partnership is being properly calculated and reported by each of the partners.) The partnership information form must be filed by March 31.

If your business is a corporation

If your business is incorporated, the corporation is a taxpayer and has to file its own income tax return — Form T2, Corporation Income Tax Return — together with information from the corporation's financial statements. (See Chapter 17 for more about financial statements.) Form T2 serves as both a federal and provincial income tax return — except in Alberta and Quebec, where a separate provincial corporate tax return must also be filed. Ontario corporations must also file an *Ontario Corporations Information Act* Annual Return. For Quebec taxes, search out the Corporate Income Tax Return section of the Revenue Quebec website (www.revenuquebec.ca) for corporate tax return forms and pertinent information.

The corporation will have to file a corporate income tax return within six months after the end of the corporation's fiscal period or taxation year. Unlike a sole proprietorship or partnership, a corporation can choose any date for its year-end.

You will also have to file your personal income tax return. Your return must be filed by April 30, because you are not considered to be self-employed when you're running your business through a corporation.

A corporation must pay income tax in monthly instalments unless the tax payable for the year or the previous taxation year is $3,000 or less for all provinces except Quebec. (During the corporation's first taxation year, no instalment payments

have to be made.) The CRA does not calculate the amount of the instalments —
you must do that yourself, basing your payment on one of the following:

>> An estimate of the tax payable in the current year

>> The tax paid in the previous year

>> A combination of the tax paid in the previous year and the year before that

TECHNICAL
STUFF

If the corporation owes more income tax than it paid in its monthly instalments,
it must pay the balance within two months after the end of the corporation's fiscal
year (three months if the corporation is a Canadian-controlled private corporation, eligible for the small business deduction, and with an income of less than
$500,000 in most provinces). Notice that the due date to pay the balance of the tax
is earlier than the deadline for filing the corporation's income tax return.

Being penalized

Whether your business is a sole proprietorship, partnership, or corporation, you
will have to pay interest at about 6 percent on taxes that are overdue if

>> You don't make your instalment payments on time.

>> You don't pay enough in instalment payments.

>> You don't pay any balance of tax owing by the due date — April 30 for
individuals, and two (or three) months after the fiscal year end for a
corporation.

You may have to pay a penalty if

>> Your accumulated interest charges for any year are more than $1,000.

>> You file your income tax return late.

>> You fail to report income.

>> You knowingly or carelessly make false statements or omissions on your tax
return.

Penalties start at 5 percent of unpaid taxes . . . but they don't stop there. If you owe
taxes and file your tax return late, the CRA charges an additional percent for each
month late up to 12 months. For example, if you owe the CRA $20,000 and you file
your tax return six months late, the CRA assesses an 11 percent penalty. This
increases your tax bill to $22,000. Filing late taxes when you're owed a refund or
you don't owe any further tax will not, however, result in any interest, fees, or
penalties.

Keeping the proper records

Any corporation or individual who carries on a business, or is required to pay or collect income taxes, must keep books and records that allow the amount of taxes payable to be calculated and checked. You must hold on to these books and records for at least six years after the taxation year they relate to.

TIP

To easily prepare your tax returns when they are due, you should keep organized books and records throughout the year and hang on to your invoices and receipts. You can keep actual account books, or you can use small-business bookkeeping and accounting software. We tell you more about accounting for your business in Chapter 17.

Dealing with an audit

When you file your or your corporation's income tax return, the CRA reviews the return. When the CRA completes the review it issues a notice of assessment, which sets out the amount of tax payable for the year. The CRA has the right to reassess your return later, and can go back and reassess your returns for the past three years (or longer, if they suspect fraud) and ask you for more money. If you disagree with the CRA about the amount it says you have to pay, you (personally or through your accountant) can object to the assessment or reassessment, and try to persuade the CRA that you don't owe as much as they say by showing them documents that support your objection and even by visiting the local tax services office in person to argue your case. This can go on for some time, because the CRA usually takes a while to digest any communication from a taxpayer.

A tax audit is different from (and worse than) an assessment or reassessment. In an audit, the CRA goes over all your records, including records you weren't required to send in with your tax return, to see whether you've declared all your income and deducted only legitimate expenses.

WARNING

Tax returns of corporations and self-employed taxpayers are more likely to be audited than those of taxpayers who are employees, because businesses have more opportunities to evade taxes by hiding income or inflating (or even making up) expenses.

TIP

On an audit you will have to prove all your income and expenses by presenting receipts. So just in case you're audited, you should keep dated receipts and show what business activity they relate to.

If you are audited, the CRA will notify you by letter that your tax return for a stated year, or years, has been selected for review. The letter will ask you to provide specified information within 30 days (although you can ask for an extension if you need more time).

If you get an audit letter, speak to your accountant immediately. If you don't already have an accountant, get one!

You can respond to the request on your own, or you can (and probably should) hire an accountant or tax lawyer.

The auditor will then arrange a face-to-face meeting (your accountant or even your lawyer can be present), during which you may be asked to justify some of your expense claims. You'll respond by showing the auditor your supporting records and receipts. You should have your records organized so that you are able to answer the auditor's questions. Be cooperative and polite, even if you're feeling cranky and angry. (Don't bother irritating a person who has the power to assess additional taxes, not to mention interest and penalties, against you.)

When the auditor is finished, he or she will send you a letter setting out proposed changes to your income tax return, and giving you time either to accept the changes or dispute them. (To dispute the proposed changes, you will have to provide new information that you didn't have for the auditor.) Then the CRA will send you a notice of reassessment setting out what you owe and when it's due.

If you accept the reassessment, you have to pay the balance by the due date. If you can't pay by the due date, you can contact the collections department of the CRA to make other arrangements for payment. You can apply to the CRA through a formal appeals process to have any penalties or interest set aside. If you disagree with the reassessment, you can file a notice of objection with your local tax services office within 90 days after the date of the reassessment.

Sales Taxes

You've had the spy-satellite overview of income taxes, so we move on to sales taxes.

Man battle stations! The enemy is performing a flanking maneuver.

The Goods and Services Tax (GST) is a federal tax levied in all provinces and territories either on its own or as part of the Harmonized Sales Tax (HST). In New Brunswick, Newfoundland and Labrador, Nova Scotia, Ontario, and Prince Edward Island, you have to charge HST because these provinces have combined the GST with their provincial sales tax schemes to create a uniform HST.

Other provinces, such as British Columbia, Manitoba, Quebec, and Saskatchewan, kept their provincial sales tax schemes (provincial sales taxes such as PST or QST) separate and apart from the federal GST tax system. This means that in those provinces, your small business must charge, collect, and remit GST, as well as PST or QST. To boot, it must also fill out two sets of forms. As for Alberta, the Territories, Yukon, and Nunavut, there are no provincial sales taxes, so your business only has to charge, collect, and remit GST. Provincial sales taxes range from 7 percent to 10 percent; GST is 5 percent; and HST is between 13 percent and 15 percent (depending on the province).

Provincial sales tax

Businesses that sell goods or provide services on which PST has to be charged are responsible for collecting the tax from the buyer of the goods or services. Businesses are required to *remit* (send) the collected taxes to the provincial government on a regular basis. In every province except Quebec (where sales tax works more like GST, see the "Goods and Services Tax" section later), the tax is payable by the final consumer only, so businesses do not have to pay PST on goods that will be resold (although they must pay PST on goods bought for their own use).

If your business will be selling goods or providing services on which PST must be charged, you must register with your provincial government's department or ministry of finance. You will be given a registration certificate and provincial tax number. You will have to file periodic (usually monthly) returns with the ministry of finance, in which you report the amount of tax collected and remit the tax. For more information about PST in your province, check the website for your provincial Canada Business Service Centre or for your provincial government.

Your business must keep proper books and records to document the amount of tax collected, and you are subject to audits by the provincial government.

WARNING

If you fail to file returns, collect taxes as required, or remit the taxes collected, you may be charged an interest penalty. You may even be charged with an offence and hauled into court.

Goods and Services Tax

GST applies to almost all goods sold and services supplied anywhere in Canada. Unlike PST, which is paid only by the ultimate consumer, GST is charged to everyone along the production and sale chain — from the supplier of the raw materials, through the manufacturer, wholesaler, and retailer, down to the consumer. While everyone is charged the tax, the government keeps only the tax paid by the ultimate consumer. Everyone else in the chain is allowed to claim a refund on the GST they paid (called an *input tax credit*).

You'll find plenty of information about the GST on the CRA website at www.cra-arc.gc.ca.

GST categories

GST must be charged when goods and services are "supplied" — whether by sale, rental, barter, or gift. Three categories of "supplies" exist:

>> Supplies that are taxable at 5 percent, which commonly include all supplies that don't fall into the second and third categories — so chances are good that whatever goods or services you're providing are in the first category.

>> Supplies that are taxable at 0 percent, which commonly include prescription drugs and medical devices, basic groceries, international travel and transportation, precious metals, and farm and fishing products and equipment.

>> Supplies that are tax-exempt, which commonly include health care, personal care, child care, or educational services and financial services.

Are crazy people running the Goods and Services Tax department of the federal government? Why would you tax supplies at 0 percent . . . and what on earth is the difference between supplies that are taxed at 0 percent and supplies that are tax-exempt? Well, the GST people may indeed be crazy, but there's a method to their madness. The supplier doesn't collect GST from customers if supplies are taxed at 0 percent or if supplies are tax-exempt. But if a business provides zero-rated supplies it can still claim a refund on the GST it paid to get goods and services, whereas if a business provides tax-exempt supplies, it can't. Again, be sure to check out the CRA website for any changes to the inclusions to and exclusions from GST "supplies."

Registering for the GST

If your business provides GST-taxable goods and services and has annual revenues (income before expenses) of more than $30,000, you *must* register for the GST. Otherwise you *may* register. Once you register for the GST you must charge GST to your customers and remit it to the CRA, and you can claim a refund on the GST you pay to get goods and services. If you don't register for the GST, you don't have to charge GST, but you can't claim a refund, either.

Register for the GST even if your revenues are less than $30,000. You'll be able to get back the GST paid on the goods and services your business buys. Besides, you don't really want your customers to know that your business's annual revenues are less than $30,000.

You register for the GST by applying to the CRA for a *business number*; we tell you how in Chapter 6.

Collecting and remitting GST

When you invoice a customer or client for goods or services you provide, you have to invoice for GST, as well. You calculate GST on the full price your customer pays, including any customs or excise duties and transportation taxes — but excluding any provincial sales tax, and not taking into account any discounts for early payment of your invoice or interest charged for late payment.

You must report the amount of GST collected and remit it to the CRA on a regular basis. How often you remit depends on your business's annual sales, as follows:

>> If your annual sales are less than $1,500,000, you must report and remit GST annually, although you can choose to report quarterly; you can also choose to report and remit monthly.

>> If your annual sales are between $1,500,000 and $6,000,000, you must report and remit GST quarterly, although you can choose to report and remit monthly.

>> If your annual sales are more than $6,000,000 (here's hoping!), you must report and remit GST monthly.

On the GST form, you show the GST your business charged on the goods and services it provided, as well as the GST your business paid on the goods and services it bought. The difference between what you charged and what you paid is the amount you must remit to the government. If you paid more than you charged, you are entitled to a GST refund.

You must keep books and records, including invoices, to document the GST collected and any refunds claimed, for six years.

If you fail to report or remit GST as required, you will be charged interest and penalties. If you willfully fail to pay, collect, or remit GST, you can be charged with an offence, and if you're convicted, you can be fined or imprisoned.

Harmonized Sales Tax

Hey, what's that sound? Could it be "The Ride of the Valkyries"? Actually, it's the humming of the Harmonized Sales Tax (HST), the name given to the combined GST and provincial sales tax charged in New Brunswick, Newfoundland and Labrador, Nova Scotia, Ontario, and Prince Edward Island.

If your business supplies goods or services in these provinces, you are required to collect and remit HST of between 13 and 15 percent (depending on the province) to the CRA. When you register for GST, you're also registered for HST, which works the same way as GST.

Payroll Taxes

Payroll taxes are taxes levied by the federal government and some provincial governments on businesses with employees. The federal payroll taxes are Employment Insurance (EI) and Canada Pension Plan (CPP). Employers must make contributions to EI and CPP on behalf of their employees, as well as withhold and remit the employees' contributions. Provincial payroll taxes include health insurance and workers' compensation premiums.

We tell you about payroll taxes in Chapter 15.

Business Taxes

In addition to income taxes, sales taxes, and payroll taxes, federal, provincial, and municipal governments levy other business taxes:

» The federal government levies a large corporation tax on corporations with over $10 million of taxable capital in Canada.

» Some provincial governments levy a tax on the paid-up capital of corporations. Paid-up capital is the total amount paid to the corporation for all the shares that have been issued to shareholders.

» Municipalities levy taxes on businesses. Businesses that own real estate in the municipality have to pay property taxes, but in some municipalities, even businesses that rent rather than own are required to pay taxes. These taxes may be based, for example, on the annual rental value of the property or the square footage of the premises or the value of the business's stock-in-trade.

TIP

Your accountant can tell you more about these matters, or you can contact your federal, provincial, and municipal governments or visit their websites.

Chapter **17**

Close Encounters with Accounting

D on't run away in terror just because you saw the word accounting and bright lights started flashing before your eyes. Accounting is, in essence, the language of business, so try to learn and embrace it. (Or at least flip through this chapter to start conquering your fears.)

To be successful, a small business owner has to keep track of what the business earns and what it spends, and what it owns and what it owes. That means that every small business owner has to know something about accounting. But we're not going to inflict an entire accounting course on you — we're just going to tell you about the absolute basics. We're talking Accounting 101 here! If you find yourself yearning for more information, you can turn to *Accounting For Canadians For Dummies*, by John A. Tracy and Cécile Laurin, and *Bookkeeping For Canadians For Dummies*, 2nd Edition, by Lita Epstein and Cécile Laurin (both published by Wiley).

What's Accounting and Why Is It Important?

The essence of accounting is keeping track of financial transactions. Accounting is a process that begins with the collecting and recording of information about transactions and continues with the sorting of the transactions by category and ends in the preparation of financial statements and income tax returns. Accountants call this process the *accounting cycle*. Some of the steps in the accounting cycle will be carried out by you, others will be carried out by your bookkeeper and/or your computerized accounting system, and still others will be carried out by your accountant.

Accounting is important in the day-to-day operation of your business because it helps you

» Collect your accounts

» Pay your bills

» Pay your taxes

» Keep track of your inventory

» Prevent theft and fraud by your associates, employees, and customers

Accounting is also important in the long term because it helps you

» Assess how your business is doing

» Collect the information you need to plan and make decisions

» Give lenders the information they want before they will lend you money

» Give investors the information they want before they will invest in your business

» Give a buyer the information he or she wants to see before buying your business

» Show the government that you are complying with tax laws

Bookkeeping

Bookkeeping is the information-gathering and record-keeping aspect of accounting. No matter how much professional or computer help you intend to have with your bookkeeping, keeping track of all the financial transactions of your business is up to you — such as making sales, buying inventory, paying salaries, and borrowing money.

REMEMBER

Your first chore as a bookkeeper is to keep all the pieces of paper, such as invoices, sales slips, and credit card slips that document business transactions (and the more organized you are about it, the better). You should also keep a record of these transactions.

Creating and saving source documents

The basic facts of every financial transaction of your business should be documented by a *source document* — in either paper or electronic format — at the following times:

>> **Whenever your business provides a service or sells a product:** You should generate an invoice. (You may have the kind of business where you prepare invoices only on a weekly or monthly basis.) Most if not all accounting software can generate invoices. If it does not, buy software that does. The invoice is a critical document, and a handwritten invoice will not look professional. If you're in a retail business, your cash register or computer point-of-sales terminal will generate a sales slip that you can print out. Send or give the invoice to the customer or client, and keep a copy for your records.

>> **Whenever your business incurs an expense or makes a payment:** No matter how small the payment, you should get a bill, invoice, or receipt. If the receipt doesn't indicate what the sale relates to or show the date the payment was made, make a note on the receipt identifying the transaction more clearly.

TIP

For income tax purposes you have to keep a copy of both the bill and a copy of your cheque as proof of payment.

You must save every last one of these source documents. If you generate paper documents, you can just throw all of them into a file, and let your bookkeeper and/ or accountant sort them out later (and charge you for the extra work), but it makes more sense for you to set up a system for filing them by category. For example, you may want to set up separate files for

>> Invoices you give to your customers when you provide a service or product

>> Inventory purchases

>> Office supply expenses

>> Car expenses

>> Entertainment expenses

>> Accounting expenses

Recording your transactions

The next step in the bookkeeping process is to make a written or electronic record of the financial transactions, taking the information from your source documents.

Open a business bank account

TIP

If you want to keep track of and have a record of your business transactions, you should open a bank account that is just for your business. Open a separate account even if your business is a sole proprietorship or partnership. (Refer to Chapter 6. If you're a sole proprietor or partner, your business is not legally separate from you as an individual.) You might think that it doesn't matter if your business and personal accounts get mixed up — but reading this chapter will persuade you to keep your business affairs to themselves.

The bank account should be a chequing account that gives you a monthly statement and that automatically returns your cancelled cheques, or gives you copies of the cheques. Unless you will be using a computerized accounting program that will prepare and keep track of your cheques (see later in this chapter), order cheques for your new account, and get a *cheque register*. (This little booklet for recording transactions in your account usually comes with your new cheques or can be wheedled out of a teller at your bank or trust company.) An alternative to the booklet is a chequebook that has stubs — smaller pieces of paper attached to each cheque that are bound together in numerical order. You enter on the stub key information that you wrote on each cheque, such as whom you paid, the amount, and the date. (And enter a description of what was paid for, to remind yourself later.) Cheque stubs also give you space to keep a running balance in your bank account.

Pay into and out of your business account

Whenever you receive a payment for goods or services provided by your business, deposit the entire amount immediately in your business account. Enter the payment received in your cheque register or on the running bank balance on the cheque stubs.

TIP

As much as you possibly can, make any payments for your business by cheque. If you like to make payments by credit card, consider getting one card that you use for nothing but business purposes. Always pay your monthly bill for that card out of your business account.

TIP

If you have just one credit card for both personal and business purposes, you can pay the monthly bill out of your personal account and then write a cheque to yourself on your business account for the business portion of the bill. On the cheque stub for the total repayment, make a note of the individual amounts and the supplier's name — that way your accountant (or your auditor) won't have to go through your personal records to verify your expenses. Similarly, if you happen to make a cash payment out of your personal pocket for a business expense, write yourself a cheque on your business account to repay yourself.

Whenever you make a payment, enter it in your cheque register or cheque stub. Document the business purpose of the payment in case the tax man wants to get up close and personal with your business in the future.

REMEMBER

If you operate this way, you automatically create a record of all your business's revenue and expenses. In accounting language, you are *recording* entries into a *cash receipts and cash payments journal*.

Cash accounting or accrual accounting?

When you record a business transaction in your cheque register, you are not recording the transaction until you actually make or receive a payment. This is called *cash accounting* — you record revenue when you actually receive it and expenses when you actually pay them.

In *accrual accounting*, you record revenue when you earn it (when you send out an invoice for the service performed or product supplied), and you record expenses when you incur them (when you receive a service or product). You'll actually receive the revenue or pay the expenses at some later time.

You can choose either the cash accounting method or the accrual accounting method to record your business transactions. However, when you report the business results on your personal income tax return, you or your accountant will have to adjust your business records to the accrual accounting method, as the Canada Revenue Agency (CRA) requires.

TIP

Speak to your accountant about how you plan to keep track of your business's transactions and what role your accountant will play in preparing the final financial statements.

Sorting your revenue and expenses by category

The next step in the accounting cycle is to sort your business's financial transactions into categories. You need to know what categories your revenue and expenses fall into in order to prepare your income tax returns and financial statements, and to keep track of how your business is doing and to make decisions and plans.

Sorting your revenue

All money your business receives is not identical. For example, when you receive a payment from a customer or client, most of it will be payment for your product or service, but some of it will be payment of GST or HST and/or provincial sales tax (PST).

Your business may receive other kinds of money, as well, such as:

>> Advances from the bank under a loan to your business

>> Refunds for goods your business has purchased and returned

>> Payment from an insurance policy for losses your business has suffered

>> Cash you receive from selling a business asset, such as a vehicle

>> Interest you receive from money you have invested

>> Rent from a tenant

>> Refund of a security deposit given when you entered into a lease

>> Money you or your family invest in the business

TIP

You need to sort revenue by category, because different kinds of revenue are treated differently in preparing financial statements and for tax purposes.

Sorting your expenses and other payments

You also need to sort your expenses and other payments by category, because different kinds of expenses are treated differently in preparing financial statements. (Chapter 16 has more about expenses and taxes.)

Here are some of the categories of expenses you will want to keep track of:

>> **General expenses to run your business:** This includes expenses such as:

- Rent

- Interest on borrowed money

- Legal and accounting fees

- Office supplies

- Professional or trade association fees

- Wages for employees (including deductions)

These operating expenses are fully deductible from income in the year the expense occurred. They are sometimes called *overhead*.

>> **Costs incurred to produce a product you manufacture:** These costs are fully deductible from income in the year the cost occurred too, but they show up in a different place on financial statements, so you might as well stick them in a different category from the beginning.

>> **Inventory:** The cost of the inventory that is sold is also fully deductible from income, but it too has a special place on a financial statement and is called *cost of goods sold*.

>> **Auto expenses:** If you use a vehicle partly for business purposes and partly for personal purposes, only the business portion is deductible. So keep auto expenses separate from other expenses so that you or your accountant can calculate the deductible portion at the end of the tax year.

>> **Home office expenses:** You can deduct only a portion of your home rent or mortgage and utilities if you're running your business out of your home. So keep these expenses separate from other business operating expenses.

>> **Business entertainment:** Only 50 percent of a business entertainment and meals expense is deductible from income, so don't just toss it into the general expense pile.

>> **Capital purchases:** (These are purchases of capital property, which is property with a long-term value, such as equipment, vehicles, and furniture.) You can't deduct any portion of a capital purchase in the year of the purchase, and after that you can deduct only a specified percentage as capital cost allowance (also known as depreciation). So definitely don't let your capital purchases get mixed up with your operating expenses. (Refer to Chapter 16 for more about capital cost allowance.)

>> **GST/HST payments:** Keep track of the amount you pay for GST/HST separately, so that you can incorporate input credits into your calculation of how much you owe at the end of each reporting period.

In accounting language, these categories are called *accounts*.

Record keeping

TIP

In order to sort your revenue and expenses by category, you need to keep separate records for the different types of revenue your business receives and the different types of expenses it incurs. (This is in addition to keeping a cheque register.) Ask your accountant about the categories your business needs to keep track of.

TIP

At a minimum, you'll need different file folders to hold the source documents for each category. But you should also keep a written record of revenue and expenses. At the most basic level, you could keep these records on sheets of lined paper. At a slightly more sophisticated level, you could keep the records in account books or ledgers purchased from a business supply store such as Grand & Toy (which accepts online orders only) or the local Staples store. These days, however, most businesspeople use accounting software, which does the bookkeeping and creates the records automatically from the entries that you make. But both ways serve the same purpose and create the same record.

Handling the bookkeeping burden

As you can imagine, proper bookkeeping involves a great deal of detailed work. How are you going to get it done?

You have three options.

Keep your own books manually

This tried-and-true method is cheap and easy to set up (you can buy manual bookkeeping ledger and journal systems, with directions, from any office supply store), but difficult and time-consuming to maintain.

You have to make all the journal entries by hand, and then post the changes to the proper *accounts* (see the sidebar "More accounting jargon"). If you need to generate a summary or financial statement, you have to work it out yourself.

If you decide to go this route, ask your accountant to help get you started.

Keep your own books using accounting software

You can use accounting software designed primarily for personal use, such as Quicken or Microsoft Money, or a more sophisticated system designed with small businesses in mind, such as QuickBooks, or Sage Simply Accounting.

The personal-use systems are basically electronic cheque registers, with the added ability to sort expenses into categories and to generate income statements and balance sheets. When you enter your business's financial transaction into the program, the changes will be posted automatically to the appropriate accounts.

A good business system will also generate sales invoices, track and report GST/HST/PST, track and age your accounts receivable, help keep track of your inventory, and compute employee payroll.

Ask your accountant for advice on the accounting software that's best for your business. You should also consider speaking to a computer consultant to make sure that you have the computer required to support the software you want to buy, and to ensure that the software is installed properly.

MORE ACCOUNTING JARGON

We've already introduced you to some accounting jargon in this chapter . . . now we're adding a sidebar for those who'd like to see more of it.

In accounting language, the place where you record your day-to-day transactions (whether relating to revenue or expenses) as they occur is called a *journal*.

In a small business, all transactions of every description could be entered into one journal called a *general journal*. As the business gets bigger and more complex, it might need several journals for different types of transactions, such as:

- A *sales journal* for sales on credit
- A *purchases journal* for purchases on credit
- A *cash receipts* journal for receipts of cash
- A *cash payments* journal for payments of cash
- A *payroll journal* for payroll expenses
- A *general journal* for special or unusual transactions

The bookkeeper *records* transactions into the appropriate journals, in the order in which the transactions occur.

The revenue and expenses recorded in the journal(s) are periodically sorted into categories by *posting* the transaction to the appropriate *account* for each category of expense. The accounts are recorded in *ledgers*. Ledgers classify and summarize the information taken from the journals. The ledgers will later be used to prepare the financial statements and the business information to be reported on your personal tax return.

Use a freelance bookkeeper

If you can't or don't want to do your bookkeeping yourself, get someone to do it for you. When you first start your business, you probably won't need . . . or be able to afford . . . to hire a full-time bookkeeper. So contract with a freelance bookkeeper who will work only the number of hours that your business actually needs.

Your accountant is your best source for finding a bookkeeper. In fact, your accountant probably has a bookkeeper either in-house or by referral with whom he or she works on a regular basis and who is familiar with the accountant's requirements. Using this bookkeeper helps to ensure that the bookkeeper and accountant are on the same page, saving you time and money down the road.

THE MYSTERIES OF DOUBLE-ENTRY ACCOUNTING REVEALED RIGHT HERE — AND ALSO OVER HERE

Accounting operates on the theory that every business has on the one hand *assets* (property like equipment, inventory, money) and on the other hand equal and offsetting *liabilities* (claims against the assets in the form of money borrowed from lenders or *equity* invested by the owner — all assets are either owed to the lenders, or owned by the owner). This theory is expressed in the basic business accounting equation "Assets = Liabilities + Equity."

Every financial transaction of a business affects both sides of the business accounting equation. If the assets of the business increase, so does either the claim of the owner or the claim of the lenders. Result: invention of *double-entry accounting*. The essence of double-entry accounting is that every transaction is recorded in two places, to maintain the overall balance between the Assets side and the Liabilities + Equity side of the equation. (See this in action in the financial statements covered later in this chapter.)

Double-entry accounting also recognizes the give-and-take nature of every business transaction. For example, if a business spends $1,000 to buy $1,000 worth of inventory, the total value of the business hasn't changed — but its cash-on-hand decreases as the value of its inventory increases.

Inventory Accounting

If you're not in a pure service business, one of the things you want your accounting system to do is to keep track of your inventory so that you know when to buy replacement inventory, and also what kind and how much. You need to know what sells and what doesn't in order to know what to buy in the future.

The best way to get this information is by using inventory-tracking software. If you have a retail business, you want a point-of-sale system that makes adjustments to your inventory records when sales are entered at the cash register. As we tell you in the section "Handling the bookkeeping burden" earlier, some computerized bookkeeping packages include inventory-tracking features. If you prefer a low-tech approach, ask your accountant to help you develop a manual inventory-tracking system.

VALUING YOUR INVENTORY

In addition to knowing what you have in your inventory, you need to know how much it cost. This isn't easy to figure out if you bought identical inventory items at different times and prices throughout the year. (You can't just shrug this question off because it affects the Cost of Goods Sold figure in your income statement and the Inventory figure in your balance sheet. See below under "Financial statements.")

Because specifically identifying your inventory is generally impossible, you address this question by using one of two accounting methods. The *First In, First Out* (*FIFO*) method assumes that the inventory you bought earliest is sold first. Under this method you value your inventory at the most recent price you paid for it. The other method is the *average-cost method*, which values the inventory based on the average cost of the units on hand. Your accountant will advise you which method you should use.

TIP

Whatever system of inventory tracking you use, be sure to do physical counts of your inventory two to four times a year. Compare the results of your physical count with what your financial records show.

Internal Controls

Think no one associated with or working for your business will ever stick a hand in the till? Think again. Although shoplifting gets more attention, internal theft and fraud cost businesses far more each year. In consultation with your accountant, establish and enforce *internal controls* — a system of checks and balances — to discourage and detect both honest mistakes and dishonesty. Here are some examples of internal controls:

» Inspecting and counting shipments from suppliers before accepting delivery and paying for them

» Requiring two signatures on cheques over a certain amount

» Having outsiders or employees who aren't normally involved do surprise inventory counts and compare them with inventory records

» Having one person record sales and collections while another person records and takes the deposits to the bank

» Requiring every associate or employee to take a vacation, during which time someone else does that person's job

Preparing Financial Documents

Your bookkeeping efforts will soon be put to good use. In no time at all you'll find yourself filing CRA forms and returns and needing financial statements to track your business's activities.

Tax and related returns

Go to Chapter 16 to find out more about your tax obligations — but briefly:

>> If you've registered for GST/HST, you'll have to file statements (usually annually), and calculate whether you have to pay GST/HST (and how much) or whether you're entitled to a rebate because you've paid out more in GST/HST when making purchases than you've taken in when charging GST/HST on your goods and services.

>> In every province except Alberta (which has no provincial sales tax) and Nova Scotia, New Brunswick, Newfoundland, Ontario, and Prince Edward Island (all of which have HST), you will have to file provincial sales tax returns (usually monthly), in which you report the amount of sales tax you have collected from your customers or clients, and remit that amount to the government.

>> If you have employees, you must complete and file with the CRA a remittance voucher called a Statement of Account for Current Source Deductions (Form PD7A) on a regular basis (either monthly or quarterly, depending on the amount of your remittances). In this statement, you report your gross payroll for the remitting period, the amount that you are paying on for income tax, Canada Pension Plan (CPP), and Employment Insurance (EI) that you have withheld from your employees, and your contribution toward your employees' CPP and EI. At the end of each calendar year you will have to file a T4 Summary form (Statement of Remuneration Paid) in which you report your total payroll for the year and all amounts you have previously remitted.

Depending on your province, you may also have to file returns with your provincial workers' compensation board or provincial health insurance commission, setting out the amount of your payroll.

>> After you've been in business for a year, if you've had any kind of success at all, you'll have to pay your income tax quarterly in advance. So you need to put aside an appropriate amount out of revenues at the end of each week or month so that your payment is ready when the quarter-day comes around (March 15, June 15, September 15, December 15).

>> At the end of the year, your personal income tax return will have to be prepared including the income of the business. If your revenue is all ready to add up, and your expenses are categorized so you can easily include them and enter them in the correct lines, preparing your return should be a breeze (either for you or for your accountant).

Financial statements

Your records will also be used to prepare financial statements. Businesses use financial statements for a number of purposes:

>> To help you track the progress of the business, and plan for the future.

>> To provide information that may have to be included in income tax returns for the business.

>> To show to lenders when you're trying to persuade them to lend you money. A lender will want to know how profitable your business is, and to see trends in the revenue and expenses of the business — and so will want to see your financial statements, over several years if possible, and your cash flow projections. A lender will also be very interested in how much debt your business has.

>> To show potential buyers when you're trying to sell your business. A prospective buyer will want to see the financial statements for your business for the past three to five years. In Chapter 5 we discuss what buyers look for in your financial statements.

TECHNICAL STUFF

Businesses have historical financial statements and forward-looking financial statements. *Historical statements* report actual results of the operation of the business after they've taken place. The income statement and balance sheet are the main types of historical financial statements. *Forward-looking statements* (sometimes known as *pro forma* financial statements) are used to plan for the future, and they include forecasts of revenue and expenses and cash-flow projections.

Historical Financial Statements

The income statement and the balance sheet are the main types of historical statements. You use these statements to track the progress of your business and help you plan for the future.

Creating financial statements

If you have accounting software that prepares financial statements and you've faithfully recorded all your transactions, you can generate accurate financial statements by clicking a button.

You can also create financial statements by hand. But that would be cruel and definitely outdated. (In the good old days this was the only way to create them.) In the following discussions about income statements and balance sheets, we explain the process to you in case you want to try it yourself — but we mainly want to give you an idea of what's going on inside your computer . . . or your accountant's head.

The income statement

The *income statement,* also called a *profit and loss statement* or *statement of operations,* sets out the business's revenues (or sales) and expenses over a stated period of time (a specific month, quarter or year). The business's *revenues* are the money that its customers or clients pay for its products or services. Its *expenses* are the costs incurred in doing business. The business's profits (or income) equal its revenues minus its expenses.

How do you prepare it?

In Table 17-1 are our instructions for preparing an income statement. (At the end of the chapter is a completed Statement for you to look at; see Figure 17-1.)

If you are in a retail or manufacturing business, start with Gross Sales (which is all the money you took in minus GST/HST and any PST charged) and then deduct the Cost of Goods Sold, which is what you paid directly for your inventory, either to buy it or manufacture it — Gross Sales minus Cost of Goods Sold equals Gross Profit or Gross Margin. (If you are a service business, you will not have a cost-of-goods-sold expense.) Then set out and add up all your expenses of operating the business other than those directly related to creating or acquiring the product you sell (that's your overhead), and subtract the total from Gross Profit to find your Net Income or (Net) Profit before taxes are taken into account.

TIP

You can find a version of Table 17-1 online (look for Form 17-1) that you can fill in to create a statement of income and expenses for your business. (Turn to this book's Introduction for instructions on how to find the free downloadable content.)

TABLE 17-1 ## Statement of Income and Expenses

	Prior Year (or month or quarter)	Budget (for current year or month or quarter)	Current Year (or month or quarter)
Gross Sales MINUS **Cost of the Goods Sold** EQUALS **Gross Profit**	As a start-up you won't have a prior year, month, or quarter until you've been in business for a while.	Your budget is the projected statement of revenue and expenses that you prepared before the start of this year. See below for forecasting revenue and expenses.	These are the actual figures from the records you've kept for the period.
Expenses (such as)			

Accounting/legal, Bank charges, Depreciation, Insurance, Marketing, Rent, Telephone, Wages Total Expenses

Net Income or **Profit** (Subtract Total Expenses from Gross Profit)

You prepare a budget for an upcoming period by preparing a *forecast of revenues and expenses*. It is meant to be a realistic prediction of the revenue you will earn and the expenses you will incur over that period. Before you start your business, your revenue and expense forecasts are based on a combination of research and hope. (Projecting your expenses is easier than projecting your revenues before your business is actually up and running. We give you some advice in Chapter 9 about forecasting revenues and expenses.) After your business has been in operation for a year, you'll be able to make your forecasts based on past performance and your knowledge of trends in your field.

What can it tell you?

By comparing the current year's (month's, quarter's) Gross Sales figures to the previous year's (month's, quarter's), you can tell whether your sales are going up or down. By comparing current Expenses to previous Expenses, you can tell which of your expenses have gone up or down.

By looking at your Gross Profit and Expenses together, you'll see whether you're generating enough through sales to cover your operating costs.

By dividing your Net Income or Profit by your Gross Sales, you'll find out what your return on sales is. That gives you an idea about how efficiently your business turns a dollar's worth of sale into a profit.

By dividing your Gross Profit by total sales made to find your gross profit margin, you can see how much profit you earned on sales before taking into account your expenses to sell the products.

By dividing your Net Income or Profit by your total sales, you can find your net profit margin or profit margin. A low net profit margin may indicate that the business isn't being efficiently run, that the selling price of the product or service is too low, or that the cost of what you are selling is too high.

TIP

The acceptable profit margin varies with the type of business. Ask your professional or trade association what a decent profit margin is for your type of business.

The balance sheet

The balance sheet lists a value for everything a business owns (its *assets*) and everything it owes (its *liabilities*) as well as the *equity* belonging to the owner at a specified date, usually the last date of the company's *fiscal* (financial) year, referred to as its *year-end*. It's called a balance sheet because the total assets have to equal the total liabilities, plus the owner's equity. It measures the financial condition of your business at a given point in time. (If you come up with a balance sheet where assets don't equal liabilities, you haven't created an imbalance sheet; you've just done it wrong.) In Canada, you can't choose the date of the fiscal year-end of your proprietorship or partnership. The CRA forces to you use a calendar year-end of December 31.

How do you prepare it?

You create a balance sheet by setting down the account balances of the business's assets, liabilities, and equity in a recognized order.

Start with assets, which are categorized as *current assets* or *fixed assets*. Current assets are cash or assets that are intended to be and can be converted into cash easily. Fixed assets are assets the business intends to hold on to for a long period of time.

Then list liabilities, categorizing them as *current liabilities* or *long-term liabilities*. Current liabilities are debts that are expected be paid within a year, such as accounts payable, current wages, GST/HST payable, and the current portion of long-term debt. Long-term liabilities are debts that will not be paid off within a year.

Then you show *owner's equity* — what belongs to you, the owner, after your business's debts are deducted from its assets. (It's that double-entry accounting thing again.) Take a look at Table 17-2.

TIP

Use the version of Table 17-2 online (look for Form 17-2) to create a balance sheet for your business. (The Introduction has instructions on how to find this free content.)

TABLE 17-2   ## Balance Sheet

Prior Year (month, quarter)	Budget	Current Year (month, quarter)
Assets:		
Current Assets		
Cash		
Accounts receivable		
Inventory		
Total Current Assets		
Fixed Assets		
Furniture and fixtures		
Equipment		
Total Fixed Assets		
Total Assets		
Liabilities:		
Current Liabilities		
Accounts payable		
Short-term notes payable		
Total Current Liabilities		
Long-term Liabilities		
Long-term notes payable		
Total long-term liabilities		
Total Liabilities		
Owner's Equity or Net Worth (Subtract Total Liabilities from Total Assets)		

What can it tell you?

By dividing the Total Liabilities (the total debts of your business) by the Owner's Equity or Net Worth, you'll get the debt-to-equity ratio of your business. This ratio will tell you what percentage of the business you own and what percentage your lenders own. Generally speaking, you don't want the ratio to go above 1:1

(that is, you own as much of your business as your lenders do). If it goes above 2:1 (your lenders own twice as much as you do), borrowing money may be difficult because even the most optimistic lender can't be sure of getting the money back out of the business. Keep in mind, though, that if you have too little debt, you may not be realizing the full potential of your business — because you can use borrowed money to expand and improve your business and make it more profitable.

By dividing Current Assets by Current Liabilities, you'll find your *current ratio*. It tells you how *liquid* your business is — how quickly you can come up with cash if you need to. A 1:1 ratio means that your business has a dollar in current assets to cover every dollar of current liabilities. You don't want to fall below 1:1, and you'd like to stay at 2:1 or higher. By dividing the Current Assets minus Inventory (that is, only Cash and Accounts Receivable) by the Current Liabilities, you'll come up with the *quick ratio*. The quick ratio will give you an idea of how quickly you can come up with cash without selling off your inventory. You want your quick ratio to be at least 1:1.

By dividing the Net Income or Profit (from the income statement) by the Equity or Net Worth of the business (from the balance sheet), you can find out what your *return on equity* or return on investment is. You'd like a return at least equal to what you'd get if you just sold the business, invested the cash, and collected interest or dividends. (But if you look at your return on equity and panic because it's low, remember to take into account any money you are getting from the business as salary.)

Case Study: E.T.&T. Telecommunications Inc.

Let's put into practice what we've just discussed and look at some completed financial statements (for E.T.&T. Telecommunications) to see what the figures tell us.

Have a look at the sample income statement shown in Figure 17-1.

You can see that E.T.&T.'s Gross Sales went up in the current year, but not as much as predicted in the budget, while the Cost of Goods Sold went up more than predicted. As a result, Gross Profits went up, but not as much as the owner had looked for. In addition, while some expenses went down, wages went up by 20 percent (the owner had predicted that they would go up by only 10 percent). (These wages included a salary for the owner of $40,000.) Overall, expenses went up at a higher rate (by over 15 percent) than sales, which went up by only about 6 percent. The business made a profit of $23,560 on total sales of $160,000, or about 14.75 percent. Looks like the owner of E.T.&T. should be thinking about:

E.T.&T. Telecommunications Inc.
Income Statement
For the year ending December 31, 2011

	Prior Year	Budget	Current Year
Sales	$150,000	$165,000	$160,000
- Cost of goods sold	50,000	52,000	55,000
- Gross profit	$100,000	$113,000	$105,000
Expenses			
Accounting/Legal	$2,000	$2,500	$2,250
Bank charges	1,500	1,500	1,500
Depreciation	1,450	1,115	1,115
Insurance	650	675	675
Marketing	1,000	1,500	1,500
Printing	750	750	500
Rent	12,000	12,600	12,600
Telephone	1,200	1,200	1,300
Wages	50,000	55,000	60,000
Total expenses	$70,550	$76,840	$81,440
Profit (before tax)	$29,450	$36,160	$23,560

FIGURE 17-1:
Income
statement.

>> Increasing sales

>> Finding a less expensive source of inventory

>> Cutting the number of hours worked by employees other than the owner

Now look at the balance sheet for E.T.&T shown in Figure 17-2.

The Net Worth of E.T.&T. went up by $22,445. (That increase is equal to the profits for the year of $23,560, shown on the income statement, minus the amount by which the furniture, fixtures, and equipment went down as a result of depreciation.)

The profit of $23,560 is over 45 percent of the equity of the business. When you consider that the owner also took a salary of $40,000, that's a healthy return on investment.

E.T.&T.'s Current Assets amount to $62,510 and its Current Liabilities to $5,500, so its current ratio is approximately 11:1 — this business can easily come up with cash to pay off its debts. E.T.&T.'s debts total $15,500 compared to Owner's Equity of $50,945, a ratio of about 1:3. This is a healthy debt-to-equity ratio. Maybe a little too healthy — is the owner failing to take advantage of loans or outside investment in order to expand and become a more serious player in the field . . . or even to move into a related field?

E.T.&T. Telecommunications Inc.
Balance Sheet
For the year ending December 31, 2011

	Prior Year	Budget	Current Year
Assets			
Current assets			
Cash	$29,450	$55,860	$24,010
Accounts receivable	1,000	0	500
Inventory	16,500	18,250	20,000
Total current assets	$46,950	$75,110	$62,510
Fixed assets			
Furniture & fixtures	$3,200	$2,560	$2,560
Equipment	1,850	1,375	1,375
Total fixed assets	$5,050	$3,935	$3,935
Total Assets	$52,000	$79,045	$66,445
Liabilities			
Current liabilities			
Accounts payable	$3,500	$500	$500
Short-term notes payable	5,000	5,000	5,000
Total current liabilities	$8,500	$5,500	$5,500
Long-term liabilities			
Long-term notes payable	$15,000	$10,000	$10,000
Total long-term liabilities	$15,000	$10,000	$10,000
Total Liabilities	$23,500	$15,500	$15,500
Owner's equity (net worth)	$28,500	$63,545	$50,945
Total Liabilities and Net Worth	$52,000	$79,056	$66,445

FIGURE 17-2:
Balance sheet.

Cash-Flow Projections

Revenue and expenses rarely match each other exactly. Your revenue may come in a few times a year, whereas your expenses are likely to be fairly steady on a month-by-month basis.

As a result, knowing how much money your business is going to earn is not enough. You must also know when you are actually going to receive this money. Likewise, knowing how much money you'll need to operate your business is not enough. You also have to know when you'll need it. A cash-flow projection charts not only how much money you can expect to receive and pay, but when.

You use a cash-flow projection when you first start your business to help you calculate how large an operating loan you need until you can establish revenue flow cash that more closely match the amount and timing of your expenses. Cash-flow projections remain useful, if not essential, even after your business is established. While some of your expenses are fixed and occur on a regular basis, you have some control over the timing of other expenses. Cash-flow projections help you plan, both to put off expenses you have control over until you expect to have the revenue to cover them, and to borrow money to cover expenses you can't put off. You should make cash-flow projections for at least six months into the future, updating them every month.

TIP

If you borrow money, the lender will want to see your cash flow projections to help decide whether and when you'll be able to repay the loan.

Refer to Chapter 9 for more about cash flow, including an explanation of how to build a cash-flow table.

Hiring an Accountant

So, does your business need an accountant? If you've paid the slightest attention to anything in this chapter, you're likely screaming "Yes!"

Considering what an accountant does

Although you don't have to have an accountant as a permanent member of your staff, you need to consult an accountant on an ongoing basis:

>> **To help you set up your bookkeeping system** — either a manual or computerized one, and to build in internal controls to help reduce errors and to prevent and detect theft and fraud

>> **To prepare various financial statements** — such as budgets, cash flow statements, income statements, and balance sheets, based on a review and analysis of financial data

>> **To prepare your personal income tax returns** — based on a review and analysis of financial data in the context of income tax law

>> **To deal with the CRA from time to time** — if you experience difficulties arising out of your income tax returns or with respect to your GST/HST or employer payroll remittances

Determining what kind of accountant you need

In Canada, anyone can call himself or herself an accountant. What you want is a Chartered Professional Accountant (CPA). CPAs have a professional designation and belong to government-recognized self-regulating bodies, just as lawyers do. If you seek the advice of a CPA, make sure that he or she has experience in supporting small businesses and isn't just a tax expert.

For more information on finding and dealing with professional advisors such as accountants and lawyers, refer to Chapter 14.

4

What Does the Future Hold?

IN THIS CHAPTER

» **Considering what "doing more business" means to your business**

» **Knowing when not to do more business**

» **Finding more business**

» **Financing your business expansion**

» **Managing a bigger business**

Chapter **18**

Getting Bigger

Y ou launched your business some time ago, and now your business is expanding, or you'd like it to be. In any case, you have to have some idea of what you're getting into when your business expands, and how you can finance an expansion and manage a bigger, busier business. And if you aren't expanding but want to, you have to know how to find more business.

What "Doing More Business" Means

If you're thinking that "doing more business" means "making bigger profits," "having access to more opportunities," or "becoming a more important player," you're right. But that's not all. They say that every action has an equal and opposite reaction — well, in this case the reaction can seem bigger than the action! Here are some of the things that go along with doing more business:

> » **You'll probably do even more work than you're doing now.** And it may be different work from the work you're doing now, too — you may be doing less of what you think of as your business . . . and more managing. Better ask yourself if you want this.

» **You may have to travel more.** Do you enjoy business travel? Does it fit in with your current lifestyle? (Maybe you went into business so you could stay at home with the kids or the goldfish . . . or wouldn't have to do any more commuting.)

» **You may have to create new lines of products or services to entice customers and clients to your business (or to satisfy their demands).** That may mean doing more research and development and making a new marketing plan — go to Chapters 4 and 11 if the thought of that doesn't scare you.

» **You'll probably need new accounting and bookkeeping and/or inventory control systems to handle the increased business.** (Refer to Chapter 17 for more on accounting matters.) Unless you planned for this expansion when you originally set up your business.

» **You'll need a more sophisticated (and costly) system of management controls and automated business processes.** That's because you won't be able to have your eyes on everything at once, so your business will have to have "systems and processes" to protect its assets.

» **You'll need employees, or more employees, to help you.** (Refer to Chapter 15 on hiring employees.) Will your customers or clients accept new people? Maybe your business and you have been very closely identified with each other up to now, and customers and clients will resist dealing with someone other than you. And you'll have to worry about finding capable people who can handle some of the important functions of your business.

» **Your employees will need training, or more training.** They'll need it to deal with the added business and the things that go along with it.

» **You'll need more equipment.** The new employees will use it, and increased production will demand it. (Refer to Chapter 7 for information about equipping your business.)

» **You'll need more inventory if you're in the retail or wholesale business.**

» **You'll need bigger premises to hold the new employees, new equipment and increased production capacity, new product lines and increased inventory, and to provide larger areas for client meetings.** We talk about choosing a place of business in Chapter 8.

» **And last but not least, you'll need money.** You'll need it to hire the employees, buy the equipment, lease the premises, and so on. So you've got financing concerns. We deal with financing a business in Chapter 9.

Haven't we been here before? Most of these issues look strangely familiar.

WARNING

Expanding a business will upset its equilibrium. You and your business will probably have trouble coping, at least in the beginning. In fact, you may never be ready to cope. Sometimes expansion is just not the best thing for you, and you and your business will be happier if things stay the way they are.

Don't Do More Business If . . .

In the previous section we aren't telling you not to do more business, we're just showing you that more business doesn't happen in a vacuum — it has consequences, and some of them you may find unpleasant.

In this section, on the other hand, we are telling you not to do more business — if doing more business would just get you into financial trouble. And in financial trouble is where you'll end up if you expand because your business isn't profitable now and you think doing more business will make it more profitable. This is the type of scenario where you should really seek the counsel of a professional accountant and trusted business advisor.

Lack of profitability is the result of low margins. Your margin is the price you sell your goods or services for minus the cost of providing the goods or services. Your business may have low margins for two possible reasons. One is that expenses are too high, and the other is that prices are too low.

If you expand an unprofitable business, you'll end up with a bigger unprofitable business . . . which means you'll go down with a real thud later on. Remember the joke about the dot-com companies? "We lose on every transaction but we make it up on volume." Don't allow the glorious martyrdom of the dot-coms to have been in vain. Learn from their example: Become profitable before you think about becoming bigger.

Lowering expenses

Controlling expenses is a two-step process. You have to audit your business to find out whether you're spending money on things you shouldn't be spending money on, and you have to review your expenses to see whether they're higher than necessary.

Audit your business activities

Sit down with your account books and do some thinking. Ask yourself, for example:

» **Do you have expenses that you could pare down?** Are you over- entertaining clients or potential clients? Maybe a business meeting in the client's office would accomplish as much as or more than lunch at a good restaurant. Are you doing unnecessary travelling? Combine several activities into a single trip (on a single plane or train ticket or gasoline bill). Are you buying premium-quality equipment and supplies when ordinary quality would do the job just as well? A desktop PC or laptop may be as much as your business needs, and that top-of-the-line computing device is perhaps more about your love of neat gadgets. Are you spending money you can't afford on furnishings for your office or on a company car? A desk is a flat surface to work on, you don't need cherry wood with a matching credenza. A $20,000 car will get you the same places as a $40,000 car . . . and a taxi could take you to a lot of them, too. Are you renting premises that are too expensive for you? Could be time to move back home.

» **Are you spending your time inefficiently?** Is important work not getting done (like billing) because you're too busy with other things? If you need help with accounts or inventory control or payroll, buy a software package to do the job. Or outsource the work to another business or bring in a temporary or part-time worker. If your files are disorganized, you may be wasting time hunting information down instead of using the information to do business. Spending a few hours organizing your files properly may save you dozens or hundreds of hours over the course of the year.

» **Are you making good use of your employees?** Are you paying someone full-time to do part-time work? Are you paying someone to do work that he or she can't or isn't doing? Don't take on employees until they'll make money for your business rather than cost money — don't hire somebody to do work that you (or software or another business) can do more cheaply.

Review how much you're spending

Even if you're sure that you need everything you're currently paying for, you need to make sure that you're getting it at the best price. Make it a habit to re-price your supplies regularly. Before you make a purchase — equipment, lease for premises, business loan, telephone services, insurance, and everything else — get three or four quotes from competing suppliers. If you find a cheaper supplier, though, make sure you'll be getting comparable quality before you make the switch.

In some businesses, you might consider becoming your own supplier of certain products if an analysis indicates that you can provide your own supplies more cheaply.

TIP

Always ask suppliers for itemized invoices, and go over them carefully for mistakes.

Raising prices

Your prices are not fixed in stone. Review them whenever you notice an increase in demand or an increase in competitors' prices. And review them annually to see whether your costs are creeping up on your prices.

WARNING

Before you raise your prices, consider whether higher prices could translate into lower sales, as customers go elsewhere for lower prices. Are your customers with you just because of your prices, or do they take into account other factors such as your expertise or your location?

If you decide to raise prices, start with your lower-priced goods or services, or with the ones that you don't think need to be competitively priced to sell.

If you're a manufacturer, think about opening your own retail or wholesale outlet or becoming your own distributor — if you eliminate the middleman you can charge middleman prices yourself.

How Do You Find More Business?

If you're reading this section, you probably want to expand your business and you believe that expanding won't lead to disaster. So how do you go about increasing the amount of business you do so you can get on with the expansion process?

Some enterprises are born with more business, others have more business thrust upon them. But some have to achieve more business. If you're not flooded with work but you'd like to be, you can proceed in four ways:

>> Do more of what you're already doing for the customers you already have.

>> Find new customers for the work you already do.

>> Do new work for the customers you already have.

>> Find new customers for new work.

See if you can do more of the same work for existing customers

TIP

This is the most cost-effective way to expand. You already know your product and your customers. Doing more for the customers you have costs a lot less than going out and finding new customers or hunting down or creating new products. That's because you'll have to spend additional time and money to find new customers and develop new products, as opposed to simply connecting with the customers you already have.

The first place to start in your quest to do more work for your customers is to review your customer turnover rate and, if it's significant, to find out why customers aren't coming back to you. Speak to non-returning customers, if you can. Ask what they like about the business they're dealing with instead of you, and if they'd be interested in doing business with you again if you made some changes. If you can't talk to the lost sheep, chat with the customers who're still with you and try to get a sense of what they like and don't like about your business. Make reasonable changes as required.

Next, go to work on the customers you've got. Try to "generate new demand" by getting them to use more of your products or services, or use the same amount but more frequently. Apart from persuading your customers or clients that they'll benefit from using more of your products or services (for example, be healthier, smell cleaner, save money), here are some moves you can try out on them:

>> **Make sure they know everything you can do for them.** Bring their attention to your complete line of products or services by posting them on your website, mentioning them in conversation or in reporting letters or social media channels like Twitter and Instagram, sending around newsletters, brochures, and special promotion letters about them, even listing them on your packaging. When an opportunity comes up for you to do something or provide something the client hasn't requested, ask directly for their business.

>> **Reward your customers.** Offer them discounts for volume, rebates on certain items, or gifts for buying a pre-set amount. Make sure they know you're handing out rewards. A simple thank-you can go a long way, too.

>> **Bundle your products or services.** For example, offer a service contract with the product, or complimentary products as a package (for a slightly lower price than if they were purchased separately).

>> **Make your product or service more appealing.** For example, make it easier to use. Or make the packaging more attractive. (Customers can be pretty shallow.)

>> **Come up with new uses for the product or service.**

>> **Switch to autopilot.** Make your product or service more convenient to get. Have an online catalogue loaded with useful information for customers. Automate your delivery, via a monthly or annual contract, or through an e-commerce platform that enables end-to-end online order processing. Or at the end of an appointment or meeting, set up the next one. Or send reminder letters or emails or make personal reminder phone calls for customers or clients to make their next appointments.

Overall, one of the most important things you can do is to develop a good relationship with your customers. Make them your friends. Listen to them — and give them lots of convenient ways of talking to you, such as voice mail, your URL, email, a 1–800 number, and, if possible, regular opportunities to meet face to face. If they have complaints or concerns, respond to them. If they have suggestions, pay attention to them.

Don't waste or lose any information from your clients. Keep a customer information file for each client (or at least for the best ones or up-and-coming ones) that includes notes and records of the following:

>> Which products or services the customer buys, how frequently the customer buys, and how much the customer spends

>> How the customer makes the purchase and payment (and any interesting collection history) and takes delivery

>> Any complaints the customer has made, and what you did in response

>> Which products or services you provide that your customer buys from someone else, and why; and which products or services you provide that your customer doesn't buy at all, and why

>> Any notes about the customer's plans (that might tie in with your goal of providing more to the customer)

>> Any of the customer's special interests and important dates (these may not involve flogging any of your products or services; remembering them may just be good customer relations)

>> Any ideas you have about how you might persuade the customer to buy more of your products or services

Customers and clients will be pleased that you consider them important enough to remember details of past transactions, and they'll be thrilled if you remember something about them that isn't immediately linked to making a sale. This is why data mining and analysis has been one of the hottest business trends in the last decade. Businesses that "know their customers" tend to do well.

Find more customers for the same work

If you're sure that your current customers are satisfied with the work you're doing, then you can go out and look for new customers in similar situations or business sectors. You can also look for them in a new geographic area or in a new target group. When you go into a new area or after a new group, focus on it and make a good job of capturing it before you move on to another area or group. Don't try to expand on too many fronts at once.

You can hunt for new customers, either geographically or by group, by:

>> Creating a new marketing campaign (see Chapters 5 and 11), which might include repackaging your product or service under a new label.

>> Acquiring customer lists from another business.

>> Luring customers away from the competition with goodies such as rewards for switching over, or with the usual incentives (see Chapters 4 and 11) such as lower prices, better service, and so on.

>> Getting new premises by renting in a new location or buying an existing well-located business. If you're a manufacturer, you can open a retail outlet.

>> Going into the export business. This involves a lot more trouble because you have to assess market opportunities in the new country and comply with local laws and regulations, as well as physically deliver your goods or services. We get exhausted just thinking about it, so we won't wear ourselves out further writing about it. Check out the information on exporting at the Government of Canada's Business and Industry web page. Go to www.canada.ca/en/services/business and click the International Trade and Investment link to get there.

Do new and additional work for existing customers

Don't go wild if this is the route you decide to take! Just because your customers love what you're doing with their stock portfolio doesn't mean they'll also be eager to buy pedicures and facials from your business. The best way to proceed is simply to ask your customers what more they'd like from you — or even just listen to what they're saying in your regular contacts with them. You'll probably find that your customers and clients are the best sources of new ideas for you.

When you bring in new products or services, consider having a testing period with free samples or with an "on approval" arrangement. This will give your customers a chance to try out the new product or service without any financial risk (to them, that is).

Find new customers for new products or services

If you're looking for new customers and new products, it almost means you're starting over again! So you'd better go back and read Chapter 11.

But steering your business off in a new direction isn't as hard as setting up a new business, because you've already got some things going for you, such as:

>> Experience in product or service development and delivery, and in business management

>> An understanding of how the marketplace works

>> A few hard-earned skills in dealing with customers

>> A name in the business community, and a history of operations

In addition you may have some money that you've made and set aside that can fund this venture. Or your business may have more capacity than it's using right now — maybe you could produce more, or sell other products through your existing channels.

Alternatively, you may be nervous about keeping your business based on one product or service and you want to branch out as a form of insurance.

How Do You Finance Your Expansion?

Earlier in this chapter, we talk about the kinds of things you'll need money for in an expansion. Now we talk about where to get the money. Essentially, you'll go to the same sources we send you in Chapter 9. Prying money out of them — especially the commercial sources — should be easier this time, because you've got a track record as a business.

In addition, you have some new sources of financing, which we cover in the upcoming sections.

Sale or sale and leaseback of equipment

If you already own equipment, you can sell it to a leasing company and then lease it back. Or you can sell one thing, and then lease something else. Or you can sell and not buy anything. Whichever way you go, you free up some cash for other purposes.

Retained earnings

Retained earnings are money you've set aside out of the profits of your business. As soon as you can, you should start building a fund from your profits for unforeseen problems and for expansion . . . instead of blowing every penny that comes in on fancy office furniture or by taking all your profits as salary.

Equity investment

An *equity investment* is capital for your business in exchange for partial ownership of your business. (In Chapter 9, we talk about this as arm's-length investment.)

Venture capital and angel capital

You're no longer a start-up, but you're still eligible for an investment from an angel or from a venture capital firm. In fact, you may be more eligible because you've been in operation for a while and it will be easier for an investor to tell whether your business is going places (or not). Venture capitalists will probably see you as looking for "first stage financing" (to increase production) or "second stage financing" (to increase production and expand your markets). Heck, you may even be ready for "mezzanine financing" (to expand prior to an *initial public offering* — see "Investment from outside the business" — or a buyout of your business by another business).

Investment from within your business

TIP

If you bring in new people who are going to run the business with you, you'll usually ask them to buy a partnership share (if your business isn't incorporated) or to buy shares in the corporation (if it is incorporated). This gives you some fresh capital to play with. The new guy may have to take out a loan to make the purchase; the interest payable on the loan is deductible from his or her income.

If your business is incorporated, you can set up a stock plan that allows employees to buy shares in the business. This not only brings in capital, but also gives employees an incentive to work hard to make the business more profitable. However, to get much money via employee investment, you'll probably have to sell a significant percentage of shares, and even though you make sure you keep at least 51 percent of the shares, you can still end up with conflict about control of the corporation.

Investment from outside the business

Under provincial securities laws in Canada, up to 50 people who are not employees of the corporation can own shares in a private corporation. So you can go looking for a few individual investors. But if you want more money than 50 outside investors can provide, you'll have to "go public" or make an *initial public offering* (IPO) — in other words, become a corporation whose shares are traded on a stock exchange such as the Toronto Stock Exchange (TSX) or the Canadian Securities Exchange (CSE).

WARNING

If after reading that last sentence you're already toying with the idea of taking your business public and are daydreaming about what your stock symbol will be, we've got some cold water to pour over you. An IPO is complicated and costly to set up, and you aren't guaranteed to get any money out of it. As a result, there aren't many IPOs in Canada. In 2017, there were only about 40 issues from Canadian companies or companies listing on Canadian exchanges. That's a very low figure.

Here's how an IPO works. After collecting numerous expensive outside advisors including an *underwriter,* lawyers, accountants, auditors, and investment relations specialists, you prepare a *prospectus,* which you file with the Securities Commission or regulator in any province where you're making your offering. The prospectus provides detailed information to both the Securities Commission and potential investors about your business, the stock to be issued, and the purpose for which the money raised will be used. It has to give full disclosure of all important information. The underwriter, after looking over your business even more carefully than a venture capitalist would, agrees to buy shares from the corporation and then resell them (taking a commission) to the public for a short period of time, usually just a few days. The price set for the shares will depend on various things, including your business's financial history, how glamorous your industry is, and current share prices of other public companies in your industry. Depending on your agreement with the underwriter, the offering may be cancelled if not enough shares are sold within a specified period.

After the IPO is completed, the shares that have been sold trade on the stock market without affecting the value of the payment your corporation received for the shares. So if the value of the shares drops dramatically, that's not good news for your business, but at least you don't have to make refunds to purchasers.

WARNING

After you become a public corporation, you're required to provide information to the Securities Commission and to the public on a regular basis about things you might actually prefer to keep secret, such as important changes to your business whenever they occur, quarterly and annual financial statements, the amount of compensation for senior executives, and share purchases or sales by insiders (people who have access to special knowledge of the business, particularly employees and their immediate families). And you have to worry about keeping your investors happy, or else they'll sell their shares and drive down the value of your business.

If this all sounds like a massive pain, it is. And this description of the IPO process has only scratched the surface.

How Do You Manage a Bigger Business?

The bigger a business grows, the more managing, and the more expert managing, it needs. Poor management is probably the most common reason for a business to fail.

TIP

The first thing we talk about is how to manage yourself. If you can't manage your own time and work efficiently, you're going to have a lot of trouble managing anybody else. And because you're the most important person in the business at this point, you won't have a business to manage if you can't keep it together personally.

Learning personal management techniques

As your business expands, you're going to have more and more to do and less and less time to do it. So you're going to have to make the time you do have go further. Here's some advice about managing your time and work.

Schedule your time wisely

TIP

Don't rely on your memory! You haven't got one anymore — it drowned in the sea of details that a business floats in. So plan ahead in writing. Plan your year, your month, your week, your day. Keep a calendar or daybook — just one, if possible! — or a calendar on your computer or smartphone. If you have more than one calendar, make sure that they're always synchronized. Otherwise, you'll end up with two incompatible schedules. When you plan:

>> Include your personal as well as business commitments and intentions, so you don't end up with conflicts, or miss dental appointments.

>> Schedule more than appointments in your calendar. Also schedule phone calls you intend to make and matters you intend to deal with. Make lists of to-do jobs for the day, week, or month (some calendar systems incorporate to-do lists). At the end of each day, week, or month, cross off the jobs done and carry forward the ones not done or not finished.

Schedule as efficiently as you can:

>> Schedule meetings and work that require your full concentration at the time of day you're at your sharpest; schedule mindless tasks for the time of day when you're mindless.

>> Schedule in the right order. For example, if a client wants to talk to you about the poor quality of a product you provided and what you're going to do about it, don't schedule that appointment before making an appointment to talk to the supplier of the product first.

>> When you're on the road, plan your trips so that they cover a number of tasks. For example, if you have to travel to another city to meet a client, see whether you can also meet with other clients, or a supplier or potential investor you have in that city. Plan even short trips to accomplish several things — on a drive to meet with a local client, work in other destinations that aren't too far off your route, like the gas station, business supply store, or dry cleaner's.

>> Combine some of your down time — lunch, golf, a hockey game — with a low-key meeting with a client, supplier, or investor.

>> Allow yourself some flexibility in your schedule so that you don't end up running late or wasting time. Some meetings take longer than planned; others get cancelled. So don't plan important meetings back to back, and always have a plan B if you unexpectedly have extra time.

TIP

Remind yourself what you're supposed to be doing now or next — have a tickler (reminder) system. Use your calendar or organizer to enter reminders of what you have to do in a day, week, or month, such as following up on a letter you just sent. Get into the habit of glancing frequently at your tasks for the month, week, and day. Every night before you close up shop (or before you go to sleep, whichever comes first), look over your schedule and to-do list for the following day. If you don't, you'll end up missing a morning meeting or phone call.

REMEMBER

Whenever you do something, keep a record of the action taken. Otherwise, a day or two later you won't remember whether or not you've done something, and what you did. And when a matter has been finally disposed of, put documents relating to it in your storage area, not in your active files area, so you won't be wondering if you're *still* supposed to do something.

TIP

Meetings can be terrible time wasters. So always make sure that a meeting is necessary, and that a phone call or an email can't replace it. Then make sure that you're properly prepared for the meeting . . . and that everyone else is too:

>> In preparation, review your files, gather any additional information that's necessary, make notes about what you've done and what you want to talk about.

>> If you're hosting the meeting, send around a detailed agenda, so everyone else knows what the meeting is about and what each of them should do to prepare for it. If you're not the host, request an agenda. If you don't get a response, circulate a suggested draft to the participants. If you get an inadequate agenda, send it back with suggested additions.

>> At the end of a meeting, prepare *minutes* (a summary of what was said or what happened at) of the meeting, or request that someone else provide minutes, and send them around to all the participants. The minutes should include an "action agenda," so that everyone knows not only what's been discussed and decided but also what the participants are supposed to do and by when.

Screen and bundle

Don't let your phone and email and faxes and mail and drop-in associates or employees rule your time. Organize your day so that you have blocks of time when you give your full attention to matters that require thought and concentrated effort, and other blocks of time when you read and answer your mail and return phone calls. Let customers or clients and suppliers know that you return phone calls and emails within 24 hours, but that they should not necessarily expect an instant response.

>> Don't answer your phone every time it rings (or at least get caller ID if you're afraid of missing important calls). You've got voice mail, let it do its job. Don't check your email every ten minutes (or ten seconds). Emails will wait quietly until you reply. Don't leap up every time you hear the sound of the email alert.

>> Screen incoming voice messages, emails, faxes, and letters according to whether they are urgent and should be dealt with immediately, or should be dealt with within your normal 24-hour period, or should be answered within 24 hours but require longer to deal with, or can be delegated to someone else. Some items can probably be filed without a response or even completely ignored (like junk mail).

>> When you check your messages, emails, faxes, and letters, group them by category and deal with them by category. For example:

- Matters you can deal with by phone. Sit down and make all your phone calls at once.

- Matters you can deal with by email. Send all your email at once.

- Matters that you can deal with by writing and mailing a letter or sending a fax. Write all your letters at one time.

- Bookkeeping matters that require you to enter expenses or write cheques or create bills. Enter all your expenses together, write all your cheques in a group, and put aside time to run bills.

Put off procrastinating

Putting off work that must be done is one of the biggest thieves of your time. So no matter how much you DON'T WANT TO DO IT, start your work right away — and finish it too.

Here are some tips for the hard-core procrastinator who's looking to reform:

>> **Divide up complex work into smaller segments.** Avoiding a daunting task is all too tempting — but you'll be surprised how much you can accomplish if you do a task in bites instead of trying to swallow it whole.

>> **Don't avoid starting something just because you won't be able to finish it in one sitting.** If you know that a task will take six hours, don't wait until you've got six hours free. Say to yourself, "I can spend half an hour now, and tomorrow I can fit in an hour, and the next day I can do two hours," and so on.

>> **Set a deadline.** If your client (or the Canada Revenue Agency [CRA] or whoever wants this work done) hasn't set you a deadline, set one yourself. Tell your client you'll have the work done by such-and-such a date, and then deliver on your promise.

>> **Reward yourself.** Promise yourself that if you finish this matter, you can have a cup of coffee, or can do some work that you enjoy doing more. Yes, these are pretty feeble rewards. Maybe you can persuade yourself that if you finish this matter, one day a multinational corporation will buy you out for $100 million.

>> **Get an employee or business associate or family member to nag you.** You do not want your clients or customers (or the CRA) to have to nag you.

>> **Live in fear.** Keep in mind that if you don't do your work on time, your business will fail and you'll end up penniless and starving on the street, your name cursed by all who once knew and respected you.

Delegate

TIP

Do what you do best, and delegate the rest. If you're not a secretary and you're doing a lot of secretarial work; if you're not a bookkeeper and you're doing a lot of bookkeeping; if you're not a salesperson and you're making a lot of sales calls; if you're not an office manager and you're spending all your time marshalling employees and ordering supplies; if you're not a janitor and you're doing a lot of cleaning — you need to hire someone to do these tasks. Your time is better spent doing what you're expert in. Try outsourcing this work, or hiring a temp or a part-time worker, before you hire a full-time employee.

WARNING

While we're on the subject of delegation, don't let people you've hired delegate to you! "Upward delegation" is a sneak attack. If someone you've delegated to isn't doing the work right, don't do it for him. Provide more training, or give guidelines for correcting the work and have the person try again until he gets it right. Otherwise you'll end up doing the work *and* paying someone else to do it.

Just say no

The word *no* has a lot of power. Sometimes you have to use it to keep other people from hijacking your time and your energy.

>> **Whenever someone makes a demand on you, consider what's in it for you.** What will you gain if you do it, and what will you lose if you don't? Will attending a community event or giving a presentation help you find more customers? Will turning away a potential client who wants you to perform a time-consuming low-paying service destroy your business? Will telling a supplier to check her own files before you check yours ruin your relationship?

>> **Don't hold or attend useless meetings.** When someone suggests a meeting, consider whether a meeting could be replaced by a phone call or email, or a brief informal chat, or an information document that can be circulated.

>> **Discourage drop-in visits from colleagues and clients.** Sure, visits are more fun than work, but you don't get paid for visits and they interfere with your carefully planned day. If a client drops by at an inconvenient time, have a short stand-up meeting and make an appointment for a real meeting later.

>> **Tell your family and friends not to call you all the time to chat.** Now that you're working for yourself, everyone thinks you can spend the whole day shooting the breeze. (You can, but your business will flop.) This is especially true if you have a home office, where spouses, children, and pets will not just call but will also show up in person.

And don't forget to take care of Number One

TIP

Finally, make sure you keep yourself in good shape to run your business:

>> **Take time off to refresh yourself.** Leave the office for a coffee break, go for a walk, take evenings and/or weekends off.

>> **Eat properly!** Low blood sugar won't do anything for your concentration — and neither will a blood sugar high if you get tired and try to cure the problem with cookies, doughnuts, chocolate bars, and lots of caffeine.

>> **Get enough sleep.** Lack of sleep won't help your concentration or your mood — or your looks.

>> **Get regular exercise.** Your exercise program can slide when you're busy, but you need to be healthy to keep the business running. And you want to stay alive to enjoy the fruits of your labour.

Learning business management techniques

As your business expands, it's turning into an enterprise that needs professional management. You may be able to turn yourself into a professional manager, or you may need to bring managers on board. While you wait to discover whether you have what it takes to be a professional manager (management may be something you left your employed life to avoid), you can think about the issues we talk about in this section.

Give up control (at least a little)

Giving up control isn't something you want to hear about — unless, of course, someone's buying you out for an obscenely large amount of money. One of the reasons you went into business for yourself was so you could run things the way you wanted to! But the fact is that you can't do everything yourself, so you're going to have to share some of the responsibilities with others or even hand responsibilities over entirely.

Start off slowly, if you like:

>> **Have brainstorming sessions to solve problems.** You may find that you come up with better solutions when you get two or three other people to help you think.

>> **Take your time to think about important matters, and gather information and get advice before you make a decision.** Look at the matter in the context of your goals and vision for your business, rather than making it personal.

>> **Make yourself redundant.** Your business has many critically important areas, and if an area is entrusted to just one person (even if that person is you), you're putting your business at risk. What if you get sick, or you're injured? What if you want to go on a vacation? So find yourself an understudy, or even hand over primary responsibility to someone else (whom you've carefully chosen, of course).

>> **Set up formal systems to make business decisions.** That means bringing your associates and/or employees into the process. Maybe it's even time for you to get a board of directors for your corporation, including some experienced businesspeople from outside your business who can help you with your expansion.

Set goals

You've probably had goals all along. But do they still match the direction your business is taking? Are you following the right strategies to reach them? Review your goals, and set new ones if that makes sense. Rethink your strategies if your goals are fine but you're not making headway in reaching them.

Your goals should take into account the underlying values of your business (such as fairness, honesty, reliability) and the purpose of your business. They shouldn't focus purely on making money, or you'll find yourself going astray pretty quickly.

When setting your goals, keep in mind that they should be "SMART":

>> **Specific** — but with enough flexibility built in that you can go off course if the right opportunity arises.

>> **Measurable** — use actual numbers. And build milestones into your plan so that you'll know as you go along whether you're going to meet your target.

>> **Achievable** — so that you can stay motivated to reach a realistic target.

>> **Relevant** — so that your goals align with the nature of your business and its overall strategy.

>> **Time limited** — set a deadline to meet the goals.

As an example, after reviewing your profit and loss statement, you might set a goal to increase sales by 5 percent in one year, or to reduce expenses by 10 percent within six months. Your milestone #1 to increase sales might be to identify a specific number of new customers or identify customers for whom you could do more work. Milestone #1 for reducing expenses might be to perform an audit of your business activities. You'd create a document setting out your goal and the tasks involved in reaching the goal, your deadline, your milestones and milestone dates, and assigning the appropriate people to take charge of the tasks. You'd circulate the document, meet with the people in charge of the tasks, and you might also hold a general staff meeting to explain the plan for reaching the goal.

Focus on your strengths

TIP

Focus on your areas of strength. Have you heard of the "80/20" rule? It says that the most significant areas of your business (whether significant for good or bad reasons) actually make up a small percentage of your business. For example, about 20 percent of your customers give you about 80 percent of your business, about 20 percent of your products bring in about 80 percent of your revenue, and about 20 percent of your employees do about 80 percent of the work. (And about 20 percent of your clients and employees give you about 80 percent of your headaches.)

So concentrate on your best customers, your top-selling products, and your best employees. If you can't move your unproductive customers into your Best Customer category, maybe you should gently try to find them another home. If you've got products that aren't moving and you can't get them moving, maybe you should drop them and free up shelf space. If you can't get more work out of an employee, maybe you should encourage the employee to depart. Don't spend a lot of your time and effort on customers, products, and employees who aren't going to generate a return on your investment.

Learn to live with change

In fact, go beyond living with change and learn to embrace it. Change brings you opportunities as well as challenges.

>> **Keep your eyes open at all times.** What is the economy up to? What is the market up to? What are your customers up to?

>> **Be ready to act on a change.** You'll need to reinvent your business, or pieces of it, constantly to keep up with the changing world you operate in. And if you get used to coping with small changes all the time, you'll be better prepared to cope with the big changes that sometimes shake an industry, or an economy.

>> **Assume change will happen even when things look pretty stable.** For example, when you invest in new technology, leave yourself some growing room. If a technical product is just right for your business now, you may outgrow it before too long.

>> **Learn from your mistakes.** Analyze what went wrong, make recommendations about how to avoid such a mistake in the future, and then implement any necessary changes.

Make good use of employees

You're the boss. If you hire people to work for you, make sure you help them do a good job.

>> **Communicate clearly.** One of your duties as an employer is to tell your employees what to do (see Chapter 15). Making sure that your employees know what their jobs are and how they're supposed to perform them is also

sound business practice. So tell them clearly what you want done, and give the same story to everyone — the employee, the employee's superiors, and the employee's subordinates.

>> **Encourage employee input.** They know quite a lot about your business, so their input is extremely useful. And if you pay attention to their input they'll feel more commitment to carrying out their duties because they're helping to make or at least refine the plans.

>> **Don't discourage employee output.** By output we don't mean work (although we don't want you to discourage work, either), we mean questions. Tell your employees that no question is stupid. But stupid mistakes can arise from ignorance and could cost your business a lot of money.

>> **Run a tight ship — but not too tight.** Don't let your employees treat your workplace as a social forum — they're not there to have extended non-business chats with co-workers or to take nonessential personal phone calls, or to surf the Net or play computer games. But at the same time remember that employees who aren't allowed to speak to their fellows or call home to see how a child or elderly parent is doing are going to be unhappy and unproductive because they'll be cranky and worried. And try to restrain yourself from telling your employees what they can and can't do on their lunch hour or break, even if it involves using your business's computer equipment (as long as they're not doing something that could lead to complaints from co-workers, like visiting porn websites).

>> **In fact, try not to be a control freak in general.** Give your employees responsibility and make them accountable for their work. Tell them that the buck stops everywhere. Let them know in advance what the rewards for achievement are (such as a bonus). (Avoid dwelling on punishments for failure — it's bad psychology. But if you have an employee who does a lot of failing, keep notes — you'll need them when the time comes to fire him or her.) Follow up so you'll know whether they're succeeding.

>> **Don't let the sun set on employee conflicts.** Warfare among your staff will cripple your business. You must try to resolve conflicts, and the earlier the better. Don't tell yourself that whether employees get along is their business. It's *your* business.

IN THIS CHAPTER

» Evaluating if running a cannabusiness is right for you

» Finding the industry, regulatory, and legal information you need to get started

» Brainstorming a good new idea in the cannabis ecosystem

» Examining some existing types of cannabusinesses

Chapter **19**

Starting a Cannabusiness

I f a Bay Street businessperson picks up the dictionary, he or she will find that the term *cannabusiness* means "the commercial activity of selling cannabis or cannabis-based products." If a hipster goes to the Urban Dictionary, he or she will see that *cannabusiness* means "the fine art of selling weed." Either definition is fine.

Cannabusiness is becoming a real powerhouse force in the Canadian economy. A discussion about its somewhat long history in Canada is beyond the scope of this book, but it's worth noting that this sector truly awakened in 2018 when use of recreational cannabis became legal. The Cannabis Act is the law that legalized recreational cannabis use in Canada, in tandem with its companion legislation Bill C-46, An Act to Amend the Criminal Code. When this act was passed, Canadians witnessed the birth of a whole new business sector!

Ever since, and a bit before, Canada's leadership in the marijuana sector has made the world stand up and take notice. We hear an endless stream of news — good and bad — about the issues surrounding this sector. As we all know, where there is change, there is also opportunity, and Canadian small business entrepreneurs and those who want to be "cannapreneurs" are stepping up to the plate to consider taking a swing at the opportunity. If you're one of those folks, this chapter is for you!

Determining If You Have What It Takes

In Chapter 1, we outline the upsides and downsides of small business ownership. If cannabusiness is the industry sector you're interested in, the principles we discuss in that chapter don't change. However, because this is a brand-new frontier for Canadians, both the upsides and the downsides may be more pronounced than they are for existing and longstanding industries in Canada. Uncertainty fuels the volatility and velocity of change, as well as how pronounced the impacts of that change may be. So, if you're interested in getting into the cannabusiness sector, you need to be able to tolerate a little volatility, and go with the flow, man.

If you've never experienced the culture of cannabis, you may be at a disadvantage. To catch up, check out our section "A plant by any other name: Learning the lingo" to at least *pretend* you regularly talk the talk! If you want to do business in the legitimate marijuana ecosystem, you need to speak two languages — one related to the traditional cannabis subculture, and the other that of the real business world. With a mix of grow-culture speak and MBA-style business savvy, you'll do well in the legitimate cannabis ecosystem.

Your success is also most likely to crystallize if you and your employees are able to adapt to changes in the cannabis industry, and keep up with growing amounts of legislation at both the federal, provincial, and territorial levels. It also helps if you have a creative streak in order to adapt your existing skill set, background, and experience into a brand-new small cannabusiness context. Do you have these and other similar traits?

Another acid test (no drug pun intended) is to really ask yourself if you're "just sort of" interested in cannabis, or if you're totally amped about it. If it's the former, success may be harder to find. That's because starting a regular and traditional business is hard enough in longstanding industries, let alone in the undiscovered country of cannabusiness. Participating in the cannabis industry requires that you're committed to the hard work and effort associated with understanding dozens of aspects of the sector.

TIP

A good approach to making sure you have the right stuff is to leverage what you're really good at. Wield your very best *soft skills* (such as interpersonal and relationship building skills), and leverage your tangible background and experience. Get other outside experts or your own employees to help you with the rest. For example, creative agencies can build your website, and graphic designers can help with your marketing materials.

Be one of the three musketeers and adopt an "all for one, one for all" philosophy. Collaborate when you must, join forces and resources, and work as a team to maximize your chances for greater market share.

Seeking Out Helpful Business Information

In Chapter 2, we show you how to search for relevant information about business in general, as well as investigate your own field (in this case, cannabusiness). We also show you how you can build your skill set with online and other resources, as well as find experts to help you. We cap that chapter by showing you how to look for potential customers and suppliers. If you haven't read that chapter yet, take a quick look — it's a logical reference point for this chapter.

If you want to start a cannabusiness, knowing the rules of the game is critical. We cannot stress this enough, so we repeat this critical success factor throughout this chapter. The laws, rules, and regulatory framework for opening a cannabusiness are incredibly complex, growing, and fast-changing. The pace of legislative change, combined with the fact that this is an emerging industry and sector, make knowing the regulations, risks, and theory around cannabusiness imperative to your business success. There, we repeated this point already!

Industry information

A good place to start your quest for knowledge of cannabusiness is to understand the theoretical side of the legal marijuana business. In this section, we cover the basics, as well as cannabusiness industry trends.

A plant by any other name: Learning the lingo

You may have heard the terms *marijuana* and *cannabis* and wondered about the difference. We did, and our fogginess wasn't even because we smoked any of the above. Here's the deal: *Marijuana* refers to the plant scientifically known as *cannabis* — more specifically, to three recognized species that include *Cannabis sativa, Cannabis indica,* and *Cannabis ruderalis.*

The cannabis plant is a source of hundreds of compounds. Two in particular, called delta-9-tetrahydrocannabinol (THC) and cannabidiol, are the most widely tested elements for medicinal and recreational uses. *Hemp,* another term you hear lots about, is a variety of the *Cannabis sativa* plant species that is grown specifically for the industrial uses of its derived products.

So, next time you hear news stories about marijuana, you'll likely hear about these terms. You'll also realize that marijuana and cannabis refer to the same plant, so from here on, we use the terms *cannabis* and *marijuana* interchangeably.

Cannabis looks weird. The shredded flowers, buds, and leaves of a marijuana plant comes in a green, brown, or gray mix. It's smelly, too. Cannabis is presented in various ways and forms. Marijuana that is rolled up like a cigarette is called a *joint*, and if you roll it like a cigar, it's a *blunt*. Marijuana can also be smoked in a *pipe*. Some Canadians incorporate marijuana into cookies or other foods, or brew it as a flavoured tea. Canadians who smoke oils from the marijuana plant practice what is referred to as *dabbing*. Other slang names for marijuana include *pot, weed, grass, herb,* or *boom.*

Getting hip to what's happening with weed today

It's also interesting to note that smoking weed isn't the main trend. Actually, quite a few pot users are turning away from the smoking variety of marijuana. The smoke has a problem: People's lungs get coated and choked with tar under long-term use. More and more users are tending toward new ways to consume pot. These alternative ways to consume, not all legal yet, include vaporizing, eating cannabis-infused foods like crackers, drinking cannabis-infused lemonade, ingesting oils taken in capsules or added to food or drink, applying tinctures directly under the tongue, and using topical lotions and balms. Do you see the brand-new industries cropping up like we do? The trend is your friend. Know the trends if you want to pursue cannabusiness success.

WARNING

This is not a health book or chapter. We get that. But do know about what people, perhaps your customers, may experience. Cannabis can make you feel relaxed, silly, sleepy, and happy. It can also make you nervous and scared. Your senses of hearing, sight, and touch may be altered. Your judgement may also be significantly impaired.

Knowing why you may want to invest in a cannabusiness

As with any new industry, there are good opportunities to be found for Canadian cannabusinesses entrepreneurs willing to do their research, and who recognize the advantages and trends. One advantage is the fact that Canada has provided other countries with a legal and operational template for politicians and producers to mimic. In other words, the fact that Canada has first mover advantage in a politically friendly context make the opportunity to invest in this industry undeniable. But, of course, the risks of doing so are still many.

It's also an advantage that medicinal pot is already entrenched in the Canadian healthcare industry, so it already has a small but important installed base market. What better endorsement is there than a hospital or doctor sanctioning its careful — and we emphasize the word *careful* — use? As all this slow but steady acceptance is happening, the investment community has swooped in for a piece of the action. The flow of capital is vital (and something you need to watch) in order for any emerging sector to grow and flourish.

In the following sections we look at what cannabusiness may have to offer in terms of an investment opportunity.

LOOKING AT THE PAST AND PRESENT

The trend is your friend. Let's take a look at where we've been so far, with numbers, which always tell part of a story. Arcview Market Research, a prominent marijuana market research company, reported that legal pot sales way back in 2017 were $10 billion in North America. The company has since estimated that by the end of 2021, sales could reach $25 billion or more. That's a big enchilada of a number. At the time of this writing, there are more than 100 publicly listed companies in Canada supporting this ecosystem, with a market capitalization value of $35 billion.

TIP

Go to the Marijuana Index (www.marijuanaindex.com) to access indexes for the North American, U.S., and Canadian marijuana stock markets. Why stock markets? Because stock market indexes are excellent indicators of what investors think of the potential of a sector, industry, or individual company. It's a great proxy for the health of the weed sector as a whole. It's also a great site to visit for basic news information on the sector. Four hundred companies are listed!

CONSIDERING FUTURE INDICATORS

The basic infrastructure — access to financial markets, the ability to produce marijuana, and lots of smart visionaries with sound business plans — is now in place, and the ecosystem is thriving. Now that cannabis is legal, other indicators of growth to watch for include new listings of large Canadian cannabis companies on major U.S. exchanges like the New York Stock Exchange (NYSE) or Nasdaq. Tilray, Inc. (TLRY); Canopy Growth Corporation (CGC); Cronos Group, Inc. (CRON); and Aurora Cannabis (ACB) have all benefitted from listing with our friends south of the border. Many others are applying.

Also, watch for merger and acquisition activity for a barometer of industry health. Recently, Aurora Cannabis made a $3 billion all-stock offer to buy its rival and licensed producer MedReleaf to create an 800-pound gorilla in the cannabis sector. Together, the combined company is poised to produce over 600,000 kilograms of cannabis annually, representing about 50 percent of expected Canadian demand in 2021.

What other countries do is critical as well. Look for developments in Italy, Sweden, and of course the United States to see if their markets will further open up domestic, as well as foreign, supply of medical and legal marijuana. And see how many U.S. companies are seeking listings on Canadian exchanges. If banks like BMO and others support the industry, that's another great sign that the sector will continue to thrive. It will help point you to promising business ideas and areas.

Although U.S. laws and Food and Drug Administration (FDA) regulations are still in a state of flux, you'd be wise to wonder if the United States represents the next big opportunity and super-catalyst. If so, then Canadian suppliers are uniquely poised to capitalize. That's because Canada is one of only two countries — the other is the Netherlands — that currently exports cannabis (if you have a licence and the purpose is medical or scientific) to well over 20 countries. It also helps the future of this sector that the number of companies that have been authorized by Health Canada to produce medicinal marijuana across the country has been steadily increasing.

TIP

To get statistics and market forecast information, check out the Statistics Canada website at www.statcan.gc.ca and use the search tool with the term *cannabis* or *marijuana*. We found lots of current and helpful information on this rapidly evolving industry sector.

Legal and regulatory information

Whether you use marijuana or simply want to start a business in this budding (sorry, we couldn't resist) industry, you can get into real legal or financial trouble. But that trouble only comes if you don't know and follow the rules, be they rules about growing, processing, retailing, or any other aspect such as licensing. A good starting point to avoiding trouble is knowing the specific rules and regulations in place about marijuana today — and, of course, reading this book to learn about starting a cannabusiness and risk principles germane to this industry!

Canada was a pioneer in the legalized use of marijuana for medical purposes as far back as two decades ago. Today, and as we mention in the introduction to this chapter, it's also legally permitted to purchase, grow, and possess limited, regulated, and tested amounts of cannabis in Canada. Way back in 2014, it was actually already legal for Canadian medical patients to possess medical marijuana from a licensed distributor, but only with a prescription provided by a still-practicing Canadian physician. Soon after, legislation evolved to allow patients possessing a prescription from a doctor to grow their own medical marijuana plant and use the bud. They could even designate a third-party grower to grow it for them. The Cannabis Act, together with provincial and territorial legislation, currently prescribe the number of cannabis plants that can be grown per household, as well as any other key restrictions.

Canada now possesses a draft but rigid legal framework to oversee the production, distribution, sale, and possession of cannabis across Canada. This framework has allowed for the legal, efficient, and effective production and cultivation of cannabis. The good news is that the new legislation is aimed at restricting access to cannabis by underaged Canadian youth, deterring and reducing crime around it, and protecting the users of the drug through strict safety requirements and quality control measures. Also, the legacy program for accessing cannabis for medical purposes will continue under the new act. As you can see, it's really important for cannapreneurs to understand the ever-changing legalities — and opportunities — surrounding the medical marijuana industry. It's crucial to be a good cannabis ecosystem citizen!

REMEMBER

Regulations in Canada and the United States differ from the municipal, provincial, and state levels all the way to the federal level.

WARNING

If you're like most news-watching Canadians, you've undoubtedly heard about occasional raids on pot dispensaries on Queen Street in Toronto, West Hastings Street in Vancouver, and elsewhere all across Canada. That's because, even under the new law, some dispensaries may be operating illegally. Canadians who buy medical marijuana from an unproven dispensary are also placing themselves at risk of possible exposure to pesticides, heavy toxic metals, and nasty pathogens. Starting a cannabusiness is complex!

Why following the rules is so important

Knowing the rules really well is the first step to making sure you don't break them. This is important because the penalties for breaking drug, health, and safety-related rules are much more severe than they are for breaking other laws of the land. These penalties include large fines and even jail time. To manage the legal and regulatory risks of noncompliance with the rules, you first have to identify and understand what those rules and, therefore, risks are. In addition, legal and regulatory risks are just one of many risks that cannabusinesses face. We deal with these risks throughout this chapter.

To start and run your cannabusiness, make sure that you and your employees possess a sound understanding of how the regulations work and how and where to get more information when necessary.

REMEMBER

When the rules become overwhelming, we *strongly* recommended that you hire an experienced lawyer with cannabis-related expertise to help you along.

The cannabis industry is still in its infancy and many new regulations are still hot off the press. This makes networking with local institutions and industry associations important in order to get their guidance and insights. The next section shows you some starting points and approaches to help.

Government of Canada resources

To stay on top of the shifting sands of federal legislation, check out the Government of Canada's Cannabis in Canada website (www.canada.ca/cannabis) for key details that will expand your knowledge of the industry. These details include essential information about law, medicine, and educational resources pertinent to cannabis.

For example, the website advises you not to travel with cannabis across the border, and identifies the risks of impairment on the road and at work. For cannabusinesses, the key tab to check out on this website is What Industry Needs to Know; here, you can find out how the Canadian legal and regulatory framework may impact your cannabusiness.

REMEMBER

There are federal rules and provincial and territorial rules. Whether your business will transact in only one province or in several provinces, you need to know what is legal in each province and territory across Canada.

IDENTIFYING INDUSTRY REGULATIONS

After the Cannabis Act and its supporting regulations became law on October 17, 2018. Health Canada became the main government entity accepting applications from those who want to become cannabis licence holders and comply with the act.

At the time of this writing, Health Canada was in the process of making amendments to the cannabis regulations that would enable licensed processors to produce and sell three new classes of cannabis: edible cannabis, cannabis extracts, and cannabis topicals. The legal production and sale of edible cannabis, cannabis extracts, and cannabis topicals is expected to be permitted by October 17, 2019.

APPLYING FOR A LICENCE

As indicated on the Cannabis in Canada website (www.canada.ca/cannabis), cannabis licence holders may actually need not one but two licences: one from Health Canada and, possibly, one from the Canada Revenue Agency (CRA).

You're required to have a licence from Health Canada if you want to grow cannabis commercially for sale or produce cannabis products commercially. You also need a licence from Health Canada if you sell cannabis for medical purposes, conduct scientific tests on cannabis, and/or conduct research with cannabis. On the Cannabis in Canada website (www.canada.ca/cannabis), click the What Industry Needs to Know link, and then click Apply for or Amend a Licence. Check this website regularly for any changes to the requirements.

The federal government requires that cultivators, producers, and packagers of cannabis products obtain a special cannabis licence from the CRA. It doesn't stop there. After you obtain a licence, you're also required to buy and apply cannabis excise stamps (explained at www.canada.ca/en/revenue-agency/campaigns/cannabis-taxation) to your products (if you package cannabis products), calculate the duty on your sales, and file a return and send the excise duty to the CRA. Fun!

TIP

Health Canada runs an online Cannabis Tracking and Licensing System. This system allows you to submit and view the status of applications. It also allows you to submit amendments to licences. You can access it at www.canada.ca/cannabis by clicking the What Industry Needs to Know link.

FOLLOWING THE PACKAGING AND LABELLING RULES

Your cannabusiness has to follow plain packaging and labelling standards in order to protect against accidental consumption, to ensure that products are not appealing to minors and youth, and to provide consumers with key information they need to make informed decisions prior to consuming cannabis. Health Canada prescribes the rules around packaging; you can find out more at www. canada.ca/en/health-canada/services/drugs-medication/cannabis/laws-regulations/regulations-support-cannabis-act.html.

UNDERSTANDING COMPLIANCE AND ENFORCEMENT UNDER THE CANNABIS ACT

Cannabusiness owners, whether they're licensed or not, absolutely must comply with the Cannabis Act and its associated and relevant regulations. This means that you're expected to know and understand the legislation and your obligations, cooperate with inspectors, and comply with orders and prohibitions from Health Canada. Health Canada's compliance and enforcement policy can be found at www. canada.ca/en/health-canada. Check it out to see what parts of the long arm of the law apply to your business idea or enterprise.

GETTING CLEAR ON PROHIBITIONS ON MARKETING AND ADVERTISING

The rules are also very tight regarding what and how you can market. The prohibitions against cannabis marketing under the Cannabis Act apply to you if you promote cannabis, cannabis accessories, and services related to cannabis. The gory but vital details can be found at www.canada.ca/en/health-canada/services/drugs-medication/cannabis/laws-regulations/promotion-prohibitions. You can also just Google the term *prohibitions for cannabis marketing in Canada* to get not just the government's website but also articles on the subject as well. The provinces and territories have something to say as well, and knowing these rules is critical. Check them out at www.canada.ca/en/health-canada/services/drugs-medication/cannabis/laws-regulations/provinces-territories. For example, Ontario recently made changes by capping the number of new retail cannabis stores that could open annually in the province. This is a significant new restriction.

PAYING LICENSING FEES

Fees apply to you on the following classes of licences:

>> Cultivation (standard, micro, or nursery)

>> Processing (standard or micro)

>> Sales for medical purposes

These fees are meant to recover costs for screening your licence application, executing security screening, and reviewing the substance of the applications to import or export cannabis for scientific or medical purposes. The fees also cover a robust review of your licence application, the actual issuance of your licences (if you're successful), inspections, and compliance and enforcement activities.

WARNING

If you're involved in the cannabis industry in Canada, you should know that the legalization of cannabis in Canada has not changed Canada's border rules. It's still illegal to take cannabis across Canada's international borders. The Canadian government's website states the following:

> [I]f you try to travel internationally with any amount of cannabis in your possession you could be subject to serious criminal penalties both at home and abroad. You could also be denied entry at your destination country if you have previously used cannabis or any substance prohibited by local laws.

EXPORTING AND IMPORTING CANNABIS

WARNING

No cannabusiness may export or import cannabis for any purposes, other than for medical or scientific purposes, under the Cannabis Act. Doing so is strictly prohibited. As a result, any company still conducting business in the cannabis industry in international markets is exposed to many risks. We discuss risks in the next section. Be sure to seek legal counsel if you plan to expand operations abroad.

Legal and regulatory risk factors

WARNING

If you've already read Chapter 12, where we discuss most of the types of risks small businesses face, you'll recall that we also touched on legal and regulatory risks. Although almost all the risks we outline there also apply to small cannabusinesses, a key, if not top risk for cannabusinesses, is legal and regulatory risk. Not complying with regulations and winding up on the wrong side of the law is serious business and serious trouble. On top of that, there are competitive, operational, reputational, and strategic risks to consider.

In this section, we stay focused on the top risks to a cannabusiness, but we advise you not to forget the other risks we discuss in Chapter 12.

The top risks that we identify for you but which you yourself must manage are

>> **Regulatory:** Small cannabusinesses sell into and cater to a highly regulated niche market. This makes demand for your products or services uncertain. The gradual easing of laws also works the other way around. As competitors grow in size, number, and complexity, you'll lose market share even if you're one of the first movers.

>> **Barriers to entry:** Licensing is still a huge hurdle that you may have to overcome (especially if you're a grower, processor, or retailer where some provinces have retail licence quotas), but there are low barriers to entry for new cannabusinesses, especially those companies that serve the ancillary marijuana market, which we discuss later in this chapter.

>> **Large competitors:** Big Tobacco, Big Pharma, and Big Food are poised to steal away customers, even from the relative minnows but true innovators that we've come to know as small cannabusinesses.

>> **Short supply:** Cannabis supply, at the time of writing, was a significant problem. You can't sell what you don't have. You can't support an ecosystem that suffers from frequent shortages. From a financial risk perspective, sure, strong demand and low supply equals profits. After all, shortages increase the per-gram price of cannabis. Yet, despite the rapid capacity expansion of many growers who anticipated the passing of legislation, most projects won't be fully operational until the end of 2020.

>> **Long-term oversupply:** What goes down must come up. Although undersupply is a bit of a problem now, oversupply may be a problem down the road. Estimates from analysts suggest that four of the largest cannabis producers — Aurora Cannabis, Canopy Growth Corporation, Aphria, and the Green Organic Dutchman — are poised to collectively grow and produce 1.5 million kilograms by 2020, and grow even more beyond that time. On the bright side (from the perspective of entrepreneurs), perhaps this excess supply will be absorbed by foreign markets if and when exporting laws become more clear and relaxed.

WARNING

Government can definitely get in the way of recreational marijuana production, sale, and use. This risk is political. Political interference on hot-button issues like this can and ought to be expected. The issue is the nature and extent of the meddling. Given the recent legalization, industry momentum, and demand (read: votes), there is still some residual risk.

Finally, enforcement risks (enforcement is a good thing for the industry) are high, so you'd better operate a legitimate business. This means paying extra attention to avoiding certain behaviors and risks. For example, to steer clear of trouble, your cannabusiness must have zero tolerance for

>> Distribution of marijuana to minors

>> Profits from the sale of cannabis going to criminal enterprises

>> Diverting marijuana from areas where it's legal to areas where it is not

>> Government-authorized cannabis activity used as a cover for the trafficking of other illegal drugs or other illegal activity

>> Violence and the use of firearms in the distribution of marijuana

>> Drugged driving

>> Growing marijuana on public lands and the related safety concerns

Getting Clear on Your Big Product or Service Idea

Canadians today are witness to the birth of an entire industry. This environment of innovation, ideas, animal spirits, and change has given rise to many opportunities — both known and yet to be discovered. When you start a small business in any sector or industry within that sector, a unique idea that meets demand is obviously an essential and fundamental ingredient to reach small business success. As we explain in Chapters 3 and 4, your business will be in deep trouble if you offer a product or service that no one wants or is interested in. In this chapter, essentially a case study on starting a cannabusiness that puts theory into practice, we help you avoid those landmines. We want this section to be your idea factory and to give you practical tips on how to develop a product or service tailored for your target customers.

Before diving into some specifics about ideas pertaining to the cannabusiness sector, we urge you to take a quick look, if you haven't already, at the principles we cover in Chapters 3 and 4. In those chapters, we discuss how you can brainstorm business ideas, be watchful of using existing ideas that have possessive owners, safely leverage the ideas of others, and protect your very own ideas. Yes, intellectual property issues can live in the marijuana world! In addition, we also discuss in those chapters whether your small cannabusiness should sell a product, service, or both. We show you how to think about your target pot market as you develop a product or service, how to get your product or service to the right people, and how to price your product or service.

In the upcoming section "Exploring the Opportunities," we outline some ideas that have already been exploited and explored by others. We get there shortly to help you along. But more important, what we'd prefer to do is to first induct you into a few brainstorming approaches that hold true to all ideas, and that may help you generate brand new ones. The next few subsections give you some big-picture tips to do just that. After that, we get to the really interesting stuff that others have already thought of but which you may be able to improve!

Generating a unique cannabusiness idea

When you brainstorm ideas, it's useful to start at the top of the idea pyramid. Okay, maybe second from the top. If you already decided to jump into cannabusiness, you've already picked a sector — cannabis. The next step is to figure out the industry within that sector. For example, weed growth, distribution, and retail are core industry components of the broader cannabis sector, much like software and hardware are industries within the broader technology sector. Industries can be further divided into subsets and so on and so on. We find it's most helpful to start at the top of the idea pyramid and work your way to the bottom. It's not the only way to brainstorm, but it is logical and methodical.

If you're totally new to the sector, you'll likely think about dispensaries and grow ops if only because that is what's in the news a lot. However, the cannabis industry includes much more than that. Other cool ideas in the news include "bud and breakfasts," which are cannabis-friendly lodges and facilities. News is a good source of ideas.

You may want to brainstorm in terms of what you know best. For example, if you're into food or have a background associated with restaurants, you may look into making a unique line of edibles. Again, at the time of this writing, legislation prohibited such edibles. But change is coming, and getting in front of change may give you first-mover advantage. Leverage your strengths!

As we recommend throughout this chapter, check out the legal requirements first, preferably with the second opinion (or first) of legal counsel experienced in this sector. Cannabusiness entrepreneurs absolutely need to make sure that their idea is legally viable in addition to offering a compelling and unique product or service.

TIP

If you prefer to dip your toes instead of diving in head first, a less risky type of small cannabusiness to launch is one that doesn't directly touch the "bud." When you look at the Cannabis Act, much of the regulations pertain to cannabis growers, processors, and retailers. This makes ancillary marijuana businesses an appealing option because they're less burdened with red tape and high taxes. We discuss some of the ancillary businesses in a separate section later in this chapter, but the list of opportunities is endless.

WHO'S MAKING MONEY?

According to the Marijuana Business Factbook, and in those few parts of the world where cannabis has been legal for some time, about 85 percent of operating dispensaries and recreational marijuana stores, infused products companies, and wholesale cultivators and growers — important components of the marijuana space — report that they're "profitable or at least breaking even."

The cultivation and infused products sectors are especially successful, with about 30 percent of wholesale growers and 25 percent of infused companies reporting that they are "very profitable." Cultivators can hit profitability fairly quickly, but start-up expenses can be very high. They can also be moderate to high for infused product companies. Of all these industry components, 90 percent of infused products businesses reported that they're at the very least operating at break-even profitability.

Considering start-up and ongoing costs

Startup costs should be one of the first things you need to consider. The nature of the cannabusiness you're thinking about (which we discuss in the upcoming section "Exploring the Opportunities") and extent of its size (staff, space, scope, and scale) are the real drivers of start-up costs. Sure, it's great to start a vast cultivation operation that stretches to the horizon, but unless you have access to a bank vault, it's not going to come cheap.

As you think of an idea, research its costs and compare that cost and effort to your financial risk appetite. For example, conventional wisdom and experience has been that start-up and operational costs are significantly lower for infused product companies as compared to cultivators and larger retailers, making profitability more likely and speedy. If the costs you come up with are too scary, quickly move on to another brainstorming session to generate other ideas.

Evidence to date points to a hung jury when it comes to ancillary cannabusinesses. Companies that provide services to the cannabis industry and its customers are thriving, with almost half reporting meaningful profitability. On the other hand, ancillary products (not services), as well as technology firms, are still searching for a pot of gold in their pot-related businesses. About a quarter of this group reports losing "some or a lot of money." Why? Many of these companies must invest a significant amount of money to get started, and they face stiff competition once launched.

Understanding your consumer base

When you come up with your idea, you'll have already thought about your consumer base. What we want to point out in this section is that now you have to take a deeper dive into understanding this base. It's vital to know exactly who is going to be interested in your products or services and to really understand their particular wants and needs.

REMEMBER

When starting a cannabis business, two things are especially critical in addition to start-up costs and other considerations:

>> Understanding the unique challenges of this sector and industries within the sector

>> Understanding your consumer base and the unmet need you're satisfying for them

TIP

The cannabis industry is different from any industry you've ever worked in. The unique legal, regulatory, operational, financial, taxation, marketing, and reputational stigma elements of cannabusiness will take a big bite out of your profits and will siphon your attention away from the more fundamental and core elements of your business. Be aware of these unique challenges.

WARNING

It's precisely because the legal cannabis space is becoming crowded that you need to have a targeted consumer segment to focus on. Know who your core consumers are and what they want from the products and services you plan to provide.

TIP

The cannabis ecosystem is very connected and interrelated. It's not the best place for a lone-wolf small business to be. Success is tied to the connectivity, relationships, and leadership that you and your cannabusiness will cultivate with the local cannabis community.

Exploring the Opportunities

Before delving into specific cannabusiness opportunities at the "shop" level, which we do in this section, it's useful to see what larger industry "buckets" your cannabusiness may fall into. This parcelization is really important because it represents the particular ecosystem, and the players, partners, and associations within it that you'll need to know very well. The more defined an industry is, the better you'll be able to operate your business within it.

TIP

Business usually defines the *primary sector* as the one that produces raw materials, the *secondary sector* as carrying out manufacturing, and the *tertiary sector* as the one providing product sales and services.

TIP

Another way to look at cannabis industries within the marijuana sector is to segment them beginning with those that "touch the plant" — industries like biotechnology, cultivation, processing, retail, hemp, and similar areas. A second segment may be the "direct support" basket, which includes agricultural technology, real estate, and secondary services industries. The "ancillary" product and service segment, yet another lens, includes consumption devices, investing and finance, technology, and media.

The Marijuana Index (www.marijuanaindex.com) breaks out its industries a bit deeper than this, although its sectors include many of the same segments. This website uses about ten segments, which we present in Table 19-1. This list is likely to grow. The Marijuana Index's list is not exhaustive — it really only focuses on those industries or segments where the public companies being tracked are currently found. Segments that have done great things for the Canadian cannabis ecosystem but may not be listed at this site include venture capital firms, individual angel investors, investment firms, and the accounting and legal practices that support thousands of ecosystem companies and businesses.

Table 19-1 is the abbreviated version of how The Marijuana Index breaks down its segments, along with a very brief snapshot of each. (For more detailed descriptions, click the Sectors tab at the top of www.marijuanaindex.com.)

TABLE 19-1   **Cannabis Industry Segments**

Industry Segment	Types of Companies within the Segment
Agricultural technology (AgTech)	Companies that provide technologies, equipment, and supplies to assist in the cultivation and production of the cannabis plant. Includes automated growing systems, greenhouses, farming products, nutrients, hydroponics, fertilization systems, horticultural expertise, LED/lighting technologies, air filtration systems, and climate control and energy efficiency systems.
Biotechnology	Companies focused on the research and development of new drugs and products using cannabinoids, the active compounds within cannabis.
Consumption devices	Companies that develop and sell personal consumption devices like cannabis vaporizing devices and alternative cannabis delivery methods like inhalers.
Cultivation and retail	Licenced producers (companies) that grow and sell the cannabis flower and products related to the flower.
Hemp products	Companies that produce and sell hemp products, which have lower concentrations of the psychoactive tetrahydrocannabinol (THC) compound and higher concentrations of the non-psychoactive cannabidiol (CBD) compound. Examples of hemp products include paper, textiles, clothing, food, beverages, and medical CBD products.

Industry Segment	Types of Companies within the Segment
Investing and finance	Firms and financial services providers that offer capital infusions and financing options for companies in the cannabis sector.
Marijuana products	Companies that extract, develop, and sell marijuana-infused products, including infused food products, drinks, oils, extracts, and lotions.
Other ancillary	Innovative and creative companies that provide products and services related to the broader cannabis ecosystem and economy that simply don't belong in other categories. Examples include breathalyzers, testing kits for consumers and regulatory organizations, medical clinics, hospitality and tourism providers, and much more.
Real estate	Companies that develop, own, and/or lease commercial real estate properties to licensed cannabis enterprises.
Secondary services	Companies that provide consulting and other services directly to marijuana growers and retailers. Examples include experts in licensing processes and cultivation, and professional service providers such as branding, packaging, bottling, compliance, lab testing, distribution, and insurance consultants.
Tech and media	Companies that provide hardware, software, and other information technology solutions for cannabis companies and consumers. Examples include seed-to-sale systems that track cannabis cultivation up to the points of sale and delivery, as well as enterprise software, e-commerce trading platforms, communication, and mapping services. Also includes media companies that provide cannabis-related marketing, including news, social networking, games, and entertainment.

Source: The Marijuana Index (www.marijuanaindex.com)

Now that we've touched on the sector segments, industries, and even very specific examples of the exact types of cannabusinesses that are out there in the cannabis economy, we dive deeper into several selected and specific examples of business opportunities. This is the fun part!

Producing, cultivating, or growing cannabis

A logical place for us to begin our exploration of cannabusiness opportunities, assuming all your licensing and regulatory obligations are in order, is the growing (cultivation or production) of cannabis. After all, it doesn't just appear in the ground like a weed. Okay, wrong choice of words! Nevertheless, you should know that a fundamental option you have is to be the first step in the process: to farm or grow the plants that supply the companies that go on to process marijuana into other ingestible products.

Considering cost

Before we even continue, you've probably, and correctly assumed that the cultivation of cannabis is not only time consuming — what with the patient waiting associated with growing the plant and getting a licence — but darned expensive!

Whether you grow cannabis outdoors, indoors, or in greenhouses, initial one-time capital expenditures can begin at about $200,000 (for land and facilities). The ongoing annual electricity, water, labour, growing solvents, administrative, marketing, and other operating costs can begin at $400,000, and we're really low-balling this figure. The total cost varies widely depending on the scale. For example, public companies you can search on The Marijuana Index (like Aphria) report annual costs in the tens of millions of dollars! We try to steer clear of actually costing out opportunities presented in this book, but we just want to let you know that this is one of the more expensive ones. Costs for any option can vary widely.

Now we present the sunnier news about the profitability of cannabis producers: Many studies and public filings show that on a contribution margin basis (revenue minus variable costs) and profitability basis (we discuss the income statement in Chapter 17), the cultivation industry is particularly lucrative. In that segment, about 30 percent of wholesale growers report that they are "very profitable." Remember that this profitability, and break-even, only kicks in once start-up costs like facility and equipment costs are first recovered. It also depends on how well the business is run and even luck, such as good weather and effective cultivation practices.

Cultivating cannabis is indeed one of the most rewarding aspects of the legal marijuana business process. Much like farmers take great joy in seeing their crops grow successfully, the same holds true for cannabis cultivation. Now that it's regulated, the guilt aspect of being a grower may be removed.

Identifying the different ways to harvest and sell the cannabis flower

There are different ways to harvest and sell the cannabis flower:

>> Selling harvests "as is" to processors (which we discuss in the next section), which produce concentrates, edibles, and other derived products

>> Breeding cannabis seeds and selling them to other growers

>> Producing cannabis clones and selling them to dispensaries

REMEMBER

The seed-versus-clone debate is a common dispute referenced by marijuana cultivators. There tend to be camps on each side. Will you use seeds, which despite providing a higher yield, grow more slowly and also risk growing male plants? (Yup, you heard that right.) Or, will you select a faster-growing "clone" certified to be female but susceptible to disease and pests? (We can't believe that seeds have genders, but you should know that a cannabis clone is a small cutting from a mother plant and has developed its own root system. It's all in the family!)

Recognizing some hurdles you'll need to jump

Operating as a cultivator is complex business. One hurdle is that licensing bodies at the federal, provincial, and municipal levels all have something to say about it. For instance, the regulatory body or licensing committee will likely need to verify that your location meets all the requirements and restrictions. Yes, you heard that right, one oversight body or another assumes that you already have the place rented out or purchased before the application is even submitted. If you don't, sure they'll accept your application. But the licence is less likely to be granted to wishful thinkers. This is a very big hurdle especially if your dream involved running a large grow op.

Another hurdle is that production will depend on the one strain you select to harvest. Alternately, you may grow different strains of the cannabis plant. Also be aware that the growing method you use, experience of your staff, and how well growing conditions are maintained affect success. Sales revenue will also depend on the weight and variety of cannabis grown. The most potent marijuana may command the highest sales price, but may not necessarily yield the greatest amounts.

Considering where you'll grow your plants: Indoors or out?

Outdoor cultivators in Canada produce one harvest annually, in the fall. Indoor cultivators produce year-round and can produce up to five or six harvests annually. Greenhouse cultivators can have between one and three harvests annually. As you can see, you have even more decisions to make here. Whatever you decide, options within the grow op area abound! We also want to remind you again that in addition to possessing basic knowledge of agriculture and horticulture, you'll want to make sure you adhere to the federal and local laws.

Craft cultivating: Starting small

In addition to different *ways* to cultivate cannabis, there are different *scales* of operations! The Cannabis Act recognizes both large-scale and small-scale growing operations, or grow ops. That changes everything because this book is all about starting a "small" business, and the Cannabis Act has something just for you! It's called *craft cultivating* and *craft processing*, and we discuss these opportunities in this section and the next.

Under Health Canada regulations, which permit both micro-cultivation and micro-processing, a craft micro-cultivation licence lets you possess a plant canopy of 200 square metres. Security regulations are a bit less onerous than those faced by large licensed producers, which are currently allowed to grow for medical users, as well as other licence holders. But both standard and micro-cultivators are not allowed to sell directly to the public for recreational use. Cultivators instead sell to companies possessing standard processing or micro-processing licences. These processors, in turn, sell the finished processed product to provincial distribution bodies like the Ontario Cannabis Store (www.ocs.ca) or BC Cannabis Stores (www.bccannabisstores.com). The Cannabis in Canada website (www.canada.ca/cannabis) has all the current rules.

TIP

Another legal and operational route to consider is for a micro-cultivator to apply for its own micro-processing licence. If you opt for this route, this would allow you to *process* up to 600 kilograms of dried cannabis per year by packaging it or making it into other products such as cannabis oil. We discuss processing in the next section.

Most Canadians have witnessed the rapid rise of the craft brewing industry in Canada. Molson and Labatt, while still the titans of the beer guzzling sector, are losing market share to craft brewers. The same "go craft" phenomenon appears to now be taking hold in the still growing cannabis sector. Canadians are selective in their beers, wines, and foods, and now they're selective about their cannabis options. At the same time, Canadian produce farmers who want to supplement their "traditional farming" revenues are diversifying into cannabis crops. Other entrants are black-market growers looking to go legal. This is good news because regulations translate to better safety and wellness for the consumer. As a potential small cannabusiness entrepreneur, you may be able to distinguish yourself by growing better-quality cannabis than Aphria and its giant competitors — by running a craft micro cultivation business.

WARNING

Another hurdle you should be aware of if you want to pursue this opportunity is that obtaining municipal approval and zoning permissions, which is an absolutely essential requirement of licensees, is still difficult! That's because many municipalities, towns, regions, and cities haven't yet established zoning rules. Those that have set rules often have quotas on licences granted. Many cities and towns are either not ready or reluctant to allow microcultivation, and many still communicate and adopt a strong "not in my backyard" (NIMBY) philosophy.

WARNING

Check with a lawyer, one who is experienced with and preferably specializes in the Cannabis Act, to get a legal opinion on the impacts, risks, and other matters you need to be aware of in this very complex and fast-changing component of the cannabis sector. We cannot stress this enough!

TIP

Although this resource does not replace legal counsel, do check with Health Canada's website for the latest developments in cannabis legislation and regulations (www.canada.ca/en/services/health/campaigns/cannabis).

Exploring cannabis processing

A second fundamental part of the business process of growing and selling finished cannabis products is processing the cannabis into derivative products. If you want to be a processor, you're expected to take the raw material plants grown by marijuana cultivators and prepare them to be ready to convert them into medical or recreational use products. Processors are also referred to as manufacturers, extract technicians, extract artists, or edibles chefs, depending on the position of the moon!

Understanding the rules of processing

As we mention in the previous section on cultivation, the Cannabis Act recognizes both large-scale and small-scale processing operations. If you're setting your sights on a smaller business operation, which is germane to the title and purpose of the book, you can get a permit for micro-cultivation, as well as micro-processing. The licence offered by Health Canada is called a "micro-processing licence." This licence allows you as an individual small-scale manufacturer to legally manufacture, package, and label cannabis and certain cannabis-derived marijuana products that are earmarked to be sold to the general public. Micro-processors would also be permitted to sell these processed products to other cannabis industry business operations.

REMEMBER

According to Health Canada, a "standard processing licence" is required for a facility that is processing more than 600 kilograms of dried flower. You need to keep up with ever-changing regulations as to what and how much you can process (www.canada.ca/en/services/health/campaigns/cannabis).

Knowing what you're allowed to process

Cannabis processors have to follow specific rules we mention in this chapter, and if this part of the cannabis ecosystem interests you, know the rules cold! That means seeking legal counsel and checking the Heath Canada website for regulations about what you can grow, and produce or process. However, common processed products that are found around the world include topicals, concentrates, and edibles.

Looking at the array of processed products

In this section, we take you through a selected range of cannabis products that were derived by cannabis and processed into other products. We have no desire to take you through any crazy paths of uber-weird products, although these do exist and you may even think of one yourself! Instead, we focus on what is already being produced today and present mostly the types of products you would expect to find in the medical marijuana space. This territory is a safer and better regulated ecosystem and is generally underpinned by strong regulations, which is actually a good thing for the long-term viability of these products. To be sure, not all the options we present are medical — some options are health-oriented, while others speak to uses who have nothing to do with health. We begin with the basic and move down a more complex processing chain.

FRESHLY CUT MARIJUANA

One of the very first ways that cannabis can be consumed may be the simplest, and may involve a lower amount of actual processing. Many people don't realize that a cannabis plant's raw flowers, stems, and leaves may actually be picked right off the plant and ingested. This means someone can eat the plant (add it to a salad, for example, or juice the raw plant with berries and fruit) to receive certain medical effects. When consuming the plant in the raw form, psychoactivity is greatly reduced.

One aspect of raw marijuana you may notice when you look at cannabis flowers is that they possess what are referred to as *trichomes.* The trichomes are the parts of the flower where cannabis oil is found. As you look at the plant, you'll see very small and whitish crystalline structures spreading across the surfaces of the leaves and flowers. The trichomes are a lot like dew resting on grass or leaves. Trichomes generate cannabinoids, and they're also sticky, shiny, and carry a strong smell.

DRIED FLOWERS

The consumption of freshly cut marijuana may be the most common thing you may think of when you think about someone smoking marijuana. It's what you expect to see when watching an old Cheech and Chong movie. But even with this type of smoky consumption, you can rest assured that there will be processing backed by standards and regulations. Again, it's a good thing.

To be more precise, cannabis flowers (and especially cannabis for medical use) go through a rigorous flush and curing process throughout the growth cycle. This helps to ensure that the dried flowers are free from fertilizers and other chemicals and that the flavor is attractive. The ideal end result is that there is a good collection of trichomes, a pleasant flavor, and significant medical benefit. This medical benefit may include pain management, better sleep, enhanced appetite, reduced inflammation, and enhanced mood during depression. Only a medical doctor can guide you on the stated medical benefits, so be careful here.

When the processing is complete — *voilà!* — a finished product! These products, derived from dried flowers, perhaps ground and pre-rolled, may include cannabis flowers or "buds" that can be either smoked or vaporized. Cannabis oil that is ready for ingestion is another product, as is an oral spray, which is essentially a fine spray of cannabis oil that is ready for ingestion. Cannabis oil can be placed or processed into pill or gel cap form, also ready for ingestion. There are even more possibilities, but you get the picture.

COLD-EXTRACTED CANNABIS

In addition to humidity and dryness, there is the element of temperature as a catalyst to process cannabis and produce finished products with it. Heat is an efficient and common ingredient to cannabis production, but there are also methods of extracting the trichomes without heat, all with the end purpose being that the cannabinoids and other by-products remain in their raw, acidic forms.

Processing cannabis may result in the following end-products:

» **Hash (hashish):** The word *hashish* means "grass," and the extraction and production of hash is generally based on using cold water and ice. Special micron bags are sometimes used to filter and extract the trichomes. The four general types of hash in order of increasing purity are: bubble, full bubble, melt, and full melt. Full melt is a collection of virtually pure trichomes that fully melt when exposed to heat with almost no residue.

» **Kief:** This is sort of like the cannabis equivalent to draft beer. It's residue-based. Plant matter and trichomes that fall off of the raw plant are captured. Kief is a loose collection of cannabinoids and by-products that may be smoked or properly cooked.

» **Essential oil:** This type of oil is produced using a solvent to cold-kick the trichomes right off the plant. The solvent is then removed. Essential oils are typically consumed by vaping (which has its own dangers), but they can also be processed into edible cannabis products. Oils also come in different types such as crumble (dry and loose), budder (viscous, sticky, and resembling butter), shatter or glass (looking like hard candy and cracks when handled), sap (yup, looks like sap from a Canadian Maple), and taffy (more firm than sap).

» **Slurry:** A cold extraction of cannabis using olive oil or alcohol and typically ingested raw. Processing it involves steeping and soaking raw cannabis flowers in alcohol or olive oil.

HEAT-EXTRACTED CANNABIS

As we mention earlier, heat is an efficient and effective processing state or medium and is used to produce the following finished products:

» **Edibles:** There's tons of news about edibles because cannabis can be infused into just about any food or beverage. Processing the cannabis (flower, hash, or essential oil) involves dissolving it by heat into fats, oils, or butter, that can then in turn be used in many recipes. Edibles may even be created with vegan, gluten-free, or other dietary needs in mind, or with specific strains of cannabis each with different therapeutic effects in mind.

REMEMBER

Health Canada has strict regulations on the disclosure of active ingredients to help ensure consumer safety and product consistency. Be sure to obtain legal counsel for ingested products.

» **Oil:** A production process is used involving slowly heating cannabis into medicinal or organic oil (olive or coconut).

» **Tea:** This process involves steeping leaves from various cannabis plants in hot water just like most other teas. This tradition has been around for centuries.

» **Tincture:** A liquid suspension of cannabinoids and terpenoids (a by-product) that is typically included with alcohol or glycerine. Tinctures are one of the most common ways of consuming cannabis for medicinal purposes.

» **Topicals:** Includes lotions, creams, and patches used for certain muscle, skin, and joint aches and pains, as well as inflammation and arthritis. Processing topicals is straightforward — the cannabis flower or oil is heated at a low temperature into an emulsifier like beeswax or natural oil. Topicals can be found at many herbal skin stores and the product creation opportunities are plentiful.

Many products can be produced with cannabis and many remain undiscovered. Current and forthcoming product categories include beauty products, colas, beer, cannabis-infused coffees, cannabis chocolates, weed brownies, pot cookies, and marijuana gummies. Even capsules exist to simply get the desired effect as soon as possible.

Processing edibles

A recent Deloitte survey provided a glimpse of what edibles would be popular with Canadians. In order of the extent of "interest in using the product," the survey found that 51 percent would be interested in baked goods, cookies, and brownies. Another 43 percent would dabble in chocolates. And 37 percent of adults (a key word here) would be willing to try hard candies, lollipops, or gummies. For beverages, 31 percent would be interested followed by 25 percent interested in honey products. Other edibles categories enjoying at least a 19 percent interest were popsicles or freezies, ice cream, potato chips, biscuits, and olive oil.

For the beverage market, we've seen beer companies making investments in cannabis companies. In 2018, Constellation, a beverage company, invested a whopping $5 billion into Canopy Growth Corporation (a 38 percent stake), which is one of the world's largest marijuana growers. It did so to experiment with and develop a roster of infused beverage products that Canadians would like. One challenge, and opportunity, will be for processors to overcome the rather bad or bitter taste of cannabis-infused drinks. Retailers that can offer better-tasting drinks, and all edibles actually, will expect to fare well with those products. Taste and intensity of flavour are critical success factors in the cannabis-infused edibles market.

WARNING

Watch out for high-risk products like chocolates and gummies where kids might accidentally eat them. Even as a producer of these products, you may be exposing yourself to legal headaches. Ask your lawyer about your compliance with relevant legislation.

REMEMBER

To stay on top of all the key rules, check out www.canada.ca/en/services/health/campaigns/cannabis.html for the latest rules and regulations about what you can produce, when, and where. Also seek legal counsel before embarking on a micro-processing enterprise.

Selling cannabis as a legal retailer or dispensary

If you want to sell cannabis, there are two primary routes to do so. The terms *cannabis retail* and *cannabis dispensary* are used interchangeably, but there is a difference. A marijuana dispensary typically focuses on medical marijuana patients who come in with a prescription. With a cannabis retail store, the focus is on the legal recreational segment. In a dispensary, "patients" enter a waiting room, and from there, they're asked to visit the sales area where a budtender can answer questions and recommend products. In a cannabis retail store, staff walk you through a selection of cannabis-related products for recreational use. Regardless of which option appeals to you as an entrepreneur, follow the rules or the police will, simply stated, raid you!

Following the rules

Health Canada's Cannabis in Canada website (www.canada.ca/cannabis) discusses Cannabis-related laws and supporting regulations from a federal perspective, but the provinces and territories have a big say in the matter. For example, in Ontario a new government changed the rules in 2018 and instituted quotas on the number of retail outlet licences that could be granted. This effectively shut out hundreds of potential retail cannabusiness entrepreneurs!

Some of that "big say" also deals with growing and producing marijuana; most of the provincial laws and regulations deal with the retail, distribution, and consumption side of things. For example, some provinces permit consumption at the age of 18; others, at 19. Much of the current provincial legislation at the time of this writing has to do with where (what retail outlets) cannabis may be sold. It also deals with its transportation, licensing, and personal safety.

On the Cannabis in Canada website, click the Cannabis in the Provinces and Territories link to find out very important legal and regulatory information and requirements you need to follow if you want to pursue the retail route. The direct link is www.canada.ca/en/health-canada/services/drugs-medication/cannabis/laws-regulations/provinces-territories. Note that provinces and territories also set rules and regulations on how cannabis can be sold (online or bricks and mortar), where stores may be located, how stores must be operated, and how personal plant cultivation can be done.

REMEMBER

You and you alone are responsible for knowing what is and what will be legal in the province or territory where you reside. At the Cannabis in Canada website, go to your provincial or territorial web link for more current, specific, and complete details about the provincial laws.

Getting organized

Before you get started, be organized in how you plan out a new retail enterprise:

>> Verify whether local, provincial, and federal laws support the sale and distribution of cannabis in the first place, and to what extent.

>> Research what retail licensing is required, and how to apply for that licensing.

>> Find a suitable and desirable location for you and your customers.

>> Figure out if you want to sell and distribute online.

>> Know the leading practices and standards around packaging, preservation, and branding.

>> Check the rules and costs out with your lawyer and accountant.

Paying attention to profitability

In very general terms, and of course depending on any number of factors, profit margins within the retail and dispensing part of the cannabis ecosystem are more moderate than for many other types of cannabusinesses. One reason is the rather high start-up and annual operational costs compared to other industries in the marijuana sector. Operating costs can easily be as high as $500,000 annually, depending on the nature and scope of the cannabusiness.

In terms of the big picture of this opportunity, and the enormous size of this sandbox, a CIBC analyst forecasted that by the end of 2020, the cannabis industry in Canada will have a retail value of $6.8 billion, almost as large as the wine market. That's not even taking into account the feeder ancillary service industries, which could be worth many billions more. In terms of the global weed market, Piper Jaffray, equity analysts for the stock market, predicted that this world market could "eventually" reach $500 billion.

On the smaller-scale end of the cannabis retail spectrum, there's a big demand for specialty packaging of a wide variety of products. Retailers and other cannabusinesses need unique packaging solutions that are protective, preservative, and childproof.

TIP

Running a cannabis delivery service

If you're willing to invest in the right transportation (safe and secure) to keep marijuana products fresh, protected, and preserved, you can dip your toes into this side of cannabusiness. You can move product from growers to processors, or from processors to distributors or to retail businesses. Or you can do all the above. Be sure to check out your provincial transportation and licensing regulations, as well as related federal and provincial legislation. As with any cannabusiness, have your lawyer review your business idea. The start-up and operating costs associated with this idea is lower than many other options we discuss in this chapter.

Providing advertising, public relations, marketing, and branding services

The Canadian government is rightly concerned about how cannabis products are advertised. This is the same concern that they have with tobacco and hard liquor products, and that's a good thing. However, if you have advertising experience and you want to leverage it in the cannabis sector, you'll be faced legal hurdles. Check out the Cannabis in Canada website (www.canada.ca/cannabis) for laws on advertising, and then check in with your legal counsel to be doubly sure. Existing laws are still opaque, and new ones are being written on a constant basis. Making a mistake here will translate into serious penalties, and a reputational black mark on your business and that of your clients.

After you have, in fact, positioned and aligned yourself with federal, provincial, and territorial requirements, you're ready to practice your craft. You can find creative marketing channels to get national or provincial press coverage for your clients. If you have strong public relations skills and you've established and built business relationships with a robust network of journalists and reporters, you could flourish. Cannabis growers, processors, and retailers have enough of a tough time keeping up with their own corners of federal and provincial laws, so your expertise with branding and bona fide advertising practices will be valued.

Offering security services

Security over small, valuable, and in the case of grow ops, "accessible" cannabis product will always be a significant concern. This reality will drive demand for security services in the cannabis industry, in both inventory protection as well as cash security. Security services that are expected to thrive in the cannabis ecosystem include

>> On-site security of crops and processing facilities

>> Armoured transport of small but valuable packages of finished product to retailers or end-consumers, or secure transport of crops for processing

>> Secure storage of cash and product in dispensaries and stores

>> Video surveillance of growing, production, and retail facilities

>> Secure record keeping for financial transactions and inventory with specialized software applications

Considering ancillary products and services

Ancillary products and services are those that are part of the cannabis sales cycle but not the foundational cultivation, processing, and other "touch the plant" business segments we discuss earlier. In this section, we introduce you to a handful of these products and services because they're very conducive to smaller-scale business operations. We begin by exploring a few unique ancillary *product* businesses, and end this section by listing some other types of ancillary products and services that you may want to delve into further.

REMEMBER

The ancillary products we note here are just the tip of the iceberg. There is nothing wrong with taking an existing product idea, like the ones we present earlier, and making a better mousetrap. Perhaps you can make that same product or deliver the same service in a more economical, efficient, and effective way. But if you want to brainstorm a brand-new idea, just walk into a mall or browse an online site like eBay (www.ebay.ca) or Amazon (www.amazon.ca) to see if there's a new and unique idea that appeals to you.

TIP

When you've decided on an idea you want to pursue further, check out the advice we provide throughout this book. In Chapter 9, we show you how to figure out your finances. In Chapter 10, we give you pointers on writing a business plan that gets you the money you may still be missing. After you've launched your business, Chapter 11 helps you make a marketing buzz. When your business is up and running, Chapter 12 will help you manage risk. Whatever your small business dream is, chase it by being informed!

Edibles

In the earlier section called "Processing edibles," we discuss *processing* cannabis into edibles. But there also exists an opportunity to be a retailer of those products. Again, even here, there are very strict rules to follow. We also previously indicated the types of edibles that Canadians are most interested in. But many other categories exist that are not yet discovered!

This is an area of opportunity where you can get creative in how you want to invent and present your own products in your very own cannabusiness. In addition to cookies, brownies, chocolates, candies, beverages, and chips, edibles can also include hot sauce, peanut butter, pies, popcorn, and more — much more. In fact, the choices are huge.

To succeed, you just have to be aware of the processes and challenges of creating, packaging, and selling edibles. You especially have to be aware of food safety regulations in Canada. Check in with a lawyer before you embark on this path. You do not want to harm consumers with overdoses and other negligent practices. The rules are strict, and many are still not finalized (in fact, most edibles are not yet permitted) at the time of this writing! Also go to the Cannabis in Canada website (www.canada.ca/cannabis) for the rules and timelines.

Beauty and skincare products

If you go into a Shoppers Drug Mart, Rexall, or Jean Coutu pharmacy, you'll undoubtedly be swamped by hundreds of beauty products. At Hudson's Bay, Loblaws, Metro, Body Shop, and just about any other large Canadian retailer, you'll also pass through a large array of beauty product aisles. Add to that all the online options for buying beauty products, and you get the picture as to just how massive this market can be. This is another area to explore.

Hemp

Hemp is an offshoot of the cannabis plant and can be refined into clothing, biodegradable plastics, paint, biofuel, food, and cosmetics. Hemp has lower concentrations of THC (the psychoactive component) and higher concentrations of CBD, which decreases or eliminates its ability to provide a high. Hemp regulation varies widely among countries and provinces and among product categories. The products you see today likely have minimal hemp content because governments regulate the concentration of THC and permit only low THC content. As Canadian regulations ease up, there will be an opportunity to explore creating and selling safe and certified products with hemp and cannabis as ingredients.

You can leverage hemp to produce many products. The Canadian Hemp Trade Alliance (CHTA; www.hemptrade.ca) can help you find out what your options are, and help you navigate through the Canadian hemp industry.

Accessories

Aside from the actual cannabis product, you can build a small cannabusiness around selling accessories. This would include vessels, rolling papers, trays, pipes, bongs, vaporizers, grinders, and filters. The accessories option lets you avoid some of the more onerous provisions of the Cannabis Act and its related provincial and territorial cousins.

Industry-specific consulting

There are probably hundreds if not thousands of undiscovered cannabusiness opportunities. Why not consider first gaining an in-depth knowledge of the cannabis sector and its ecosystem components, and then become a consultant? Maybe you can focus on the risks, or be a financial expert. Perhaps you know a lot about production processes, or how best to navigate through the regulatory framework.

As long as you have bona fide knowledge, gained through lots of research and interaction with members of the ecosystem, you can market that knowledge. You can even specialize in a certain industry component or niche such as processing, retailing, or growing. As with most businesses that provide services, the up-front and ongoing costs are typically a lot less.

A worldwide list of the top 100 cannabis websites, newsletters, and blogs can be found at http://blog.feedspot.com/marijuana_blogs. This is a great resource to get to know the cannabis sector, or specific components within it.

Other ideas currently being transformed into actual businesses include software and technology application development, specialty lodging, event planning, and the review of cannabis products on blogs or magazines.

IN THIS CHAPTER

» **Making a plan when you can't repay a debt**

» **Dealing with lack of funds to pay your rent or mortgage**

» **Coming up with a strategy when you can't pay your taxes**

» **Negotiating settlement of a dispute**

» **Using alternative dispute resolution to end a dispute**

» **Deciding when to start a lawsuit**

Chapter **20**

Anticipating Problems

N o matter how careful you to try to be with your business affairs, problems can — and do — arise from time to time.

In this chapter, we discuss some of the trouble that a business can encounter. Of course, the best way to deal with trouble is to avoid it in the first place. To do that:

» Don't borrow more money than you can realistically expect to repay on schedule.

» Do a credit check on customers before you do the work.

» Follow up on collections after you send a bill.

» Take care not to do shoddy work or provide defective products.

» Always have contracts in writing that you understand.

» Perform your contracts properly.

But when you can't avoid trouble, you have to deal with it. So this chapter is meant to help you face your problems head-on, make an objective assessment of the situation, and try to come up with a plan of action.

No Money

So your creditors are after you. They want their money and you haven't got it at the moment. Maybe

>> You can't repay a loan.

>> You can't pay for equipment you're buying on credit.

>> You can't pay your rent.

>> You can't pay off a mortgage.

>> You can't pay your taxes.

>> You are insolvent.

>> You are about to go bankrupt.

What's going to happen and what can you do?

TIP

Even though you may be broke, consider talking to your lawyer (if your lawyer will talk to someone with as little money as you have). Borrowing and lending are subject to legal rules and you may be in a better position than your creditor thinks (and your creditor may be in a worse position). Your lawyer may be able to help you negotiate an extension of the deadline for repayment, or more favourable repayment terms.

TIP

Don't fight your creditors out of sheer pig-headedness. If you lose the fight, you'll owe even more money — because creditors are usually allowed to pass on the cost of collecting their debts to you, the debtor. (And you'll still have to pay your own legal fees.)

Your business can't make a payment that's due

If you borrow money, you're expected to repay it. If you don't repay, the lender is liable to get a little exercised. But what the lender can do depends on the nature of the lender and the loan. If you end up getting sued, see the section later in this chapter on "Litigation." And, because we frequently suggest that you try to work out a deal with your creditor, check out the section further along on "Negotiation of a settlement."

A payment on a loan from a non-commercial source

You got *love money* from a family member or friend to set up your business (refer to Chapter 9) but the lender doesn't feel so loving now — maybe he needs the cash desperately, or maybe you've ticked her off by not taking her canny business advice.

Besides giving you the cold shoulder or not inviting you over for dinner anymore, the lender can sue for return of the money. This is true whether or not you have a written contract. An *oral contract* (a contract made through conversation) is as valid as a contract in writing. Although proving the terms of an oral contract is more difficult because no one wrote them down, your lender is legally able to tell the court about the conversations you had when the loan was made (the terms of the loan agreement will be the lender's word against yours). Your lender can require other people who have heard you talk about the loan to repeat in court what they heard. Also, your lender can show to the court documents such as a note or letter you wrote to the lender acknowledging the loan or saying that you would pay the money back.

So don't ignore the lender or tell him to buzz off. If you have no money to pay now, try to reach an agreement:

>> See if the lender will agree to wait a few weeks or months until you do have the money.

>> See if the lender will agree to accept smaller payments over a longer term, or smaller payments now and "balloon" payments later to make up for the smaller payments now.

>> Offer something other than money in full or part payment of the loan — something you own or the business owns, or your services for free.

>> Offer security for the loan, such as a mortgage on property you own; or offer a share in your business (although doing these things could create more problems for you in the long run).

Then put into writing the agreement you've reached, and sign it and have the lender sign it. Each of you should get and keep an original of the signed agreement.

A payment on a loan from a commercial source

If you have a commercial loan, you probably agreed to pay it off in instalments, so you may think that not being able to pay one instalment is not such a big deal. You're wrong. Most commercial term loans (refer to Chapter 9) have an *acceleration clause*. That means that the lender can demand that you repay the entire loan as soon as you miss one payment by more than a few days. And if you have a line of credit (refer to Chapter 9), it's probably repayable on demand — so you don't even have to miss one payment before the lender has the right to tell you to repay the full amount.

If a lender demands repayment and you can't repay, the lender has the right to sue you for the outstanding amount of the loan, plus interest owing, plus the lender's costs of collecting the debt from you. If you've given security for the loan (a *right against property* — again, refer to Chapter 9), your agreement with the lender probably allows the lender to realize on the security after you miss a payment. That means that the lender, after demanding repayment of the loan and waiting a few days for payment:

>> Can take property you offered as security and either keep it or sell it (or start a lawsuit for possession of the secured property if you won't let the lender have it)

>> Can demand that a person who guaranteed the loan pay back the loan (plus interest)

>> May be able to appoint a receiver/manager to take possession of the secured property and sell it, depending on the terms of the loan agreement

If a lender seizes secured property, you may have the right for a short period (a couple of weeks) to get the property back by paying what you owe plus interest and costs. If the lender sells the property, it has to make sure that it gets a fair price, and afterward has to account to you for the property. The lender is not allowed to keep more than it's owed (don't forget that this includes interest and the costs of taking and selling the property), and it has to pay you any surplus from a sale.

TIP

If you know that you don't have the money to make a payment, but you think that you'll have money soon to get back on track:

>> First, try to find the money for the payment from another source, if you can. Unless you're on really good terms with your commercial lender and have the lender's trust and adoration, avoid letting the lender know that you're in a bit of trouble. The lender might panic and pull the plug on your loan, and on any other dealings you have with that lender.

>> Then, if you can't get money from another source, talk to your lender before the due date of the payment that you're going to miss. The lender may agree to overlook your default for a short time, especially if you offer some

additional security (if you've got anything left that's not already being used for security, that is — if you don't, the lender might accept security from someone else, such as a personal guarantee from a relative or associate).

WARNING

Be careful about borrowing more money and offering more security for a loan that you're already having trouble repaying! You may be digging yourself deeper into a hole and you may lose more in the long run.

TIP

If you're in a really bad financial position and you don't think that a little extra money or a little extra time is going to do anything but delay bigger trouble, you should think about making a proposal to all of your creditors or even going bankrupt (see the section "Your business is insolvent").

A payment for an asset bought on credit

If you've bought assets (such as equipment or vehicles or furniture) for your business and are paying for them over time, you've almost certainly entered into a financing agreement such as a *chattel mortgage, conditional sales agreement, purchase money security interest,* or a *lease with an option to purchase.* If you stop making your payments, the other party to the financing agreement can:

>> Sue you for the full amount still left to pay (plus interest)

>> Seize the asset and sell it (and account to you after the sale)

The best you can do is see if the financer is willing to give you more time to pay (and then try to find some money).

A payment under an equipment lease

If your business leased assets instead of buying them outright or on time, you're not in any better position if you stop making your regular payments. The terms of a commercial asset lease normally don't allow you to stop making your lease payments for any reason — including the fact that the asset is broken or defective and the fact that you have no money. You have to make all the payments for the full term of the lease. If you miss a payment, the lessor can:

>> Sue you for the full amount owed under the lease

>> Seize the asset (and, if you have an option to purchase, sell it and attribute it to you)

Again, the most you can do is try to negotiate more time to pay, and look for some money to pay with.

You've personally guaranteed a debt for your business and your business can't pay

If you've given a personal guarantee for a business loan and your business can't make a payment, the lender can demand payment from you. If you don't pay, the lender can sue you for the full outstanding amount of the loan, plus interest. If you gave security (such as a mortgage on your home) as well as guaranteeing the debt, the lender can realize on the security you provided.

WARNING

If you've co-signed a loan with your business, the lender doesn't even have to wait for your business to miss a payment — it can demand that you make the payment instead, because you're equally responsible for the loan from the get-go.

Note that if you're a member of a partnership, in most provinces the partners are individually responsible for paying debts of the partnership if the partnership itself can't pay (Chapter 6 has more on partnerships).

Your business can't pay its rent

If you can't pay the rent owing under your commercial lease, your landlord can do a variety of nasty things to you, including:

>> Sue you for *arrears of rent* (rent owing) or for *damages* (money compensation) for breach of the lease, while letting you stay on under the lease.

>> Retake possession of the premises and terminate the lease (in which case, although the landlord can sue for arrears of rent before termination, it can't sue for any rent due after the date of termination).

>> Retake possession of the premises and terminate the lease with notice for future loss of rent. (Then the landlord can sue for arrears of rent before termination and also for damages for future loss of rent after the date of termination. If the landlord makes a reasonable effort but can't find another tenant, or another tenant who's willing to pay as much as you agreed to pay, the landlord can sue you for the entire shortfall over the rest of the term of your lease.)

>> Retake possession of the premises without terminating the lease, and re-letting the premises acting as your agent (you remain responsible for the rent, minus whatever the landlord collects from the new tenant).

>> *Distrain* (seize and sell your property on the premises) to satisfy arrears of rent. In most provinces, if you remove your property from the premises to keep your landlord from getting it, the landlord can seize the property wherever it is (if the landlord can find it) within the next 30 days and can make you pay a penalty for being such a sneak.

TIP

If your landlord terminates your lease, retakes possession of your premises, or distrains, consider seeing a lawyer to find out whether the landlord is within his rights. Landlords sometimes ignore the fine print of the law, and you may have some rights of your own. For example:

>> A landlord cannot terminate a lease for non-payment until the rent has been unpaid for 15 days or more in most provinces (and it can't terminate for other reasons without giving you proper notice and a chance to fix whatever the landlord is complaining about).

>> If the landlord terminates, you can go to court to get the termination set aside — if you can pay the arrears of rent.

>> A landlord can't distrain until the day after the rent was due, and has to carry out the *distraint* (also known as a *distress*) during daylight hours.

>> A landlord that distrains (in most provinces) can't seize fixtures, cash, property that belongs to others (such as inventory on consignment), or perishable goods, and it has to leave tools you use in the business up to a value of as much as $10,000 (depending on the province).

>> The landlord has no right to distrain if it has already got a judgment for arrears of rent, or has terminated the lease or locked you out, or if you and the landlord have agreed to end the lease.

Your business can't pay a mortgage on real property

If you took out a mortgage to buy real property for your business and you can't make your payments, the *mortgagee* (the lender) has the right in many provinces to *foreclose* on the mortgage (become the legal owner of the property), or to sell the property — under court supervision in a *judicial sale*, or privately under a *power of sale*.

TIP

If the mortgagee starts a legal action for foreclosure or judicial sale, you can stop it by paying off the entire mortgage, or in some cases by paying the payment(s) you missed plus a penalty. If you can't pay the entire mortgage immediately, you can ask the court for a delay (from about two to six months) to come up with the money. You can also stop foreclosure by asking for judicial sale. If the foreclosure goes through, in most provinces your mortgage debt is cancelled and you don't owe the mortgagee anything, even if the property is worth less than the debt you owe (however, the mortgagee doesn't owe you anything if the property is worth more than the debt you owe). If the property is sold in a judicial sale, any money left over after payment of the mortgage debt plus interest plus legal costs is yours; but if a shortfall remains, the lender can require you to make it up.

Most mortgagees prefer to act under a power of sale, if they can, because they don't have to go to court to sell the property. The lender has to notify you that it's going to exercise its power of sale, and you'll be given a short time (about a month) to stop the sale by paying off the mortgage or, in some cases, by making up the payment(s) you missed. As with a judicial sale, the proceeds from the sale will be used to pay the outstanding amount of the mortgage, as well as interest and costs; the mortgagee can sue you for any shortfall, but if money is left over, the mortgagee has to return it to you.

TIP

If the mortgagee wants to sell the property, see if it will let you try to sell the property yourself first. Buyers may think they can get a good deal and may offer a lower price when they see it's a judicial sale or sale under a power of sale. The more money the property sells for, the less you'll owe the mortgagee or the more you'll get to keep.

Your business can't pay its taxes

The Canada Revenue Agency (CRA) has a *statutory lien* against the personal property (as opposed to real property, or real estate) of a taxpayer who does not pay taxes or remittances that are due. This lien lets the government seize your business's personal property — which is your personal property, if you're a sole proprietor or partner — after giving 30 days' notice (during the notice period you can pay up and avoid the seizure).

If you own real property in a municipality and you don't pay your property taxes, the municipality will almost certainly add interest charges and penalties to your property tax bill. If you still don't pay your taxes, the municipality has the right to sell your real property. (The municipality doesn't get to keep all the money from the sale, only the amount that you owe in taxes.)

Your business is insolvent

Your business is insolvent if it owes at least $1,000 and cannot pay its debts and obligations as they become due. Being insolvent in itself isn't so wrong (apart from the fact that you have no money), but if you're insolvent, you're in danger of being forced into bankruptcy. A creditor to whom you owe more than $1,000 and who has no security from you for the debt can petition your business into bankruptcy if your business commits an act of bankruptcy — such as not paying a debt when it's due or not complying with a court order to pay a creditor who's won a lawsuit against the business, or telling a creditor that you're not going to pay your debts, or hiding or disposing of property to avoid paying a creditor.

If you're dealing with unsecured creditors

If you're insolvent, what can you do before someone petitions you into bankruptcy? You can try to reach some kind of agreement with your creditors — for example, that they'll give you more time to pay, or accept part payment of your debt. Put any agreement into writing. By the way, your creditors won't likely be interested in cutting you any slack unless your business has decent prospects.

TIP

If your business does have prospects, it might be wise to get some advice from a lawyer who specializes in insolvency, or from a *licensed insolvency trustee* who deals with businesses (rather than with consumers). Your advisor might recommend making an informal offer to your creditors, or a formal proposal under the *Bankruptcy and Insolvency Act* (see the next paragraph).

If you're dealing with secured creditors

If you're insolvent and a secured creditor notifies you that it's going to realize on its security, you should consider making a formal proposal under the *Bankruptcy and Insolvency Act*. If you do nothing, your secured creditors are going to make off with the secured property, and you probably need it to keep your business running. You should get a trustee in bankruptcy to advise you and to file in bankruptcy court a *notice of intention to make a proposal*. After the notice is filed, your business has some protection from secured and unsecured creditors for at least a month:

>> Creditors can't seize any property.

>> Companies that supply utilities such as electricity, heat, water, and telephone can't cut off service.

>> Parties to contracts with your business can't terminate the contracts or invoke *acceleration clauses* (an acceleration clause makes a debt you're paying off in instalments come due all at once).

On the downside, you have to pay cash up front for any supplies you buy.

WARNING

After you file your notice of intention, you have to file the actual proposal, and then your creditors meet within about three weeks to vote on it. Here's another downside to the proposal process: If your secured creditors reject the proposal (even if your unsecured creditors don't), they can immediately realize on their security. In addition (as if you needed an addition at this point), your business is deemed to have made an *assignment in bankruptcy* (a transfer of its property to the trustee in bankruptcy) and will be officially declared bankrupt.

You can choose to go bankrupt

TIP

You can be forced into bankruptcy, but you can also choose to go into bankruptcy by making an assignment in bankruptcy. Why would you actually want to go bankrupt? Well, when a court declares you bankrupt, your trustee in bankruptcy deals with your creditors. You don't have to look at their judgemental and sour faces anymore. Your trustee will make arrangements to sell the business's property to pay the debts. And you'll be able to start over again.

If you're carrying on business as a sole proprietorship or a partnership, you'll go bankrupt as an individual. If you're carrying on business as a corporation, the corporation will go bankrupt. As an individual you'll probably be discharged from bankruptcy after nine months, and if you receive an absolute discharge, almost all of your debts are cancelled. (If you receive a conditional discharge, you'll still be responsible for repaying certain debts — income taxes, for example.) A corporation can't be discharged until it has paid all its debts, but you can always start up a new corporation (however, you may find that the creditors you stiffed won't be very eager to deal with your new corporation).

See the next section for more (hooray!) about bankruptcy.

Bankruptcy

After the bankruptcy court has made an order that your business is bankrupt, it appoints a trustee in bankruptcy. The trustee becomes the legal owner of all the unsecured property that formerly belonged to your business (and to you if your business is a sole proprietorship or a partnership — refer to Chapter 6) and it uses the property to pay off debts. Your secured creditors keep their rights over secured property — it doesn't go to the trustee.

If you're a sole proprietor or partner and you go bankrupt, you'll be allowed to keep some personal property — about $5,000 to $10,000 worth (depending on the province) of clothing, furniture, and other household items, as well as "tools of your trade" and, in many provinces, a car.

WARNING

If your business is a corporation and you're a director, you may not escape having to make some payments personally if your business goes bankrupt. You'll be held responsible for up to six months' worth of unpaid wages for employees, for unpaid amounts owed to the CRA for income tax and GST/HST, Canada Pension Plan and Employment Insurance, and for unpaid provincial sales tax owed to your provincial department or ministry of finance. And that's on top of paying any business loans for which you gave a personal guarantee.

If your business disposed of any property to save it from creditors, you can be personally charged with a criminal offence. And your trustee in bankruptcy can sue to get his hands on property that was improperly transferred away from the business, so that it can be distributed among the creditors.

WARNING

If a person or business is an undischarged bankrupt, he, she, or it can't borrow more than $500 without telling the lender about the state of bankruptcy (and not telling is an offence punishable by a fine or imprisonment). If a person is an undischarged bankrupt, he or she cannot be the director of a corporation.

Disputes

Talking about money troubles is depressing. Let's talk about something more cheerful, like fighting with your customers, suppliers, and neighbours.

Somebody doesn't like what you've done (or what you've charged). Or you don't like what somebody else has done (or charged). Maybe you feel like a fight . . . maybe you don't. But you're a businessperson, not a doormat, so you have to do something.

Disputes can escalate and end up in court, but they don't have to. (On the other hand, some disputes belong in court.) In this section, we lead you gently through the mechanisms available for resolving a dispute. They range from negotiation of a settlement through mediation and arbitration, and all the way to litigation. We won't get into the messy illegal stuff like baseball bats and cement shoes.

TIP

But before we go any further, we want to say two things about any dispute you get into:

>> **Wrap it up in writing.** If you and the other side reach an agreement, write it down. You may need or want a lawyer to draw up a formal contract or release, or maybe a scribbled note signed by both sides is enough, or you may simply write a letter or send an email to the other side confirming that you reached an agreement (and setting out the terms of the agreement). A written document will help keep the resolution from unravelling and will be valuable evidence if the dispute erupts again.

>> **Learn from this experience.** Ask yourself what you can do to prevent a dispute like this from occurring again. For example, you may want to make sure that in the future you have written contracts that cover all the essential details, or that you get payment in advance for part of the work you do, or that you investigate a potential customer or supplier more thoroughly before making a deal.

Negotiation of a settlement

When you find yourself in a dispute, before you start shouting "I'll see you in court!" (or before anyone else starts shouting it), consider whether the dispute can be cleared up through negotiation.

The traditional way to negotiate a settlement is for each side to state what it wants and then use whatever power it has at its disposal to persuade or force the other side to agree. The sides sometimes exaggerate what they want so they'll have maneuvering room if they're forced to make a compromise. The purpose of traditional negotiation is to win, not necessarily to solve the problem effectively.

We give you some help to learn how to be a successful negotiator without upsetting the traditional negotiation pattern too much. We do this by showing you various negotiation techniques, including how to focus not on what you want (or on what the other side wants) but on interests that you and the other side may have in common.

Preparing for negotiations

If you want to be successful in your negotiation, you can't just rush in punching as soon as the bell sounds — first, you have to prepare to negotiate. Preparation involves two steps: studying the situation and planning your moves. When you study the situation, you will:

TIP

>> **Gather information about the matter in dispute.** You should know the facts backward and forward and sideways. If you've got the facts at your fingertips you'll be much more effective at arguing for the resolution you want. You would also be wise to know the law relating to the dispute, so consider speaking to your lawyer about the matter even if you plan to handle the negotiations yourself.

>> **Separate your *position* in the dispute from your short-term and long-term business *interests*.** Your position, for example, might be "I want to be paid the full amount for the work I did." Your interests are a lot more various — they might include needing X dollars to keep the business running, or wanting to keep a customer (or wanting to get rid of an annoying customer without damaging your business's reputation), or wanting to maintain your personal reputation for doing good work at a fair price or for never backing down when you're under pressure.

>> **Think about what the other party's business interests are.** (You may already know their position or you may be waiting to hear it.) Just like you, they have lots of different interests, and you can use that fact to help find a solution that gives something to both parties. You may be able to give up easily something that the other party wants badly, and vice versa.

>> **Think about your goals in this negotiation.** Again your goals are different from a position. For example, a position would be "I want to be paid the full amount for the work I did." Your goals might be getting as much of the full amount as possible while keeping the customer, and not appearing to back down when a customer turns purple in the face and starts screeching at you. Choose some objective criteria that will allow you to decide whether an offer is acceptable and meets your goals — that way, you won't give in just because you're being bullied. Objective criteria might include things like:

- *A fair market price:* What do other businesses charge for this product/ service?

- *Legality:* Is their offer legal?

- *Accepted standards:* Is the offer in line with the other side's own standards, or standards in the business generally, or legal standards in court decisions, or scientific standards, and so on.

TIP

>> **Gather information about the other party in the dispute.** Get information about the business *and* about the individual you're going to be dealing with. Talk to people who know them or have dealt with them. Find out what their strengths and weaknesses are, and how they're likely to behave during the negotiation (and how others have handled their behaviour). Google their business name to see what else you can come up with by way of useful background information. This background tells you what might be influencing the other side's position (such as little-known financial difficulties, or general distrust of businesses in your field).

>> **Think about the side problems you may encounter in the negotiating process and how you might deal with them.** For example:

- *A history of bad blood exists between you and the person you'll have to negotiate with.* If you can't find a way of negotiating with that person's associate or superior instead, you'll have to try to focus on the problem to be solved and not on the personalities involved.

- *The person you're supposed to negotiate with doesn't have authority to make a deal with you because he or she isn't high enough up in the organization.* Try to find a way to negotiate with someone who does have authority to make a deal with you.

- *The other party doesn't give a damn about you — as is sometimes the case with large businesses that haven't trained and motivated their employees properly.* You'll have to try to find a way of making the other party give a damn.

- *The other party has a lot of power over you that is not related (or not closely related) to the issue in dispute.* You'll have to try to get them to focus on the problem in dispute and set aside other power issues for the time being.

- *The time for negotiations is limited and it favours the other side, not your side.* Sometimes deadlines cut both ways, so don't automatically accept the other party's story that only you are adversely affected by the deadline. And if a deadline is being used just as a pressure tactic, it can often be extended or ignored by the party that set it.

>> **Think about the leverage you can use to argue for your interests.**
No matter how grim things look for you in the dispute, you've probably got something to use. Leverage includes things like:

- Contract wording that supports your position.

- Law (either legislation or court decisions) that supports your position.

- *Precedent* that supports your position — what you want has been done before (either by the other side or by a similar organization).

- The desire of both sides to maintain a decent relationship.

- The desire of the other side to get the matter settled quickly and quietly. You could have a lot of nuisance value if you start writing to and phoning people in the organization, or if you talk to others about the problems you're having with the person or organization, or if you drag matters on into the next budget year.

Planning

Next, you plan — but if you did all that preparation, the planning is easy. Here are the steps:

1. **Create a list of alternatives to the position the other side is taking or is likely to take.** Consider your interests and the probable interests of the other side, and try to come up with alternatives that would satisfy at least some of the interests of both sides. Then, when they announce their position, you'll have some maneuvering room — and you'll be able to offer them some maneuvering room, too.

2. **Choose your own opening position.** Make it realistic, based on the information you gathered about the issue and the analysis you made of your interests.

3. **Marshal the arguments you think you can use to persuade the other party of the strength of your position.** Use the list of leverage you made in the planning stage. Don't argue using general statements, use specific facts. (For example, "I did a lot of work for you and got as good a result as could be expected" should be ditched in favour of "Here is a list of the work I did for you, here is the problem I had to deal with, here is the result I got, and here is the less favourable result obtained when you took your work to someone else.")

Opening discussions

TIP

Don't let discussions get under way until you're ready. If you haven't finished your planning and preparation when the other side announces that it's ready to negotiate, tell them that you have to look into the matter and will be back in touch as quickly as possible. If they won't go away, encourage them to chat about the problem. If the issue is personal to the other party, he or she can blow off a little steam; and you may be able to get valuable information about the other party's position, interests, and side issues just by listening to the person talk.

But after you're ready to discuss the problem via a meeting, Skype call, or phone call:

>> **Start by getting personal, if possible.** See if you can make a connection with the other individual if you don't already know (and hate) each other. Some brief preliminary remarks about the weather (always a popular and acceptable topic in Canada), or the failings of a local sports franchise, or the news, or a mutual acquaintance ("I hear you know my colleague Joe Blow quite well") help set the tone that you're both human beings.

>> **Don't be in a hurry to state a position or describe your interests.** Let the other side go first. (Most people can't wait to open their mouths and start talking, so going last is pretty easy.) You're in a better negotiating position if you know what the other side wants before you tell what you want or are ready to give. And when you do talk, the other person will be more likely to listen to what you have to say.

>> **Be courteous to the individual you're dealing with.** And definitely don't make any personal attacks.

>> **Do your best not to get aggressive, angry, or upset.** Try to remain objective and composed throughout the discussion.

>> **Really listen to the other side.** Show them that you're listening and understand what they're saying (whether or not you agree with it). Asking for clarification of vague or ambiguous statements or summarizing what they've told you are two ways of showing you're listening. Get them to explain their position in detail and what they don't like about your position.

>> **Admit that the other side has reason to be annoyed with you and/or your business, if the reason is legitimate.** Apologize if you think an apology will remove a barrier to reaching a solution.

>> **Focus on your interests and champion them.** Don't let the other side talk you out of your important interests, and don't get sidetracked from the issue under negotiation.

>> **Look for ways of putting your interests and their interests into the same basket.** You may or may not have interests that you actually share, but you almost certainly have interests that fit together even if they don't overlap.

>> **Deal with solvable issues.** If the dispute is made up of several issues and some of them seem unsolvable at the moment, put those aside and deal with the solvable ones. If you can reach an agreement on some or most of the solvable issues, the previously unsolvable ones may then appear more manageable.

>> **Avoid using threats or pressure tactics against the person or organization.** Use offers instead. (Have you ever heard the expression "You'll catch more flies with honey than with vinegar"?)

>> **Offer the other side ways of moving from its original position toward your position.** Your list of leverage items will come in handy here — for example, "The contract seems pretty clear on this point," or "You've done this before," or "Doing this for me won't set a precedent in other cases because . . ." or "In the long run this will save you money."

Calling it quits

Quit while you're ahead. But how will you *know* when you're ahead?

>> **Use the objective criteria you dreamed up in the planning stage.** With any offer, ask yourself whether it meets those objective criteria. If it doesn't, explain to the other party why it doesn't meet your criteria. They may not agree on the criteria you've chosen, but you may get them to agree with you that a decision should involve objective criteria and not mere pressure.

>> **Ask yourself what your best alternative to a negotiated agreement may be if you don't agree to the other side's offer.** Your alternatives might include

 • Further negotiations (but are they likely to lead somewhere or will they just go on forever? Your time, money, and emotional energy are not infinite.)

 • Accepting a less favourable offer from the other side

 • Accepting a more favourable offer from a third party

 • Getting outside assistance to resolve the dispute, from a mediator, an arbitrator or the courts (see the upcoming sections on "Alternative dispute resolution [ADR]" and "Litigation")

 • Ending the relationship between the parties (this might or might not seem like an attractive alternative)

>> **Ask yourself whether you and/or the other side will be able to or will want to go through with the terms of the deal.** A deal that's going to be broken right away isn't a good deal. Also ask yourself about the repercussions of a particular deal. For example, will the other side pay up but say nasty things about you in the business community . . . or even vandalize your property someday?

For more information

You might like to read these books on negotiating:

>> *Getting to YES: Negotiating Agreement Without Giving In*, by Roger Fisher, William L. Ury, and Bruce Patton (published by Penguin). This is the famous book about negotiating that grew out of the Harvard Negotiating Project and that everyone has heard about. We based a lot of our advice about negotiating on this classic. If you want to know more about the Harvard Negotiating Project, you can go to its website at www.pon.harvard.edu/research_projects/harvard-negotiation-project/hnp.

>> *Swim with the Sharks Without Being Eaten Alive*, by Harvey Mackay (published by William Morrow and Company).

>> *Negotiating For Dummies* by Michael C. Donaldson (published by Wiley).

If you'd prefer something more hands-on, you can probably sign up for a negotiation workshop offered in your community.

Alternative dispute resolution (ADR)

The "alternative" in alternative dispute resolution means alternative to going to court. Litigation is expensive and usually leads to bad feelings between the parties — and just because you're facing a dispute doesn't mean you want to spend as much money as possible to resolve it or end up never doing business again with the other side.

The two usual forms of ADR are mediation and arbitration.

Mediation

In *mediation*, a neutral third person (a *mediator*) meets with the parties to try to help them reach an agreement. Mediation is negotiation with a kind of coach present. The parties choose the mediator — someone who has experience in the particular area of the dispute and who has good mediation skills. (Ask around for recommendations.) The mediator doesn't take sides and doesn't judge between the parties as to who's right and who's wrong, but merely tries to help the parties find a solution that meets everyone's needs. The solution can be more flexible than one the parties could get by going to court. (Courts are best at awarding money to one side, not at coming up with creative answers to problems.)

Mediation is *useful* if the parties:

>> Want to save face by not backing down on their own (a mediator will be able to point out the issues that aren't worth arguing about)

>> Want to save time and money by not going to court

>> Want to maintain a good business relationship

WARNING

Mediation is *not useful* if:

>> One of the parties does not want mediation — the parties both have to have some desire to settle the matter and must both be willing to meet with a mediator

>> One of the parties has a lot more power than the other and is going to use it to impose a solution on the weaker party

In some provinces, the parties to a lawsuit are required to go to mediation shortly after the lawsuit starts, to see if the matter can be settled without going any further through the court system.

Arbitration

Arbitration gets closer to court proceedings. In *arbitration,* a neutral third person, the *arbitrator* (sometimes three arbitrators are involved), is chosen by the parties to hear both sides' stories. The parties can design their own process, or they may prefer to conduct proceedings under provincial arbitration legislation. (As part of the design, the parties can agree on rights to appeal the arbitrator's decision to a judge or can agree that the decision cannot be appealed.) After listening to each side's presentation, the arbitrator makes a decision that one side or the other has won, and usually makes the kind of order that a court would make in the same circumstances. The decision can be registered with the court and enforced the same way as a judge's decision.

The advantages of arbitration are that:

>> Arbitration can be faster and cheaper than a lawsuit (although the bigger and more complex the dispute, the closer arbitration costs get to litigation costs).

>> Parties can choose an arbitrator who has expertise in the area of the dispute (instead of just hoping that the judge they draw knows something about it). This can be very important in specialized areas of business.

>> Arbitration proceedings are private and confidential — unlike court proceedings, which are public.

>> Arbitration decisions do not set precedents (establish examples that have to be followed in later cases) the way court decisions do.

Litigation

When disputes arise, the parties often think of a lawsuit as the first option. As we discuss earlier in this chapter, a lawsuit is just one of several options and may even be the last option. In this section, we talk about deciding whether a lawsuit is your best option.

Should you sue?

TIP

If you're the injured party, you decide whether to take the dispute to court. You need to talk to a lawyer about deciding whether to sue. Your lawyer will help you make the decision, based on the following matters:

>> **What are your chances of winning the lawsuit?**

- Is the law on your side?

- Do you have the evidence you need to persuade a judge to help you?

- Are you in time? A time limit applies to starting any lawsuit — it varies according to what the dispute is about, and in some cases you've only got a few days to get started, although in most cases you've got several years. Only a lawyer can tell you how long you've got, and starting from when.

>> **What will you get if you win?** If you want money, will the court give you enough to make the process worthwhile? If you don't want money, the court can give you other things — but none of them may be what you really want. Besides money (called *damages*) to compensate you for losses and maybe even to punish the other party, the court might be able to give you

- An *injunction* — to prevent someone from doing something; or a *mandatory injunction* — to make someone do what he or she promised to do

- An *order for specific performance* — to make the other party honour its agreement with you (such as an agreement to sell you a piece of land)

- In certain special cases, an order requiring the other party to do something such as sell property and divide the proceeds with you, or allowing the court to oversee some activity that the other party is carrying out

If what you really want is an apology, or the other party to parade naked through town carrying a sign that says "I'm evil," you won't get much satisfaction from a court.

>> **What's this going to cost?** The short answer is . . . a lot. Litigation is very expensive — and that's if you win. The losing side is usually ordered to pay some of the winner's legal fees, but not all of them (except in rare circumstances). In the meantime, before you win (if you do) your lawyer will be asking you for payment of her fees as you go along. If you lose, you'll have to pay the amount of any judgment the court awards against you, very likely at least part of the winner's legal fees, and all your own lawyer's fees.

>> **Where's the lawsuit going to take place?** If the other party doesn't live in or carry on business in your province, you may have to start the lawsuit wherever that party *does* live or carry on business — maybe another province, maybe another country. Extra cost and extra uncertainty.

>> **What are your chances of making the other party carry out the court order if you win?** For example, if the court awards damages, collecting the money is up to you. (Court officers such as the sheriff will help but they won't do it all.) If the other party doesn't have any money, or is really good at hiding it, you'll probably never see a penny. And you can spend quite a bit of money on collection.

WARNING

>> **Will you be able to stand the litigation process?** Your lawyer won't do everything — he'll have you digging around for documents and providing information and attending meetings. And your lawyer can't do some things on your behalf, such as undergo questioning by the other side before trial (the *discovery* process). Even if you've got the time (and money) to carry on a lawsuit, you may not be up to coping with the emotional stress involved in preparing for trial . . . and many people are terrified at the thought of testifying in court and being cross-examined by a lawyer for the other side.

If you do decide to start a lawsuit, you'll be happy to know that most lawsuits do settle. Only a small fraction actually go to trial.

If you decide not to sue, you can still try to settle the matter through negotiation or mediation (possibly with the threat of court proceedings hanging over the head of the other side).

What should you do if you're sued?

If you are sued, your options are narrower than if you're the one deciding whether to sue. You can put in a statement of defence and then defend the action vigorously, or you can put in a statement of defence and then try to negotiate a settlement. In some cases you can put in a statement of defence and a *counterclaim* (a lawsuit against the other side) or a *third-party claim* (a lawsuit against other people who were really responsible for causing the problem in the first place — hey, the more the merrier, right?). Or you can do nothing.

WARNING

Doing nothing is a poor option. If you don't defend, and the other side continues with its lawsuit, the court will quickly enter judgment against you and the other side can start trying to enforce the judgment right away. However, doing nothing is a possibility if:

>> **Your business has nothing to lose.** If the plaintiff is looking for money and your business has no cash or other assets, defending the action is a waste of your time.

>> **You have nothing to lose personally.** If your business has nothing, but you're on the hook to pay debts that your business can't pay, you should defend . . . unless you don't have any cash or assets, either. But be aware that even if you have nothing now, the plaintiff will be able to grab money or property that you get in the future.

TIP

In the no man's land between doing absolutely nothing and responding formally to the lawsuit, you could see a lawyer and try to:

>> Settle the matter before the deadline for putting in a defence has passed (the defendant usually has several weeks after being notified of the lawsuit to file a statement of defence, but sometimes the allowed reaction time is much shorter).

>> Persuade the other side to call off the lawsuit even if the dispute can't be settled right away.

Chapter **21**

Closing Up Shop

You've had your Big Bang (when you started up your business). Things didn't work out quite the way you expected . . . and now your business could be heading for the Big Crunch.

It may seem strange in a book about starting a business to talk about getting out of business. But you may have good reasons to get out of business sooner than you planned. Some business philosophies even promote the concept of "failing fast." In other words, in certain situations where all hope appears to be lost, cutting your losses and getting out of Dodge may be a good idea.

There are actually many other reasons to close the shutters. Here are some of the most common drivers of a business exit:

» **Someone wants to buy you out.** Your business is so hot that a buyer approaches you. Or you decide to try to find a buyer because you can make more by selling your business than by running it.

» **You want out.** Although business is fine, you're ready for a change. Maybe you're bored. Or maybe you hate your business. Or maybe you love your business, but hate your spouse, and have to sell your business to settle property claims in the divorce. Or maybe you love your business and your spouse, but you and your spouse are moving to another city and your business can't. Or, like one-fifth of small business owners, you're planning to retire.

>> **You have to get out.** A lot of new businesses fail, so your business may not be as successful as you had hoped. A buyer (if you can find one) may be able to turn the business around, or you may think it best just to put your business out of its misery. Or your creditors may take over your business to pay off the debts you owe.

>> **You keel over and die.** We saved the most alarming possibility for last. Starting a business doesn't offer you any special immunity from death. (If you incorporated, your corporation theoretically has perpetual existence, but you as the shareholder don't.)

In this chapter, we tell you about what's involved in selling your business as a going concern, going out of business voluntarily, being put out of business by your creditors, and making arrangements about your business in the event of your death.

Parting from Your Business May Be a Joint Venture

What happens to your business if you want out will not be yours alone to decide unless you are in business by yourself, either as a sole proprietor or as the only shareholder of a corporation.

If you have business associates, either as partners or as fellow shareholders, they will have something to say about what happens. You won't be able to sell the entire business to an outsider or hand it over to family members without their agreement. Actually, if you have associates, they're the real market for your share of the business if you want out, because outside buyers aren't likely to want a share in someone else's business. But just because you want to sell to your associates doesn't mean they have to buy — unless you have a partnership agreement or shareholders' agreement that covers this situation (refer to Chapter 6).

For the purposes of this chapter, we assume that you're the sole owner of your business, either as a sole proprietor or the only shareholder in your corporation, or that you have the full agreement and cooperation of your associates for your plans.

Tax Considerations When You Get Out of Business

In Chapter 16, we tell you more than you really want to know about taxes on your business. But we don't tell you everything. We deal only with the taxes on an ongoing business, and we don't talk about the special tax considerations that arise when you get out of business.

The special considerations have to do with *capital gains*.

Taxation of capital gains

When you sell your business, either by selling the assets (property) of the business or by selling your shares in the corporation that carries on the business, you are selling *capital property,* which is property with long-term value. The profit you make from selling capital property is called a *capital gain*. A capital gain is not taxed the same way as the profits you make from running your business. The entire profit you make from running your business is taxed as income. But only one-half of a capital gain is taxed. (If you have a *capital loss,* one-half of it can be used to reduce your capital gains, although it can't be used to reduce your other income.)

Calculation of capital gains

A capital gain or loss is calculated by comparing how much you get when you sell the property to how much it cost you when you bought the property. If you sell property for more than it cost you, you have a capital gain. You don't use just the raw sale price and the raw purchase price when you're making this calculation, though. You use the *adjusted sale price* — which is the sale price of the property minus the expenses associated with selling it (like business broker commissions), and the *adjusted cost base* — which is the purchase price of the property including any additional expenses associated with originally buying it.

TECHNICAL STUFF

The calculation gets a bit more complicated (What? You thought it was already complicated?) if you sell capital property against which you have claimed *capital cost allowance* (CCA). You can't claim the full cost of capital property as a business expense in the year of purchase because its usefulness to your business lasts for more than one year. However, its usefulness doesn't last forever, so you can claim a percentage of the cost as an expense every year over a period of several years until the entire cost has been claimed. The amount you are allowed to claim on capital property each year as an expense is called capital cost allowance.

If you've claimed CCA on property that you then sell, you have to take the CCA you've claimed into account when you calculate the adjusted cost base of the capital property. If you sell the property for more than its *undepreciated capital cost* (its residual value on your business's books after you've claimed CCA) — and this is quite possible to do because an asset's book value is not necessarily the same as its market value — then you've claimed too much capital cost allowance, and you have to pay back the excess to the tax authorities.

TECHNICAL STUFF

The excess capital cost allowance is taxed fully as income of your business, not just one-half as a capital gain. (That's because you used the CCA as an expense to reduce the income of your business, and now the government wants to collect the tax you should have paid.) Taxing excess capital cost allowance is called a *recapture* of capital cost allowance . . . picture the tax officials chasing the capital cost allowance around with a net. On the other hand, if you sell capital property for less than its undepreciated capital cost, you did not claim enough capital cost allowance over the time the business owned the property, and you may be able to deduct the entire loss — called a *terminal loss* — as an expense from the income of the business.

Dealing with the tax bill

WARNING

When you sell your business — especially if it's been successful and has increased in value — you may have to pay tax on half of the money you get from the sale (and on all the excess capital cost allowance you claimed on assets purchased for your business). As if you hadn't already paid enough tax when you were running the business — refer to Chapter 16. So the sale proceeds aren't pure profit to you. Don't go on a spending spree until you've figured out how much belongs to the Canada Revenue Agency (CRA) and until you have consulted a Chartered Professional Accountant (CPA) with taxation expertise. We talk further along in this chapter, however, about ways of reducing the tax consequences of a sale. See the headings "Sale of assets or sale of shares," "Allocation of purchase price if you sell assets," and "Consulting agreements."

Now that we've given you a headache by talking about taxes, we turn to the actual process of parting from your business.

Selling Your Business as a Going Concern

If someone approaches you about taking over your business, or if you want someone to take over and run the business, you're looking at selling your business as a going concern.

In Chapter 5, we talk about buying an existing business. Now we look at the transaction from the seller's point of view.

Knowing what your business is worth

If you are selling your business, you need to have a good idea of what it's worth, both to set a reasonable asking price and to decide whether or not to accept any offer that a buyer might make.

When you sell your business as a going concern, its value is based not only on what its physical assets are worth, but also on the value of its *goodwill*. Goodwill, which can be defined as the likelihood that the business's customers will come back, is usually valued by looking at the past earnings of the business. (Chapter 5 tells you more about how assets and goodwill are valued.)

TIP

The best way to figure out what your business is worth is to find out how much comparable businesses have recently sold for. You may be able to get this information from industry publications, your accountant, lawyer or other consultants, a business broker, or a professional business appraiser.

Finding a buyer

TIP

Unless a buyer approaches you, you'll have to find a buyer. You can:

» Place an ad in your local newspaper or industry publication under Business Opportunities or Businesses for Sale, or on websites like Kijiji (www.kijiji.ca) and others that list businesses for sale.

» Read the ads in your local newspaper or industry publication under Businesses Wanted, or check the Buy a Business section of websites that list businesses for sale.

» Tell your lawyer, accountant, financial advisors, consultants, bank manager, or people in your industry that you're interested in selling.

» Use a business broker to find a buyer for you — but keep in mind that business brokers charge you a commission (a percentage of the sale price).

Dealing with prospective buyers

No one is going to just show up at your door and say "I'll take it! Show me where to sign." Any prospective buyer is going to have lots of questions about your business, and you have to be prepared to answer them.

For example, a buyer might want to:

>> Know why you are selling the business

>> See the lease for your business premises

>> Know whether you're aware of any plans by the municipality or landlord that will affect traffic, parking, or access to the premises

>> See the business's audited financial statements for the past three to five years (Chapter 5 discusses what the buyer will be looking for in your financial statements.)

WARNING

You may or may not be asked to give a lot of information about your business to a prospective buyer, but if a buyer asks you a question, you must answer it honestly. Don't make any false statements about your business. A buyer who decides to buy your business based on your false statements may be able to set the sale aside or sue you for financial compensation if he or she suffers losses after the deal goes through.

TIP

Don't agree to show a prospective buyer around your premises, answer questions about your business, or let the buyer see any business documents, unless the buyer first signs a *confidential disclosure agreement* under which he or she agrees not to tell anyone else what he or she finds out about your business and not to use the information for any purpose other than assessing the business for possible purchase. You'll find a sample confidential disclosure agreement in the free downloads available online; just look for Form 3-1. (Refer to the Introduction of this book for instructions on how to access this material.)

Putting the deal together

If you find someone who wants to buy your business, you'll have to negotiate a deal with the buyer. That will involve deciding between a sale of assets and a sale of shares if your business is incorporated, deciding on a purchase price for individual assets if you go for an asset sale, arranging to pay off the business's debts out of the sale price, and working out the terms of a non-competition agreement and possibly a consulting agreement.

TIP

Get advice from your lawyer and CPA before entering into any agreement to sell your business.

Sale of assets or sale of shares

You can sell a business in two ways — by selling the property the business owns (the assets) or by selling ownership of the whole business.

If your business is a sole proprietorship or partnership, you have no choice — you must sell the business by selling its assets. If you sell the assets of a sole proprietorship or partnership, you personally are the seller and you personally receive the sale proceeds. The proceeds will be taxed in your hands as a capital gain (or loss). Any recapture of capital cost allowance will be taxed in your hands as income.

If your business is a corporation, you have a choice between selling the assets of the business and selling ownership of the corporation by selling the shares of the corporation:

>> **If you sell all the shares of the corporation,** the buyer will become the owner of the corporation. The corporation will continue to exist, and will continue to own all its assets and owe all its debts. The corporation will continue to carry out any contracts it entered into, including any lease on business premises (unless the lease includes a "change of ownership" clause — then the landlord can decide whether to terminate the lease).

>> **If you sell the assets of the corporation,** the buyer will be the owner of the assets, but you will continue to be the owner of the corporation because you still own the shares. The corporation will continue to exist, even though it won't have much in the way of productive assets (instead it will have cash from the sale of the assets) — but will still owe all its debts. The corporation will have to carry out any contracts it entered into, including any lease on business premises, unless the corporation *assigns* (transfers) the contracts to the buyer of the assets (which can be done only with the consent of the other party to the contract).

TIP

The choice between a sale of shares and a sale of assets will be based mainly on the tax consequences. Consult your lawyer and CPA to help you decide between the two and to find out how to reduce your taxes as much as possible. The cost of their services will be far less than the amount you save by making the right tax and strategic decisions.

If you sell the shares of your corporation, you are the seller and you receive the sale proceeds personally. The sale proceeds will be taxed in your hands as a capital gain (or loss). If you sell the assets of your corporation, the corporation, not you, is the seller. The corporation receives the sale proceeds, and pays tax on any income or capital gains resulting from the sale. You get your money from the corporation in the form of a dividend on which you will pay tax as income (subject to the dividend tax credit).

Owners of a corporation usually prefer to sell shares because:

>> The sale of shares (rather than assets) doesn't involve the recapture of capital cost allowance (CCA). Remember that recaptured CCA gets added to the seller's income and is 100 percent taxable — whereas capital gains are only 50 percent taxable.

>> The capital gain (if any) on the sale of your shares may be tax-free up to $500,000 because of the capital gains deduction available for some small business corporations (and no equivalent deduction is available on the sale of assets).

>> The buyer has to buy all the corporation's assets and can't just pick and choose the assets he wants.

>> The buyer takes over the debts and liabilities of the business.

Keep in mind, though, that the buyer may well prefer an asset sale because:

>> He'll have a better chance of rejecting assets he doesn't want.

>> She doesn't have to take over the debts and liabilities of the business.

Allocation of the purchase price if you sell assets

If you sell the assets of your business, negotiating the price has two parts. First, you have to decide on an overall price. Second, you must *allocate* the amount of the purchase price among the various assets included in the sale (in other words, you must assign a price to each asset).

TECHNICAL
STUFF

The way you allocate the purchase price among the assets will affect the amount of tax you pay on the sale:

>> You will want the price allocated to each asset to be less than its undepreciated capital cost (its value on your books after deducting the capital cost allowance you have claimed). If you allocate a sale price to an asset that is higher than its undepreciated capital cost, the recaptured capital cost allowance (the extra amount of CCA that you claimed over the years) will be taxed as income in your hands.

>> You will also want to allocate as little of the purchase price as possible to the business's inventory. That's because 100 percent of any amount allocated to inventory will also be taxed as income.

As it turns out, the buyer will want to allocate a higher price to the very assets to which you want to allocate a lower price, because that allocation will save him or her taxes down the road (refer to Chapter 5).

Paying the debts of the business (if you sell assets)

When you sell all the assets of your business, your business remains responsible for its debts. Your business is you personally if it's a sole proprietorship or partnership, or your corporation if your business is incorporated.

After a business sells off its assets, it has no way of earning money to pay off its debts. So creditors of a business can get the short end of the stick when a business sells off all or substantially all of its assets. For that reason, every province has legislation to protect creditors. This legislation — called the *Bulk Sales Act* in most provinces — requires the buyer and seller to make arrangements to pay the creditors out of the proceeds of the sale. Usually that means that the proceeds of the sale will be paid directly to the business's creditors, and the owner who sold the assets (the corporation or the sole proprietor or partner) will get only what's left over. So if your business has debts, be prepared to see the sale proceeds shrink or even vanish!

Non-competition agreements

When you sell your business as a going concern, whether by share sale or asset sale, the new owner will want to make sure that you don't set up a competing business nearby and take away all the business's customers. To keep you from doing this, the buyer (if he or she is on the ball) will want you to sign a *non-competition agreement* — an agreement not to enter into a competing business within a specified distance for a fixed period of time. A cautious buyer is likely to want an agreement that prevents you from opening a business anywhere in Canada and anytime for decades.

WARNING

If you sign a non-competition agreement and then start up or join a competing business, the buyer's remedy would be to sue you, either for compensation for the business he loses to your competing business, or for a court order to stop you from competing. But a court will enforce only a reasonable non-competition agreement — in other words, one that keeps you from setting up a similar business for a reasonable period of time and within a reasonable distance of the business location. What's "reasonable" will depend on the nature of the business. It's usually much less than the buyer would like.

Consulting agreements

A consulting agreement keeps you on as a consultant with the business for a limited period of time after the sale, and allows you to turn some of the purchase price of the business into consulting fees spread out over the period of the contract. You'll pay tax on the part of the purchase price that's paid in consulting fees as income rather than as a capital gain — so you'll pay tax on 100 percent of the amount rather than on 50 percent — but you'll get to spread the tax payable out over two or more years.

Going Out of Business

If business is bad, you may not be able to find a buyer to take it over as a going concern. Then your only choice is to close the business down and try to sell off as many of its assets as you can. You'll need to find buyers for the business's inventory, fixtures, and equipment. If you're lucky, you'll raise enough cash to pay off the debts of the business before you close the door and turn off the lights.

Here's some advice on how to go out of business with your head held high and without leaving a bad smell behind.

Finding buyers for your business's assets

If you are in a retail business, you can have a "going out of business" sale to sell off your inventory, and perhaps some of your store fixtures.

Speak to your landlord and your municipality before holding any sort of liquidation sale. Most commercial leases state that the landlord's permission is required, and many municipalities require a permit or licence before a going out of business sale may be held. Also check your lease to make sure that your store fixtures don't belong to your landlord.

Also speak to your lenders before holding any sort of liquidation sale. Most commercial loan agreements state that a going out of business or liquidation sale is a breach of the loan agreement. If you hold a sale without first getting permission, your lender may demand immediate payment of all your loans. And if you have given security for the loans, the lender may seize the property that is the security (refer to Chapters 9 and 20).

When it comes to your machinery, computers, office furniture, office supplies, and so on, you can try offering them to business associates, or family and friends. If you don't get any takers, you can place ads in the newspaper or Internet classifieds, or try to find a dealer who buys used equipment. Businesses sometimes end up giving their assets to charity for a tax credit, or simply giving them away to anyone who's willing to remove them from the premises.

TERMINATING THE CORPORATION (IF YOU SELL ASSETS)

If your business is a corporation and you sell its assets, you'll still have the corporation on your hands when the sale is completed unless you terminate its existence.

If the corporation has no assets left in it at all, you can do nothing, and eventually the government that incorporated it may *dissolve* it (end its existence) for not filing documents and/or not paying fees.

If the corporation still has assets that must be used to pay off debts of the corporation or that the shareholders want returned to them, the shareholders can vote for the *winding up* (or, in some provinces, for *voluntary dissolution*) of the corporation. When a corporation is *wound up* or *liquidated*, arrangements are made to pay its debts and distribute any remaining property to the shareholders. Then documents are filed with the incorporating jurisdiction (the federal or a provincial government — refer to Chapter 6) that allow the corporation to dissolve.

A provincially incorporated corporation may need the consent of the provincial department or ministry of finance before it can terminate its existence. Since the minister of revenue is no dummy, no consent will be given until all provincial corporate taxes have been paid. You don't have to have the consent of the CRA to terminate the existence of your corporation, but you should get it anyway to protect the directors and officers of the corporation from being held personally liable to pay federal taxes owing by the corporation.

TIP

If you don't have the heart to sell off the bits and pieces of your business personally, you can hire a business liquidator to sell your inventory, equipment, and supplies for you.

Unloading leased equipment

If your business has leased equipment, you can't just return the equipment and stop paying. Your obligation to make the lease payments continues for the full term of the lease (refer to Chapter 7).

Speak to the *lessor* (the business that leased you the equipment) to find out whether you can arrange for someone to take over your lease. Perhaps the lessor knows of someone who may be interested. Or see if you can negotiate some sort of payment to terminate your lease.

Paying off your debts

If you sell all or almost all of the assets of your business, you will have to comply with your province's *Bulk Sales Act*, which is designed to protect the creditors when a business sells all or substantially all of its assets. You will have to make arrangements to pay your creditors out of the proceeds of the sale. Usually the proceeds of the sale will be paid directly to the business's creditors, and the business will get only what's left over.

If nothing is left over from the sale proceeds but more debts, you're in trouble. How much trouble will depend on whether or not your business is incorporated. If your business is a sole proprietorship or partnership, your business's debts are your personal debts and you will have to use your personal assets to pay off any debts left over after you use up the assets of the business. If your business is incorporated, you won't have to use your personal assets to pay the business's debts unless you gave a personal guarantee for the debts of the business (refer to Chapter 9). Chapter 20 offers a fuller discussion of what happens when you can't pay your business debts.

Notifying your clients or customers

TIP

Let your customers and clients know that you are shutting down your business. If you are a service provider, finish off whatever work you are doing and send your customers a final bill. If you have property belonging to your customers in your possession, tell them to come and pick it up. As a final act of customer relations, thank your customers and clients for their business over the years, and, if possible, refer them to another business that can offer them similar goods or services.

WARNING

In some professions, you must find another professional in the field to take over your clients. Speak to your professional organization to find out what your obligations are when you close down your business.

Notifying your suppliers

Tell your suppliers that you are closing down your business. Return any goods that you have on consignment. If you have purchased supplies or inventory outright, ask if your suppliers will take anything back and give you a refund.

See if your suppliers will agree to cancel any ongoing contracts for the regular delivery of goods or services. You may have to pay something to get out of these contracts.

Pay off your outstanding accounts if you are able. You may not be able to pay off your accounts until you sell off the assets of your business. In that case, let your suppliers know what you are doing to see that they are paid.

Negotiating with your landlord

WARNING

If you have leased business premises, you can't just close up shop and walk away. Your obligation to pay rent continues to the end of your lease, and your landlord can sue you if you don't keep on paying. So you'd better have a chat with your landlord.

Unless your landlord is willing to let you out of your lease (which is unlikely), you will have to find someone who is willing to take over your lease. Your landlord may know of someone who is interested in your space. If not, you will have to find a new tenant yourself.

WARNING

You can place a classified ad in the newspaper or on a website that lists premises for rent under the headings Commercial, Industrial Space; Office, Business Space; Stores for Rent; and so on. Or you can place a For Rent sign in your window. (Make sure you have your landlord's permission.) Or you can use a real estate or leasing agent who specializes in industrial, commercial, and investment properties — but you'll have to pay a commission.

If you find someone who wants to take over your premises, your landlord must give consent to the *assignment* (transfer) of your lease.

Being Put Out of Business

If business is really bad, you won't be able to pay your debts. Once that happens, the decision to go out of business may be made for you by your creditors.

When you started your business you probably borrowed money. In fact you probably took out several different loans, such as:

>> A capital loan to pay for your business's start-up expenses

>> An operating loan, perhaps a line of credit, to help you cover the ongoing expenses of your business

>> A loan to help you pay the purchase price of a particular piece of equipment

You may have other debts as well: an outstanding balance on your business's credit cards or money owing to your business's suppliers. (For more about borrowing money, refer to Chapter 9.)

When you borrowed money (whether through a bank loan or on your credit card or by being given credit by your suppliers) you entered into a contract to repay the money. If you don't repay the money as promised, the lender has the right to take steps to collect the money that you owe. The steps that a lender can take will depend on the terms of your contract and the kind of security the lender holds. If you owe money to (and are not paying) a number of lenders, they'll probably all be taking steps to get their money back at the same time. And some of those steps may put you out of business.

In Chapter 20, we tell you about all the nasty things your lenders can do to you if you don't repay your loans. Here we tell you about only those things they can do that will put you out of business.

How your secured creditors can put you out of business

Your secured creditors are the lenders to whom you gave *security* (which is the right to take specified property from you if you don't repay the loan).

TECHNICAL STUFF

When you borrowed money and gave security, you may have signed a *general security agreement* or given a *debenture,* both of which give the lender security over all your business assets, including equipment, vehicles, machinery, inventory, and accounts receivable. Under a general security agreement or a debenture, the lender has the right to take possession of all this property (including the right to collect your accounts receivable) if you don't repay your loan. Many general security agreements and debentures give the lender the right to appoint a *receiver/manager* to take possession of the secured property if the loan is not repaid.

After your lender appoints a receiver/manager, you are effectively out of business. The receiver/manager will take over your business and either liquidate it or run it for the sole purpose of taking possession of the secured property, which will then be sold to pay off your loan.

How your unsecured creditors can put you out of business

WARNING

If your business can't pay its debts as they become due, and it owes at least $1,000, your business is *insolvent.* If your business is insolvent, any *unsecured creditor* (a lender who has no security from you for the debt) to whom you owe more than $1,000 can *petition* your business into *bankruptcy* if your business commits an *act of bankruptcy.* Not paying a debt when it's due is an act of bankruptcy.

If the court makes an order that your business is bankrupt, it will appoint a licensed insolvency *trustee.* The trustee becomes the legal owner of all the unsecured property that belongs to your business and will use the property to pay off your debts. Once the court appoints a trustee in bankruptcy, you are (again) effectively out of business. The trustee will take over your business and liquidate it or run it for the sole purpose of taking possession of the unsecured property, which will then be sold to pay the business's debts. If you're a sole proprietor or partner, the trustee will take over your personal property as well as your business property (with some exceptions, so that you don't freeze to death) and sell it to pay your debts (refer to Chapter 20).

Dying to Get Out of Business

Thinking about dying is not very pleasant. We cover this topic quite briefly, so you're probably not in danger of having an emotional breakdown before you get to the end of the chapter. If, however, you're keen to know more about how to arrange your business and personal affairs before you pass on, you should read *Wills and Estate Planning For Canadians For Dummies* (Wiley).

If your business is worth anything, you'd probably like to pass its value on to your family when you die. You can do that by leaving it to family members to run or by making arrangements to sell it to someone outside the family and leaving the proceeds to your family.

The decision whether to keep your business in the family or to sell it is a complicated one. If you're thinking of keeping it in the family, you have to consider the nature of the business, the abilities and interests of your family members, and your own temperament:

>> **Is your business one that can be passed successfully on to family members?** Can your business exist without you, or will it simply collapse without your personal presence? Is it worth enough to pass on? Will your estate or your family be able to pay the tax on any capital gain that results if you leave your business to family instead of selling it to an outsider? (The CRA says that a "deemed disposition" — a kind of pretend sale — of a taxpayer's property occurs when the taxpayer dies, and the taxpayer's estate has to pay capital gains on any increase in value of property.)

>> **Can your family run the business without running it into the ground?** Does anyone in your family have both the desire and ability to run your business?

>> **Can you do whatever is necessary to ensure a smooth transfer of control of your business to your family?** Can you choose a successor? Are you willing to hand over some control to your family while you are still alive?

>> **Will all hell break loose?** If you have more than one family member, can you leave the business to all of them, or only to one or two? If you leave the business to only some of your family, do you have enough other property so that everyone gets something and no one is seriously prejudiced by your arrangements?

Short-term planning versus long-term planning

You're just starting up your business at this point. Practically speaking, you're probably not yet thinking about whether your family should take over and run the business or whether it should be sold to an outsider. But, again practically speaking, you should still make some sensible short-term plans about what should be done with your business if you were to die suddenly (or even if you were to become seriously ill).

TIP

Whatever your long-term plans for your business, you should have someone on tap who can step in and run your business, at least temporarily. (The best way to maintain the business's value is to keep it running; and even if it's not going to run for much longer, it still needs to be properly shut down.) That person can be your spouse, your adult child, another family member, a trusted employee, or a manager hired by the *executor* of your will (the person you name in your will to handle your estate).

The person, whoever it is, will need access to enough information about your business to be able to operate it on short notice for a period of time. If the person you have in mind is a family member or employee, you should keep him or her informed about the business's activities. You should also keep your business's financial records and documents in good order and together in an obvious (but secure) place.

TIP

In addition, you should consider whether you need life insurance so that you have enough money to:

>> Pay the debts of your business.

>> Pay for someone to help your family run the business.

>> Help cover the business's expenses if its income goes down because of your death.

>> Pay any capital gains tax that result from your death.

TIP

Finally, you'll need a properly drafted will so that the assets of a sole proprietorship (or partnership) or the shares of a corporation are passed on to the appropriate person or people to allow the business to continue to operate or to close down in an orderly fashion. If you don't have a will, provincial legislation determines who gets your property after your death. This government agency is called a Public Trustee in some provinces. Speak to your lawyer about drafting a will. Speak to a CPA for tax implications.

Keeping it in the family

Now back to planning for the longer term.

TIP

If you want to pass your business on to your family, you must plan how and when to do it. If you want family members to run your business successfully after you die, you may have to transfer ownership or part-ownership of your business to them while you're still alive. When the time comes, you'll have to consider whether you can afford to retire from the business and/or whether you can afford to pay the tax on any capital gain that results from a full or partial transfer of ownership. (Even if you don't take any money for handing over a share of the business, the CRA says this is another "deemed disposition" or pretend sale that triggers capital gains.) If you can't afford to transfer ownership of your business before you die, you should still think about bringing your family into the business (as employees, for example), so that they can have the opportunity to learn about the business from you and to get to know your clients or customers.

Bringing your family on board has a legal side, too. For example, if you're a sole proprietor and you want to share ownership of your business during your lifetime, you'll have to transfer legal ownership of all the assets of the business jointly to yourself and to the person or people you have in mind as successor(s). If you want to hand over full ownership of your corporation, you'll have to transfer legal ownership of all the shares of the corporation to your intended successor(s). If you want your family to take things over only when you die, you will need a properly drafted will leaving the assets of the business or the shares of the corporation to your intended successor(s).

TIP

You'll need the advice of both your lawyer and your professional accountant about bringing your family into the business.

Selling to an outsider

If you want to sell your business to an outsider — so that when you die your family gets the proceeds of the sale of the business instead of getting the business itself — you have two choices about when to sell. You can sell while you're still alive, or you can let your executor sell after you die. If your business is worth more as a going concern than as a collection of assets, its sale value will probably be greatest while you're in the land of the living. But you may not be able to afford to retire from business, or to pay the tax on the capital gain, if you sell the business while you're alive.

If you want to sell your business during your lifetime, you'll have to find a buyer and then legally transfer ownership of all the assets of the business, or the shares of the corporation, to the buyer. (As you may recall, we talk about selling your business earlier in this chapter.) If you don't want to sell your business until you die, you will need a properly drafted will directing your executor to sell your business and then leaving the proceeds of the sale to your family. Either way, you'll need the help of your lawyer, CPA, and other professionals to sell your business.

5
The Part of Tens

Chapter 22

Ten Questions Every Prospective Small Business Owner Should Ask

Want to be sure that small business ownership is right for you? Here are ten questions to ask yourself before you make the big leap.

Do I Have the Right Personality to Run My Own Business?

Take a long, hard look at yourself before you put a lot of time, effort, and money into a business. A small business owner needs most of the following qualities:

>> Confidence in yourself and your abilities

>> Knowledge of your goals

- » Desire and ability to be your own boss
- » Independence and self-sufficiency
- » Ability to survive without a social group
- » Skills for getting along with people and dealing with conflict
- » Determination and persistence
- » Self-discipline
- » Reliability
- » Versatility
- » Creativity
- » Resourcefulness
- » Organizational talents
- » Risk-management instincts
- » Nerves of steel in a crisis
- » Pick-yourself-up-itiveness
- » Knack for recognizing opportunities when they come along
- » Drive to seek out new opportunities
- » Success-management instincts
- » Objectivity
- » Courage to live without a regular paycheque
- » Good health and physical stamina

If you don't have all these qualities yet, you'd better get to work on them if you want to be a successful small business owner. Chapter 1 talks more about the qualities of an entrepreneur.

What Should My Business Produce or Sell?

Your business needs a product or service to sell. And it needs to be something that customers or clients want to buy. Chapter 4 discusses selecting your product or service.

You can get ideas from potential customers, trade shows, trade journals, TV, blogs, newspapers, or the web. Or you may come up with an idea of your own. Whatever your idea, you must decide whether:

- >> The idea is right for you and your business personality.
- >> A market exists for the product or service you've come up with.
- >> You can compete successfully.
- >> The idea is financially viable.

Should I Buy an Existing Business or Start from Scratch?

Starting your own business from scratch is a lot of work. You have to:

- >> Come up with a business concept
- >> Find a location for your business
- >> Buy equipment
- >> Find customers or clients
- >> Set up management operations
- >> Expand the business through your own efforts

If you buy an existing business, you may find that

- >> You can eliminate a lot of the early work involved in building a business.
- >> You can benefit from the knowledge of the original owner, who may be willing to give you advice about how to run the business.
- >> You have an easier time borrowing money.

However:

- >> A successful business does not come cheap.
- >> The business may not continue to be successful for you.

If you still aren't sure whether to get into your own start-up business or to buy an existing business, we give you more to think about in Chapter 5.

Should I Incorporate My Business?

Here are the main advantages of incorporating a business:

>> Limited personal liability if the business fails, because a corporation exists as a separate legal entity. *However*, most lenders will require your personal guarantee before lending money to your corporation.

>> Tax advantages, because the highest corporate tax rate is lower than the highest personal tax rate. *However*, if your business makes only a small profit or loses money, your tax situation will be better if you don't incorporate.

Incorporation does have a couple of disadvantages:

>> Corporations are expensive to set up.

>> Corporations are expensive to run.

If you want to read more about incorporating a business, we talk about it in Chapter 6.

How Will I Finance My Business?

Start-up operations may be able to get money from the following sources:

>> Personal assets — your own money or property

>> Family money — money from family and/or friends

>> Money borrowed from commercial lenders — by way of credit card, a mortgage on your home or cottage, a commercial loan, a micro-credit loan

>> Credit — from suppliers and/or customers or clients

>> Sale of accounts receivable — at a discount

>> Grants and loans from government

>> Investment from external sources — angel investors or venture capital companies

That's a respectable-looking list — somewhere among all these possibilities you should be able to find a buck or two. Refer to Chapter 9 for more information about financing your start-up business.

Should I Work from Home?

When you're starting out, your main goal in choosing your place of business should be to spend as little money as possible while making sure that your location satisfies the needs of your business. Without a doubt, working from home is the cheapest way to go, but is it right for you? In Chapter 8, we help you think through the decision.

Working from home has the following advantages:

» You can claim an income tax deduction for a portion of the expenses of running your home.

» You save time commuting to and from work.

» You have flexibility to deal with children, aging parents, or pets.

However, working from home does have disadvantages:

» Limited, if any, room for expansion

» Lack of space for employees

» Inability to have the facilities and services you need

» Isolation from others in your business industry

» Potential for interruptions by family and friends

What's the Best Way to Market My Business?

A successful marketing strategy will mix and match promotion, advertising, and publicity, using both traditional and web-based methods. We get you buzzing about marketing in Chapter 11.

Promotional activities include:

» Networking by getting out and meeting people

» Providing useful information in a public forum such as teaching a course, giving a talk, writing a newspaper or magazine article or a book, putting out a newsletter, creating your own website or blog or contributing to someone else's, and using social networking sites such as Facebook, Instagram, or Twitter

You can advertise in many different ways, all of which cost money:

>> Direct mail

>> Telephone solicitation

>> Print ads

>> Ads on websites

>> Flyers, handbills (delivered by hand or by Canada Post's direct mail service), and street posters, or posters in other businesses' stores or offices

>> Business cards or brochures on display at other businesses, community centres, and so on

>> Billboards and bus boards

>> Radio

>> TV

Publicity is harder to come by than promotion or advertising because it is harder to control. But here are some publicity-generating ideas to try:

>> Issue a press release about the opening of your (interesting and innovative!) business or about some significant activity you're undertaking or some event you're planning.

>> Contact an appropriate editor or journalist and invite him or her to an event you're staging, or ask if he or she is interested in writing about your business.

>> Contact an appropriate editor or journalist to let him or her know you're available to be interviewed as an expert on a particular subject.

How Can I Keep My Customers Happy?

The first step in keeping your customers happy is to do what you agreed to do. However, just doing the work isn't enough if you want to be paid promptly and get repeat business and referrals from your customers. You must also keep an eye on customer service in the following ways:

>> Don't make promises you can't keep.

>> Keep the promises you make.

>> Document changes if your customer asks for changes to your original contract.

>> Give your customer regular updates about the work you're doing for him or her.

>> If you make a mistake or miss a deadline, deal with it.

Even if you do everything right, you're still going to encounter unhappy customers. Remember these key points in dealing with a difficult customer:

>> Listen to what the customer has to say.

>> Show that you understand the customer's problem.

>> Try to solve the customer's problem.

Even if you decide that you never want to have anything to do with a particular customer again, and you're pretty sure the customer won't give you any referrals, try not to send the customer away angry. You don't want him or her badmouthing you to potential customers. Check out Chapter 13 to get inside the minds of your customers or clients.

When Should I Take On Employees?

Sooner or later, you're going to need some help. You may start off using computer software and contractors who provide services, but the time will come when you need another body around full time.

But before you decide to take on an employee, you'd better have some idea of what will happen when you do. (We tell you more about being an employer in Chapter 15.) As an employer, you have to do the following:

>> Pay the employee.

>> Give the employee time off with pay.

>> Make regular payments to the federal and provincial governments on behalf of your employee and your business.

>> Provide a workplace that's safe, and free from discrimination and harassment.

>> Take legal and financial responsibility for your employee's actions.

>> Be a human resources manager.

>> Maintain records about your employees.

>> Establish fair and reasonable policies for dealing with your employees.

>> Let go of an employee if your business doesn't do well or if the employee simply doesn't work out.

What Professional Help Do I Need?

Planning a business start-up takes a lot of work. But you don't have to do it all alone. You can and should get professional help with many of the tasks involved. (Turn to Chapter 14 to meet some of the professionals who can help you.) At the very least, you'll need a lawyer, an accountant, and an insurance agent or broker. Depending on the nature of your business, you may also want help from

>> An advertising firm and/or a media relations firm

>> A marketing consultant

>> A computer systems or computer applications consultant

>> A website designer

>> A management consultant

>> A human resources specialist

>> A business coach

Whatever kind of help you're looking for, you want to find someone who has experience in small business matters, someone with whom you'll feel comfortable, and someone who will charge you a reasonable fee.

Before you hire a professional, you should take these steps:

>> **Get recommendations.** Ask your friends, relatives, or business associates for names of good people.

>> **Investigate.** Call each recommended person's office to find out more about his or her area of expertise, experience with business start-ups, fees, and location (if the person doesn't make client calls but expects you to come to him or her).

>> **Interview.** Meet the top two or three candidates in person. A face-to-face meeting allows you to get more information than you collected in the preceding bullet and allows you to see how you personally react to each individual.

Chapter **23**

Ten Key Documents for a Small Business

M ake life easier for yourself as a business owner! Don't try to keep all the information you need in your head, or all the agreements you make in a handshake. Using the documents we list in this chapter can help your business matters run more smoothly and protect you if problems arise.

Partnership Agreement or Shareholder Agreement

These critical documents set out how your business is run. (See Chapter 6 for more about them.) In most provinces, the law makes certain rules about how partnerships are run. The laws include the following terms:

» All partners have an equal say in management of the partnership business.

» All partners are entitled to an equal share of partnership assets.

» All partners share equally in the profits of the partnership.

» All partners are equally responsible for partnership debts.

>> If one partner dies, goes bankrupt, or withdraws from the partnership, the partnership is at an end, even if the partnership has more than two partners.

>> All existing partners must consent before a new partner can be admitted to the partnership.

If you want to customize these terms to suit your own partnership, you need a *partnership agreement*. This document can do a number of things, including let you and your partners:

>> Own the partnership property unequally

>> Define how the work will be divided among the partners

>> Divide the partnership profits unequally

>> Divide responsibility for partnership debts unequally between the partners

>> Have the partnership continue even if one partner leaves, goes bankrupt, or dies

Similarly, if your business is a corporation, provincial statute law makes rules about how to run it. If your corporation has two or more shareholders, you may want a *shareholders' agreement* that sets out mutual rights and obligations. A shareholders' agreement can deal with matters similar to those in a partnership agreement, as well as other matters such as the right of a shareholder to be or to appoint a director and how to resolve voting deadlocks.

Lease for Your Business Premises

A *commercial lease* for your business premises (refer to Chapter 8) will cover a whole slew of matters that are important to you, including the following:

>> The size of the space — you need to know how much room you'll have, but you also need to know the size of the space because rent is usually calculated by the square foot.

>> The cost of the space — basic rent plus any other costs you'll be responsible for.

>> Leasehold improvements — what needs to be done to renovate or decorate the premises, and who pays?

>> The term of the lease — how long does the lease run?

- » The use of the space — can you use the premises for all the activities your business needs to carry out?

- » Protection against competition — in a shopping centre, will the landlord agree to prevent other tenants from competing with you?

- » Hours of business and hours of access to the premises.

- » Facilities in the building — such as elevators, and security, cleaning and other services.

- » Insurance policies that the landlord requires you to take out.

- » Your right to transfer the lease to someone else or sublet the premises to someone else.

Insurance Policy

You need insurance to manage the risks associated with carrying on your business. (Chapter 12 tells you more about insurance matters.) Your insurance policy will tell you:

- » Who's insured (a corporation or individuals) — so you'll know whose problems are covered by insurance.

- » What perils (risks) you're insured against — depending on the kind of coverage you choose, risks might include physical injury to others, damage to your property or others' property, damage to your business's computers, your or others' financial loss, defamation, false imprisonment, the death or disability of a key member of the business — so you'll know whether a particular problem is covered by insurance.

- » What your exclusions are — so you'll be absolutely clear as to what is *not* covered by your insurance policy.

- » Whether you have actual value or replacement cost coverage — so you'll know how much money to expect to receive from the insurance company if you make a claim.

- » What your premium is — so you'll know what you're paying per year for your coverage.

- » What your deductible is — so you'll know how much is coming out of your own pocket if you make a claim.

Business Plan

We walk you through business plans in Chapter 10. Before reaching into its pocket and giving you a lot of money, a lender or investor will want to be sure of getting its money back later on. So the lender will want you to answer some basic questions about your business and your plans for the business's future; for example:

>> How much money do you want and what are you going to do with it?

>> What does your business do, and what industry does your business belong to?

>> Why can your business compete successfully? What's your strategy for competing?

>> How does your business run (or how will it run) on a day-to-day basis, and who are the business's managers?

>> What's the state of your business's finances, including projections for income and expenses? What's your personal financial status?

Traditionally, a business plan wraps up all this information.

Loan Documents

If you're borrowing money (refer to Chapter 9), a *loan agreement* sets out what you need to know about the loan, including:

>> The principal amount of the loan

>> The lender's obligation to continue giving you loan funds if you're receiving the loan in instalments

>> The interest rate

>> The repayment terms and any right you have to pay off the loan early

>> The kind of security to be provided

>> Any promises you make to the lender (apart from promising to repay the loan), such as a promise not to dispose of any major assets of the business or to change the nature of the business

>> What constitutes default under the loan (and will cause the loan to be immediately due and payable), such as breaking any promises made to the lender, not making payments in full and on time, becoming insolvent or going bankrupt, or not paying your debts to other lenders as those debts become due

>> What the lender can do if you default, such as seizing assets that you've provided as security for the loan, or appointing a receiver

Standard Customer Contract

Providing goods or services to customers is what your business is all about. (See Chapter 13.) A standard contract with your customer or client should cover:

>> The parties to the contract.

>> A detailed description of the goods being sold or the services being provided.

>> The quality of the goods or services, and what your responsibility is to the customer or client if the quality isn't up to snuff. A contract for goods should also cover the customer's right (or lack of right) to return the goods even if quality is not an issue.

>> The price to be paid for the goods or services, and the amount of the GST/PST or HST.

>> When and where the goods are to be delivered or the services are to be performed.

>> When payment is to be made — before, upon, or after delivery of the goods or performance of the services. If you agree to accept payment after the date of delivery of the goods or performance of the services, the contract should set out the terms for payment, including the amounts and dates of the payments and the interest rate being charged.

If you're supplying goods and they will be shipped to your customer, the contract must also deal with:

>> The method of shipping

>> Who pays for shipping

>> Who bears the risk of damage or loss to the goods during shipping

If you're performing services, the contract should also deal with:

>> The rights of the parties to change or end the contract before the services have been fully performed.

>> What happens if you cause injury to someone or cause damage to property. You may want to limit your liability to compensate the injured person or the property owner.

As you deliver the goods or perform the services, your agreement will serve as a checklist of what you are supposed to do. And if a dispute arises later on, a detailed written contract is evidence of what you and your customer or client agreed to.

Employment Contract

When you hire an employee, you both need to know and agree on the terms of employment. A written employment contract (refer to Chapter 15) should include:

>> The job title

>> The employee's work duties

>> The date the job starts and how long it lasts

>> The employee's hours of work

>> The employee's rate of pay or remuneration

>> The employee's right to paid vacation days and statutory holidays

>> The employee's right (if any) to paid sick days and whether the payment is in whole (short-term disability or illness) or in part (a percentage of wages kicks in after a period of time and payments may last several months)

>> Any employee benefits (such as extended health care or dental care or group life insurance)

>> A period of probation (a period of time, often three to six months, during which the employer can terminate employment without having to give a reason, notice, or compensation for termination)

>> Any rights of the employer to discipline the employee (for example, to dock pay, suspend, or terminate the employee if policies such as those that address harassment, code-of-conduct violations, or conflicts of interest are not complied with)

>> A promise by the employee to devote his or her full time and attention to the employer's business

>> A promise by the employee not to reveal trade secrets or other confidential information obtained during the course of employment

>> An agreement by the employee not to compete with the employer after termination of his or her employment

Confidential Disclosure Agreement

If you need to show or tell others confidential information about your business — for example, if you're telling a potential investor about your invention (Chapter 3), or giving financial statements or an outline of your marketing strategy to a lender (Chapter 10), or sharing trade secrets with an employee (Chapter 15) — before you make the disclosure you should have the other person (or business) sign a promise not to reveal the information and not to use it themselves for their own purposes. Otherwise, you may find that someone else has made off with your ideas and information and is putting them to good (and profitable) use.

Non-Competition Agreement

If you buy a business as a going concern (refer to Chapter 5), you want to keep the business's customers — so the last thing you want is for the seller to set up a competing business next door. Similarly, if one of your associates or employees leaves your business (refer to Chapter 15), you don't want that person setting up his or her own shop and nabbing the customers you worked so hard to get.

To make sure that doesn't happen, you must have a *non-competition agreement* with the seller or your colleagues and employees. Without one, the seller is free to compete with you and take your customers away, and you may not be able to stop your former associate or employee from tempting customers away, either.

A non-competition agreement will stand up in court only if it's reasonable — you'll be able to prevent the seller, colleague, or employee from setting up a similar business only for a reasonable period of time and only within a reasonable distance of your business location. What's reasonable will depend on the nature of the business.

Privacy Policy

Under federal and provincial privacy laws, you must establish a privacy policy and follow federal and provincial privacy protection rules if your business will be collecting any personal information about any identifiable individuals such as your customers or clients. (We cover more about respecting and protecting privacy in Chapters 11 and 13.) The policy must set out how your business collects, uses, and discloses that information.

Your policy should address the following matters:

>> Defining the purposes for which you collect personal information

>> Ensuring that you collect only the information that you need for those purposes

>> Limiting your use and disclosure of the information to those purposes

>> Ensuring that the information you collect is accurate, complete, and up-to-date

>> Advising your customers or clients of any intention to disclose information to anyone else

>> Obtaining consent before collecting any personal information

>> Establishing adequate methods for safeguarding the information

>> Developing a policy for destroying information after the information is no longer needed

>> Establishing a policy for dealing with questions and complaints

Chapter 24

Ten Internet Resources You May Find Useful

The Internet provides a wealth of great resources to help you start, run, and carry on your business. We think the websites in this chapter may be particularly helpful to you.

The Government of Canada

The Government of Canada's website (www.canada.ca/en/services/business or http://canadabusiness.ca/starting) contains information about business-related programs and services of federal and provincial agencies. The site allows you to input your province, industry, and/or demographic group and receive information tailored to the location and nature of your business. It also provides links to the individual websites maintained by some provinces. The main site contains information on such topics as:

>> Starting a business

>> Looking at growth and innovation in your business

>> Getting financial assistance through grants, loans, and financing

- » Managing federal and provincial taxes
- » Complying with business regulations
- » Obtaining licences and permits
- » Exporting and importing
- » Hiring and managing staff
- » Creating a business plan
- » Managing and operating a business
- » Conducting market research and getting access to statistics
- » Doing marketing and sales
- » Managing intellectual property
- » Exiting your business

It also provides links to the provincial Canada Business Service Centre websites — where you can find and register for business workshops and seminars — as well as links to other useful websites.

Provincial/Territorial Government Websites

Each provincial and territorial government maintains a website. Some of the provincial sites contain good general business information, as well as information about provincial programs for small business, and laws and regulations.

- » **Alberta:** www.gov.ab.ca
- » **British Columbia:** www.gov.bc.ca
- » **Manitoba:** www.gov.mb.ca
- » **New Brunswick:** www.gov.nb.ca
- » **Newfoundland and Labrador:** www.gov.nl.ca
- » **Northwest Territories:** www.gov.nt.ca
- » **Nova Scotia:** www.gov.ns.ca
- » **Nunavut:** www.gov.nu.ca

- » **Ontario:** www.gov.on.ca

- » **Prince Edward Island:** www.gov.pe.ca

- » **Quebec:** www.quebec.ca

- » **Saskatchewan:** www.gov.sk.ca

- » **Yukon:** www.gov.yk.ca

Innovation, Science, and Economic Development Canada

The Innovation, Science, and Economic Development Canada website (www.ic.gc.ca) is particularly useful in the preliminary stages of starting a business because, in addition to general business information, it contains information on a wide variety of businesses, organized by sector. This federal government website contains information on a wide variety of businesses, organized by sector, in addition to general business information. Each type of business has its own page, with additional pages on a number of subtopics. The subtopics vary for each business category but include areas such as the following:

- » **Company directories:** With links to lists of Canadian companies carrying on business in the field

- » **Contacts:** With links to major trade associations in the field

- » **Electronic business:** With links to a variety of information about e-business and e-commerce

- » **Events:** With links to major trade shows in the field

- » **Industry News:** With links to Canada and U.S. trade periodicals

- » **Regulations and standards:** With links to relevant government regulations and standards organizations

- » **Statistics, analysis, and industry profiles:** With links to North American Industry Classification definitions and to selected Canadian statistics on topics such as the Canadian market, imports, and exports

- » **Trade and exporting:** With links to relevant international trade agreements and export information

Business Development Bank of Canada

The Business Development Bank of Canada website (www.bdc.ca) has information about its lending programs and activities. Pay it a visit if you want to drool over some money.

Canada Revenue Agency

You don't find fun and excitement on the Canada Revenue Agency's (CRA's) website (www.cra-arc.gc.ca). But you do find forms and information galore about income tax, tax credits, customs, and GST/PST or HST. Visit this website whenever you want to get the butterflies in your stomach stirred up — or, of course, whenever you need some information about tax, GST/PST or HST, and so on.

Bank and Trust Company Websites

The major banks' and trust companies' websites have information about the products and services they provide to small businesses. Some have information about general business topics as well. For example, the Bank of Montreal site (www.bmo.com) contains links to a number of small business resources such as podcasts, planning guides, articles, tips, Internet resources, and business FAQs.

The Royal Bank website (www.rbcroyalbank.com) is particularly good because it contains information about many general business topics such as starting a business, expanding a business, and business succession. It also has a page for women entrepreneurs. In addition, the Royal Bank website gives you access to the "Big Idea," an online guide through the steps of developing a business plan, including sample business plans for several different types of businesses. Other banks, such as CIBC (www.cibc.com), TD (www.td.com), and ScotiaBank (www.scotiabank.com) have similar resources.

The Yellow Pages

If you're looking for a business in a particular field and/or geographic area, let your fingers do the walking (across your keyboard instead of through the phone book)! You can find the Yellow Pages at www.yp.ca.

Top Ten Reviews

Can't decide which computer printer to buy? Don't know which accounting software package to choose? Check out reviews for these and many other small business products and services at www.toptenreviews.com. Their slogan is "We do the research so you don't have to."

HowStuffWorks

HowStuffWorks (www.howstuffworks.com) is a great site if you're trying to figure out how all your office tech and electronic gadgets actually work.

Mashable

Trying to figure out how social media works so you can use it to spread the word about your business, or connect with customers, clients, and suppliers? Mashable (www.mashable.com) is a great site for information and news about social media, technology, and Internet culture.

Index

B

D

D&O (directors' and officers') liability insurance, 260
dabbing, 394
damage to premises, 247–248
debentures, 175, 456
debt-to-equity (debt-to-net-worth) ratio, 85
dedicated work spaces, 150
defamation, 326
delivering/distributing cannabis, 417
Dell, 128
Deloitte, 328, 336
delta-9-tetrahydrocannabinol (THC), 393
demand loans, 174
depreciable capital property, 332–333
depreciation, 84–85, 332–333
desks, 122
desktop publishing software, 129
direct costs (variable costs), 71
direct mail, 205
directors, 105–107, 116–117
directors' and officers' (D&O) liability insurance, 260
disability insurance (critical illness insurance), 259–260
disclaimers, 212–213
discrimination, 308, 325–326
disputes, 431–441
  alternative dispute resolution, 437–439
  learning from, 431
  litigation, 439–441
  negotiation of settlement, 432–437
  written agreements, 431
distraint (distress), 426–427
distribution, 69–70
distributors, 70
Domain Name System (DNS), 210
domain names, 56–57, 134, 209–210
  choosing, 56–57, 210
  overview, 210
  registering, 210
  using someone else's, 57
double-entry accounting, 356
Dragon Speech Recognition, 129
dried flowers, 412–413

E

e-commerce, 11, 377
edibles, cannabis, 413–415, 419
effective interest rate, 172
EI. *See* Employment Insurance
"80/20" rule, 388–389
email
  accounts, 131–132
  etiquette for, 133
  screening and bundling messages, 384
  signatures, 133, 140
  spam, 133
email marketing, 214–219
  developing and maintaining lists, 215–216
  maximizing deliverability, 216–217
  newsletters, 217–218
  professional help with, 218–219
  strategy for, 215
email marketing service providers (ESPs), 218–219
employees
  controlling expenses, 374
  employer's responsibility for, 308
  establishing policies for, 322–323
  federal requirements for employers, 320–321
  hiring, 309–319, 469–470
  maintaining records of, 321–322
  making good use of for expansion and growth, 372, 389–390
  managing, 319–320
  paying taxes for, 307
  paying wages to, 306
  providing paid vacations and holidays for, 306–307
  providing safe workplace for, 307–308
  provincial and territorial requirements for employers, 321
  terminating employment of, 323–326
employers' liability insurance, 260
Employment Insurance (EI), 307, 346
  bankruptcy, 430
  as business expense, 332, 335
  financial documents, 358
engagement letters, 302
EPO (European Patent Office), 49
Equilease, 138

U

UFile, 329
undepreciated capital cost, 446
underwriters, 381
unified messaging, 132
United States Copyright Office, 58
United States Patent and Trademark Office (USPTO), 49, 53–54
University of Calgary, 35
University of Toronto, 35
U.S. National Inventor Fraud Center, 65

V

valuing/pricing businesses, 86–89
variable costs (direct costs), 71
venture capital, 179–180, 380
videoconferencing software, 129
viral, 225
virtual private networks (VPNs), 135
visible contracts, 266
VistaPrint, 142
Voice over Internet Protocol (VoIP), 125
voice recognition software, 129
voluntary dissolution, 453
VPNs (virtual private networks), 135

W

wages, 306
warranties, 295
web monitoring, 227–228
web presence, 207–228
    blogging, 219–220
    consistent branding, 207
    email marketing, 214–219
    social media, 221–227
    top broad search categories, 207
    web monitoring, 227–228
    websites, 208–214
website ads, 205
website designers, 38
websites, 208–214
    attracting visitors, 214
    content, 211–213
    design, 213–214
    domain names, 209–211
    importance of, 208–209
    online presence, 134
    software for, 129
    web servers versus web hosts, 209
WeChat, 132
WhatsApp, 132
WHOIS Lookup, 57, 210
wholesalers, 70
widgets, 208
Wi-Fi, 127
winding up, 453
WinZip, 129
word processing software, 129
WordPress, 220
workers' compensation, 260
working models (prototypes), 178
Workopolis, 311
World Intellectual Property Organization, 58
written materials, 57–60
wrongful dismissal, 325
WYSIWYG (what you see is what you get) website creation software, 213

Y

Yahoo!, 287
Yahoo! Mail, 132
Yellow Pages, 288, 482

About the Authors

Andrew Dagys is a Chartered Professional Accountant and risk management expert. As a best-selling author, he has written and co-authored more than a dozen books, mostly about investing, personal finance, business, and technology. Andrew has contributed columns to major Canadian publications. He is a frequently quoted author in many of Canada's daily news publications, including *The Globe and Mail,* the *National Post,* and the *Toronto Star.* He has appeared on several national news broadcasts to offer his insights on various current events and topics. Andrew considers writing books, and collaborating with talented publishing partners, to be one of life's most truly amazing experiences.

Margaret Kerr and **JoAnn Kurtz** are lawyers, and they are also both entrepreneurs — and they have the bumps, bruises, and scars to prove it. Occasionally, they find a minute of free time here and there, which is how they came to be the authors of, among other books, *Buying, Owning and Selling a Home in Canada* (now in its second edition); *Canadian Tort Law in a Nutshell* (with Laurence Olivo, also in its second edition); *Legal Research: Step by Step* (with Arlene Blatt, another one in its second edition!); *Make It Legal: What Every Canadian Entrepreneur Needs to Know About the Law*; and *Facing a Death in the Family.* They're also the authors of another excellent *For Dummies* book that's to die for — *Wills and Estate Planning For Canadians For Dummies.*

Dedication

Andrew dedicates this book to his wife, Dawn-Ava, and their three children, Brendan, Megan, and Jordan. He thanks God for them all and for all of life's blessings.

JoAnn dedicates this book to her father, George Kurtz, with love.

Margaret dedicates this book affectionately to Bree and Poppy (although they didn't offer much help).

Authors' Acknowledgments

We thank Tracy Boggier, our acquisitions editor at John Wiley & Sons, Inc. Tracy is a consummate professional who provided us with yet another opportunity to co-author an amazing book and who recognized the exciting changes in the Canadian small business landscape as a story that needed to be told. Tracy's insights throughout this project were valued and tremendously appreciated.

We also thank Elizabeth Kuball, an extremely talented project and copy editor, for her tremendous insights and valuable guidance. She is a professional who sees both the importance of details as well as the bigger picture. It was a pleasure to have worked with her on this edition.

We also thank Brent Barr, our technical editor, for his ongoing quest for factual accuracy, his expertise, and his great suggestions. We commend him for his dedication and diligence toward this book. Additional thanks go out to all the dedicated people at Wiley who work so hard behind the scenes to create a success story. We wouldn't have gotten it quite right without all of you.

Publisher's Acknowledgments

Senior Acquisitions Editor: Tracy Boggier

Project Editor: Elizabeth Kuball

Copy Editor: Elizabeth Kuball

Technical Editor: Brent Barr

Editorial Assistant: Matthew Lowe

Sr. Editorial Assistant: Cherie Case

Production Editor: Magesh Elangovan

Cover Image: © Tonktiti/Shutterstock, Canadian flag © alexsl/iStock.com

Leverage the power

Dummies is the global leader in the reference category and one of the most trusted and highly regarded brands in the world. No longer just focused on books, customers now have access to the dummies content they need in the format they want. Together we'll craft a solution that engages your customers, stands out from the competition, and helps you meet your goals.

Advertising & Sponsorships

Connect with an engaged audience on a powerful multimedia site, and position your message alongside expert how-to content. Dummies.com is a one-stop shop for free, online information and know-how curated by a team of experts.

- Targeted ads
- Video
- Email Marketing
- Microsites
- Sweepstakes sponsorship

20 MILLION PAGE VIEWS EVERY SINGLE MONTH

15 MILLION UNIQUE VISITORS PER MONTH

43% OF ALL VISITORS ACCESS THE SITE VIA THEIR MOBILE DEVICES

700,000 NEWSLETTER SUBSCRIPTIONS TO THE INBOXES OF

300,000 UNIQUE INDIVIDUALS EVERY WEEK

# of dummies

Custom Publishing

Reach a global audience in any language by creating a solution that will differentiate you from competitors, amplify your message, and encourage customers to make a buying decision.

- Apps
- Books
- eBooks
- Video
- Audio
- Webinars

Brand Licensing & Content

Leverage the strength of the world's most popular reference brand to reach new audiences and channels of distribution.

For more information, visit dummies.com/biz

PERSONAL ENRICHMENT

9781119187790
USA $26.00
CAN $31.99
UK £19.99

9781119179030
USA $21.99
CAN $25.99
UK £16.99

9781119293354
USA $24.99
CAN $29.99
UK £17.99

9781119293347
USA $22.99
CAN $27.99
UK £16.99

9781119310068
USA $22.99
CAN $27.99
UK £16.99

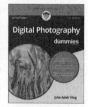
9781119235606
USA $24.99
CAN $29.99
UK £17.99

9781119251163
USA $24.99
CAN $29.99
UK £17.99

9781119235491
USA $26.99
CAN $31.99
UK £19.99

9781119279952
USA $24.99
CAN $29.99
UK £17.99

9781119283133
USA $24.99
CAN $29.99
UK £17.99

9781119287117
USA $24.99
CAN $29.99
UK £16.99

9781119130246
USA $22.99
CAN $27.99
UK £16.99

PROFESSIONAL DEVELOPMENT

9781119311041
USA $24.99
CAN $29.99
UK £17.99

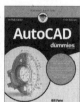
9781119255796
USA $39.99
CAN $47.99
UK £27.99

9781119293439
USA $26.99
CAN $31.99
UK £19.99

9781119281467
USA $26.99
CAN $31.99
UK £19.99

9781119280651
USA $29.99
CAN $35.99
UK £21.99

9781119251132
USA $24.99
CAN $29.99
UK £17.99

9781119310563
USA $34.00
CAN $41.99
UK £24.99

9781119181705
USA $29.99
CAN $35.99
UK £21.99

9781119263593
USA $26.99
CAN $31.99
UK £19.99

9781119257769
USA $29.99
CAN $35.99
UK £21.99

9781119293477
USA $26.99
CAN $31.99
UK £19.99

9781119265313
USA $24.99
CAN $29.99
UK £17.99

9781119239314
USA $29.99
CAN $35.99
UK £21.99

9781119293323
USA $29.99
CAN $35.99
UK £21.99

dummies.com

dummies
A Wiley Brand

Learning Made Easy

ACADEMIC

9781119293576
USA $19.99
CAN $23.99
UK £15.99

9781119293637
USA $19.99
CAN $23.99
UK £15.99

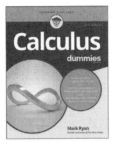

9781119293491
USA $19.99
CAN $23.99
UK £15.99

9781119293460
USA $19.99
CAN $23.99
UK £15.99

9781119293590
USA $19.99
CAN $23.99
UK £15.99

9781119215844
USA $26.99
CAN $31.99
UK £19.99

9781119293378
USA $22.99
CAN $27.99
UK £16.99

9781119293521
USA $19.99
CAN $23.99
UK £15.99

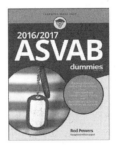

9781119239178
USA $18.99
CAN $22.99
UK £14.99

9781119263883
USA $26.99
CAN $31.99
UK £19.99

Available Everywhere Books Are Sold

Small books for big imaginations

9781119177173
USA $9.99
CAN $9.99
UK £8.99

9781119177272
USA $9.99
CAN $9.99
UK £8.99

9781119177241
USA $9.99
CAN $9.99
UK £8.99

9781119177210
USA $9.99
CAN $9.99
UK £8.99

9781119262657
USA $9.99
CAN $9.99
UK £6.99

9781119291336
USA $9.99
CAN $9.99
UK £6.99

9781119233527
USA $9.99
CAN $9.99
UK £6.99

9781119291220
USA $9.99
CAN $9.99
UK £6.99

9781119177302
USA $9.99
CAN $9.99
UK £8.99

Unleash Their Creativity